SUPER CAR

Also by Mark Christensen

The Sweeps: Behind the Scenes in Network TV (with Cameron Stauth)

Mortal Belladaywic

Aloha

Wildlife

THE STORY
OF THE XENO

MARK CHRISTENSEN

THOMAS DUNNE BOOKS
ST. MARTIN'S GRIFFIN ⚏ NEW YORK

SUPER

CAR

THOMAS DUNNE BOOKS.
An imprint of St. Martin's Press.

www.stmartins.com

Lyrics from "Eve of Destruction" by Barry McGuire reprinted by permission of MCA Music Publishing, Universal City, CA.
Lyrics from "Ride My Harley" by Jonathan Winters reprinted by permission of Jonathan Winters.

Book design by James Sinclair

Library of Congress Cataloging-in-Publication Data
Christensen, Mark.
  [Build the Perfect Beast]
  Super car : the story of the Xeno / Mark Christensen.
    p. cm.
  ISBN 0-312-26873-4 (hc)
  ISBN 0-312-30246-0 (pbk)
  1. Natural gas vehicles—Design and construction.   2. Experimental automobiles—Design and construction.   3. Pugh, Nick.   4. Automobile engineers—United States—Biography.   5. Christensen, Mark—Friends and associates.   I. Title.

TL228.C5 2003
629.222'092—dc21
[B]

2002192722

Originally published by St. Martin's Press / Thomas Dunne Books under the title *Build the Perfect Beast*

First St. Martin's Griffin Edition: April 2003

10 9 8 7 6 5 4 3 2 1

This book is for
Kathleen Christensen
and
Deborah Wenner.

CONTENTS

He who strives never perishes.
—Mahatma Gandhi

Beware of suicide pacts.
—Dick Tracy's Crime Stoppers

SUPER CAR

PART ONE

GREAT
EXPECTATIONS

PROLOGUE: 1999

"Who believes in progress and perfectability anymore? Who believes in master builders or formgivers?"
—Robert Hughes, *The Shock of the New*

What, I used to wonder, would happen if I could allow a singularly gifted visionary to pursue his spectacular vision, loose from the constraints of common reality and free to do, pretty much, whatever he damn well pleased?

Los Angeles is not so much big as it is endless, a small town that goes on forever, burg after burg, all its burgs mostly the same burg, palm-shaded service station by minimall by fast-food plaza, and the trip to So-Cal Speed takes an hour. My eleven-year-old son Matt beside me in my dad's big old Mercedes, I take freeways from our home in Long Beach to Pomona, a town known for oranges, drag racing and crime.

A trek. Years ago, back in the days when I had a nice new house in Portland and a nice old Porsche in Long Beach, before my partners decided to reinvent America's automotive energy policy, I had determined to create an ultimate high-performance car built to look great and go fast well, a 700-horsepower suicide machine emitting fewer toxic fumes than a new Honda, and able to turn a quarter mile from a standing start in a tenth of the time that it takes to read this sentence.

The Xeno III was born out of my idea to get the best high-performance experts in the auto industry to create the best car ever—an ambition that has devoured what I pray will be only the center of my life—and today will be the first time Matt has seen the car since it was nothing but a tube chassis and a pipe dream.

I swing off the freeway. At the red light above Reservoir Road, standing like a sentinel is an old longhair on crutches, smoking. He looks mummified by the sun, cigarettes and alcohol, a citizen from a Southern California not a cover page image on tourist brochures. We drive into town under San Gabriel Mountains made craggy ghosts by the smog, bump across railroad tracks and swing into the parking lot before a big, low building. A little lizard darts the gray wall and a chicken is running loose between the parked pickup trucks. Across the street a goat has his goateed chin propped on a barbwire fence. The middle of rural industrial park nowhere, but So-Cal Speed—land of the $10,000 paint job—draws car collectors, designers and automotive executives from all over the world.

The shop specializes in hot rods "built before Elvis but after the Bomb." Framed on the wall in the front room inside are automobile magazine covers featuring So-Cal Speed cars—sixteen covers in the last year. Founded in 1946, So-Cal Speed is the oldest and most respected hot rod builder anywhere. During the late 1940s and early 1950s, their racing team was a dominant record breaker at the California dry lakes and Bonneville salt flats, establishing the American land speed record in 1951 and establishing too a "clean machine" design style that has set a standard for custom high-performance cars for almost fifty years.

There is no place better to construct an ultimate automobile. So-Cal Speed cars have appeared in everything from MTV videos to the half-time show at last year's Super Bowl; their owners number rock stars, movie stars and whoever, I suppose, is king of the latest dot com soufflé. The So-Cal Speed proprietors occupy three positions in the Hot Rod Hall of Fame and have spent years variously as writers, editors and art directors. One So-Cal Speed manager, Tony Thacker, is also a publisher whose books about hot rods, concept cars and rare autos command up to $200 apiece. The general manager, Jerry Forster, a religion major in college, spent days in silence training to be a Buddhist monk before discovering this more rigorous calling.

Matt pushes through the door to a service bay as big as a gymnasium and as clean as a hospital operating theater. Eight *concours*-quality hot rods and race cars are scattered around in stages of polished undress, cars as carefully constructed as hydrogen bombs. Among them, the late Bob McGee's stoplight red 1932 Ford. So clean, powerful and precise. Completed in 1946, restored here fifty years later and headed for either the Petersen Automotive Museum or the Smithsonian, the roadster is an explosive steel poem all about creativity, individuality, technology, speed, craft and the democratization of prestige.

Wearing a T-shirt with FUCT written across it in the style of the Ford logo, Nick Peixoto Pugh is leaning over the Xeno III on his knees, so that when Matt and I walk in it looks almost like he's praying to it. Nice looking and with the wiry physique of someone who rarely stops moving, Nick is—in our retrograde design time—a rare soul, a thoroughbred futurist who believes cars are as valid a medium for art as canvas or stone.

His impact on the auto industry has been profound. The new Mercury Cougar, with its sleek, lunging body and crisp diagonal lines, evokes Pugh's style, as does the new Mustang, the Cadillac EVOC concept car and the outer-spacey new Toyota Celica sport coupe. Greg Brew, BMW Design Director and Acting Head of Transportation Design, Art Center College of Design in Pasadena, has put it nicely. "Nick Pugh's original Xeno model was the concept design of the 1990s. Only Taru Latte's Focus for Ghia was in the same class—pure sculpture. The whole Ford's New Edge design program is based on Nick Pugh's design language and owes its ancestry to Nick Pugh. In the car world his influence is felt everywhere. The question is, what will he do next?"

This.

Nick reaches over the little black Indy 500 steering wheel, says "Wish me luck" and twists the ignition as our fabricator, Greg Petersen, adjusts the modified Holley Dominator carburetor squatting on top of the car's supercharger. Chevrolet Racing gave us its new-generation Rat motor, the 502-cubic-inch big block V-8 that stands behind the driver's seat. The Xeno III is a platform for "overt technology"— twenty-first-century cooling systems, power systems, computer systems, you-name-it systems and because this engine is fueled by natural gas, its tuning is tricky. The starter rachets and the motor, as big as a doghouse, shudders and shrugs, then jumps to life in a rip of explosions that settle to a stuttering roar. The coiling metal snakes of the exhaust headers shade from raw silver to glowing copper and dusky gray and— where they join the huge Chevrolet's cylinder heads—a molten red.

I ask if the motor is making too much heat.

"Nah," Greg says, peering over the top of his glasses at the temperature gauge. "As long as we hold at one seventy-five or so we're okay."

When I tell Nick that Ross Spires called me, his eyes narrow. "What about?"

To get this far, we have met every other genius and crook in the transportation technology business—some working out of the same rib cage—and Spiro "Ross" Spiros is a dicey subject. Beak nose, round baby-bird eyes, an explosion of Albert Einstein hair, a mangled hand from an "experiment" gone wrong, the Mad Scientist made real.

"He said," I say, "investors have put up eight million dollars for his water-powered motor"—an engine to make it possible to drive cross-country at a fuel cost of ten cents—"and he wanted to know if we needed money."

I get a look to cut glass. "We don't need Ross," Nick says.

"I thought you two were pals."

"Ross was the crown jewel of our stupidity."

"He asked me," I add, "what we were going to do about Ford."

Nick puts a finger to his convict-short hair. "This time, keep everything right up here."

Secrecy is very important in this realm. Nick, who was designing Corvettes for General Motors before he knew what the V and the 8 meant in V-8, is paid very well to design cars no one will ever see, by clients he does not know, designs destroyed as soon as they are assessed. We met when he was the number one student at the number one automotive design school in the country, the Art Center College of Design in Pasadena. He had already worked in Paris as a designer for Renault. Then twenty-one and freshly sponsored by Mazda, Nick had, during the previous month, drawn his first sketches of the Xeno I. An automobile another student at the Art Center would soon copy to create Ford's Synergy 2010—their so-called car for the new millennium, the centerpiece of Ford's New Edge design program.

Ford took the design and made it theirs. So far we have come up with no good idea what to do. File a lawsuit? Ask the Detroit police to arrest the Ford design staff for, so to speak, grand theft auto? Though Nick is very ambitious and has strong drives I suspect are more common to babies and dictators, I doubt he could lie, cheat or steal if his life depended on it. Having his best ideas lifted has left him perplexed—left him feeling like human shareware, and he has come up with nothing better than to keep the Xeno III hidden out here, about as far from Detroit as you can be and still remain in the continental United States. When design teams from the automakers come trolling through So-Cal Speed, as they do, looking for hot, hip new performance ideas, Nick has the car draped under tarps. Finished, the Xeno III will look like a crystal knife. It has been built to last one hundred years by engineers who have created everything from components for the Freedom Space Station to race car components for Paul Newman and Mario Andretti. Mario even gave us a steering rack from a car he'd totaled at the Indy 500 and that, for some reason, he didn't want to use anymore.

Nick intends the Xeno to provide a primer for a new design language to ignite the next generation of car design, a design language* that will make his previous work look like "a high school football team compared to the Oakland Raiders." The radical aspects extend to the engineering. Nick is an environmentalist. But a new kind. He foresees a hydrogen/solar economy and doesn't want to conserve petroleum energy, just to use it. "All that means is less dead dinosaurs." So the Xeno's monster racing engine has been designed to ignite its fuel so thoroughly that all that will shoot from its exhaust is superheated nothing.

Sure, there are problems. This minute, the unfinished Xeno is about as safe as a time bomb, and there are questions too. Like, where will we find the money to make the Xeno more than just dangerous, and whose soul will have to be sold to do so? Also, there are lawyers after me and suggestions that I make Don Quixote look like Alan Greenspan and that I've sacrificed my writing career and the financial future of my family to chase an impossible dream.

Nick got here at dawn. His days are divided into four three-hour work sections punctuated by breakfast, lunch, dinner, sleep and his girl-friend. He plans to create the best cars ever made, and to use those cars to change the world. He has designed the Xeno III to be the first of a whole new generation of cars, cars that will be sentient and which "the passengers will wear like a coat," cars that are engineless and driven

---

*Design language is a referential set of idioms that allow an object to tell the story of the way it looks, an alphabet of individual but complimentary visual cues that allow the object to express a congruent whole. These cues may be as basic as a reoccurring set of triangulations, as overarching as an automobile silhouette that appears to lunge forward or as specific as a car's signature set of air scoops, vents and grill. The guidelines for creating a design language are tremendously varied. The design language defining a jet fighter plane is almost totally determined by function, aerodynamic and otherwise. An 18th-century grandfather clock, on the other hand, may be constructed from a design language that is almost wholly decorative.

Nick Pugh's design language will attempt to establish cues that are "self similar" at every level. In simple terms, that means that if he'd been the Egyptian who designed the Pyramids at Geza he might have had them constructed of countless little triangular bricks.

instead by a closed-loop system roughly analogous to the human digestive system, cars that will be grown rather than manufactured.

He has dedicated his life to the car, even given up a chance to art direct the new *Star Wars*. Requiring the attention to detail necessary to construct an eleven-foot-long Swiss watch, the Xeno III and making money to make the Xeno III take all his time. Professionally, Nick Pugh is usually hired to invent the future. He developed one of the very early commercial websites, Pepsi's. He was hired recently by *The New York Times* to predict what the world would be like one hundred years from now.

But his biggest hit has been patents he developed courtesy of grants from public utilities and the Advanced Research Project Agency (ARPA)—the people who developed the Internet—patents that will allow a car like the Xeno III, in fact most any car, to double or even triple its onboard fuel-storage capacity by way of $26 worth of chassis modifications. Play this card right and we'll soon be living the life of banana daiquiris.

The Xeno III has no skin and—with its big, high-pressure fuel tanks and trapezoids of tubing—looks like a cross between a bomb-ladened, streamlined jungle gym and a chunk of the Mir space station.

"You gonna ride with your dad?" Nick asks Matt.

Though my son still can miss a connection ("Is there marijuana in pot?"), be reckless ("Floor it over the speed bumps") and spacy ("Do you realize how hard it is to unfocus your eyes and stare at nothing?"), he's basically as nailed down as an astronaut. "Oh yeah," he says.

"If Matt likes it," Nick announces, "it's all worth it."

I hope. Blonde, skinny as a swizzle stick, handsome, winner of a Bill Clinton Scholastic Achievement Award, a surfer, snowboarder, lizard owner and two-time Tournament of Champions pitcher in Little League and .346 hitter so far this season—I want him to love cars, to be inoculated today with the need for speed, to leave here, with luck, blessed or cursed forever.

"Just take it easy," Nick says.

"Sure," I affirm. "Why press my luck the first time out?" I am a good bad driver, but later I'll wonder why I didn't take my own advice.

"All right." Nick grins. He's almost as tall as I am, and gets into the car in sections. "Dude, the brakes," he says, depressing them.

"They're not real great," Greg Peterson admits. He is balding, maybe forty.

Nick hoists himself back out. "Then let's not push it."

Matt climbs in gingerly. Even without a body, the Xeno is beautiful, the frame revealing angles and space as evolved as the Hope diamond or a house by Greene and Greene. Nick has willed his estate to the car, in case he dies before it gets finished, and he plans to sell it for a million dollars.

The engine screams *raaaa-haaaa*, *raaa-haaa* as Greg tweaks the throttle lever on top of the blower. But when Greg takes his hand away the motor slows to a gasping *lub*, *lub*, *lub* and, so it won't die, I reach in, crack the throttle and—there is a loud *pop* and the motor is silent. "Shit," I say.

"Backfire," Greg clarifies. "No biggie." But when he hits the ignition again all it does is make a sound like a muzzled dog trying to bark.

"The problem is," I say, "if it backfires the wrong way—" I point to the top of the engine. "Everything in there—the blower blades—could be shredded."

"Bye-bye, five grand," Nick says.

"Nick," Greg says, "reach in and hit the ignition again."

Nick does and, though the V-8 makes nothing but the *are-are-are-are* sound of the starter turning the flywheel, Greg, his ear blushing against the Whipple blower, a supercharger that drives its fuel mix into the combustion chambers at many times hurricane speed, says, "Nothing sounds broken. Lemme call Whipple."

Waiting, Nick paces. We're $200,000, maybe $300,000 into the car now. I lost the courage for the bookkeeping ages ago. Each headlight and taillight will be an intricate assembly of halogened LED arrays, held in a setting machined out of billet aluminum by an engineer who created prototype flight controls for the Y-22 fighter and Apache helicopter. These headlights and taillights will cost $4,000 apiece. The car will have more onboard computer systems than an *Apollo* moon ship and host a cellular connection for streaming audio, and MP3 stereo with ten hours of music playback (at one point we considered the installation of speakers you could play so loud you'd have to wear ear plugs to listen to them [Nick also toyed with the idea of turning the driver's seat into a speaker for a more physical stereo effect]). The nose of the Xeno—which occupies, roughly, the space that would be taken by a tipped-over garbage can—has consumed enough money to send both my children through college and, at the moment, I am in debt. More to the point, if you and I are on a first-name basis, I owe you $2,500. I've borrowed $2,500 from everybody I know and currently my wife and I, using credit cards, are able to pay money back only to those most likely to either starve or sue.

Across the shop, Greg is on the phone, nodding, nodding, nodding, frowning, pushing his glasses off the bridge of his nose.

An exploded blower won't make our lives any easier.

The biggest new market of the twenty-first century is up for grabs and, among other things, the Xeno III is being created to show that natural gas is the best potential successor to petroleum. At the current rate of consumption the United States will likely be sucked dry of domestic oil by 2020 and, while Birkenstock America rhapsodizes about electric power, electric power will be impractical until—Dean Kamen and/or the hybrid people not withstanding—batteries weighing no more than bowling balls can provide 250-mile range to vehicles bigger than a golf cart. Natural gas—never mind temporary recent price hikes—could cut our annual trade deficit by $100 billion, and is a fuel our sponsors hope to help make preeminent in an automotive energy market worth a half-trillion dollars a year.

Greg returns from the phone. "Got it, got it, got it, got it," he says. He makes a few more twists and turns to screws atop the carburetor, tells Nick, "Hit it" and the motor starts right up. Nick climbs back into the car, bops the accelerator. Exhaust screams and mutters through the coiled snakes of the exhaust headers.

Nick is behind the wheel, and the car rolls past Doanne Spencer's 1932 Ford roadster, winner of the inaugural Pebble Beach Historic Concours d'Elegance hot rod class. Paint as clear as water, chrome polished to a hard sparkle, it looks zapped from a time machine, as new as a baby . . .

. . . Past the Pierson Brothers' '33/4 Ford. Its top is chopped so low the windshield is a glass squint. Fifty years ago, it was a record setter at the Bonneville salt flats, running on a home-brew alcohol fuel . . .

. . . And over a tiny grease slick created by a long-gone Bondo-packed Mercury lead sled owned by Johnny Depp.

Nick gooses the Xeno III between So-Cal Speed's big metal sliding back gates toward a broad alley beside the building, an alley that serves, on occasion, as a pocket drag strip. He eases the car into the parking lot, turns it around, hits the accelerator. The engine yells, the rear tires squirt smoke and the low, little machine shoots past in a metal flash.

Matt squeezes my hand. "It's so fast!"

I'm glad he likes it. When I was his age a great fast car was a tangible Christ. A hot foretelling emissary sent from a bigger and better place. If not heaven, at least California. At eleven I saw a world full of Chevys and Fords and Mercs dying to be torched, cut, chopped, channeled and made lower and faster, sleeker, prettier, better. Made Art before I could spell it. But, for me, Art Delayed. Building the hottest car in the universe may be a kid's dream, but I didn't reach the height of my emotional immaturity until the dawn of middle age.

"How was it?" I ask Nick, as he climbs out.

Nick is laughing. "The brakes are nowhere, but it rips."

I fold myself into the cockpit, the motor burbling and quaking behind me. Re-engineered by Don Bass, who created superstock V-8s for the first factory stock car race teams in the 1950s, the 502 V-8 generates enough horsepower to launch a boxcar to the moon. There are no seat belts, and the seats are plywood boards that would shame a soapbox derby racer. If we hit anything . . . in this car, everything is behind you. It is like riding the nose of a rocket tipped on its side.

Matt climbs in. His tan face is mostly a big white grin. What teeth. Like sugar cubes. No father has ever had a better son, we haven't had three cross words. Though his mother dotes on him, he practically raises himself, and I want to make an impression. When I was a kid going through cars like Kleenex, I figured I was never going to die, and so what if I did? One place I still feel immortal is at the wheel of a too-powerful automobile.

I slip the engine in gear, let the car tug forward. The brake pedal goes down forever before it grabs. But we'll be going nothing but straight, and the alley stretches to the San Gabriel Mountains in the distance.

I press the accelerator, the car surges beneath us, the engine making a hard, dry languid howl that says "Punch this thing and it'll catch the horizon." Instead, I just give the accelerator an extra tap but the car rips toward those ghost mountains anyway, so fast it's like being in a film with a dozen frames cut. Alley whams by. A city block of asphalt just gone, the road is a jetting abstract of shapes and flashes, and suddenly, like a car cuckoo popping from a cinder block cuckoo clock, an old red Toyota shoots from the walled exit of a parking lot down the alley. I have time to see a Mexican family, who have time to see me—the kids' eyes and mouths round as zeros—as I hit the brakes. There aren't any. "No," Matt says as I yank the steering wheel, and we fly off the road.

1

At First

Under stars, at dusk, cars fell from the sky. Junkers, jalopies trailing strings of flame and smoke, their doors flapped open like failed wings, beaters, old humpbacked Fords and Chevys and Dodges and Mercs, tumbled down the face of the cliff, ticking and bouncing off the rocks until they crashed on the dirt and rock floor of the Hyster proving ground.

I was younger than my son is now, a thin, hot-tempered eight-year-old standing with my grandfather at the graveled lip of his wide driveway. We'd been watching *I Led Three Lives* on TV and had left Philbrick's chill, gray purgatory of traitors and Communist cells for this fiery sight. My grandparents lived across Marine Drive from Rocky Butte, an inland Gibraltar stabbing to the East Portland sky. Rocky Butte was also the site of the Multnomah county jail, handsome, stone and castlelike, tucked in a hollow 100 yards down from my grandparents' house and the asphalt paved grounds of my granddad's construction company, United Contracting.

During the day, inmates dynamited the jagged rock face of the monster cliff, charges going off hundreds of feet up while below—away from the falling debris—orange Hyster construction equipment wheeled around next to the boulder-tossed field, where the prisoners hammered up rocks.

It was the Fourth of July, 1956. A hot rod club was setting these old machines on fire and pushing them off the Butte for some good cause and a crowd was within the fence surrounding the proving ground, paying a dollar or so for the privilege. But I didn't like it. Watching the old cars twisting and flaming and popping off the cliff on their way to smithereens I wanted to yell, "Save one! Give it to me, so I can fix it up!"

They continued to fall and crash, fire swirling from hoods and doors. When it was over, dark, and people were leaving, I asked my granddad if we could walk over and check out the place where the cars hit, maybe there at ground zero of the beater apocalypse there might be a survivor, like a live baby found beneath a collapsed skyscraper after an earthquake. Maybe one of the cars could be salvaged. It would need work. Three hundred feet was, after all, three hundred feet. But get a crowbar and some body putty. Why not? Didn't my grandfather have a huge machine shop at his service not a hundred feet from his front door?

No, my granddad said, standing in his twill slacks, a toothpick in one corner of his mouth; that was "pritnear impossible."

Odd, given his powers. Powers that said: Machinery runs life. My granddad ran a lot of machinery. We'd just gotten back from one of his jobs. Beneath a huge blue sky beside the Columbia River, he had let me hold TNT. A red cylinder that looked as it did in *Roadrunner* cartoons. A mile or so away the stuff had gone off, blasts like an artillery barrage making way for United Contracting's construction equipment.

Eisenhower was president and roads were needed everywhere. My grandfather was field supervisor for United and his crew carved lines through fir trees with tall, yellow earth movers and graders, laying long floors of gravel which were then carpeted by squat, smelly, boxshaped machines that oozed wide ribbons of fresh asphalt behind their rear wheels. I rode on bulldozers with steel blades bright as ice and taller than I was as they ripped sheets of clay from the ground, laying a path for car civilization through the Oregon and Washington woods. My granddad's dynamite made hills pop apart, then the blades would slice away long curls of earth and busted rocks. Sometimes I'd have to watch from the timekeeper's trailer—not allowed to walk around alone because of rattlesnakes.

A trim, informal man, Roscoe Kellogg had been a gold miner and a logger. He had a moustache and a gray crew cut. At night I'd sit on his lap and—with an aquarium of whiskey, lemon, water and ice perched on the arm of his chair—he'd read me Robert W. Service poems:

A bunch of the boys were whooping it up
in the Malamute Saloon . . .

The morning after the fall of the jalopies I followed my granddad past a rock crusher as big as a house, down the winding dust roads of the Hyster proving ground to the foot of Rocky Butte where, among dry scrub grass that came to my chest, the wrecks were arrayed like the aftermath of an automotive battle of Tobruk. A humpbacked four-door Mercury, its paint oxidized to a dusty blue, sat listing to one side, its fenders smashed in on themselves and its seats black from fire. An old Ford rested on its back, like an upended turtle. I gazed at the X of its frame and the rusted tangle of its exhaust. I told my granddad we could fix it. That only the top was squashed. In my eight-year-old heart I saw the Ford unsmashed, unrusted, un-just-dropped from a three-hundred-foot cliff. No, my grandad repeated, that would be "pritnear impossible." Really? We walked back up to the house among grasshoppers popping out of the scrub, me still thinking about the cars. I wanted one bad. To fix up and make perfect.

My grandparents lived in a white, stately shack. A black iron coal-burning stove, corrugated metal siding crawling with plants and spattered with flowers, a tar roof and linoleum floors. In the cellar was a white beer keg of a washing machine, rollers on top. Wet laundry was squeezed between them, flattened to soft plates my grandmother hung from the clothesline in back.

The house was at the edge of a patched-up, tarred-up old asphalt lake. Bulldozers, their blades rashed with clods of dirt, sat in bays a pebble toss away from the front porch. My grandfather was the boss of men who rolled their cigarettes and had fingers, some of them, that stopped at knuckles. The ones who worked in the deep shade of the machine shop seemed like big trolls in their black grease-painted overalls, old, sunless men who lived among the big basics of machinery, machinery with spoked gears and shafts and belts that, for all I knew, had been born, like maybe even the men themselves, straight out of the earth.

My grandmother gave me paper, on which I drew pipe-barreled revolvers and cars designed like airplanes. A tall, thin, iron ghost of a woman with a strange, strong will, she was among the first women to graduate from Oregon State. Her high forehead, pale skin and fine features allowed her to look aristocratic in a house dress. My job on occasional afternoons was to stand above her with tweezers while she sat on a chair, find gray hairs and pluck them from her head. She and my grandfather despised each other, but I didn't know that yet.

Here I'd sit in United Contracting's fine old trucks, trucks stored in open garages below my grandparents' huge cherry and plum tree garden. There sat the 1920s and thirties open-fendered Fords and GMCs that would be worth good money today, more had I not "customized" them by taking pliers and yanking out—twisting out, breaking out— their grilles. I wanted to change these machines as I had seen machines changed wildly in the pages of *Hot Rod* and *Rod & Custom*. I would somehow conjure otherworldly "custom dump trucks" because old dump trucks were all I had and the pliers were my only tool.

I'd sit in the cabs on split leather seats spilling horsehair stuffing, gaze at the old clocklike gauges and yank at rigid shift levers that sprouted from their transmissions and daydream of taking the trucks apart to host new V-8 engines. Their rusted bodies would be made magically new in metallic reds and greens. Many parts could be chromed, the body nosed and decked. Meanwhile, I could pull and pry and peel off all the hood ornaments and insignias, dreaming of a machine light-years beyond my grasp.

One night in my parents' kitchen, on the little Formica-topped kitchen table, my father drew:

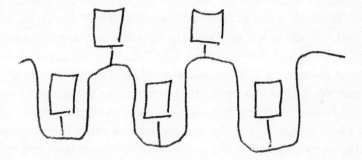

Though it may have looked like something on a caveman's wall, this was a glimpse of the internal order of the world. This was the crankshaft, he said. On top of each section of the crankshaft was a piston. Each time a piston descended to the bottom of the compression chamber a valve would open, gas would squirt in, be compressed by the piston as it rose, be ignited by a spark plug, blow up, drive the piston down, another valve would open, the exploded fuel—exhaust—would be released, the piston would begin to rise again and the whole thing would repeat itself.

Did I understand? Good. Because this was the ballet that powered the world: cars, trucks, planes, ships all used this fundamental blueprint for the engines that drove them.

My father's lessons were basic. There is no God. Frank Sinatra is a thug. Never lie. Great cars are art. The year after I was born my father bought my mother a new 1949 Cadillac. The son of a saw sharpener in a saw mill, he was, so to speak, new himself. Tall, slender, a handsome, quietly charismatic young eye surgeon fresh out of Columbia University. He had already been a developer of microsurgery and, by the early 1950s, had some money. My mother's gift was a Series 62 fastback—the roof and trunk were a single swoop—and it was a car that started an automotive revolution.

"You'll learn from the very first mile," Cadillac ads read, "why we say from victory on the battlefield to victory on the highway." The great prewar American luxury sports cars—Auburn, Cord, Duesenburg, Marmon and Pierce-Arrow—were gone, and Packard was going. But Cadillac had just sold its millionth car and was not shy about promoting its product.

Cadillac declared the Series '62 coupe "the world's most beautiful and distinguished motor car"—and it proved to be the first of a twenty-year series of extravagantly designed American high-performance automobiles. Sleek, the first car with tail fins, the first car with a curved glass windshield, a car as solid as a wedding ring, the Series 62 was equipped with the new four-speed Hydra-matic automatic transmission, power steering and, according to Cadillac, "the greatest automobile engine ever built," a 160-horsepower, 331-cubic-inch overhead-valve V-8 that would ignite Detroit's two-decade-long horsepower race, the first production "high-compression" engine. With the intake and exhaust valves on the top of the compression chamber instead of at the side, the entry and exit of the air-gas mix was faster than before. The Cadillac compression chambers had been redesigned to create more pressure within, so that when the sparkplug fired, an even more furious and powerful explosion occurred, driving the piston down with much greater thrust. These new motors would make America a force at Le Mans and on the European racing circuit for the first time ever.

My father's 1953 Oldsmobile 88 was even more powerful. Lighter than the Cadillac and parent to the muscle cars of the 1960s, the Olds 88 had recently racked up five hundred National Stock Car Racing Association (NASCAR) victories, and inspired the first rock 'n' roll song, "Rocket 88," sung by Ike Turner and produced by Sam Phillips, who would soon give the world Elvis Presley.

My father bought the car in Detroit and drove it across the country to Portland with stops for just food and gas. But the Olds's V-8 vibrated like crazy and by the time he got home the car had nearly shaken itself apart, and within months he traded it in for an even more powerful new Hudson Hornet. The Hudson insignia was a chrome rocket bomb and Hudsons were the new kings of the rapidly expanding NASCAR racing circuit. They were forcing Oldsmobile out of competition, having gone on what would later be described as "a racing rampage" that had made the Hudson "invincible." Despite the fact that the Hudsons weighed thirty-five hundred pounds and employed a six-cylinder flathead motor, they beat the best of Detroit's new overhead valve V-8s, largely because Hudsons handled so well due to the car's "step down" construction that put the center of gravity low over the wheels.

Instead of sitting above the frame, the Hudson's body was draped over it, the passenger compartment sunk within the car's frame rails. This was a tremendous advance in automobile design, my father explained, and it gave the Hudson an advantage on circular race tracks. In one race 150 miles long, Dick Rathman finished six miles ahead of the number two car, also a Hudson, which, in turn, finished *five miles* ahead of the rest of the eighteen-car pack.

Cars already provided me the power, steel and flash for a technicolor fantasy life. We lived above a creek in a wooded hollow in the hills above Portland, where by second grade I was convinced life was an illusion, that every night when I went to sleep I woke up somebody else. Thank God for TV. My hook to reality. I realized, for example, one reason for hot cars was to melt the heart of Annette Funicello. Spin and Marty, the teenage stars of the Mickey Mouse Club's *Spin and Marty Show*, planned to win this moon-faced nymph by way of a Ford Model A that might appear, to the untrained eye, to be a Three Stooges flivver stripped by orangutans. But already I knew better. Spin told Annette the jalopy was a hot rod. Naked. No fenders. No hood. Everything on display. It was as if you were God and you'd built a transparent human so everybody could just look at the pancreas and see what an almighty genius you were in rigging it up.

Already, barely eight, I was a boy possessed.

A $100,000 bolt from the blue to build the car of my dreams. This offer came from my friend and emergency room physician, Gideon Bosker. Gideon is also a screenwriter and author or coauthor of books on food, pharmaceuticals and design. While still in his twenties, he was one of the first journalists to recognize that AIDS was more than the latest doom du jour by the dust ruffle set.

He is unusual: even in a suit he looks, as my adolescent daughter Katie says, "like somebody in a band" and one of the last times I saw him was when he threw a party in a Portland art gallery. On display, Gideon's collection of medieval psychomachia. Ancient dioramas hung on cathedral walls like stations of the cross. Each scene depicted a lively cruelty. Humility stabbing Pride. Truth tearing the tongue from Falsehood's mouth. The gluttonous being force-fed toads and rats. In the middle of the room was a pile of babbling plastic. Portland's municipal bureaucracy was getting a new telephone system, and Gideon had all the old phones trucked to the gallery, plugged in and squawking. Excellent wine, excellent noise, the best party ever.

Now, seated in a chic Hollywood bar next to a Smothers brother, he asks me: "What would you do if you could do anything you wanted?" And I reply: "Build the greatest car in the world."

He says, "Let's do it."

How this greatest car in the world was going to materialize was hardly an issue, Gideon only wanted to know: "If I put up a hundred thousand dollars, will that cover it?"

Of course.

I feel what Leopold must have felt when he met Loeb and felt also, as I did when I was eight: All things are possible.

If I could tell that boy of my faraway past of my friend Gideon Bosker's offer—a chance to build a car of my dreams—the boy would have been delighted. Though, in telling the tale I'd have to tell this boy other things about that future that would have delighted him less.

2

THE WINTER NATIONALS, 1989

The night after he felt the machine that made him the quickest man alive leave the ground at 250 miles per hour and begin to flip, bust and rip apart while he sat strapped inside there in his "office" in front of a 4,800-horsepower engine, Eddie Hill had a dream. In it the accidents that had nearly killed him during almost forty years in racing appeared in sequence, from the time the engine in his 1950s dragster fire-balled and the flaming gas cooked his face to when Eddie, the only man to ever hold—simultaneously—both water and land speed world records, hit the surface of Lake Foxfire face first at 217 miles per hour. Water was driven, behind his eyes with such force that his eyes popped from his skull. The dream was not precise, because Eddie could remember little of the reality: Only starting the race and then seeing a light on the roof of the ambulance as paramedics raced him to the hospital.

Americans have always excelled at creating horsepower at $1.99 a pound and, Dr. Bosker's promise of $100,000 burning a hole in my pocket, I figured: If you want power, go to the powerful. To the Ferrari/Fangio *Car and Driver* crowd, drag racing is greaseball stuff, but drag racers like Eddie Hill developed computer powered management systems that have made them among the technological leaders of motor racing.

I want to keep my dream car's mission simple: A) Start; B) Hit the horizon. I'd create as much power as sanely or—forget sanity—mechanically possible, construct a Chevrolet 454 big block Rat motor, cousin to the engines used in Pomona. Lovely in the theater of my brain pan but difficult to actually do.

Seeking counsel, I stand beside Hill at the Winter Nationals, the World Series of drag racing. We are in a tent church. The Pomona drag strip is the best-known drag strip in the world, born out of a country that used to go to the moon and that drove cars with twice the power most cars have today. Morning light makes the tent's cloth walls as bright as blank movie screens. Outside, skyscraper effigies of Marlboro cigarettes and Budweiser beer—rubber bags shaped like packs and cans—loom a hundred feet above grandstands that tip in two-block-long slabs on either side of the track.

The strip provides religious services for the racers and their crews and families. The minister, a beefy man with pretty eyes, stands before a cardboard hand holding a Budweiser as big as a refrigerator. His wife, tall in her heels, sings "I Believe" and the minister offers the parish of three hundred racers a chance to go to Israel for $1,700 and "walk the path that Jesus walked."

I hear the crackling thunder of the first cars firing up in the pits. An institutionalized stoplight street race, drag racing is crime made legal, science for the outlaw, a galaxy of precision systems (ten computer-directed clutch adjustments in a top alcohol dragster made in the time it takes to sneeze, a motor whose eight cylinders altogether fire up to fifteen thousand times a minute) in thrall to mayhem. An expensive proposition. A pair of cylinder heads on a top fuel dragster can cost as much as a Volkswagen and may enjoy a working life of less than ten minutes. It costs roughly $10,000 a second to race these machines and a single sponsor can easily put a million dollars on a car whose total competitive time in an entire year spans less than a minute and a half.

After the service, fans trail Eddie Hill like children after Santa. You might recognize him, his face stares out from magazine ads looking hawkish, cocky, younger than he is. He has a thick eave of light hair that looks blond in photos but is white. Modest, a "Texas shade tree mechanic" who is used to creating his own parts from the ingot, he is the last of what he calls "the privateers."

We walk past the pits. Dragster after dragster after dragster after dragster. Engines here are being ripped down to nothing, autopsied and reassembled in under fifty minutes.

Beside the crew of a top fueler—imagine a wheeled arrow with a huge engine grafted to its middle employing an alcohol-based "Top Fuel" that would seem better suited inside a bomb than a gas tank—a muscled man in shorts and a gray apron, rimless glasses at the end of his nose, leans over a Keith Black Hemi head V-8, tearing it apart with the speed of a coronary surgeon cracking open a rib cage prior to an emergency bypass. A young woman swabs bleeding grease off cylinder heads as he spins out spark plugs. A big logger of a guy squats in front of the engine, popping open a little door on the side of the chassis and hooking up a computer to determine previous race RPM, crankshaft stress, blower pressure and cylinder temperature while the grease-stained doctor completes his leak-down test, to figure out if the giant $40,000 engine has what it takes to explode one more time through the traps. "My guess," I hear him say to the girl, "it'll blow before a thousand feet."

All great hot cars are created from a trinity: power, craft and style. In America the power part usually comes from a V-8 engine, a device conceived by a Rube Goldberg and executed by an Albert Speer—a complex system of belts and valves and bearings reduced to the most efficient and coordinated form to satisfy this formula: Volatility x volume x pressure x spark / weight = acceleration (gear ratios fit in there somewhere, but they make the equation less elegant). Here everything is done to make the numerator big and the denominator small. Valves 50 percent larger than stock, a twin magneto ignition that could power my house. Otherwise, these engines are stripped to their essence, are not even water jacketed, not cooled at all. Run one five minutes and what happens next is a puddle of aluminum in the middle of the street.

Lose control of a motor like that and your life changes quickly. At his trailer, Hill signs autographs on pictures of the crash in which his machine is flying vertically across the finish line at 271 miles per hour and ripping apart in the air. He jots, *Don't try this at home—Eddie Hill.*

Hill is known as "the first in the fours" because he was the first to accelerate from a dead stop and complete a quarter mile in a piston engine car in under five seconds. He did it in 1989 in a machine able to go from zero to a hundred miles an hour in one hundred feet. "These plugs," Eddie indicates a set in a box on his lap, "are from the world's fastest drag race. A couple blew apart at the end. I may not have even been running on eight cylinders when I hit the finish line. But I still had enough things going to break a world record.

"A lot is trial and error. You want more power, you adjust your cam to have less overlap between intake and exhaust. That'll raise the cylinder pressure so you'll either have more power or blow up. Usually the only way to find out is to just go out and try it."

He sits down in front of his computer. "Each race is won or lost by the alignment of at least twenty different factors. Reaction time at the start, track condition, timing of the different stages of the clutch." His monitor blinks to life. On it is a graph of the quarter-mile track, its length broken down in quadrants across the bottom, various functions: engine RPM, G-force, et cetera, appeared vertically.

"The computer lets us re-create every race. G-force." His fingers pluck keys. "See the arc on the screen, within the first couple hundred feet I was pulling 4.59 gees." Meaning, in less than a second Eddie's weight in pounds jumped from 170 to over 800, his drag racer accelerating quicker than fifty miles an hour per second. He taps a key, a new image jumps to the screen. "This is me getting killed yesterday. The arcs representing G-force and RPM overlap and cross, G-force dipping, RPM climbing."

On the monitor I watch Hill spinning his tires at 270 miles an hour, screaming across the finish line at, relatively speaking, nothing but a walk.

Later, Hill and I cross the parking lot, under the huge, floating beer cans and toward the stands where the fifty thousand greet him with a roar. Eddie is guest of honor, introduced as a "living legend, impeccable, unbeatable."

At the top of the sky a man jumps from an airplane. A red, white and blue parachute erupts and the parachutist unfurls, as he drifts earthward, a huge American flag. Hundreds of pink and white balloons spill up from behind the stands into the blue.

Here it is: Hell meets the fun house. At dusk, smoke wanders the sky from the last run. A guy wearing wrap-around shades and a bandit's kerchiefed mask sweeps the asphalt while another guy with a tank torches it to burn off grease. The evening light pinks everything. There have been four wrecks so far. Fireballs. In two of those fireballs the racers were lucky to get out alive.

Earlier Eddie Hill raced in the quarter finals. His yellow spear of a drag racer detonated off the starting line and he spun his huge rear tires with such incinerating force that smoke rose like a mainsail as he shot crazily down the track, tires spinning and not gaining traction as the dragster beside him ripped to the finish, its perfect O of a parachute popping open in victory. Later, we sat in the parking lot in Eddie's car—not his race car but the car he drives to the grocery store—and listened on Eddie's radio to a news broadcast of the semifinals going on no more than a hundred yards away.

Rice hull ash has been spread across the track to lift up oil, and a jet engine mounted on wheels roves the quarter mile, burning off any that remains. Rosin and VHT traction compound has been broomed over the track. My shoes stick to the pavement.

The enraged thunder of the burnouts begin. Funny cars are lined up in pairs, their engines pulse wildly before their back tires spin, smoke jetting and the sound rippling the air so violently it is like an electric shock. A green light and they fly down the track, burning 4,500 horsepower off nitro methane, their sleek, stretched $90,000 carbon fiber bodies mock the cars on which they have been based.

World Champion Kenny Bernstein's Buick funny car rolls to the starting line, a long, low distortion of a Buick chopped and extended in the name of acceleration—it is a Buick like it is a horse. A blower juts from its hood, fuel lines hanging off the blower's side as thick as snakes. These machines can kill you. No doors. Next year Bernstein was moving up to Top Fuel. "I can't wait to kiss funnies good-bye," Bernstein's girlfriend told me earlier. The only way out of a funny car is a hatch on top. A fire burns up the driver's oxygen in a second.

Build my car for $100,000. Right. Racers spend a million dollars apiece just to be here. The car, the crew, the equipment, the maintenance. Racing fuel goes for $22.50 a gallon and the engines—each twenty times more powerful than the average street-legal V-8—suck up the nitro methane propellent at a rate of forty gallons per mile, a thousand times faster than a conventional engine.

If I drive such a machine across country as Gideon has suggested, his $100,000 may not even pay for my gas.

Two funny cars ignite. The explosion is knives through my head, a blast so loud that even with my fingers in my ears it is noise from the end of the world.

3

FLORIDA

My life is in the starting lights and I can move nothing except for my head, my hands and my feet. Behind me, the engine fires up, not so much starting up as exploding, then detonating over and over and over, its exhaust blasting straight off the manifold through pipes arcing up from just in front of the rear wheels. I ease the car forward. It was designed to go fast and nothing else. The rear tires are huge, barely inflated rubber bags that, when the rear wheels begin to spin, flatten against the pavement for extra traction. This makes the machine un-stable. Jiggle the steering wheel and you'll be rocking back and forth like a butt wiggler in a row boat. At 140 miles an hour, that can be more exciting than Russian roulette. Flooring it, I begin my burnout. The Super Comp sling dragster's rear tires—big, soft-sided drag slicks two feet wide—spin crazily and the sound of the big block Chevy V-8 is shot from hell's heart. Smoke leaps from the wheels to a fat, speedy cloud, my rear tires go a hundred miles an hour standing still and the car is jerked sideways by the power of their loony whirl.

No lottery jackpot, sex kitten or Nobel Prize could offer the snap thrill of sitting behind the wheel, foot to the floor, of a really too-powerful car, and I'm here in Gainesville to learn how to "pull the trigger and ride the bullet." I plan to build a street-legal version of what I'm driving now—I'll race it. So best to learn how.

Three days before the New Year, Jacksonville, Florida, was colder than Anchorage. At the airport, long, flat shards of ice lay scattered around the runways like sheets of broken glass. I'm sick. My throat feels like housecats have fought in it, I spent half the night driving skinny roads in a rent-a-car whose lights revealed little more than signs for taxidermy shops, roadhouses and state prison farms. Talk about demagnitized. Gainesville is one of the oldest towns in North America, dating to the 1600s, but it seems strangely impermanent, as if it could be swallowed tomorrow by the jungle and swampland around it. The empty streets feel haunted at night. At Cape Canaveral a few years ago reporting on a Space Shuttle launch, I saw alligators take their prehistoric time jaywalking the highway outside of Coco Beach. They knew who was in charge. Someone once described Florida as just "California without the ideas." Well, maybe. I go to a liquor store for a can of beer and when I walk inside I see that all the liquor, even the beer, is behind bars. So is the hippie clerk. When I ask why, he smirks. "Guess," then nods up at the back tall wall, where, just below the ceiling, a fat man is sitting behind an indoor window. "He's got a ten gauge up there that'll blow your mind."

It is as if the state were not in the hands of people, laws and civilization, but animals, criminals and ghosts.

At my motel, feverish, I spit blood into a toilet bowl. That had never happened before. The next morning, the fields beside the Gainesville Raceway were gauzy with frozen dew as I drove to the drag strip downing aspirin like M&Ms.

Nothing weird about the parking lot, or the grandstands beside a half-mile-long drag strip that provide a quarter mile to accelerate and another quarter mile to figure out how to stop. Otherwise, just a shop, and a building being used as a classroom. Still, it is a little unnerving. *"No previous racing experience?"* I was asked when I finished filling out my liability forms.

Alka-Seltzer leaking from my throat, I watched a TV screen alive with sling dragsters smashing and scything themselves to rags on the walls and metal guardrails. Then Frank Hawley said, "A four-second car is no fun. Freeze a race at half track, pull off the driver's helmet and see if he's smiling. It'll never happen. Whatever you anticipate, it won't be that. These cars are quicker than any race car—any stock car, formula car, or Indy car—the only thing quicker is a more powerful dragster."

On the television a funny car ripped and exploded to fire and confetti as it flipped end over end down the track. "The main thing you're going to have to get by is fear. Fear is only an idea. All it does is take up space in your brain. People who see some poor racer die say, 'He must have been terrified.' Forget it. There's no fear, because up till the second he's dead, he's busy."

Stocky, thirty-six, with his short hair and brush moustache, Hawley looks more like an accountant than a two-time National Hot Rod

Association (NHRA) World Driving Champion. He said, "Tires. The rear tires on a Super Comp dragster are ten times the size, by volume, of a street tire. They only understand one thing: Going straight. Which is all you want to do out there, go straight. Because anything but straight is trouble. The steering wheel is there not to create movement, but to prevent it. The object in drag racing is for the driver to do as little as possible. If you look at these films you'll see most racers crashed from their corrections, not from what went wrong in the first place."

We were in a classroom like most any classroom except for a huge painting of Kenny Bernstein's red Buick Budweiser funny car air-brushed across the back wall. The instruction was precise, sort of like being in a canine obedience school where you are the dog.

We—Frank and his seven students—went outside to the drag strip, where four Super Comp dragsters sat side by side. Above, a buzzard kited the sky. Black rubber turds lay scattered over the asphalt in the staging area, tread ripped from spinning drag slicks. Hawley said, "Some of you are going to get into this thing and not like it. You'll be strapped down very tight, wearing a helmet. You can't see, can't move, can't breathe and you have to remember all the time that at any moment, any second, any part of a second, something can go wrong—and by 'go wrong' I mean crash."

Okay. I've been in a dozen wrecks, no big trauma. But wrecks are unexpected, quick. If you haven't killed or been killed, what's two hours in an emergency room? Generally, I don't have the attention span to be a coward. But here there is lots of time to think about the worst.

We went into the shop and pulled on fire suits and full-face helmets. Hawley took a welder's torch, lit it, and passed the long, blue arrow of flame over a piece of cloth made of the same material as our fire suits. The material did not ignite or char but, instead, just went orange with the heat. Like an electric grill left on high. What this means, he explained, is that in case one of us goes up in a ball of fire, we'll be well protected. Or at least more poached or baked than barbecued or fried.

We were strapped into the cars. The cockpits are so small I had to climb in backward and screw myself down to the seat. The steering wheel is no bigger than a saucer and a touch will make the car veer left or right. I was belted in, pretty much sewn into the machine, by a small, young member of Hawley's crew. He cinched me down at the shoulders, crotch and forearms so that if I flip the thing I'll remain knotted inside the chassis. No question though: I could barely see, move or breath.

A Super Comp dragster is a rocket. Needle-nosed, spoked wheels up front—like the front tires on a tricycle. It has the same basic power train I'm after. A B&M hydromatic transmission bolted to a 454-cubic-inch Chevy big block 700-horsepower Rat motor V-8. I'll use a Super Comp drive train—the engine placed behind the driver's head. Because there is no more rugged geometry than this. The big Rat motor is a torque factory, the B&M hydro is grandson to the original tough-as-rock/smooth-as-butter Hydra-matic that ran in my dad's Cadillac, Hudson Hornet and Olds 88, and the mid-engine configuration is the shortest, best way to get the power from the engine to the rear wheels.

I hit the switches I was told to hit and the engine blasts to life behind my head. The shift stuck up between my legs. Though it had only five positions, low, high, neutral, reverse and lock, it had a complicated mechanism to make sure it could not be thrown into the wrong gear by mistake. I drove the dragster around the track under its own power. A jolt of the accelerator and I felt the power of God.

Next I was taught the burnout: how to ease the car to the starting line, eye the lights on the Christmas tree, rev the engine up to 2,400 RPM while jamming the brake down to hold the car still and then, as the light popped from red to yellow to green, let the brake off so the car can go wild. The idea was for the tires to rip and spin into the pavement in order to heat them for better traction once the race began.

The engine screamed, smoke flew, the dragster zipped and slithered a hundred feet down the track. It was like going berserk without getting angry. Next, the start. I waited, the engine jumped to 2,200 RPM and the machine straining against the brake, as the lights made their descent: two yellow stage lights, string of ambers, green. *Boom!* Sixty miles an hour in a proverbial heartbeat. I backed up blind, the track receded in front of me as I sped up, directed by the hand signals of the crew chief and found myself at the starting line, nothing else but ready to go.

Frank Hawley says, "Your run was very dangerous. For the first four hundred feet, your car was all over the track. Out of control. One thing would go wrong and you'd try to correct it by doing another thing." He reruns the tape at high speed. He and the starter appear on the screen, moving around the dragster like Charlie Chaplins as the cars move backward and forward and, finally, stops when Hawley freezes the tape. "You were way too busy out there. When you get busy in drag racing, there's only one thing to do: Shut down. Quit. Stop. Right now. Otherwise you're going to stuff your car into a wall."

Day three. In the classroom Hawley is talking to Jon, a stocky, black-haired, white-skinned scrapyard worker who drag races on weekends, who paid Frank Hawley $1,000 in cash, and whose luck has been running out. He'd blundered by shifting too quick off the line, then jammed the shift lever back in low in a panicked attempt to correct his error.

I feel sorry for Jon. He tries hard but has a handicap: He can barely read. "I'll look at a story in a book," he tells me, "and I can go, 'The . . . rat . . . came . . . into . . . the . . . house . . . and . . . ate . . . the . . . ice . . . cream,' but that is about as good as I can do.' " Jon has come here to learn how to become a professional drag racer so he can change his life.

I am doing okay; in fact, am the teacher's pet. Hawley points to me on videotape. "Jon, you could teach a chimp these skills. Burnout, banana, prestage, banana, stage, banana, cut the light, banana. High gear, banana. It's easy. See what Mark does? Nothing. When his car accelerates, he's a bag of bricks. He just sits there. In drag racing, that's the secret of success."

Outside, the end of the quarter mile looks far away. I watch other drivers make their runs. Alternately hot and cold, I move from sun to shade, shade to sun, zipping and unzipping my fire suit, part of me all for hiding behind the skirts of somebody else's larger, better disaster. But when Jon sends his dragster fishtailing all over the track, its rear end swerving toward the concrete retaining wall protecting the bleachers, it isn't a balm. "Scary," one of the three women here, a small thin mechanic, says.

Yeah. You can make more bad mistakes out here in four seconds than you have in the last four years. Hawley puts a hand on my shoulder. "A little advice. All of a sudden you're starting to think too much. I'd like to cut out half your brain." Then: "Are you okay? Your shoe is untied. You look like a lost little kid."

I know that if I say, "I'm sick and on fire and you look like vapor," he won't let me get back in the car. A half hour later, I am strapped in again. Hawley approaches. "You're ready for the quarter."

"I thought we were supposed to go eight hundred feet first."

"You've got good control. You're ready."

I get back in my car, feverish. I feel made out of hot paper. Strapped in, I think: This must be what it feels like to get belted into the electric chair. Wheeling onto the course, the engine crackles behind my head. The burnout, backup, the crew chief waves me forward, the machine blubs and crackles to the starting line. Prestage, stage. Lights descend. I shoot off the line, slam against the horizon. Cones flashed to either side and I push the shift to high.

The empty stands spew by. The finish line whaps beneath me. I snap the parachute release and cut the engine. What has happened? I feel like I just went a million miles an hour, like I've lost a new virginity. My mindless monkey fingers fool around under my chin, yank at the crash helmet strap as the crew guys swing by in the van to tow me back to the pits. When they ask me how I did, I yell and scream who-knows-what.

4

Machine Dreams

We were flying. On my dad's lap, the Hudson Hornet's steering wheel as big as a world in my jerking nine-year-old's grasp, fir trees whipping by above the arc of freshly tarred Woodside Drive, our new ranch house looming as long as a little aircraft carrier through the windshield as I swung the car off the road and into the driveway, both my feet stabbing for the brake.

My dad's Hudson was an upside-down bathtub of a car whose 308-cubic-inch flathead six sported a three-quarter racing cam and "twin H-power"—dual carburetors. Shaped like a streamlined Sherman tank, the Hudson's doors must have weighed two hundred pounds. Still, it drove like a cut cat.

My legs tangled in my father's legs, we whizzed through the driveway, through the breezeway, past the garage in back, over grass and, *splash*, into the jungle of rhododendrons. Home sweet home. "Holy Cristóbal," my dad said, getting out. I waited for him to get mad, but wrecking the hedge didn't seem to bother him a bit.

The house I'd nearly crashed into was a five-bedroom home designed by local architects known for their sleek and solid use of wood—and built among tall fir trees in Raleigh Hills—a pretty place, farmland twenty years before—where if you were black you were here to do floors. Big, low, new custom homes. The suburbs. Highballs, bark dust, Herman Kahn, Velveeta, IBM stock splitting every six months. The first day in our fresh neighborhood the tan, little, agile-as-a-monkey architect's daughter next door came pedaling across the road on her bike, skidded a comma of puffing dust on the gravel and told me, "Tell your dad my dad told my mom your mom's a dish."

At school I was already thinking the unthinkable, after having sat in class before a whirring projector, watching a cartoon of Sputnik tumble confidently above a gory blue-and-orange earth and, at home, on TV, a pop of light and the majestic roil of a mushroom cloud. Soon we'd incinerate or be incinerated, that was the jist.

A good life for a boy. My father worked dawn to dusk but on weekends he would throw a football toward orbit. He'd stand on one side of the house, I'd wait on the other. The football would shoot above the roof, like a shivering flying saucer, ascending into the white Oregon sky, then drop spiraling into my spidery hands. He was an athlete. He could ride a bike standing on its seat, could drive a golf ball three hundred yards off a tee and when he won the Members Handicap Tournament at the Portland Golf Club, he brought home a silver chalice as big as a sink.

But the best thing was his fast driving. Calm as a corpse, my dad would fly through traffic, whip the Hudson through Oregon's windy roads as surely and silently as if the Hudson were mounted on railroad tracks. The key: "No matter how fast you go, your tires should never make a sound." What I would give to be able to drive so fast and soundless.

Anything. I was a fairly disconnected child. I kept expecting to pick up the newspaper in the morning and read the headline:

SORRY, YOU DON'T EXIST.

See Details Inside.

I had awful ideas. For example, somehow, maybe because she seemed to be all of a sudden spending a lot of time in her nightgown and robe and didn't seem very happy, I was convinced that there was something wrong with my mother.

But what? TV had taught me to fear the big three: divorce, nervous breakdowns and cancer.

Divorce made no sense. My parents never fought and besides, my mother was a hardcore Catholic. Before she met my father, she'd been engaged to the science fiction writer Frank Herbert—who would later write *Dune*—but broke the engagement off because Herbert had been divorced. So that was out.

What about a nervous breakdown? No, the craziest thing my mother did was draw in bed. She was an artist and soft, gray flowers and babies and dogs emerged from the swift strokes of her pencil. But that was the thing, she was in bed too much. So, when I saw a TV show in which a boy's dad got cancer, that convinced me.

To escape this loony dread, I lost myself in fantasy. I'd ride my bike the mile or so to where the Kienow's shopping center had sprouted among the fir trees and pluck from the magazine racks *Car Craft, Hot Rod* and *Rod & Custom*. I'd thumb past the letters to the editor. Some genius writing in about his "custom" Clinton V5703 lawn mower painted with flames and equipped with a "hot cam and a milled head." I'd glance at big ads for *Music from Mr. Lucky* and *Eddy Arnold Sings Them Again*, ogle ads for racing equipment—the $29.95 Acura Shift floor shifter displayed under another spinning Sputnik—and then on to where the cars were displayed like the bunnies in *Playboy*: gleaming voluptuous "customs" like the "Thunderlet," a '57 Chevy with a '59 Thunderbird grille mounted below '59 Dodge front fenders and '57 Ford quarter panels mated with '59 Plymouth gravel pans that formed a chic rocket ship rear end. A photo of the Thunderlet's creator was there, behind the wheel, black hair combed to a tidy little storm surf and his smile more gum than teeth. My thought: This nincompoop has created his own dream machine. Why couldn't I?

At night I'd read. On my wall, moonlight provoked the OO OO wheels of the wild 1912 Oct-o-Car. My dad had given me framed drawings of that eight-wheeled wonder—those wheels, were arranged OO OO, four in line to a side—and a Stanley Steamer.

I couldn't turn on my bed lamp because I was supposed to be asleep. There wasn't enough moonlight to illuminate my stack of car magazines, so I had to resort to the dime-sized pink light on my electric blanket control.

I was hooked on speed and I inhabited race car books. Reading by the tiny pink electric blanket light, I risked frost bite with Henry Ford when in 1904 he became the first American to hold the land speed record. Piloting a contraption that could have been two bicycles sandwiching a tractor engine, he raced Michigan's frozen Lake St. Clair. A track was laid in burning coals for his tires. *Ice.* But no other surface was flat enough to facilitate Ford's record-breaking 91.37 miles per hour. Ford nearly lost control of the car and his triumph so terrified him that he vowed never to climb into a racer again.

Then, another book propped by the pink electric blanket light and curled up in bed, I was again transported—baked in Utah's blinding white 1937 desert, my skin blistering with sunburn, beside the leviathan

British streamliners, there with George Eyston when he brought his eight-wheeled, seven-ton, thirty-eight-foot-long Thunderbolt to Bonneville salt flats. The Thunderbolt housed two V-12 thirty-six-liter 2,350-horsepower Rolls-Royce aircraft engines—equivalent to thirty standard Cadillac V-8s—a combination that punched him over the salt at over 311 miles per hour. Though my dad said England's parliamentary democracy was superior to ours, I wasn't big on the British, with their pith helmets, failed dreams of empire and safari shorts above fish-belly white calves. No Yankee wog, I was with them there on the white, hot salt but not of them—I took tea at three.

All that bookish, snaggle-toothed bravado. Plus, hadn't they hanged whoever said "I regret that I have but one life to give for my country"? With an American rope, no less. Since 1927 all land speed records had been established by the British on American soil. American racers weren't coming in close.

How could this be? We had crew cuts, biceps, better technology—the Sabre jet fighter, color TV, the new Kent menthols and better dentists. Our only hope seemed to be Mickey Thompson. Thompson was preparing a four-engined streamliner, the Challenger. It was hot rod-like, small by British standards. In fact, the British were already talking about breaking the sound barrier in locomotive-size rocket cars. Supersonic Redcoats. Only Thompson stood in their way.

A guy who in his photos looked like a white pug boxer off a Wanted poster, Thompson was a hot rodder, and hot rodders represented the me I wanted to be. Hot rod history, I already knew, was the history of the junkyard availability of the Ford flathead V-8. Anybody, even a boy, could have one. Introduced in 1934—after Henry Ford considered an X-8 option, four cylinders on top, four on the bottom—the original flathead V-8 displaced only 221 cubic inches. It was a tenth the size of some British motors, but provided bargain basement power. Now the Mickey Thompsons of the world were honing their machines on the drags strips of Southern California, mostly former airfields around Los Angeles. Flatheads had given way to overhead valve high-compression V-8s like the one in my mother's Cadillac. Eddie Hill had already raced a four-engine dragster and Thompson, employing four Pontiac V-8s in the Challenger, was taking the four-motor concept to a showdown with the Crown in Bonneville.

Hot cars were getting hotter. I lusted after "cars of the future," with jet tail fins and Plexiglas canopies that looked designed to shoot down MiGs, cars like sharks or knives or UFOs. Like the Ford X-1000, designed to house an engine either in front or in back, it had three seats arranged triangularly with the driver in the center, and onboard radar. Or, better, yet, the Ford Nucleon, a nuclear-powered car with a range of five thousand miles. Cars that steered sideways, cars that flew, cars that were dynamic, ingenious and sure-footedly insane.

In my mind I kept seeing cars drop from Rocky Butte. If they'd just saved one. This ripping off '57 Chevy quarter panels to slap on Ford fenders and jerking off bumpers to substitute inverted Plymouth dust pans to make "Thunderlets" didn't look so hard. I'd done it tons of times—I spent all my money on AMT hot rod models. They were $1.39 apiece. I'd break all the little parts off white plastic trees. I'd have six going at once, my objective always to build wilder and wilder cars. Using a razor blade and soldering gun, I'd chop the tiny tops, cut the frames to lower the wheels to the ground. Then the goddamned glue would creep like an amoeba across the clear plastic windshields and the spray paint would run and puddle into candy apple red and lime green goo. I got better at these surgeries but no matter how nice the cars turned out, they were never the cars I'd imagined. Often I'd get bored and not finish what I'd started and the table where I'd assemble the little machines looked like a Lilliputian's junkyard.

At night in the tiny shine of the pink electric blanket light, I read Henry Gregor Felson's classic car novel, *Hot Rod*. What romance: Behind the wheel of your Ford rocketing down some godforsaken lost American highway, your baby doll girlfriend beside you, loyal to your quest for something superpowerful and heroic that might appear to be, to the unschooled eye, blithering idiocy. I wondered: Why couldn't that be happening to me?

Maybe it could. I had a new friend, Dick Donaca. He was a short, round-faced boy whose crew cut was combed up in front to a spike fence by butch wax, which clung to his hair like pollen. He resembled the current subteen Disney movie idol known as Moochie, and was outspoken. In class my teacher, Mr. Davis, a former professional baseball pitcher, asked me a multiplication question along the lines of, "What's twenty-two times eight?"

"Let's see: eight times two is sixteen, carry the one—"

"Mark, come on, it's not that hard—"

"That's what *she* said," Dick piped up.

"Donaca," Mr. Davis said and aimed his wood pointer at Dick as though it were a sword. "I suppose you know the answer?"

"Elementary, my dear Stiff Arm: one hundred seventy-six."

Dick went by the names "Sir Cedric Seed" and "Dick Tator"—as in "Dick Tator and the Tator Vine Boys," his gang of fourth graders. To whom he instructed, "Don't let your pie go dry," "Elvis! He's the king!" and "On your feet or on your kaaa-nees!" He lived with his mom and dad and three older brothers, Bill, Dan and John, in a mechanical Garden of Eden above a gulch about a mile from my house. The Donacas' split-level was a museum of the future of everything that had a motor and was dangerous. Hot rods, motorcycles—*stacks* of them, everything from a gorgeous old JAP to a state-of-the-art Gilara racing bike—go-carts, a sleek yellow airboat with a huge German cross painted on the tail, model airplanes that looped and zapped in circles around the Donacas' backyard like big, pissed-off mosquitoes. If it floated, flew, drove or exploded, the Donacas had one. Dick and his brothers raced their motorcycles out at "Sidewinders" racetrack. The two oldest, Bill and Dan, on big Matchless bikes and Triumphs. Dick, the youngest, on his Gilara. I'd go along, eat hot dogs and breathe Castrol from the spewing exhausts. Now and then a brother would slam his machine into the hay bales surrounding the track. It looked fatal, but was only exciting.

The Donacas had a dirt track in their big backyard and Dick convinced his brother John to let me drive his go-cart. John was a year older than I. He wore his T-shirt sleeves rolled to his shoulders, jeans, pointed black shoes and his hair was combed to fins and scoops. A chubby boy Elvis, but tough, and not a kid to cross.

"How do I do this?" I asked.

"Elementary, my dear Stiff Arm," Dick said. "Get in and aim it. We do the rest."

I climbed into the cart. It had direct drive—a chain straight off the motor's crankshaft to the axle. To start the motor, Dick and John had to lift the cart up in the rear, run down the track with me steering and drop the cart so that the rear wheels would spin on the dirt, which would spin the chain, which would spin the motor, get it to fire—and *pop, bang, rrrrrrrrrrrrrrrrh*, dust flying everywhere, my foot to the floor, the cart was caroming over the dirt so fast I saw house, field, woods, house, field, woods only in flashes as I blasted around the track, Dick and John waving through the haze for me to stop. But I didn't know how.

Finally, stomping on the brake, I slowed down enough so John could snatch the roll bar and wrestle the cart skidding across the dirt like a steel rodeo steer. He was screaming. "Why didn't you hit the kill switch! I told you to hit the kill switch."

I climbed out of the go-cart, legs spaghetti, John was barking words that had to be swearing but that were too complicated for me to understand. I'd done eight, ten, twelve laps, who knew, John could beat me bloody, I didn't care. All I was sure about was I had combined speed and stupidity and survived.

5

1990

I live in Belmont Shore, a California beach town populated mostly by Yuppies, though close to a Mexican ghetto where the only Yuppies are the cops, and just south of Los Angeles, a city my friend Gideon Bosker identified to me in a recent letter as "an ex-paradise where opulence is an accessory and where looking for a window of opportunity qualifies as a genuine job description."

My wife, Debbie, and I had moved from Oregon to California before the heyday of political correctness, back when cocaine was still good for you. Our exit from Portland was speeded, however, by the idea that it was time for a healthy change. For example, after I found myself in a house with Big G Little O and Ronnie Jo, two high school friends— handsome, bright, athletic, ex-All-American boys—who had just bought $10,000 cash for $500 cash. Good deal. The only difference between the $10,000 they bought and the $500 they bought it with, was that the $500 didn't have red teller's dye squirted all over it from a bank robbery.

We came here so that I could write a book about TV. California has been fine. My cheery toddler son appeared as "triplets" in *California* magazine, my daughter was selected out of her Brownie troop by a casting scout mom to appear in a nationally televised oil company ad, Deb was just on the cover of *California Business* magazine in the guise of a California businesswoman—which, as an interior designer, she actually is—and at our first Hollywood party I was asked how I liked being "Mr. Deborah Winger" after some soul of unction mistook my wife for the famous young actress.

So here we are. Saddam Hussein has just beaned Kuwait. Gideon says this means war—but I figure that's doubtful. Whoever this guy is he'll pull his troops out as soon as he secures whatever economic concessions he's after, as nobody but a complete idiot would take on all of NATO. Returning from the grocery store today, I see a familiar stocky, red-haired figure standing at parade rest by my front door. It is my friend Chuck, a defense industry analyst, who has told me that he would "kill" to have my wife and kids, and this morning he has frightening news: The end of the cold war has left all our neighborhood's secret underground Soviet Spetznas agents unemployed. When I ask him what he is talking about, he is blunt. "Waiters, used car dealers, high school teachers, a network of Green Beret–style Russian spies disguised as harmless Americans, but poised to take over Southern California at the start of World War Three. Gorbachev just fired 'em and they're pissed." Chuck follows me inside my duplex. "So look out." He draws a finger across his throat.

In the living room my blonde, three-year-old Matt is rapt to the sugary schemes of Brainy Smurf on TV. He's a very good little guy. Co-ordinated. He can already bump, grind and gyrate to the stereo like a little Little Richard, and the other day, driving home from day care strapped in a baby seat in the back of my old Porsche, he asked me, "Is this you car?" as if to say, *I'm pretty new from the womb, let's get acquainted,* and when I said yes, he smiled and said, "I lige it."

A voice from the back of the house. I see my wife's small face and a flash of her wavy copper hair behind our doorless kitchen door. Deb is on the phone. A client, for tax reasons, has to redecorate his house fast. Thank God, because we live like students—this minute I'm not making as much as the guy who delivers my mail—and we can use the money.

I sit down at my desk. I have been trying to reinvent my ideas for the car. The problem is that what I originally imagined isn't original or really imagined at all. At age nine it would have been easier. I haven't drawn for years and my hands are mitts.

"What's that?" Chuck asks, peering over my shoulder.

"My dream machine." I had blueprinted a coupe made of the best aspects of classic cars. My grille was lifted from the 1953 Jaguar XK120. A simple chrome oval, perfect. I stole the front fender shape from a Porsche 944, the rear flank from the hips of a Shelby Cobra, my tail from the round butt of a 928 Porsche, the top from a 1963 Corvette split-window coupe. But the car that had looked so great inside my head went south as soon as it saw paper. A crafty quilt of plagarisms, not awful, actually—except my drawing stunk, and my wife has already voiced her doubts: "If you plan to create the best car ever designed and built by the best people in the car-making business, isn't it egotistic to think the best designer could possibly be you?"

A waterfall moustache and nest of scraggly hair. C. H. Luigi Colani, oyster-eyed Renaissance man, towering bon vivant, electric son of Kurdistan, who claims to be weighted by "four thousand years of culture like a monkey on my back," designer of Ferraris, BMWs, zeppelins and "the most important beer mugs in Europe," the man *Stern* magazine hailed as "the Leonardo da Vinci of the twentieth century."

I am on a talent search. I need to secure Gideon's $100,000—Gideon having made it clear that, "We must have the best people involved from the very beginning" or no hundred grand. Fortunately, I have met a foremost designer of our age. Dressed in clothes from three centuries, Ben Franklin suede-tongued shoes, celluloid starched collar, fin-de-siecle boating jacket and white linen, unstructured (wrinkled) disco jammies, Colani had arrived at the Art Center College of Design with his own Chautauqua: House-long trucks full of his dream cars and promotional hats, Luigi Colani shampoo and a *Last Supper* contingent of stylish apostles, young men with complex haircuts wearing white CO-LANI T-shirts who have names like Ari, Sergi and Lars.

Sunny, cool California winter in the mountains above Los Angeles. The Art Center provides this country more than half its automobile designers. Their promotion literature informs me that Art Center graduates include Henry Haga, director of GM Advanced Concept Center; Jack Telnack, chief of design at Ford; Willie G. Davidson, design director for Harley-Davidson; Mark Jordan, designer of the Mazda Miata; Richard Soderberg, head of Porsche's Advanced Concept Studio. The basic message appears to be: The next time you're stuck in traffic look around and know that most of what you're seeing was designed by Art Center alumni.

The Art Center is hosting a Colani symposium. There are over a thousand people here in his honor, executives from everywhere from Apple Computer to Walt Disney Imagineering. For Colani, who spends "two months every year underwater, looking at fish, thinking," is a car visionary. "I was one of the first to use carbon fiber," he tells me. "Twenty years ago. Mother Nature, however, beat me by eighteen billion years." Maybe eighteen million. English is not Luigi's mother tongue.

Walking down halls arrayed with the swooping, wheeled visions of Art Center wunderkind, I follow Colani to a room where his models are displayed like *objets d'art*. There he informs a senior vice president for Volvo America, "You build junk. Garbage."

The gray-suited executive, his plump face going both pale and red under an eave of boyish blond hair, replies, "I don't know what you mean."

"I mean," Luigi says, "a car is not just a stupid metal beast! A car can be a beautiful useful thing!"

The vice president wants to answer, but his mouth is imploding as Colani goes on: "You must design the new car. The car for the new century. Or you are finished. People will go to their garages, look at their automobiles and shoot them."

I sympathize. Trying to design the car myself, I'd looked at the best new auto designers for inspiration. But what I'd seen were not so much cars of the future as cars of tomorrow. Cars one step ahead of the cars we are driving today, cars that looked more like appliances than Louvre-quality sex machines.

"You are not a civilization," Colani advises, "you are a technological society. That is why I like America. Specialists are everywhere."

He plans a fleet of cargo-carrying airships: "We will live again to see the day when people are dancing slowly in the salons of dirigibles floating two thousand meters above the pure white snows of Siberia,"—and one thousand-passenger, ten-engined jet airliners that look like man-eating sharks. Also, he is building an asymmetrical sailboat designed to go sixty miles an hour and new computer keyboards shaped like the twin globes of a woman's bottom because "that is what mankind's fingers are designed to feel."

He shows me a model of his "supertrain," being built in Germany to go four hundred kilometers an hour. It is driven by a single wheel seven feet tall and its engineer "dressed traditionally for tradition's sake—but with the skills of a Formula One racer" will sit in a pod above this wheel. The train's cowcatcher resembles a huge duck bill and is designed so that "if the train runs into something it forces the engineer to eject out the back. He is surrounded by an inflatable ball that automatically blows up and sends him bouncing along the countryside for miles, laughing."

But cars are Luigi's passion.

He is spending four million dollars for a 1,000-horsepower turbo-charged nitrous oxide–assisted machine built around a modified Corvette chassis. A car similar to what I have in mind for my own tin utopia. Though, for his part, Colani is designing his Corvette after the Disticus Marginaus, a water bug. One that, propelled by grasshopperlike back legs, shoots through the water at a meter per second. But he likes my more modest plan. "You have the mind of a Colani," he says. "You must come visit me in Bern."

Outside, Colani cars are strewn around a tiny grass valley at the back of the school. Beside his space-age semis, the Utah 12. An eighty-foot-long two-headed hydra, the Utah has a snout below housing a behemoth 15,070 cc Mercedes truck engine, and a snout above—a cockpit of curved clear Plexiglas. The Utah 12 ferries Luigi's roadshow, "Au-tomorrow," across America. Twelve cars of the future, everything from man-powered, streamlined "auto-bikes" to high-horsepower racing cars, the most radical of which looks—with its two streamlined sets of wheels set at the corners of a body so sleek it's almost invisible—like two globs of falling spit brought huge and horizontal. The problem, as much as I like—and am even in awe of—Colani's other designs, most of these cars look less visionary than extreme.

I drive my old yellow Porsche home through smog bad enough to be a special effect.

6

BOY WONDER

Like poetry and murder, auto design is often mastered young. I've returned to the Art Center, where twenty-two-year-olds have, for decades, seen their hallucinations made the design clichés of the future.

Above me in the classroom are two sketches on the wall of a fantastic car, fore and aft: soft and rounded in back, sharp in front. Its tail looks like something recently alive, its knife-edged snout like the thing that might have killed it, a fat, low silhouette pregnant with vows of power and speed. The designer's influences are subtle, though I can see the plump, rounded ghost of my 1964 Porsche in his rear and the thrust of a classic, slab-sided Avanti up front. The car makes a new impression from every angle and presents, overall, a weird, exciting kind of voluptuous austerity. Regal, both severely futuristic and elegantly retro, as if it were from a past that has not happened yet. This bladed vision is wild but almost perfectly controlled, created as part of a Mazda-sponsored project to design a luxury sports coupe to attract "the new old," men thirty-five to forty-five. It is the most beautiful car I've ever seen.

The car's designer, Nick Pugh, drifts into the room. Slender, in jeans and a black T-shirt with Mickey Mouse grinning off the front, he looks more like a grown-up mall rat than someone who, as I am about to be informed by General Motors Head of Advanced Concepts Jerry Palmer, "will be designing the cars we drive in the year 2000."

When I ask Nick about the car, he says, "I wanted to break away from the rounded, simple aero look of cars today—a Mercedes looks like a Lexus that looks like a Cadillac—where everything is developed to blend together. You know, like if the fender has a teardrop shape, the door handle will have a teardrop shape, you get sleek homogeny that's neat for a minute, then boring. I wanted to design a car that sent a lot of different signals, that had movement when standing still, the feel you get from a cheetah or an old Auburn Boattail Speedster. I used a small top juxtaposed to a massive body to get a missile effect. It's not a 'fuck you' car—it's meant to be shocking but attractive."

He shows me his portfolio. Nick is the inventor of "vaginal air-scoops" and an "eumorphic mind-controlled sex machine for any sexual preference" and I see a "robot assassination creature capable of injecting lethal doses of cyanide and carrying enough plastic explosives to obliterate a 747," and a naked, bullet-breasted nymph in the clutches of a purple octopus creature. The "octopus" is making love to this beautiful, idealized and ecstasy-drunk young Candice Bergen. I say: "Nice-looking woman," and Nick's friend Dean Robinson replies, "It's actually Nick's girlfriend."

I ask Nick about the cars that influenced his design and he says, "It wasn't cars so much as natural stuff, organic, beautiful things. Insects and women. A car is an emotional sculpture, and creating one is as passionate as having sex. It's all from the most primitive part of your reptile brain. I want my car to make sense the way a cloud makes sense or a tree, design with nonlinear symmetry. To do something completely new."

And when I say his cars are scary, like cars from an excellent nightmare, Nick is delighted. "Like a babe who has soft curves but talon nails, who could maybe kill you. I want my cars to be both spooky and inviting, because that makes for thinking and excitement." He shows me a sketch of his idea for a new Porsche. I say it looks Japanese and Nick exclaims, "Exactly! I drew it in the style of an old Japanese watercolor and nobody besides you ever realized that."

It is as if this kid is designing the cars I would have designed had I not given up on design—he's got the best ideas I never had. He doesn't lack for good notice either. One of his friends says he's the prototype of the creative idealist. "Totally honest and dedicated to the big vision of 'I want to make the world a better place.' Nick'll work all day on his own design, then spend all night helping somebody else on theirs."

Pugh's instructor Geza Loczi, head of Volvo Design America, tells me, "Nick shakes up the tree. His Mazda-sponsored car gave the others here permission to explore the completely untraditional. It's a totally original design, nothing based on normal perceptions. He's the guy who goes into a museum, turns a sculpture upside down and says, 'Now what if we look at it this way?' "

"He's the best new car designer I've seen in years," Ben Salvador, designer of the new Chevy Caprice, told me. When I called Jerry Palmer, designer of the current-generation Corvette, he concluded, "He's already a complete designer, analytical, very demanding of himself, exciting, uninhibited. We have a job waiting for him if he wants it."

Nick asks what I know about car design. Only the basics: A) That the language of car style was first written with the alphabet of speed. That early car builders attempting to increase performance learned to shape their machines aerodynamically to go faster, quicker, but aerodynamics had little to do with automobile aesthetics until Finley Robertson Porter applied aerodynamic touches—winged fenders, a rounded cowl—to the 1908 Mercer Runabout and achieved a very purposely pleasing visual effect; B) That in 1922, Alfred P. Sloan, founder of General Motors, wrote a memo to his staff noting that ever-changing car designs would be important, because technologically the car had stopped evolving quickly enough to spur needed sales, an insight that did more to promote the world's variety of automobile design than anything else; C) That five years later, General Motors designer Harley Earl (I've been told) created the first car ever born from design rather than engineering, the Cadallic La Salle. It was a tremendous success; D) That in 1937, Earle introduced the first "dream car," the Buick "Y-Job," which gave to the world the power convertible top, power window and, for the first time, fenders which "flowed" into the body. The Y-Job— whose name, awkwardly, was taken from that of experimental aircraft— served a far more important function, however. For the first time, the public was baited with a steel promise from the automobile future. Not a car that you could buy, just a car that you could dream of buying; E) That dreams, even preposterous ones, became a staple of American auto sales, and that the reason midcentury European cars have had a more lasting influence is their designers looked to European race cars for inspiration, while American designers snubbed function and looked to jets. This after Harley Earl introduced the first auto tail fins—those on my mother's 1949 Cadillac, modeled on the twin fins on a P-38 fighter plane; F) That however flamboyant or even dumb a lot of these American designs were, their designers wielded tremendous clout, not only within the auto industry, but over popular culture as well; G) That Nick Pugh is a throwback to the great audacious designers of the flamboyant hot car past; H) But that now, in the age of "aero drab" design, car designers face brick walls as soon as they step into their careers.

Days later I stand in the Art Center gallery and watch as Nick's model is presented to the chiefs of Mazda, Pugh's sponsor for the project.

Nick, his dark hair swept back in a sheet, wearing a zootie-looking suit and surrounded by student-designed cars of the future, points to his own car—a device resembling a trilobite designed for Le Mans—and informs the heads of Mazda that he has sought to break new ground, to use "fractology" in a new approach to "angular graphics to create a car that is subtly spooky." The Japanese laugh.

"The car," he says, "integrates faceted crystalline edges with a sweeping form."

He moves a hand above the flank of the silver little machine. About as big as a big breadbox, taller in the rear than at the front, it seems to crouch forward, as if it would like to jump off its pedestal. "I didn't want to violate its shoulder," he says, explaining why the car has a finned front end. "I wanted a leaping look. So that the lines defining the sides of the car are like the arms of a diver."

"This design is astonishing," the president of Mazda Design America, a curly-haired Japanese-American named Tom Matano, exclaims.

"I've treated the front as an elegant arch, like the entrance to a building." Nick then admits to "certain unrealistic aspects."

Mazda's general manager of Design, Shigenori Fukuda, a slender, sharp-jawed man in a metal-colored suit, indicated the swollen rear of Pugh's car. "Is that the front or the back?"

"The back," Nick says. Fukuda and his assistant look puzzled and I can see a look on Pugh's face that says, *I'm talking calculus in an algebra class.*

Then Tom Matano cut in. "This could be the future, right here."

7

SUDDEN DEATH

Summer 1957. The money flew up in the air, and I dived in. Vague coins, and a lot of them, rained down through the water as I paddled frantically to the bottom of the swimming pool at the Portland Golf Club. A year had passed since I had watched the hot rods tumble off Rocky Butte; it was another Fourth of July. A lifeguard had chucked a bucket of change out on the water and members' children got to dive for it. I clawed the bottom of the pool, bumping and elbowing other kids in desperate slow motion and came out with a few nickels, quarters and dimes. Model money.

On my walk home that afternoon, beside the wide, black ribbon of Scholls Ferry Road that ran past the sixth hole, I heard a sound. Way down Scholls Ferry something low and squat was rippling out of the July heat. It got bigger and I knew what it was. In this neighborhood boys would nose and deck junker Fords and Mercs, remove insignias and fill the holes with lead. Lead bonds uncertainly with steel and often would separate and crack the paint, leaving hairline maps of unknown continents on the hoods and trunks. I could see, on the nose of the Mercury, that separation now. I could hear too, the heavenly too-loud sound of its engine as it snarled by. I wondered: What kind of motor did it have? Guys were ripping out the old flathead V-8s and replacing that outmoded engine with overhead valve motors taken from Cadillacs, Oldsmobiles and Chevrolets. A single-stock two-barrel carburetor might be discarded for a big four-barrel or "tripower"—three two-barrel carburetors in a neat little row down the middle of the engine— bigger carburetors or more carburetors meant the car could drink more gas, and more gas meant more power. Stock exhaust headers would be replaced by big, thick snakes of steel tube exhaust that allowed the exhaust gases to escape quicker and gave any hot rod, and this one that just howled by, a throaty roar. I was punched with longing.

Not a good time. My mother had been in the hospital. One day out of the shower and wrapped in a blue bath towel, she had shown me not her missing breast but the explosive surgical damage above it. She had had a radical mastectomy. A whole muscle had been removed below her shoulder and the scars were red and splashy. I had been, so to speak, dead on the money. She had cancer. Not serious cancer, that cancer had been cut out, but cancer nevertheless. Though everybody said she was going to get better, she was now in bed more often than not, and our Catholic church had provided us with a live-in. Fifteen, Iris was a girl of the va-va-voom school whose dad had been crushed in a logging accident and who gave my younger brother Scott and me the blow-by-blow on all the top sex acts while she unpacked her suitcase. Iris had a twenty-three-year-old boyfriend, Dick, who had a low explosion of greasy black hair and drove a candy apple red '49 Ford that had been lowered to the dirt and had chrome exhausts—lake pipes—snaking from front wheels to back. But it was the candy apple red paint that killed me. To a nine-year-old the effect was literal. The paint made the car look delicious.

Iris and Dick would sit on the couch in our living room frisking each other and I'd watch from the kitchen, thinking, If I had a candy car like Dick's, I too could have a teenage girlfriend whose chest led the rest of her like the bow of a ship.

At school, addled by worry about my mother, I drew suavely impossible cars whose profiles were so low you'd have to be a midget or maybe even a baby to drive one, as knowledge passed around me. I had no idea what to do with myself, no idea even if I really was.

At sunny Lost Creek, under a veil of alders and cedar, my father's fly rod whipped back and forth on the slender axle of his wrist. The leader made a zipping S above us, and sent a hand-tied Royal Coachman flying over the clear water.

My problem, he said, was that I wasn't ruthless. No, my problem was that a dozen feet of my line hung in a tetrahedral-rhomboidal mess in the branches of a tree that leaned over the wiggly little rapids where, at this moment, a trout lunged from the water, snapped up the fly and took off downstream. My dad, in his khakis and waders, let the fish run, then began tugging it gently upstream.

He could cast through anything, I couldn't cast to save my life. That was my problem. Besides, I was violent—wasn't that the same as ruthless?

No.

Was he ruthless?

That illicited a half-smile. Troubling. My dad ruthless? Impossible, and why was being ruthless important, anyway?

Because to achieve life's most difficult tasks you had to be able to impose your will on others, no matter what, he said.

That did not sound real nice.

Successful people rarely were, he replied.

But he was nice, and successful.

Again the half-smile. The trout was flopping out of the water, silver and desperate, big too, a keeper. He slipped the Royal Coachman from its mouth, leaned over and deftly bashed its head on a half-submerged rock. The only part of fishing I didn't like. Two or three times a year he would drive me in the Hudson up here under the snowy peak of Mount Hood to the strange stream, Lost Creek, that flowed underground for who knew how long—thus the name. He would carry me on his back through the water to find gravel-banked spots on the stream where we'd fish all day long. I loved it, but now, seeing blood curl in a wobbly halo around the trout's head before my dad washed the fish off and dropped it in his creel, I felt as if I were in a Grimm's fairy tale, my father doing what he seemed to be saying.

During the drive down from the mountain he said I should think about my future, but life could be rough.

He told me that art and literature were bankrupt. Ernest Hemingway was "an imposter" and Picasso nothing but a "talented schizophrenic" who had stolen his best ideas from the ancient Mayans, Incans and Africans. The future of creativity lay in science and design. But car design had gone haywire. Each fall, new cars showed up first in *Life* magazine. My dad would sit down with my little brother Scott and me and assess what he saw. Tail fins. Tail fins bigger every year; tail fins, he said, were the symbol of a nation with too much money, too many insecurities and too few real ideas.

"You could do better than that," he said.

I? Me? I could?

Yeah. He was serious. I was astounded. My father was not big on compliments. In fact, so far, he'd given me only one. He'd told me that I was a good-looking kid, and would never have a problem with women.

But design cars? Really? At school I got As in art and Bs in PE—Cs and Ds in everything else. Already I wanted to be a writer, but my dad advised against that. Though our house was practically a library, the best writers were only "watchers" he explained, the only writers with influence were "propagandists" like Goebbels and the people who ran the *Saturday Evening Post*. No, car designer would be much better. Because I had the talent. Yes. I'd design and build cars, part of the new technological world unfolding in front of us. Sleek order would be king, Werner von Braun president and Jack Webb secretary of state. Suddenly the big-motored, swooping phantasmagorias that appeared beneath the sharpened tip of my pencils took new meaning. They weren't just schoolboy fantasies, they were real and important, and suddenly I was confident that my future was assured.

Sudden Death came out of nowhere, seeming to just *appear* in the Donacas' garage one day. Sudden Death made Iris's boyfriend's '49 Ford look like, in Dick Donaca's words, "a pussy wagon." As low as a snake, dark as nothing, Sudden Death belonged to Dick's much older brother Bill. It was a 300-horsepower murder weapon. Primer black and powered by an Olds J22 V-8, it had three double-barrel carburetors and its cylinders had been bored out "twenty over." One night, Bill took Dick and me downtown to see *Journey to the Center of the Earth*. Riding in the front seat behind the snarl of the Olds V-8, Sudden Death quaking and hissing at every stoplight, I knew I could rule the world with such a machine, and in the movie theater even the sight on the screen of the unbelievable cavern whose walls were diamonds and rubies or the fact that the guys who went to the center of the earth discovered that, instead of a molten core, the earth really had at its center some kind of other Pacific Ocean, could not get Sudden Death off my nine-year-old mind, the car's lethal feel, sound and smell.

My dad could build a car like that. Sudden Death II. I tried to point him in that direction. Sunday mornings I'd ride with him to the hospital to check on patients, and after he made his rounds, we would go look at new Corvettes. Why not buy one? Because, he replied, a Corvette didn't handle like a sports car, it was basically just a "short Chevrolet." Well, so what? "Handling" had nothing to do with power or looks, "handling" was for hairdressers and dentists.

So why not a hot rod instead? He took me to the Portland Roadster Show at the big, new Memorial Coliseum to see machines less metal than desire, cars with huge tires in back, skinny chrome wheels in front, engines with lush, bulbous, chrome-covered cylinder heads the iron equal of Jayne Mansfield's chest and paint that might burn to touch.

We could build a hot rod. Couldn't we? My dad wouldn't say, though I did get clues that he was considering it. For example, one Saturday he took me to a junkyard. Dressed in his khakis, maybe the same ones—who knew—he was wearing in World War II when, firing from his PBY bomber's bubble turret at a Jap Island, he got so caught up that he sent machine gun bullets ripping into the tail wing and nearly shot down his own plane.

The junkyard was a paradise of disaster. Mountains of rust-dusted old Fords and DeSotos and Pontiacs. Sprawling archipelagos of radiators and canyons of bumpers piled up like chrome logs. I saw, transmogrified, beautiful cars everywhere. A few dollars, a little body putty. But my dad didn't want to pop $150 for a '40 Ford that looked like it had been hit with God's fist. He was there for a hubcap.

Then stunning news. My mother went to the hospital again and one night my father sat me down in a stuffed, gold chair in his den, pulled me on his lap and told me that, barring a miracle, she would not be coming back.

8

BREAK EVERY RULE

There is a hole in the market where my designs can fit in. But how can I make them make me very rich, famous and followed?
—from Nick Pugh's notebook

"You met this doctor in a bar," Nick Pugh says, "and he told you he'd give you a hundred thousand dollars to, like, fulfill your lifelong dream of building a dream car?"

"No," I correct, "he is a friend, Gideon Bosker, a doctor who also writes great books about design. He told me in a hotel bar he thinks this is a great time to create the best-designed car ever."

This minute I'm not sure whether I'm interviewing, auditioning or about to bid on this kid. I had just returned from Tom Matano's office at the Mazda Design Center in Irvine. "Nick's car was the wildest one in his class. It exudes temperature. It is very eccentric, but has warmth. You want to jump in and zoom off," Matano enthused. "This is the bold design we must have. Very sexy."

Nick's drawings have an erotic, bright, lurid and even lawless feel that elicits an enthusiasm one might reserve for a *Penthouse* pet. Selling Nick Pugh cars, it occurred to me, could be about as easy as selling corn dogs to the Donner Party.

Matano was stocky, friendly and perhaps the most admired design chief in the industry. He hired the Art Center's Mark Jordan and the result was the hugely successful Miata. He'd just hired another Art Center graduate, Craig Derphy, who designed Chrysler's V-10-powered Viper. "Nick's model is like that. What is so great about the Viper," Matano said, "is that it doesn't make sense. A V-10 engine?

Who needs that? People do! Because they want to go faster. To win! To be the best. It is the human spirit."

Now Nick and I are at the art deco–decorated cottage Nick's friend Dean Robinson shares with his girlfriend. Dean is a fabricator-turned-Jane Fonda bodyguard-turned-scholarshipped design student. His regular features, muscular torso and shoulder-length blond hair evoke a hippie Superman.

"I want to design individual cars for individual people. Car companies," Nick says, "are all art by committee. Like if you wrote a novel and your publisher said, 'We want more suspense so we're throwing in a mystery writer, and more sex, so we're throwing in a dude from *Hustler*.' No car company would allow me to design a car all by myself." Nick says he wants to be influential in a big way quickly. "But first, I want my name on a car. The only reason American designers aren't more powerful is because they say they aren't. So what is it exactly you want to do?"

"To create the most powerful street-legal machine ever. Made by the best-of-the-best fabricators and engineers in the country. The ultimate high-performance car," I reply. "Using your design."

I embroider my pitch: Nick will design the car, Dean Robinson will fabricate it and we will do everything on the relative cheap—design prototypes and concept car budgets run $2 million apiece, but we can create our own car for a fraction of that. We'll find an old rear-engined exotic sports car—a Lotus or Pantera—buy it, strip it and over the chassis create a machine that Nick can use to create his own design studio à la Bertoni and Ghia. A studio on which to build a vital career.

That's about all it takes. Nick says yes and shows me sketches of homes and buildings, plans for what could be the creation of a twenty-first-century paradise on earth.

Nick keeps a notebook. In it he has written:

* *Beauty is its own excuse for being.*
* *The Stealth bomber is as decadent as the Palace of Versailles.*
* *Less is not more, less is boring.*
* *Nothing dates faster than people's future fantasies.*
* *Working in the car industry is out of the question. The only answer is to lead my own organization. I must be in charge of my own destiny*

and not be a wrung on an endless gray ladder that leads up to corporate pinstripe heaven. I must plan on a global scale.

Under an empty sky, Nick graduates from the Art Center. He says he is glad to go, that the Art Center sent him down a route no wider than a hair. I meet Nick's trim and pretty mother: She had written a book about business and her family was, Nick informed me, the inspiration for the primordial American soap opera, *Peyton Place.* Nick's younger brother Dave is there too: sunny, friendly, blonde hair cut to a cap, long on top and shaved around the sides and wearing long, dressy knickers and black-lensed granny glasses, a natty caddie from Alpha Centauri. I am introduced to Nick's dad: He resembles the popular idea of Jesus Christ. Tall, thin, hair to his shoulders. A renowned mathematician, he demonstrated it is possible to turn a sphere inside out without breaking its surface.

Two weeks later, I find a message on my machine: "Mark. Nick. I got news from out of this world. Completely weird, great, fabulous. I can't talk about it over the phone."

I drive to Nick's apartment in Pasadena. We've been hanging around together. He's funny, seems very honest and is never not working. Though it's hard to get a fix. He knows design history back to the shape of the apple in Eden but when informed *Esquire* wanted to publish photos of his model, he said, "*Esquire*—isn't that like *Ladies' Farm Journal?*" Against both gun control and capital punishment, his politics appear to mate Rush Limbaugh with Mother Bloor. Also, according to his friend Dean Robinson, "Nick is known at school as Prince Nick, difficult when he doesn't get his way."

Nick's apartment is in back on the second floor. Leafy trees rise around me. I walk up worn wood steps to a patio. Behind glass doors Nick is hunched over a drawing table. The place looks exploded. Papers, clothes, dishes scattered everywhere.

Khaki shorts, a shirt that looks African, Nick's hair is slicked back, as if he'd just climbed out of a swimming pool. He shows me black squares the size of an old-fashioned record album but two inches thick. "I just got Seimans S.A. to donate one of their top-secret calcium chloride hexohydrate passive air-conditioning systems to the car. They're built not to exceed eighty-one degrees Fahrenheit no matter what." Stick them in our car and they will? Have a definite cooling effect, Nick supposes.

The model is there, unearthly on his desk. Mazda offered to buy the design rights but he turned them down. He suggests we call the car the "Xeno." I asked him what Xeno means. He says, "Who knows"; he went to the desert and, there, just sort of hallucinated it.

It has occurred to me that if I'm going to put Gideon's money where my mouth is, I'd better lock Nick into this. So to secure the butterfly on the pin of its own ambition, I propose a budget of $200,000—twice Gideon's $100,000—cut into ten shares of $20,000 to be sold to investors, a plan I hear for the first time as I say it. "Upon sale of the car," I explain, "profits are split between the investors and us. But we must plan everything before we build anything." Then I sketch the particulars. "Twenty thousand dollars for the body, twenty thousand dollars for engine and drive train, fifteen thousand dollars for the chassis, ten thousand dollars for wheels and front-wheel skirt assembly, ten thousand dollars for doors, fifteen thousand dollars for interior, five thousand dollars for paint, twenty thousand dollars for glass. Add ten thousand dollars for tools, fifteen thousand dollars for overhead, twenty thousand dollars for Nick—that's you—legal and promotional expenses of five thousand dollars and twenty thousand dollars for miscellaneous, and my total is one hundred eighty-five thousand dollars." That should make him happy.

It doesn't. "Realistically?" he says. "That's low. Engineering movable front-wheel skirts alone could set us back a fortune. We may have to set higher numbers. Gnarly. But maybe what we have to do to create an ultimate." Then he steps to his desk to reveal a complicated roll back plan for opening the car's doors.

I suggest. "Let's keep things simple," but can see that things won't be. The elegant S line he put on the car's flank to define the trailing edge of the door took Nick minutes. Its execution will take days. How much time will it rob from the thousand other things needing his attention—positioning of windshield wipers, plumbing the guts of the doors themselves, construction from nothing of a body that has few mass-produced parts? Nick plans to have the Xeno's steering wheel right in the middle. How much will it cost to engineer that? Also, he wants the body to be handmade from aluminum. Suddenly a voice inside my head informs me: Not only will this be spendy, but it may take a long time being spendy. *Perfection* is a word Nick uses a lot and I wonder: What if this kid gadgets me into bankruptcy?

That night he calls to report that his $20,000 design fee may be low. His mother's boyfriend Ed, who has invented a way to eliminate scar tissue, says Nick must charge substantial fees in the prospectus or investors will think he lacks confidence in his own worth. Nick is upbeat, however. "If it weren't for you," he concludes, "I'd probably already be working in a cubicle for a car company. Thanks a lot, you really changed my life."

9

MAN'S WORLD

"It killed his boy," my neighbor Mark Rosenthal, patting the truck, reveals, "so he wants to get rid of it. It's a hermaphrodite. 1955, '56, '57 grille, '57, '58, '59 cab. It's made out of everything."

We are in Newport Beach, standing in an airline pilot's backyard next to a lethal old tow truck.

Beside that tow truck squats the rotting hulk of Bob Hope's 1957 Lincoln Mark Five. The Lincoln's tires rotted to shards, the coupe is sinking into the earth. Weeds spike up around the front seats. Most of its steel is so rusted that it is no stronger than a cookie. I touch the trunk and a little chunk of it cracks off in my hand. "It's a hallucination," Rosenthal says. "You can see it, but it's so rusted out it's no longer here."

Rosenthal, with his handlebar moustache and gold hair pulled to a ponytail and in jeans and a white T-shirt, looks like a surfer pirate. He is a car collector. He'd just invested in a classic gold 1955 Cadillac Biarritz convertible. Swank-made metal. A calfskin interior and a 331-cubic-inch V-8. The Biarritz's rocket-shaped bumper guards are bigger than artillery shells, and already Mark has a potential buyer. My cousin Jerry.

Navy doctor, actor, pig farmer, Jerry's chest and stomach swell above the pedestal of his legs and he looks less a surgeon than the honcho who comes down from the Teamster office to tell you where on the docks you're going to work, what your hours are and how much you're going to get paid. Jerry'd built a '32 Ford dragster powered by a flathead V-8 when I was still falling out of my cradle and is the closest thing I have to a big brother. Without Jerry I would probably be either in jail, a mental institution, dead, or perhaps even a rich criminal trial attorney.

To my cousin, there is little that is impossible. So when he got to our house I told him of Gideon's offer: to create a fantastic high-performance car, one fabricated to uncompromised design and quality standards and how now even though Ronald Reagan is history and greed has evidently gone the way of the granny dress, the exotic car market is going wild, people are paying astronomical amounts of money for any kind of too-powerful car—Ferraris selling new for $300,000 are going for five times that I conclude, hoping that my cousin will want to invest.

Jerry suggests that to raise money, I follow his example and get into cattle ranching. When I say I lack a ranch he tells me, "You don't need one. All you need is a *Wall Street Journal* and a phone. Three phone calls is all it takes. One to buy the cows. One to get 'em to the feed lot. One to send 'em to the slaughterhouse. It's that simple. It's making me a fortune."

Good. Because fortunes need to be spent somewhere, and Jerry loves strange cars.

We go out in front of my duplex where Mark Rosenthal has parked the Biarritz. "I like this car," Jerry admits, the right exhaust of the Biarritz farting into his palm. "Are the windows hydraulic or electric?"

"Electric," Rosenthal says.

"Good. Hydraulic's a nightmare." Jerry gets up off his knees. We are behind Rosenthal's garage in the alley. The Biarritz's convertible top is down. Jerry looks at the new upholstery. "Is this all original Cadillac pattern?"

"To the stitch," Mark says and scratches at the edge of his dark blond moustache. "A Rolls-Royce guy did it." He pinches the top of the seat. "Vinyl creases. Leather doesn't." Rosenthal's seat, pinched, looks un-molested. The dickering begins.

It's 1959. Knees on the cushions, elbows on the couch's back, age eleven, I looked out of the living room window as this zombie out of the night with chopped hair and ripped jeans shouldered the door to my father's den hard, harder, and then, mouth small with concentration, jammed something in its lock and began jiggling the doorknob. After moments he strode across the patio and grabbed the door to the dining room, behind which our black live-in, Sally Stringer, a big woman above bird legs, held a butcher knife, assuring me, "That fella sticks his head inside, he's gonna lose it."*

She'd called the cops, my dad at the hospital and my cousin Jerry up at the medical school. Minutes later I saw stars flicker through the woods, then two suns whipped into the driveway and Jerry's latest '57 T-Bird skidded to a stop, dust tumbling in its headlights. His key scratched into the back door lock. He bolted into the kitchen and to his bedroom where I watched him snap together a shotgun and slip in big red shells. Sally shouted, "Hurry," the guy was running across the yard out onto Golfland. Jerry took off, but no luck, and by the time the cops and my dad got there, Jerry was mortified he hadn't been able to shoot anybody.

My cousin Jerry had come to live with us after my mother died. He went to medical school. Twenty-two, with his black crew cut, slightly squinty eyes, beakish nose and mouth built for saying loud words fast, Jerry had a real man's arms, wore white T-shirts and baggy white cords, worked construction and was somehow also in the Navy. He'd lived with Bing Crosby's sons all summer in Hollywood—when I asked what Hollywood was like, he shrugged, "A lot of haircuts," an assessment amended only by, "and a lot of jokers who are—" he made a fluttering motion with his hand. When I asked him what that meant, he replied, "Well, let's just say that if Rock or Sal or Tab invite you over for a slumber party, you take a rain check." He'd been thrown in jail in high school for joyriding without a license and he had already built his own drag racer. When he arrived, a new life arrived with him: Man's World. Beer kegs in our basement, the Kingston Trio's "Bad Man's Blunder" on the stereo, a hairless friend named Willie. Jerry took me to parties in apartments that had paintings made out of streaks and splashes, "Take Five" noodling from somewhere and women. Dolls. Beehive hairdos and steep Vs of cleavage above a little black dress and spiked heels. His pals had Porsches and long, new Mercs and Chevys—I'd ride with Jerry in a '57 T-Bird, me straddled over the transmission hump and his latest set of curves with her leg pressed to mine.

Jerry was the first person other than my dad to think I had promise. I first got his attention when I asked him to help with my math homework. I had, I thought, discovered something weird. 0 x 2 was 0, ob-

---

*She would. Sally was tough: "Doctor own this house, doctor don't run this house." She had big arms, and gleaming dental work. So friendly, her laugh flashed a gold mine. But Muhammad Ali in his prime would never have spotted her a butcher knife.

viously. But 2 x 0 was not 0, 2 x 0—my logic demanded—was 2. Not 0 like my math book said. When I asked Jerry about this, explaining, "If you have two of something and multiply it times zero, you still have two of something. Multiplying two rabbits by zero doesn't make those two rabbits go away."

Jerry grabbed my math book, studied the equation, then, grimly enthusiastic, declared that I was right, I had unearthed an earth-shattering mathematical boo-boo, and that not only would this discovery establish forever my path as a visionary on par with Aristotle, Shakespeare and Einstein, but it might undo the laws of physics as well. The minute 2 x 0 = 2 not 2 x 0 = 0 was made, dams could burst, jets drop from the sky and the earth fall from its orbit into the sun.

All we had to do, my cousin said, was check with his father, my own father's older brother Bert. My Uncle Bert was the head of the chemistry department at Oregon State and there had just been an article in the newspaper about how he was only one of a dozen people to fully understand Albert Einstein's Theory of Relativity. Once I got the thumbs up from Uncle Bert I could reveal 2 x 0 = 2 and the universe would implode.

Fantastic, but first, grocery shopping. Declaring that he was "no happy housewife," Jerry said that from now on we'd only go grocery shopping once a month. Okay. My bushy-haired little brother Scott and I piled into the Hudson, Jerry at the wheel. *Vroom, screech*, we were there. "You kids gotta eat this crap," Jerry announced, "not me, so go get what you want." Scott and I rolled four shopping carts filled with Sugar Pops, Sugar Smacks, sugar everything to the check stand, Jerry accessing to the checker, "This is nothing but candy-covered dog kibble. I want a deal."

A what? Minutes later out came the manager to say this was not a Moroccan medina but a grocery store. Jerry held up our receipt, a ribbon two feet long. "Pal, I'm buying your week's salary. But if you want, you can restock everything, I'll go down the road."

So, a cereal sale.

Jerry and my father were like father and son. Though my father was a director of the American Ophthalmology Association, who in his starched white shirt, pressed charcoal slacks and tie with tiny knights on it, looked like a surgeon from Central Casting, and Jerry was, well, not. At a time when doctors were treated like gods, Jerry took a different view: "Hospitals are dangerous places. If you're not sick when you get there, you probably will be before you leave." Mostly, people became doctors because they weren't popular in high school, he explained. He seemed to spend more time watching *Rocky and Bullwinkle* than he did studying. "Half of medicine is voodoo, and all you have to do is remember what you read. It says here that the knee bone's connected to the thigh bone and the thigh bone's connected to the hip bone. Remember enough mumbo jumbo like that and you get your M.D." According to my cousin, all a surgeon was, was an auto mechanic who'd remembered to wash his hands. "You go in, take stuff apart, fix what you can, put it all back together and send somebody a bill." Eyes, cars, no big difference. What Jerry admired was music and art. "Any fool can do a corneal transplant, but it takes real talent to play the guitar," and eye surgery would do until he could launch a career that really meant something: as a writer for *Mad* magazine.

Not to put too fine a point on it, but Jerry saved me. Before he arrived, I was falling off my little rocker. While my mother was on her death bed, her priest told my parents that unless my dad accepted the Catholic Jesus as his savior, my mother would go to Hell.

How could he accept Jesus if he didn't believe in God? But my mother in Hell? After school I'd get on my bike and scream around the block, my eyes squirt guns. But Jerry assured me that no God— even if there was one, which thank God, there probably wasn't—would send anybody to Hell "for not kissing up to the goddamned Catholic Church," and that I should stop getting "hopped up over horseshit" and follow the hot rod gospel: "Just keep things simple."

For example, Jerry said all vital human relationships could be defined by the honest answer to the question: "What do you want?" This following my own answer to that question at my school's career day. What did I want? Most kids said they wanted to become doctors, lawyers, Indian chiefs or at least firemen. But at Jerry's suggestion I had scrawled a perhaps more realistic goal on my "Great Futures" sign-up sheet: Amoral technocrat. Our busty, fiery live-in Iris got a call from my angry teacher and when, after a shouting match, Jerry had asked Iris herself the key question to define all important human relationships, she had replied, "For you to stop screwing up this kid and get the hell out of here." To Iris, a devout Catholic except where the facts of life were concerned, Jerry was a major gas station on the highway to Hell. And given the chemistry between the two it was a miracle they didn't kill

each other or start a family. Iris blew up again when Jerry started helping me with my religious training. "Do you know," he said one afternoon in the garage, his head buried under the open hood of his new
girlfriend's T-Bird, "how the good Lord got his name?"

"No." I was there to pass him wrenches and screwdrivers.

"Well," he said, ducking upright, his hands gloved with grease, "after
Mary and Joseph were booted out of the inn they had to go to the
manger. It was dark and Joseph stubbed his toe on a rock. 'Jesus Christ!'
he shouted. Then he turned to Mary and said, 'Hey, that's not a half
bad name for our kid.' Now, do you know what's going on here?"

Yeah, the T-Bird was loud and powerful. That's what was going on.
"Look," he replied in his gravelly voice, "you should know this: The
crankshaft is hooked by a chain to the camshaft, which looks like a line
of eggs on a skewer. When the camshaft rotates, the tip of each 'egg'
drives a rod up against the underside of a rocker arm resembling a
teeter-totter. One side of the 'teeter-totter' goes up and the other down,
the down side either pushes open a fuel valve to let gas in the compression chamber or pushes open an exhaust valve to let the just-
detonated gas escape."

"How's gas get from the gas tank to the engine?" I asked.

"Easy." Jerry lit a Marlboro. "A pump that runs off the crankshaft
sucks it up a line from the tank on one end and drives it up another
line to the carburetor on the other end."

"Why not just pump it straight into the cylinders?"

"Because the carburetor has to mix the gas with air to make a spray
or it wouldn't explode. A process," he waved smoke away from his face,
"that repeats over and over."

I hung on his every word. True, there'd been a slight complication
with my Uncle Bert's assessment of my revolutionary $2 \times 0 = 2$, not 0
discovery, but Jerry had stood by me all the way.

Now we were about to go on a joyride, and though I already knew
that the thing Jerry was best at with cars was crashing them, I wasn't
worried. Because Jerry looked out for me. When I choked on steak he'd
smacked me on the back hard enough to bruise and assured me that
even a kitchen knife, driven in hard enough, could make for a successful
tracheotomy—and he taught me to box, organized my rage and once,
bored, let his gloves bob down. *Smack.* His eyes went away. I thought
I was screwed, but no. He hauled me before my father with news I had
a future: Hitting people in the face. In Golden Gloves. "Len, the kid's
really got a left." My dad replied that "the kid" was also skinny as

chicken wire. "So?" Jerry said, "They match 'em by weight. He'll be two feet taller and two years older than anybody he's up against. Get the right spade trainer and he'll kill every eight-year-old in town."

Parenthetically, my cousin noted that I might also one day pitch in the World Series. I played Little League, occasionally on second base, but mostly as a citizen of the outfield, where I'd spend most of my time rereading the inscriptions I'd scrawled on the pocket of my mitt:

DO UNTO OTHERS BEFORE THEY DO UNTO YOU

IF AT FIRST YOU DON'T SUCCEED, TRY A GUN

And below that the more down to earth:

DON'T SMOKE IN BED, THE ASHES THAT FALL MAY BE YOU

and thinking about the 1,000,000,000,000,000,000,000,000,000,000,000,000,000,000 other things that were going on in the universe while I stared toward home plate watching my coach, a corporate attorney who, dressed in slacks and a button-down white shirt and resembling George Bush Senior, plead with his son to throw strikes.

Jerry and I played catch at night and my cousin was convinced that I was born to throw a curve, that the ball moved all over the place every time it left my hand (I bought that part) and that, "Len, your kid throws a baseball *nobody* could hit; you oughta go tell that jackass coach of his to put somebody on the mound that can get things done."

Jerry also explained the world to me. For instance, how they filmed those stampede-the-cattle-right-over-the-camera shots in cowboy shows, how they paid a wino $10,000 and gave him a year to spend it and at year's end he had to go out and . . .

I only saw my dad mad at Jerry twice. Once when Jerry brought home bags of skinless, frozen rabbits. Sally fried them up for our dinner and my dad was impressed—"Jeez, they taste like chicken"—until he asked how much Jerry had paid for them and my cousin replied, "Nothing, Len. I got 'em free at the med school research lab—they all died from screwed-up experiments and stuff."

The other time was when Jerry enlisted my brother and little sister to go door to door on behalf of Jerry's newly founded Poor Motherless Children's Car Wash.

Like my dad, Jerry drove fast casually, like he was just loafing at ninety miles an hour. One hand on the wheel, as if he were not driving at all but on our couch in the TV room, not watching the road, but *The Flinstones*. But riding with Jerry was even better than riding with my dad, because with my dad, no matter how fast we went, it was like riding on a roller coaster: I knew I was safe. With Jerry, I knew I was anything but. The least I could hope for was a gratifying minor injury— weeks before, beside him in the Hudson, I slammed into the dashboard after Jerry, giving the finger to a neighbor in the wake of a near collision, lost sight of the road and drove into a drainage ditch.

And we were barely out of our driveway.

Like my father, Jerry's lessons were simple: 1) Do as I say, not as I do; 2) Respect for all, awe for none. A man of action, he taught me how to blow smoke rings within smoke rings within smoke rings, and made quick work of my late mother's beautiful '49 Cadillac. One head-on and off to the junkyard.

Just old enough to vote, arms that could do endless pushups, a five o'clock shadow by noon, my cousin was the best new mom ever.*

First and foremost, Jerry knew the secret to good parenting: Hypnotism. Forget the "lie back, relax, let your cares fall away" nonsense,

---

*But my favorite thing about him was that he ruled the world. Anything he wanted, Jerry got. At Christmas I expected from my cousin, what? A carton of Marlboros. But instead, for my younger brother and me, Oregon State College football uniforms. Helmets, shoulder pads, everything—not fake plastic shoulder pads, but real plastic shoulder pads that when you strapped them on and jumped up and down in estasy because you got such an unbelievable Christmas present clacked like plastic armor.

Even my dad was impressed. How did Jerry get all this stuff?

My cousin shrugged. "I went to the clown who runs the place and said, 'You don't need all this crap you got laying around here, let me take a few odds and ends off your hands.' "

Christmas afternoon I stood holding a football beside my cousin in our big, fir tree–shaded backyard: "But, Jerry, in *Sports Illustrated*'s Pro QB Passing Tips, Johnny Unitas said—"

"What would he know?" Jerry took the ball, spun it in the air expertly between us, plopped it back into my tendril hands. "Here's how you do it. Let your fingers do the thinking. Keep your brain out of it. Hike it to me and I'll show you."

Metamorphosis. A football that was a leathery balloon in my unsteady grip became akin to a piece of sidewalk in Jerry's. Dodging mole holes while running across our lawn, I saw a brown blur and was hit in the stomach by what? A concrete spear?

My father, so precise, could drop a football into your hands from twenty or thirty yards, light as a marshmallow. Jerry passed the ball with a mean catapulting motion that I practiced until editorials at school about my throwing evolved from "spaghetti arm" to "goddamn it—you want the fucking ball to kill me?" and I was elevated from the last boy picked at recess to quarterback who led his team to not actually all that humiliating losses against the other ragtag playground teams who had eleven-year-old quarterbacks with teenaged arms and talent.

he just had Scott and me sit before a fat brown Blitz beer bottle and said, "Stare at the bottle. Okay, you're hypnotized. From now on, you little ja-bronis follow my orders." I didn't feel hypnotized, but my brother Scott claimed we were so hypnotized we didn't know we were hypnotized—mindless zombies in Jerry's total power. I asked my cousin, "You mean if I set the house on fire it is because I'm in your control?"

"Bingo."

"And if I go get straight A's in school it is because I'm in your power?"

That response took longer. But finally, "Harder to swallow, but theoretically."

But what Jerry was best at was improving my behavior. Afraid my father would magically "go to the hospital and not come back," I was wild in the streets. At school I was a fanatic for the game four square, a game where players, each in their square, slam a big ball around a four-square grid. I was good at slamming. The problem was, older boys, particularly big Elvis-like John Donaca, boss of the playground, were always pushing me out of line and taking cuts.

So what was the answer to playground conflict? Easy. Violence. "Sock 'em," Jerry said.

"Sock John Donaca—he'll kill me," I replied.

"No, he won't. He'll just beat you up. You'll live. Then if he does it again, you sock him again."

"And he'll beat me up again," I said.

Jerry blew a smoke ring within a smoke ring within a smoke ring. He was definitely the best of the best at Marlboros. "Nah. Guys hate being hit. He'll go after somebody else."

I thought about that, and what Dick Donaca said: "Either on your feet or on your kaa-neees." So the next day, when John took cuts in front of me, *smack*, no warning, I clocked him. He put a hand to his nose, and when he saw blood on his fingers he decked me.

We were sent to the boys' room to clean up. John made paper towels blobby red and said, "Listen, you skinny little fuck, do yourself a big favor. Tell the truth. You hit me first."

Then we were off to the principal's office. After school, John was waiting for me outside my class. I figured the worst, but instead, nirvana. John said I'd done exactly the right thing and as my reward I had a new job: henchman. He was naming me assistant playground bully. Now I could play all the four square I wanted, unmolested. If I wanted

to take cuts, hey, feel free, cut away. If anybody gave me any shit, all I
had to do was squeal to John.

Assistant playground bully. I've never had a better job.

One hundred miles south of Portland, in his cabin by the lake at Fern
Ridge, my pot-bellied Uncle Bert, in his baggy black bathing suit, had
laughed so hard he was crying. "Two times zero equals two, you have
to be crazy," he told his son Jerry, who had explained: "It's like this: If
I have two zits on my face"—which already worried me because, as a
demonstration tool it stunk as Jerry had no zits at all—"and I multiply
those zits times zero, that doesn't make my pimples go away. Therefore,
two zits times two zits still equal two zits."

"Mathematics isn't about acne," my uncle replied. "It's about inte-
gers—numbers, Jerry." He wiped his eyes, started laughing again. My
uncle, my father's older brother, ruled the laboratories at Oregon State,
where a rainbow ensemble of chemicals gurgled and zoomed through
glass stems and coils, their colors neon. On a locked laboratory door
was a sexy yellow-and-black DANGER! RADIOACTIVE MATERIALS sign.
Jerry said his father could go into any kitchen, mix common spices so
that, if you set a match to the mixture, good-bye neighborhood. We
were there at the lake to waterski. On the dock Jerry would slip a
banana ski on one foot, stand holding the tow rope in one hand, bark:
"Hit it!" and his dad, my Uncle Bert, would gun their ski boat, ripping
Jerry off the dock and across the water. He'd fly over the wake, skid
across the waves at fifty miles an hour, his shoulder dipping so low it
would splash off a white cap. Until this moment, I thought my cousin
could do anything, but suddenly it looked like there would be no dams
bursting, no jet planes falling from the sky, no end of the world. "I
don't want you encouraging this poor kid's fantasies," my uncle concluded. Then to me: "Markie, stick to your dream cars."

Jerry took me outside, down to the dock. "Hell," he said, "what's he
know? You multiply two of a real thing times zero of a real thing, you
still have a real thing. End of argument."

Anyway, the joyride.

The little Thunderbird's hardtop was off, and I leapt over the
door on the passenger's side. The T-Bird was a sports car for a newly

enriched middle class. Its contours were long, elegant, delicate and it came in largely feminine colors: beige, white, pale blue, even pink, but under the hood was a 312-cubic-inch engine larger than the Corvette's and, on special models, cradling dual four-barrel carburetors that made the car a screamer. Detroit had come to realize the marketing punch available on a race track. The year before, Ford, employing race car builders Holman and Moody, outfitted a four-car fleet of "Battlebirds," Thunderbird "stock cars" designed to beat Corvettes. These machines were outfitted variously. One had a standard 312-cubic-inch V-8 stroked to 348 and topped by a supercharger, its power sent to the rear tires via a Jaguar four-speed transmission and a Halibrand quick-change rear end. Another Battlebird had a 430-cubic-inch Lincoln engine and an all-aluminum body. These "stock" T-Birds beat Corvettes, no problem, and Jerry's girlfriend's little Thunderbird certainly did not lack power.

He backed out of our garage, the T-Bird's rear tires chirping, palmed the floor shifter into first gear, hit the gas and, the Thunderbird spitting gravel, we were gone, our neighborhood of expensive, low homes un-furling at superspeed, flying, tires screaming, engine howling, two-lane blacktop jetting beneath the T-Bird, going sixty, seventy, eighty, veering all over the road and, God! Where'd that blur of a truck come from? Wham, it was gone, lost in our dust.

Close one. The Portland Golf Course, ripping by and with a long curl of asphalt visible before the highway disappeared into the trees, Jerry passed two cars at a whack. What would happen if we crashed? Jerry's T-Bird wasn't his, it belonged to his brainy girlfriend Nancy Shaw, who looked like a Miss America. Maybe he'd just say he was sorry.

For Jerry, a car's purpose was to get there now—and he gave me safety tips: Posted highway speeds are only half the real safe top veloc-ity. Never pass on a blind curve, except at night. Then it's okay because if anybody is coming you can see their headlights shining the other way.

We were flying. A one-car Le Mans. I could be joining my mom in heaven in a flash.

Our pit stop was a cheeseburger back at the Portland Golf Club. The atmosphere there was stately, well-dressed golfers, blue-haired ma-trons, black waiters—the Cardigan Confederate—and we stood out. Jerry in baggy white cords and a white T-shirt, me in jeans and a white T-shirt sporting my own artwork—a winged "flying eyeball" as big as

a goldfish bowl with crow's feet and a bloody optic nerve trailing behind—and when the waiter said they didn't serve cheeseburgers after
two, Jerry said that was okay, then he'd be happy to go in the kitchen
and fry up our burgers himself.

Unreal. The waiter changed his mind. Two o'clock in the afternoon.
Four o'clock in the afternoon, no big deal. The kitchen could make
anything, any time. Burgers history, we were home in a heartbeat. Skidding into the driveway, I heard a hiss. I climbed out. Jerry had driven
the T-Bird so hard the right rear tire was sinking flat and, helping him
fix it, the rear of the car jacked up at a crazy angle, my cousin concluded
that it was a good thing that with my mother gone, he was there to fill
the void.

I was in sixth grade when my dad got a Thunderbird himself. White,
300 horsepower. The 1959 Thunderbird was very low, its interior described in Ford literature as "a sunken living room." It was the first
American car with bucket seats and had already established a respect-
able stock car racing history. That year, because of limited entries,
Thunderbird had finished third behind Chevrolet and Ford, though it
had established by far the best individual winning percentage.

The night my father brought his T-Bird home, Scott and I piled in
for a test drive. The speedometer went to 140 and the seats smelled
luxurious, all plasticky and new. Soon there would be a Fuzzbuster radar
detector mounted next to the rearview mirror, but tonight we'd just
have to wing it.

It was dusk. My father wheeled the car up into the wooded hills to
the Calvary Cemetery past my mother's grave and then back onto the
Sunset Freeway toward the beach. The speedometer arced up to 60,
70, then hovered around the dial down to 100, 110. The broken yellow
median lines flicked by us like tracer shells. A hundred and fifteen miles
an hour. My dad said no big deal, his foot hadn't even hit the floor.

10

OUR WORLD OF NOW

In our world of now, there is no beauty for the sake of beauty. It is imperative that design matures into a new age where the creative and emotional experience is as important as function.
                                    —from Nick Pugh's notebook

When I ask my new partner my cousin Jerry's key question to defining life's vital relationships—"What do you want?"—Nick replies as if it is a question he had been waiting for his whole life. "To be the best designer ever. To do the highest-quality work that is humanly possible. To have worldwide impact." Then: "Novel writing won't get our car built," he declares.

The galleys to my latest work have been mailed to my house in rolls. I could paper our walls with my book were I so inclined. "Mark, you have to dedicate your whole life to the Xeno* or the Xeno won't happen."

Could be. Writing novels is dreamworld wonderful, but I am tired of living inside my head. Nick had presented a new opportunity. He said that with all the new superdurable alloys and compounds available, our car could be built to last a lifetime. I replied, great, but it would cost as much as a house *and it hit me!* Make our car to last as long as a house, make our car *an investment* and we could charge—*as much as a house*. Forget novel writing. The creative wattage it took to conjure *make a car as expensive as a house* was no more than what it took me to come up with a bad guy *bon mot* worth nothing but the space on the page it took to fill.

*pronounced *Zee-no*

This shouldn't be so hard. Nick is a designer, my wife is a designer. I know that world. He likes our apartment and I have a helpful parable ready. "Debbie's very versatile. She's knows the difference between fashion and style, knows how to give people the most for their money. More often than not her clients become her friends, so that cuts way down on the haggling time; if they have money problems, she knows how to compromise—"

"I can't do that," Nick says.

"Can't do what?"

"Compromise. Not if we are to achieve our goal of world-changing design. The car we build must be perfect."

Okay. Wow, a reccurring theme. Nick, in purple suede wingtips and an iridescent, blade-shouldered jacket—a New Age zoot suit—is in my sunny living room with a beautiful new drawing of the Xeno when Gideon Bosker calls to say, "Mark, make no small plans. It's visual, visual, visual. A multimedia dog and pony show. CBS follows you by helicopter from Darien, Connecticut, to Phoenix, Arizona. You want, you demand, a forty-city nationwide tour, you and Nick driving across country. We're talking about the creation of a whole new phenomena. This is too *di nuovo* for words."

Gideon says the $100,000 will be forthcoming as soon as the project is nailed down. He asks how the car is going and I have good news. "Nick's the new Messiah. He signals a revolution in design, the end of bland, and he's got the Midas touch."

Nick is waving his arms, shaking his head.

"Good," Gideon affirms. "Because the investors will be buying the aura. If you go shell out fifty million dollars for Van Gogh's *Sunflowers* you're not paying for the paint."

Nick's grasp of the written word is more lyrical than mechanical— he once mistook *there* for *their* and spelled it *thier*. He put a piece of paper in front of me: *Don't exzajjurate*!

Henrietta. Nick's German girlfriend. The heiress. Worth, according to Nick "hundreds of millions." She is twenty, tall, curvy, has lots of pale, sunny hair and gave me a big smile and then considered me with long, guarded eyes. "Piggie talked about you."

Nick met Henrietta while he was teaching sketching at the Art Center in Geneva. "She was pretty hysterical. You'd go into her room and there were these beautiful gowns covered with chocolate and spilled food all over the place."

Now, apparently, she has settled down.

I had just climbed the wood stairs to their apartment after having typed this out for Nick:

```
The essence of the Xeno can be articulated in four
words: Design. Performance. Quality. Environment.
The Xeno will be timeless, a super high performance
car for the year 2000. A "coupe killer," big, lux-
urious, built to reflect the best of a century of
American automaking, designed like a Fabergé egg
and constructed, simply, to last forever.
```

We need something to promote the car to investors. I don't want to be hypocritical about this, and again a voice deep inside me has advice: Better we've fooled ourselves before we go out and try to fool anybody else.

Nick reads, his lips moving as he does, and finally says, "Bitchin' " and announces he has designed our new company stationery. "It's radical. Four inches high, seventeen inches wide."

I ask, "How do we type on it?"

"I talked to a typesetter who says she can do it."

I am puzzled. "It's not whether she can do it or not, it's whether we can type on it or not—besides, the eye can't track seventeen inches across a page."

"Awesome." He says he had a problem with reading, dyslexia, but not to worry. "I'm making my business cards. Out of aluminum. The same dimension."

"Seventeen by four? How do you fit it in your wallet?"

"Easy, if you shrink it really little." He says he wanted to make a thousand promo packets. I ask: How would we distribute the things? Drop them from helicopters? and it occurs to me Nick has never designed a real car before. This can't be Man Ray's twenty-seven-wheeled Dada sports runabout, and if—

"Piggie," Henrietta says, "I think we'd better dress up." We are going to talk to a wealthy landlord about renting "studio space" in which to build the car. Nick loans me slacks, black, cut perfectly and designed by Henrietta's father Wolfgang, "the most powerful fashion designer in Germany and boss of the biggest cosmetic firm in Europe." The three of us get in Henrietta's new Volkswagen Rabbit convertible.

Nick drives top down. Lying in back, I stare up at a dirty sky. After my cousin Jerry was done dickering with Mark Rosenthal over Mark's Biarritz, he held Nick's drawings to the light, studying them as if they were a cancer patient's X-rays, then whistled softly. "I don't know what he's doing, but he sure knows how to do it. You better hang on to this kid." I thought this might be the time to yank on the hook, a la "Jerry, can I have the forty thousand dollars you just decided not to spend on Rosenthal's Cadillac? You'd probably like Nick's car better anyway." But the problem was, nevermind my cousin's wild excursions, Jerry's dirty little secret is that he's reasonable, and I decided I better wait until this is more pounded down at the corners.

We arrive at "the Brewery": a complex of concrete buildings at the industrial edge of downtown Los Angeles. The studio has concrete floors, is big and brick walled. No heat, and a broken window. A Yuppie bus garage. For $2,500 a month. When we leave, Nick asks what I think.

I say, "Two thousand five hundred dollars a month is thirty thousand dollars a year just for rent."

Nick shrugs, "So?"

"Mark," Henrietta, tall, blonde, rich, says, "how much money do you have to build Nick's car?"

"A pledge for one hundred thousand dollars," I reply.

"That's not gonna pay for shit!" Nick crows.

Henrietta's very pretty pale face looms toward mine. "Do you have a written contract for the one hundred thousand dollars?"

"No," I admit. "It's more like a handshake deal." Except Gideon and I didn't shake hands.

We go to a dark, wood-walled restaurant in Pasadena. Nick starts talking about a design job he had for a gizmo where the client didn't care about quality and how disgusted he was and how he put eight hours extra into the project and didn't even bill the guy because, "I don't care if he doesn't care if something is done right, I do. Work must be done right at all costs."

Then he begins to thrill about how excited he is about building the Xeno—Nick, I've noticed, has the renewable evangelical enthusiasm of a guy who comes to your door to sell you a Bible or a vacuum cleaner—he goes into a thing about how a car—our car—could become a medium for transcendental, even perfect, modern art, a new vision that will attract investors, and Henrietta gets, abruptly, angry. At once a millimeter off Nick's nose and a light-year away, she exclaims, "Businesspeople care about numbers, not visions."

Nick looks at her. "Yetta, what's the problem?"

"Piggie, it is very simple." Out of the blue Henrietta now seems tired, as if she is weary from having gone down this road many times before. "You get the fuckin' money first and then you spend it. Not the other way around. We. Simply. Do. Not. Have. The. Money."

Yetta. What if she ends up a Yoko and decides to drag her man off to a cave? I glance at her and see, across the table, a long, pink, lopsided smile, long, sunny hair curving into sleepy, bright eyes that say: Okay, mister, now just who the fuck are you?

11

THE ZONE OF DESTINY

Chances were, my younger brother theorized, we Christensens were as good as—perhaps even better than—the Nazis. A fifth grader, Scott had read that *der Führer* had declared Scandinavians the quintessence of the Master Race, more masterful than the Germans themselves, and that Norway was "the zone of destiny." Scott, who had informed our little sister Laurie's teddy bear, "*Ja Voll, mein* snooks, ve haf vays uf makink you talk," revealed this after one of our cleaning ladies, Mary, a stout, dough-faced woman sporting hair woven to an oily, black croissant, announced that, local high society-wise, we were a good family but not a great one. Okay by me. But when my dad got Hitler's good news, he produced a map of Norway, and indicated, at the top, tiny white islands. Ice islands. That's where we came from. We Christensens weren't even Christensen until some Son of a Christen made the change two generations ago. We were descendants of fishermen whose idea of high tech was a barbed hook and who numbered among the most primitive people on earth.

It was 1962. Camelot. Mickey Thompson's four-Pontiac-engined Challenger had hit 406.6 miles per hour at Bonneville, topping British John Cobb's 1947 mark of 403 miles per hour, and America was riding high. John F. Kennedy was president, and I was in my sunny eighth-grade social studies class reporting to Mrs. Crandall that my father said JFK was about "form not substance," and that during the war, Jack's father had been a bootlegging Nazi sympathizer.

Mrs. Crandall was tall, casually well-dressed, maybe sixty. "Absurd," she said.

"Mrs. Crandall," Dick Donaca exclaimed, "how suggestive!"

"Quiet, Donaca," she snapped. Then to me. "What else?"

The "missile gap" was "nonsense" and—what really got her—that my dad said there was something "unusual" about Richard Nixon. Mrs. Crandall was appalled. Not at my father—he was Dr. Leonard Christensen—but at the audacity of my lies. And when I repeated my dad's opinion that the growing war in Vietnam was a war of independence from foreign domination, Mrs. Crandall said that if we didn't stop the Communists in Vietnam we'd be fighting them in Cannon Beach, a town on the coast where she owned a gift shop.

I didn't know what to do. But my pal Scary Larry Wobbrock did. He was taller than I was, looked older and had read *The Hidden Persuaders*, *The Ugly American* and *The Caine Mutiny*, and he whooped, "The Viet Cong in Cannon Beach! Mrs. Crandall, you're paranoid."

She threw us out of class.

"If you don't shape up, you two will flunk out of high school," she revealed at the end of the period.

"The Viet Cong are not going to invade Cannon Beach, Mrs. Crandall," Larry repeated.

That was it. "Not only will you flunk out of high school," she insisted, "you will flunk out of life."

That night I sat before a thicket of red, yellow, green and blue wires and buglike transistors and resistors spread across a front page of the *Oregonian*. There, for days, had been a map of the beachhead at the Bay of Pigs. At first the beachhead, above which my father was assembling a Heath Kit stereo, expanded. My cousin Jerry was dying to go fight, but was torn. The question was: for which side? Now the beachhead was shrinking fast.

"Mrs. Crandall is a jingoist," my dad said.

Did that mean "bitch"? I wondered, watching him solder. "She says without NATO the Russians would invade Europe."

My father looked at me, then asked his favorite question: "Why?" When I said as part of the worldwide Communist conspiracy, he asked, "Does Mrs. Crandall know the meaning of the word *H-bomb*? If the Russians invaded Europe, two hours later the Soviet Union would look like the face of a moon."

Then back to basics. I asked him: If we could do something as complicated as a stereo, why not a hot rod? We could do it, I told my dad. You're a doctor, you've got money.

Yes, he agreed, he was and he did and we could. His friends owned Corvettes and Jaguars and my dad was creative—he had started a restaurant chain: Hamburger Train. You sat at a counter and your burger, Coke and fries rolled out of the kitchen on flatcars pulled by model locomotives. He was also daring and determined—he'd walked the legs off an Indian guide hunting in Canada; the poor guy had to ride out of the woods on a pack horse—and our freezer was packed with frozen red boulders of moose meat. He was decisive too. When a cleaning lady's drunk boyfriend started pounding on our front door one night, my dad stuck his Navy .45 under the guy's nose and said, "Go home or die." And he did wild things. My dad had a partner, Glover, an Arkansas wheeler-dealer. They owned a big successful pancake house. When Glover was blackmailed into selling it, my dad set a trap—he agreed to sell the restaurant, but not the parking lot on one side. What had Glover done? I had no idea, just that my dad waited until Glover was somehow in the clear, then I sat in our dark, wood-paneled den while my dad, on the phone, informed the new owners that he still owned one foot of the restaurant and that they had best agree to new terms or he'd have a bulldozer repossess the wall of the building.

Next to repossessing restaurant walls, I argued, a hot rod was nothing. We could do something simple, a 500-horsepower version of his T-Bird. Why not replace his slush box with a four-speed stick, punch his 352-inch V-8 out to 390, install a three-quarter racing cam with solid lifters and two four-barrel carburetors—add chrome-spoked American Mag wheels, tuck and roll the upholstery and paint the entire thing canary yellow?

Once again my dad asked his favorite question: Why?

To get the girl next door. An angel. A dust of freckles, features both straight and soft, the whitest teeth, a wave of brown hair. Patty was sensitive—she'd step off a sidewalk if there were ants on the cement—and she loved horses and cars.

I'd walk her home after school. Between school and home was the barn that held the *Faux Pas*, the sailboat her father and my father were building together. A half block away we could hear a screaming buzz saw, and smell of wet fiberglass.

Months before the *Faux Pas*'s new hull had towered like the Ark above us, white, spare, tall as a house behind the cab of the Mack truck roaring toward my father and me at walking speed, the weight of the boat's lead keeled hull bowing the flatbed. The truck eased up to the barn blocks, where the thirty-four-foot "Chinook"–class sailboat would be completed. Its superstructure had been designed by Patty's dad, Jim Gardiner.

Maybe forty, stylish, bald, always tan, a Chesterfield smoker, he had a scar that trickled from the corner of his mouth and had recently accidentally invested in a freighter load of "hardware" that turned out to be machine guns headed from Hong Kong to South American revolutionaries. He'd also designed Portland's brand-new, round, Voss grade school, which looked like a wood flying saucer.

An architect, he had offices in Portland, San Francisco and Honolulu. His assistant was Erwin Rommel's nephew and he and my dad's plan to build the *Faux Pas* themselves had been replaced by a larger one: to have top local craftsmen build a sailboat of unmatched quality, revolutionary in its simplicity. No chrome, no glitz. Almost every surface wood, white fiberglass or brushed aluminum.

Construction finally complete, the *Faux Pas* now had a slip at the Portland Yacht Club where, as essential as a spear, it made half the other boats look like nautical trailer homes. The *Faux Pas* shot my dad to a new world, to the inner sanctum of the president of the Portland Yacht Club itself. Mr. Summers's own yacht was big enough to creak even in its slip. Not just some rich pretend sailor, but a true old salt—that is to say, a wise old leather-skinned alcoholic who drank his weekends away on his cruiser hiding from his wife and kids, Mr. Summers was so impressed by the *Faux Pas* that my dad—who probably knew how to spell "yacht" a year before—was overnight Mr. Summers's personal boat visionary, always welcome down below there in the bourbony fumes.

Saturdays and Sundays, Patty and I would sail the Columbia River, one of our dads at the wheel, she and I shoulder to shoulder on the bow. Patty was sixteen, I was only fourteen, but I was sure I was about to get what was coming to me, when one day I saw—beneath the fir trees in the sloping pine needle–strewn U of her driveway—disaster.

That summer the Beach Boys had a hot rod fantasy hit about some guy who had saved his pennies and saved his dimes and gone out and bought a brand-new 409. This son of a bitch had actually gone out and done it. For there it was, a shiny yellow slab of a car, a brand-new yellow 1964 Chevrolet SS 409. From it had emerged an alien from a distant galaxy. A man. In a madras shirt. Nineteen and there to see Patty. Another "Dick." That was his name, and what impressed Patty most about him was not his looks but his Chevy and its 409-cubic-inch V-8. "It's a big block Rat motor," she sighed, as if Dick's "big block

Rat motor" were a great love poem. Sometimes I'm sure a cigar is just a smoke, but you didn't have to be the ghost of Sigmund Freud to get the message.

At home, in my dad's bathroom mirror, what I saw in my reflected snow-white extra-large Penney's Towncraft T-shirt, Levi's worn out to perfection front view was fine: semibroad shoulders and slender hips. My side view was, how else to say it, not there.

So great. If you were a sixteen-year-old girl with the choice between somebody off a Marine Corps recruiting poster and a boy who looked like Kafka's hunger artist with Brian Wilson's surfer hairdo, who would you choose?

What could I do? Nothing. Except pull into that long U of a pine needle–strewn driveway with a better car.

There was only one possibility. My cousin Jerry had driven off to Minnesota to do his internship. The Hudson was left abandoned, and if it was no match for Dick's yellow SuperSport 409 with its Cragar Mag wheels polished to a hard sparkle and its four-speed and 325-horsepower V-8, the Hudson might be, running, enough to . . .

My dad got the battery charged and said, "If an engine can turn over and get gas and spark into its cylinders, it'll run." Sure enough, with me twisting the key in the ignition as his long surgeon's hand covered over one of the Hudson's carburetors to create a vacuum—the better to suck gas out of the tank—the Hudson made the sound of asthma times one hundred and coughed alive.

I asked for the key and my dad said forget it. I did, until he left for work, and then I pawed through his dresser drawer until I found the damn thing. But magically, the Hudson wouldn't start and its battery pooped out.

Thank God Scary Larry was there. He was forceful and advanced. Take his girlfriend, Suzanne: Her DNA maybe fifty years off the boat from Stockholm, she had a sheet of chrome blonde hair, a woman's chest and a pink petal for a lower lip; a chain smoker, blowzy at fourteen, gorgeous. But he dumped her for trying to "control" him. Nobody "controlled" Scary Larry. He and I lugged the Hudson's battery between us down suburban roads and across cow fields to the gas station by the new Fred Meyer shopping center. Heavy, it sought the center of the earth. We got it charged, lugged it back and with my fingers atop a carburetor, Scary twisted the ignition. The Hudson again made a sound like asthma times one hundred until there were no sounds at all but me screaming swear words I'd finally learned the meaning of. Goddamnit! Hadn't I provided gas and spark? What certainly looked like gas was Niagara-ing out of both carburetors and I'd shocked myself sticking a finger between a spark plug wire and the plug to make sure the little lightning bolts I was seeing were real.

So what to do? Scary, whose strong features were already giving him the face of a man, said: "Yank the battery out of your dad's T-Bird." But wasn't the T-Bird's twelve-volt and the Hudson's six? A battery's a battery, Scary replied. When I hit the ignition the Hudson's horn screamed as the twelve-volt battery sent a flood of electricity through the Hudson's circuits so powerful that the horn was blown, the radio, the starter, pretty much the works.

Okay. If I couldn't drive the Hudson, I could at least change it. Customize it. I ogled J. C. Whitney auto parts catalogs, an idiot's wish list. All white "tuck and roll" seatcover kits. Full-length "lake pipes" and "lowering kits" to put the Hudson's front bumper an inch off the asphalt, where it belonged. Sadly, this trash cost money and I didn't have any. I'd lost my allowance over my younger brother Scott's racing bicycle. Though Scott was barely twelve, he'd scrounged every nickel he could lay his hands on, bought a frame, swoopy underslung aluminum handle bars, a French *derailleur*, Italian tires, sprockets stacked on sprockets that with the help of little baby finger–size levers he mounted surgically on the frame, which delivered about one hundred forward gears and probably reverse—what was going on here? I was supposed to be my father's creative mechanical genius, Scott had bolted everything together way too expertly—that bike looked sexy, that bike looked *good*—and he raced it at a local track. One day, straddling his masterpiece in our backyard, I asked to ride it. Scott refused to say anything but "no," and I got off the bike, picked it up and threw it at him. "That'll cost you your allowance for a week," my father said. "Make it two weeks," I replied. Okay, two weeks. "Make it a month." Okay, a month. "Make it two months." I got worn out at five years.

High and dry. No way to squeeze white Naugahyde "tuck and roll" seat covers, white carpets, chrome air cleaners, Moon discs and lake pipes into my existing estate: seven dollars.

But I was determined. Nevermind that the images the Hudson evoked were upside-down bathtub, albino Sherman tank and two-ton mushroom, *I had my hands on a car*. So how to make the Hudson my own da Vinci's block of granite and rolling honeymoon suite? Easy. Rip off the chrome. Nose and deck it. Yank off the hood and tail ornaments, pull off the side trim. Toward creation of the first Hudson Hornet classic custom of all time. It would drive Patty wild.

12

MARCHING TO MARS

"Can you control him?" my wife asks, concerned about our fate.

"Him" would be Nick. "And what if," she adds, "just for the sake of argument, what if Gideon doesn't come through?"

No, I have no contract, and yes, $100,000 invested in a car created by an unproven twenty-three-year-old designer may pose Gideon "a bit of an enormous risk" as Nick himself has suggested—never mind that $100,000 will not be half the money it will take to build the car. What if, say, Gideon were hit by a truck and went off to a better place?

Well? Debbie and I own a house in Portland ($40,000 worth of the house, anyway), my little Porsche is worth $15,000 easy and my father has given me twenty thousand shares of his company, Eye-dentify, which patented a way to identify people by focusing light on their retinas. So, theoretically, you could walk into a bank naked and cash a check. Already Eye-dentify clients include the FBI and the CIA so, forget Henrietta's $250 million (and I'm not), forget Gideon's $100,000 (and I'm not), if Nick and I need our own money to build the Xeno, sale of Eye-dentify stock should do the trick.

Still, I'm worried. It would be great if Nick and Dean Robinson were partners—Dean spent years building everything from Mexican low-riders to fiberglass Duesenburgs—but Nick says no. The problem: two Michelangelos and one Sistine Chapel. So no Dean Robinson to help build the car, and if we build the car ourselves we'll need tools. A grinder, an air file, a sander, drills, band saw and a cut-off saw, disc sander, buffer, a lathe, a compressor. A new compressor can cost $16,000, the list goes on and on, and I figure everything we think will cost a dollar will probably cost two.

So, another route. I go to "Fat" Jack Robinson of Fat Jack Enterprises, a celebrated hot rodder renowned for the Fat Attack—late 1940s

Ford Rat-motored drag racers—and a man who made his bones building anything that goes too fast really well. Fat Jack is one of an elite group of high-end hot rod builders that includes Boyd Coddington, Lil' John Buttara, Sam Foose, Pete Chapouris and Jim "Jake" Jacobs. These people build hot rods the way the old master yacht builders built yachts—everything handcrafted, one piece at a time.

Asked to give a ballpark figure on creating a 700-horsepower "ultimate street machine," Fat Jack pulls on his gray twined beard and says, "That's like the exclusive hotel where if you gotta ask the price you can't stay there."

We are in Jack's garage out in the unexamined industrial flatlands of Stanton, California. Outside it is 110 degrees. Inside Jack's garage it is a cool, concrete cave. Beside us is what looks to be a 1955 Chevy pickup with new yellow paint. The truck could be a three-thousand-pound yellow mirror. It cradles a 484-cubic-inch 700-horsepower Chevy V-8.

I ask Fat Jack how much, if he doesn't mind telling me, the owner has tied up in the pickup and Fat Jack says he doesn't mind telling me at all. "Three hundred thousand dollars, give or take."

Three hundred thousand dollars for a '55 Chevy? Does God own this thing?

I have the feeling I have just shot to a new world. How, I ask, would we work out the finances?

Jack retreats to his office, plops down under framed magazine photos of cars he has built. His thick hands, crescent mooned with grease across the fingernails, tap over computer keys. "Figure it took one guy a year to build it. That's forty hours a week, fifty weeks at forty dollars an hour. What's that? Eighty thousand and that don't *even* account for parts. No engine, no body, nothin'."

How does the builder/client relationship work out?

"Do, bill, pay, do, bill, pay, do, bill, pay." Fat Jack, fat like a pit bull is fat, wipes his hands on his white T-shirt. "The fuckin' business. Nothin' but whores. Guys measure up your stuff and have machinists fabricate it for 'em. You have something new, somebody steals it. It's a damn disgrace."

Fat Jack made his name with a Rat motor–powered "Fat" 1946 Ford that turned a 150-mile-per-hour quarter mile, the most powerful street-legal car anywhere. "I ran it on straight alcohol. That first Fat Ford could make some power, but it unloaded and went away, hit a dip at nine hundred feet, did four endos and three and a half over and overs."

So what about our financing?

"See this chair?" He indicates the one under his butt. "When you don't pay," he folds his beefy hands over his generous stomach, closes his eyes, "this is what I like doing best."

I like Fat Jack's judge, jury and executioner style—it's cut and dry. Yet Jack is not without compassion. Among the last to ride in his Fat '46 Ford was a dying twelve-year-old. "As a last wish. The poor little kid was on an oxygen tank, I didn't know what to say to him; I thought, What if he had a fuckin' *stroke* in it or something? But we took him down the street, got on it a bit and he said it was the best thing ever happened to him. And I guess it was because next thing I heard he was dead."

Yes, I like Fat Jack, I like Fat Jack a lot, but Fat Jack and Nick Pugh creating the same car?

Nick has had insomnia, took "a majorly potent tranquilizer" and he's drowsy in his ART MADE HERE T-shirt, hunched over, his chest and shoulders a question mark as we drive to Paul Batista Automotive—one of the nation's best known restoration houses. Along a great pale freeway, Nick explains the rich: "It's completely nonabnormal for them to blow fortunes on stuff they never even use. You should see Henrietta's attorney in Germany. He has a whole garage full of Ferraris and Bizarrinis and all they do is sit there and get worth more."

Twenty minutes later, Vincent M. Manocchi, solid as a fireplug in a nice sport coat and shoes shiny enough to shave by, says, "The car is a mystery. What we know is this: It's a 1937 Delage D-8 120, a drophead coupe. The coachwork was by the famed Henri Chapron and it was Louis Delage's personal show car."

A consideration re: a car worth, in Mr. Manocchi's estimate, "a million two, a million five." A car built in the service of luxury, beauty and decadence. To quote the late Henry Manney, *"Un Delage, non pour la femme, mais pour la maitresse."* A Delage, not for the wife, but for the mistress.

Manocchi's stock in trade. He's head of marketing for Paul Batista Automotive, Inc., among the best and biggest classic car restoration facilities anywhere. A forty-thousand-square-foot spread located outside L.A. in dusty, flat, old-fashioned California horse country still not completely ruined by fast-food stands, minimalls and industrial parks. Here standards are jammed to absolutes. Handling about eighty cars at a time, Batista Automotive has tended to nearly five thousand restorations, including that of the most valuable car in the world, Domino pizza czar Tom Monahan's $15 million Bugatti Royale. Batista clients include Michael Jackson, for whom the company created an "all-new" 1909 electric AutoCar. It is labor intensive out here, one mechanic has been working for five years on a single "Al Capone–era" Cadillac. When it was time to reconstruct the rusted-out Cadillac's clock, Batista tracked down clock blueprints that had sat in a Cadillac file for fifty years and had every internal part of the clock remade piece by piece.

"Boys, the first thing we need to do," Mannochi says, "is define your mission profile. Do you want trophies or just a driver? On one hand, you have the flash crowd, who just want a great paint job and a snazzy set of wheels and if the brakes don't work, who cares?"

"So," Nick says, "a lot of cars are way overpriced?"

Manocchi shrugs. "A car's worth whatever a man will pay for it." And later Nick describes Batista's as a "car heaven" where the earthbound fabricator angels are "dedicated to the perfection we must achieve."

So how much will car heaven cost? Days later I sit in Paul Batista's office. He is young, wiry and wears blue jeans so new the fabric looks black. I ask, "How much if you built a car from the ground up?"

"Show me your plans," Paul says. "We'll see."

Gideon Bosker, M.D., gives over three hundred speeches a year about the danger of high-tech drugs. He lives on the road and writes letters:

> *Greetings from discredited, devastated and disturbingly dangerous Detroit, once the highness of horsepower, a mad mechanized motortown for modern times, a city where the bluster and brilliance of industrialized America coagulated, where Italians, Poles and Afro-Americans with steel-muscled forearms sculpted by sweat and assemblage, riveted, screwed and glued Impalas, Star Chiefs and Skylarks for a world in love with wheels, whitewalls and the whisper of syncromesh. Desperate and demoralized Detroit, now necrotic and narcotized, a Keynesian casualty of slicker and sweatless forearms, robotic limbs, in fact, that click and clack for Nissan and Honda in Osaka and Tokyo.*

He calls to ask, "Who'll control the money?" When I don't say, "Nick," but the more conservative, "Who knows?" Gideon says he doesn't want to be a salesman. "I'll go to the investors," he says, "as an investor myself."

I feel a sea change. "What does that mean?"

"It means I'll say to them: I'm tasting the food before I give it to you. You have got to nail things down. I can't go out with just some diaphanous plans for a diaphanous car."

It means there will be no $100,000. "Gideon, you said you'd raise the money over a ninety-day period beginning next week."

"I'll be there for the first twenty or twenty-five thousand dollars. I'm confident I can scare up another eighty grand over the phone. But what's important now is to create a mystique: You and Nick conquering the world."

"I hate cars," Nick says. "Cars are supposed to be about beauty." Nick holds up a beer. "But they're not—they're about planned obsolescence and dumbed-down design. Cars are supposed to be about freedom, but get on a freeway at rush hour and see how free you feel. I'd like to destroy just about every car there ever was."

We are at the beach. I have written a story about him in the new *Connoisseur* magazine and he says it was hard to read because of his dyslexia, that "the words looked like equations," that the only books he's ever read are *The Catcher in the Rye* and the complete works of Ayn Rand, but that "It's great how you can say I'm the best young auto designer in the world and that's enough to make it true."

This worries me a little. The *Connoisseur* story has generated considerable attention from Nick's friends and teachers, set him apart as a new, improved, bigger and vastly more important Nick Pugh and . . .

. . . when I tell him that Gideon has concerns about expenses, Nick says, "Awesome."

"So to speak. You gotta sharpen your pencil."

I can see his trip to Paul Batista's has had an impact. "If we can keep with the theme of the car. We're building an ultimate. We could spend one hundred and twenty-five thousand dollars just for glass." Nick says, then switches gears. "Creature feature," he notes, looking to the ocean where girls with beer cans totter beside the shore break. I can see the difference in our ages, almost a generation. He is wowed, but the girls just look like drunk baby-sitters in bikinis to me.

Nick, Henrietta, Debbie, my eleven-year-old daughter Katie and my blonde little boy Matt have come down to the beach from our house, which is three blocks away.

Katie takes ballet and, with her grace, long neck and perfect lines for arms and legs she looks, leaping on the beach, almost a parody of the young ballerina.

"Henrietta's way pissed at me," Nick says, pushing a trough in the sand. Yes. They fight like children. Due to Nick's watching other women. More accurately, he *tracks* them, as if he were a lion and they were gazelles.

"Dad," I hear a few beers later and feel a weightless hand on my arm, and turn to see Katie. "Henrietta's so beautiful and Nick," my daughter whispers, "he's so cute. He looks like he's from TV."

Later, Debbie too is enthusiastic. And why not? To be so young, so talented, so idealistic, so wholesome, so rich! She tells me it's great that I finally have a genius friend from the real and winning world. One who has informed me that all he wants from life is to create cars to make him the equal of Walter Gropius or the Beatles, cars to be remembered for a thousand years.

13

ORGY FOR ONE

Summer 1963. To this day I regret what I did. A Hudson Hornet is about as easy to customize as the Grand Tetons. It is what it is and what it wants to be: among the first of the great postwar stock car racers, a rare and storied automobile, the car Jack Kerouac's blue-collar Bohemians drove in *On the Road*, and I can't imagine where you'd find the chrome side stripping that my fifteen-year-old fingers peeled off that car—they haven't made Hudson accessories for forty-years. I couldn't get the chrome to just slide off, so I took the biggest screwdriver I could find and rammed it between the chrome and the body of the car itself, then, using the screwdriver for leverage, popped the chrome stripping away from the metal grommets that held it to the car. Then I removed the big T of chrome that was the Hudson's front hood ornament. Finally, imagining how I would soon miraculously learn how to use a welding torch like a magic wand to cut the Hudson down to long, low chopped-top perfection, I began swabbing the five-dollar Miracle Putty from its can and smearing it into the holes of the screws that had held the hood ornament and side chrome. Yeah, I'd pull off the big ugly slabs of chrome that were the front and rear bumpers, then I'd lower the Hudson all the way around and then—uh-oh—this Miracle Putty crap hardened superfast, before I could even smooth it out.

Oh, boy. Now, like a tiny but very long mountain range, Miracle Putty jutted all along the Hudson's sides and front of the hood.

Okay, no need for panic. Sandpaper would take care of everything. That's when I guess I realized what the "miracle" in Miracle Putty was all about. Miracle Putty didn't sand. Miracle Putty dried to the strength of steel, and all those little mountains were there to stay. The Hudson would never, ever be the same.

I was afraid my dad would be furious. But no, thank God, he had other fish to fry. He had become a murder suspect. Remember his pal, the wheeler-dealer Glover? Glover was dead. Somebody had tampered with the brakes on Glover's Cadillac, his Cadillac had crashed, Glover was killed, the totalled Cadillac had been stolen off the police parking lot and the police discovered my father was among a dozen of Glover's business partners who had life insurance policies written on Glover's life, policies guaranteed to pay off if Glover met his end. Which he most certainly had.

I felt bad for my dad. He needed more fun in his life. So why not, I suggested, buy a new muscle car, a Pontiac GTO, High Pro Mustang or four-speed V-8 Chevelle? They'd evolved from great cars like his Hudson and Oldsmobile 88 and—not exactly, my father said. Had I heard of John Z. DeLorean? No. Well, John Z. DeLorean, he explained, was a genius who had just saved Detroit from disaster. My dad revealed that recently Detroit decided America wanted low-powered economy cars, geared up to make millions of them, then discovered America didn't. Enter an obscure engineer, DeLorean. His idea: Tart up these little loser tin cans with high horsepower truck engines, loud paint jobs, bucket seats and plausible suspensions and voilà! "Muscle cars." No, we wouldn't be buying one of those.

Was he right? It made no sense. And the fact was, as brilliant as he was with eyeballs, design, hunting, fishing, throwing footballs, business and golf, some of his ideas were, how else to say it, too far out. For example: The morning when he read in the paper that North Vietnamese PT-boats had attacked the Seventh Fleet in the Gulf of Tonkin, he declared the Vietnamese "aren't remotely that stupid" and that Lyndon Johnson was perpetrating a fraud just like Adolf Hitler's fake Polish attack on Germany that started World War II.

Midnight under a black April sky. Engines screamed. Two Chevys—a new low slab of a 327 SuperSport and a jacked-up 1955 Bel Air with spoked racing wheels and a hood scoop like a shark's mouth—were lined up ready to go. The track was lit by two facing lines of hot rods, jalopies and daddies' cars, their headlights like matching lines of close-by stars.

The SuperSport had dump tubes—exhaust pipes opening straight off the motor and red sparks shot to the road behind the front tires every time the driver hit the gas.

Between the two cars stood a tall kid in a baggy snow white T-shirt tucked neatly into his Levi's. He held a beer bottle up like the torch on the Statue of Liberty. Just as the unmuffled snarl of the Chevys hit an ear-killing crescendo, he dropped the bottle. It splashed across the asphalt, to a thousand bits of white glass light. The Chevys shrieked down the track and, in an instant, were just two sets of diminishing red taillights.

Then something went wrong. The taillights become headlights, then taillights again and headlights again. Both cars—who knew who won—had run out of track, hit the grass and were spinning out of control, like two shoes thrown across a waxed wood floor.

Shit, as the old saying goes. Scary Larry and I were racing next. Scary, sixteen years old for about fifteen minutes, had conned his mother into loaning him her Volkswagen. He had taken off the air cleaner and hubcaps so now the VW was a dragster. Beside us were a carload of drunk sailors in a yellow Ford that could have been, for all I knew, a taxicab. Scary was hitting the Volkswagen's throttle—the sound the Volks made was less a snarl than something like pebbles whacking around inside an empty Coke can—and the white T-shirt guy lifted another beer bottle. Way down the track headlights from the two Chevys crossed and shot up into the night sky at a crazy angle: They'd crashed into each other and now—

"Everybody stay right where you are! This is the Portland police, you are in violation of code blah, blah, blah," came a bullhorn voiced from somewhere out of the night. *"Any attempt to—"*

—stay out of trouble is probably a waste of time.

Tenth grade. Beaverton High. Mornings, Patty rode to class with Dick in the 409, I rode on the school bus.* GIs in Vietnam were Zippoing hootches, torching villages with cigarette lighters. Scary too had a Zippo and brought the war home by setting sack lunches on fire at his bus stop. The bus would roll up and I'd see Twinkies burning in their cellophane, and bus stop schlubs chasing and cursing a Scary so spastic with laughter he could scarcely run.

Larry had bought a go-kart for $50, tuned its lawn-mower engine felony illegal and, for a time, we had squirted up and down the street in front of his house, the little machine screaming back and forth until

---

*The bus was a rolling ghetto for all the neighborhood's mouthbreathers, apparitions, future international crime czars and whacks. About the only sane and seemingly completely normal middle-class kid to ride it was the beautiful, thoughtful Paige Powell, who ended up living with Andy Warhol during the last years of his life.

the neighbors went apeshit. Lately we'd been carrying the go-kart across the farmland behind his house to the site of the industrial park about to be home to the new Handyman megastore. So nice. Wide as a freeway boulevard, flat and tarry black, the smell of fresh asphalt, Scary and me lugging the go-kart so heavy it seemed to be seeking the center of the earth, frog-throated Scary singing a Rolling Stones favorite, *"You growed up all wrong,"* nothing but Mick's chorus for the mile of rutty farm field, so repetitive and unchanging that I was beginning to take it personally by the time we reached the new industrial park heaven, where, forget the Stones, I imagined a fabulous future, the world paved, except where McDonalds and Dairy Queen stood on the rolling sea of asphalt like those new off-shore oil rigs they were building in California. Houses would be underground, your living room window would be a periscope, so when the Main Event came down— World War III, our End of the World versus their End of the World— you, cozy in your inverted split-level, could watch the Chi-Com nukes go off as if it was a super Fourth of July. It would be like living in an irradiated human ant farm, so incredible. I was designing vehicles for this new age, Harley Davidson–motored skateboards and—like 007's machine gun–equipped Aston-Martin—hot rods fitted with surface-to-surface missiles and electric-powered Gatling guns that fired titanium alloy dum-dum shells that *Popular Mechanics* said would soon blast civilization and democracy into the jungles of Vietnam. So that if a Lincoln-driving, bald-headed meat bag gave you grief at a stop light, *powpowpowpowpow-baaaawoooooosh!*

Scary Larry, for his part, just had a brush with perfect bliss. His Lutheran father was a manager at a big new Volkswagen dealership. As serious as the most be-godded clergyman, Don Wobbrock did not share his son's love for wild cars. To Larry's father, a car was not a sex machine, but an investment second only to a house. People did not buy cars from Don Wobbrock for the thrill of being lied to by a fast-talking car salesman, people bought cars from Don Wobbrock because his customers' interests were his own. He did not traffic in wild. So I had to go sit down when he rolled onto the Wobbrock driveway in a 1957 Chevrolet coupe so wildly beautiful it looked sent from pagan heaven. A branch higher on the muscle car family tree from my dad's '49 Cadillac, '53 Olds 88 and '53 Hudson Hornet, the factory four-speed, fuel-injected 283-cubic-inch V-8 '57 Chevy was a Detroit hot rod, a long, low, voluptuous, elongated box whose corners were as smoothly rounded off as anything on any femme fatale, a car Cleopatra, a car

Playmate of the Month, so let us forget the chrome-stripped Hudson. "The Greatest Hudson Custom of All Time" was a fantasy as baby-dumb as pink on a Porsche. I'd matured, had entered the real world and could see the obvious: Larry's dad would hand the sexy Chevy over to his beloved only child, and who was I, if not Scary's best friend? The Chevy would be more or less mine as well and would drive Patty nuts. I'd be reintroduced to the white frilly furnace of her teddy-beared bed-room and, soon, get what I so richly deserved.

However, that was not to be. Larry pleaded with his dad to buy it, but the car had evidently been brought home to illustrate for Larry the sin of temptation. The Chevy was not a realistic purchase, Larry's father had explained, but more like a foolish wish or unattainable dream. The next morning the driveway was empty.

On that empty driveway we played basketball after school. Boys in baggy surfer cords and baggy short-sleeved madras shirts. Scary's team was talent, intelligence and discipline, it relied on careful plans, dia-grams of feet, like at Arthur Murray Dance Studios. My team was el-bows, mayhem and cheating. We won. "You guys think you're smart, we'll see," Scary vowed. Next we had the best minds of our generation on their hands and knees scurrying around Scary's parents' living room, dining room and kitchen, like lemmings too stupid to find a cliff. Larry had promised that if they kept scurrying, and would, at every lap, "kiss the mouse"—a rubber mouse held in his outstretched hand—he'd let them see his new book *Naked Art School Girls*. As Larry's accomplice ("Sore knees, my butt, keep it moving, men!"), I believed I'd not only get to see *Naked Art School Girls* but *Naked Art School Girls* would be delivered unto me by Scary Larry as the Ten Commandments had been delivered unto Moses by God.

But after the lemmings went home, all vowing to return the next afternoon for what Larry assured would be "only about another week's worth" of scurrying and mouse-kissing, my friend confided a terrible secret. There was no *Naked Art School Girls*. He told me that *Naked Art School Girls* was only foolish wish, false temptation, an unattainable dream—not an achievable reality.

Then one day I was walking down the street in front of my house when I heard a rumble behind me and a yellow slab of steel slid right by my left hip.

"Want a ride?"

It was Patty. In Dick's new Chevy 409 Rat-motored coupe.

I opened the door, slid onto the plush black bucket seat. What a smile. Patty was better than *The Flying Nun, That Girl*, the identical cousins and Annette put together.

She greeted me with news that people could mistake me for Ricky Nelson.

If Ricky had been floating around in the middle of the ocean for thirty days with nothing to eat, maybe. But I was confident. After all, she was obviously playing to my long suit—being manipulated. I already knew from experience that no one got manipulated like I did, and what a world. A Sun tachometer on the dash, Patty's slender hand on the knob of the chrome gearshift that stood erect between us. The sanctum sanctorum. The hallowed hall. I was beginning to wonder what she and Dick actually did in here when my pornographic dread exploded in a flash. "We're going to the Midnight Drags," Patty announced, hitting the gas. The 409's rear tires made a polite chirp as she accelerated down the street.

I had told her about Scary Larry, the crashing Chevies, the police. How I had, forcefully and articulately, groveled to the cops as Scary sat beside me in his mom's Volkswagen in tight-lipped disgust.

"We're going to race," Patty said, snapping the Chevy into second. We were flying now.

I looked at her. Patty was serene. Her face smooth, perfectly pretty, more—how else to say it—aerodynamic than Annette Funicello's. Her hair, lifted by the air from the open windows, drifted back in a short dark swoop. She wore lipstick the pale pink of cotton candy.

She said that Dick would loan her the car. "We can beat anybody out there."

He must be out of his bleeping mind.

"You mean I race it?" I asked, seeing my glory—the 409—screaming off the line, tires burning, Patty beside me, my hand slamming the shift into second gear, the 409 fishtailing out of control, soaring end over end and going up in a Nagasaki fireball in the time it took Patty, snapping the gearshift into third, to reply, "No, Mark—me."

Push was coming to shove. My father said I could have a car, no problem, if I just got good grades. Easier for me to fly to the moon. I just didn't *get* school. Why ponder $35y (4s - y) + 44q (5m - 3) =$? when bigger questions loomed. Like: If Nelson Rockefeller saw a dime on a floor, would he bend over and pick it up? And so far I'd enjoyed only one academic success: a short story in the school literary magazine about a boy who comes home drunk, sneaks inside by crawling through the attic above his parents' garage and falls through the ceiling into the concrete grease pit. It was easy. The only unautobiographical part was that in real life I didn't have to die at the end.

My English teacher Mr. Dietsche said I had talent. The only hitch was that I was "always wrong," leaving, he suggested, just two likely career paths: religion and journalism. But writing was hard. The two top pastures of literature—kinky sex and war—had no attraction for me and I wasn't even a lost soul. Still, there was hope. My dad said he would talk to my instructors to work out an "understanding." I tagged along, waiting outside in the halls, knowing this could be a goldmine.

My dad didn't look radical—a white shirt, a tweed sport coat, slacks—and he was a good persuader, like a kind district attorney, quiet fact after quiet fact, a style dictated by the nature of his medical practice. His office looked like science fiction. Laserland. If you had eye problems, how else to say it? My father was the end of the line. He did surgery by referral only, cases nobody else could handle, and part of his success was the way he handled his deeply-in-trouble patients. Sitting in his waiting room, I had listened to him. His message was a smooth weave of hope, science and authority—hypnotic—and I'd only seen him slip once, after he did surgery on a kid about my age. "The boy's retinas were cobwebs," my dad told me, his eyes watering, and when I asked—alarmed—why he was so upset, he replied, "Before the surgery I told him not to worry, that everything would be all right."

Anyway, at my parent/faculty conference my father had news for my math teacher: Kids couldn't relate to algebra unless kids knew what algebra was good for, which—if I was any example—kids didn't. News for my English teacher: I didn't have to read any books by the Brontë sisters—no *Wuthering Heights*, no *Jane Eyre*—because those novels were just prototypes for the soap opera, Ernest Hemingway wasn't fit to polish the chrome on Mark Twain's Maserati* and had Mr. Dietsche by chance noticed the endless repetition in the *Iliad* and the *Odyssey*? That was because those tomes had been passed down for centuries by oral poets who reduced Homer's tales to about seventy key phrases and

---

*"Dad, what's existentialism?"
"A franchise."

improvised the rest. So the twin foundations of Western literature were not actually literature at all, but simply folk art.

But I knew what was up. My dad wasn't there just to show the flag. He was there to cut a deal for me, there to say to my teachers: Look, obviously my son is a handful, and maybe even a little thick. But he's my son and I love him and I want you to cut him some slack.

I knew the way my father often got people to do what he wanted was by impressing them with information they didn't know about their own world. On our recent shopping trip for a new Studebaker Avanti, he had mesmerized the salesman at the dealership by explaining how Raymond Loewy, the Avanti's designer, had set a standard with the Avanti's stunning slab sides that would last to the twenty-first century and, during our test drive—with me folded up in the Avanti's little backseat like a lawn chair and my dad going, oh, a leisurely 110—he further explained to the salesguy how, not to worry, the Avanti's supercharged engine was capable of 125 easy, and by the time my father had finished our drive, the salesman, scrambling out of the car, was so impressed it sounded as if he was ready to give us an Avanti for free.

"The *Iliad* and the *Odyssey* not literature," Mr. Dietsche marveled the next day. "And no novels by the Brontë sisters." He was laughing. "Your dad told your history teacher that the American Revolution was a mistake—and that if it weren't for George Washington's crowd a united England and North America would rule the world."

Fantastic. I could see myself being queried at the bus stop. *"Mark, what's your dad, a Republican or Democrat?"*

"No, actually, he's a Tory."

Mr. Dietsche was a gifted teacher. Only a few years out of college and a semipro tennis player, he drove what could have been Wilson Pickett's own Ford Mustang—sun-bright turquoise with a pure white interior—and had a knockout wife. He played Jonathan Winters albums in class, was trying to publish a book of poems by some young writer named John Updike and I watched as he flipped through a copy of the *Iliad* and the *Odyssey* on his desk. "The wine dark sea, the wine dark sea, the wine dark sea, swift Achilles, swift Achilles, swift Achilles."

"So you're not saying my dad is crazy?" I asked.

Mr. Dietsche had a smile like the Cheshire cat's. "He said most high schools were nothing but glorified baby-sitting services."

"But," I said.

"It *is* repetitious," Mr. Dietsche admitted, flipping through Homer. "Brave Ulysses wielding that sword two dozen times."

This wasn't going right. Sort of, we had been sparring around the topic of my future; sort of, it was clear that I wasn't going to be a doctor because, sort of, I really didn't like sick people and besides, I was not a student, which was taking us in a bad direction. So I made a conversational U-turn in the form of a bold proposal. My father listened, rather wide-eyed, I must say, then replied, "You'd go fight for some cowboy with two pearl-handled pistols—just to get a hot rod?"

What did he mean by that? Then I remembered. *Life* magazine had just published pictures of South Vietnamese General What's-his-face wearing matching pearl-handled revolvers, a man my father had dismissed as a "brutal fascist clown."

I was about to get my driver's license and had a great idea: I'd let my father off the hook, give up my inheritance in exchange for a four-speed '57 Chevrolet knowing that my dad—who grew up poor and who had to make every nickel on his own—appreciated independence and initiative.

His gaze told me that he was impressed. It was night, we were in his dark, wood-panelled den under an oil painting of a naked Polynesian woman given to him by an artist patient.

"You mean," he said, "you'd give up everything I've put away for you and your brother and sister for a *Chevy*?"

"Well," I said, "maybe more like a fuel-injected Corvette."

"How will you pay for college?" he asked.

"The GI Bill." We were playing chess and I was cocky, I'd actually won a game the other night and now I felt like Rommel in the desert; I had pieces deep in my dad's territory and my king was forted behind an iron wall of pawns.

"If you join the army," my father said, lifting his queen, "you'll wind up in Vietnam." I wanted to say, "Dad, so what? Do the math. No Air Force. No tanks. No bitchin' Cobra gun ships or electric-powered Gatling guns shooting titanium-tipped dum-dum bullets. How could a po-dunk country the size of Oregon take on a United States that had walloped the Nazis and Japanese?" My cousin Jerry said all we had to do was give the Viet Cong Dairy Queens and Cadillacs and then charge them for the cheeseburgers and gas and next everybody would be saying: "War? What war?" But my dad insisted Vietnam would be "Korea all over again" and that "a lot of boys are going to die."

His queen came down, *kerplop*, on my bishop, and no! I could see that my king's pawn was double forked by his queen, a bishop and a knight. All he had to do was sacrifice his bishop—and hadn't the exact same thing happened the last game?

I shouldn't have gone for the Corvette. I should have stuck with the '57 Chevy. Because all I needed in this world was a hot coupe with a 409 Rat-motor V-8 and a four speed. Was that so much to ask? I mean, why had my dad even been bothering to spoil me otherwise?

14

Twenty-Five Years for Fifteen Minutes

"Has it occurred to you that you may have no idea what you're really getting yourself into, no real idea what you're doing, but that it's too late to turn back, and that you may have made the biggest mistake of your life?"

Gideon's four-part question, posed over the phone, followed two simpler questions, "How eccentric is this kid, anyway?" and "How much do you actually know about cars, Mark?" the answers to which were, "A little" and "A lot"—though what I "know" about cars is about 5 percent fact-based and 95 percent totally notional. Gideon wants to get together right now to "see if this is going to work or not. Otherwise, let's just forget it."

Is that a joke, or what?

My friend Gideon Bosker lives in the sky and is about action—when I first met him he had hair to his shoulders. I remember him striding through a bar so fast it lifted behind him like a black flag. Now the hair is shorter and strafed with gray. An emergency room physician, he also flies the world warning other doctors about the dangers of pharmaceuticals. His basic message is: Enough Americans die from accidental misuse of hospital drugs to fill a Boeing 747 every other day. He is a missionary but very entertaining. He'll hold up a vial of pills and begin his hospital presentation with something like, "I tell my patients, 'Take two of these and call me if you wake up in the morning.'" He packs lecture halls, makes up to three presentations a day, and when he's not in front of a crowd of doctors and nurses, he's usually on a jet, maybe going to Boise or Timbuktu. He's coauthored one of my favorite nonfiction books, *Frozen Moment*, a history of Portland architecture, has had several books published on design, and high above Newport Beach in a pastel suite in the elegant Four Seasons Hotel, Gideon, in jeans and a starched white shirt, says, "Horseshoe crabs. I can see it, that whole scalloped, serrated rear end. The beach at Woods Hill, Martha's Vineyard." One well-manicured hand poised over a bag of potato chips, he is looking at Nick's drawing of the Xeno.

"Yeah, Martha's Vineyard," Nick says. "When I was a kid. But this isn't like Luigi Colani bio design, this is something more out of your subconscious."

Gideon says, "Boy, it's low. What clearance will we need?"

"Fifteen percent ramp angles. Or one bad bump and 'bye-bye rear end."

Gideon says, "Let's get down to brass tacks. Could we build more than one?"

"Sure." Nick grabs potato chips. "But each would have to be made separately. The car's too eccentric to mass produce."

Henrietta, in black-and-white striped tights, says, "Same as in fashion design. High fashion is always overstated, rarely meant to be mass marketed."

Gideon picks up a copy of the new *Connoisseur*. Nick's wholesome, handsome face stares out life size and grinning. "Drum up more of this stuff. Car and chronicle leads to cash. We need a prospectus. Construct it as a series of exhibits. Specs for the car, a broken-down budget, step by step: A, B, C, D, E, F, G. The exhibits should be all pleasure. The key to selling this is that it's a connoisseur's car. But the investor must know he's first in line for toys, rentals, use in movies, advertising, MTV. Make it clear initial monies pay off investors. Sponsors. Has anybody given you an in-kind commitment? If so, what's the quid pro quo?"

Nick says, "That's the question?"

"Question!" Gideon exclaims, "*This is cold hard cash*. What rights do they have? They'll want to see who else is involved. You've got to document sponsors."

"We have to get the best products."

"*No.*" Gideon shakes his head. "Not if the best product has a raving lunatic attached to it."

Nick smirks. "All our sponsors will be nonraving lunatics."

Gideon sighs. "Lets talk product liability. Mark, you want to race it."

Nick puts a hand up to his forehead so it shadows his eyes. "Oh, fuck. I hope not."

"But say he does. Say he flips it and Mark's dead. Who's his wife sue? Or say what if you sell it to somebody and the brakes go out and they go over a cliff? What then?"

Nick says, "Easy. We go to a custom hot rod shop, see what forms they make people sign and have whoever buys the car sign one of those."

"Yeah," Gideon smiles, showing teeth for a toothpaste ad. "But yours is twice as explicit. It says right up front: *You're taking your life in your hands the second you buy this car.*"

I feel a little edginess here and suggest we stabilize by forming a partnership.

"Better to just sell one car to one guy. A good way," Nick grins, "to launch my career."

"Nick, this isn't—" Gideon leans forward, almost shouts "—a scholarship to art school; this is giving people a chance to make a buck."

Edginess, yes.

"No problem," Nick says. "I see a hole *above* the top of the market. That of the completely individual rip-it-up exotic car. Beyond Ferrari. Beyond the Lamborghini Diablo. Beyond any car ever built."

The new studio/apartment, ceilings stories high and big as a bus garage. Nick's new Vietnamese pot-bellied pig squeals as Henrietta picks him up. Turds pop out of his bottom like gum balls from a penny candy machine. Gideon looks at Nick's drawings up on the freshly painted white walls and says, "Canonize yourself. Like Michael Graves. He was able to congratulate himself for his architectural fabulousness by hooking all his new fabulousness to all the major fabulousnesses in the past."

Nick, up thirty-six hours painting studio walls bigger than billboards to get ready for Gideon's visit, says, "The problem is there is no tradition in car design. They say so at school but, bottom line with those guys," Nick waves his arms, "it's all just *bitchin' shit.*"

Cracking his last one hundred dollar bill from "my last trust fund," Nick says, "He only works at one speed: fast. He can't crawl, he can't walk, he just runs. What if he tries to take over and tell us what to do?"

Debbie, Nick, Henrietta and I have gone to see Sam Kinison at the

Wiltern. Thundering heavy metal covers, New Age dick jokes; at intermission, amid people with bad skin and complicated haircuts, Nick buys drinks and reveals he is not taken with Gideon. "I called my mom to tell her our plans and she yelled at me. Then her boyfriend, Ed, who is an awesome scientist in the biggest way, said I have to set it up so everything favors me, then negotiate."

"Nick," I say, "if it gets down to gimme, gimme, gimme, I, me, mine, we're screwed."

"I've been waiting twenty-five years to see you get your fifteen minutes," Scary Larry reveals. "Among all the idiots we grew up with, I always figured it was you who would make it big."

Good to know. We are speeding toward Los Angeles in his rent-a-car. Dark and strong-faced, wearing jeans, a golf shirt and a green golf jacket, Scary looks less a lawyer than a middle-aged high school kid. He has fared well. He did not "flunk out of life," but went on to college, served in the Peace Corps in Africa, then taught school in the dirt-poor South before becoming a medical malpractice attorney. He's president elect of the Oregon Trial Lawyers Association and representing Alaska in its oil-spill suit against Exxon. Recently, Scary flew a planeload of medical supplies into Nicaragua with a peace group. He finds it hard to exist out of a world not detonating with crisis, so it was fortunate terrorists bombed his hotel and blew him out of bed the very first night.

But medical malpractice is exacting. "It takes two months to get the victims out of my head," he says as we drive to have dinner with Nick. "This poor woman. All she had in life was her son. Ten years old, the apple of her eye. He goes to the hospital for a tonsillectomy and of course they kill him."

"How?" I ask.

"The anesthesiologist, natch."

We just got back from the facility where his new Saleen Mustang was built, and Larry was impressed. Weighing under three thousand pounds and capable of 149 miles per hour, the Saleen comes with a stiffened suspension, a Borg Warner T5 five-speed transmission, a high-performance Ford 302-cubic-inch V-8, and is yours new for about $25,000. The Saleen is a tough economy race car built for the street, though up in Portland, Scary also races it on the track at Delta Park, former site of the midnight drags. Delta Park remains invigorating. "I was going foot to the floor last weekend," Scary tells me, "when a

Corvette shot by me and crashed straight into a wall." But what really got him excited was how well the little Saleen assembly plant appeared to be doing. "Think about it," he says, as we nose into Los Angeles, "You buy stock Mustangs wholesale for maybe thirteen grand apiece, beef up the suspension, tweak the motor and resell them for almost twice that. Saleen must be making a mint. That's what you guys could be doing."

In a bright beige restaurant in Japan Town, Nick describes a "totally uncompromised" car that is "superluxurious, superpowerful, superoriginal."

Scary nods. "Lots of people come to me for representation and guess what the problem is? They're nuts. Put together everything, models, diagrams, engineering plans before you talk to anybody with money. Otherwise you're just another deluded twenty-three-year-old. Be generous on your estimates. You can't go back to the investors once the money is spent."

When Scary gets up to use the men's room, Nick leans over the table, beside himself with joy. "We are going to do so well. All we need now is somebody to help run the business side."

I say I've already got someone. Another friend from Portland, Moon, who was instrumental in the rise of Evans Products, Avia and Nike.

Nick wants to know: Is he totally corporate, willing to work sixty hours a week, completely well organized and used to taking orders from above?

Well, no, no, no and no, but we'll get to that. I reply that Moon is "brilliant," which is certainly the truth, and am delighted to see Scary return to distract my young partner with another rave about our car.

Driving into the night, Scary says, "We'll sell people the right to give you money. But you better understand this right now. The cash you've got won't pay for the hubcaps on the car Nick Pugh has got in mind. You crowned him the best young car designer in the country and he expects you to provide the payoff. You made a deal with the devil. This kid's got an ego that could go off like a bomb."

"So—"

"—don't waste him. Don't just build a car, start a company. Like Saleen. Do it right and you'll be set for life."

MOON

Spring 1965. My dad says: If you love something, join up with some-body who does what you love best. My dad loved beautiful sailboats, so he partnered with architect Jim Gardiner to create the *Faux Pas*. My dad loved wheeler-dealing, so he had partnered with wheeler-dealer Glover to create a small fortune. I loved mindless mayhem so I had partnered with Moon to create more problems than I could possibly solve.

It was night. Moon and I were marooned at my parents' house, in the garage, in the dead Hudson, drinking beer and me one more mishap from military school. I'd lost my new driver's license for a blunder stupid enough to earn me a billion years stuck in the worst Laundromat in purgatory. I was in trouble and, in Moon's company, likely to get in a whole lot more.

I had a wonderful new mother and I'd crashed her car.

Outside in the dark, my friends' hot rods—most of them not run-ning—sat parked on the big asphalt airstrip of our driveway, including a new arrival, a 1949 Ford painted blue with a brush that could, with just a little cash, be turned into Sudden Death II.

Engineless, it stood up in front like a speedboat. My towering friend Loog had given it to me or just left it here, I wasn't sure which. Our garage was behind the breezeway of my parents' ranch-style house. A half dozen beaters were there in stages of ruin and/or disrepair, one parked over the grease pit, a five-foot-deep coffin of concrete that stretched the center of one of the bays. You could climb down and work beneath your car standing up. Hot rods all over. Water, water everywhere and—Moon and I had already had plenty to drink.

Patty and I never got to race at the midnight drags, because her father, Jim Gardiner, my dad's best friend, got cancer and had to have his larynx removed. Even that did not work. On his last ride to the hospital, he sat up front in the ambulance, bleeding from his throat. He handed Patty a note that simply read: SO THIS IS HOW IT ALL TURNS OUT, and I guess it was.

Two six-packs of Country Club malt liquor down the hatch in the Hudson. Weekends, Moon's MO was get drunk, urp, fall head over heels with some miniskirted apparition possessed of, in Moon parlance, "lush kazooms," a girl who could see in handsome, well-dressed Moon the obvious: a house in the Heights, dinners at the Portland Golf Club, until he opened his mouth.

Blue-blooded Moon—his grandfather lived in a 15,000-square-foot brick castle in the Portland Heights—appeared to be an ultimate All-American Boy—sandy hair, blue eyes, Gant shirts, mirror-shined Bass Weejuns, creases on his brushed cotton slacks sharp enough to cut— but appearance deceived. For Moon could not have cared less about being an All-American anything. In fact, Moon considered America and the rest of the world an annoying figment of his own imagination. I was a favored hallucination. We'd been friends since sixth grade, where we'd sit in class and draw cars on paper folded into our textbooks. Mine were wild, Moon's precise. To him, cars were barrooms and bedrooms. Moon didn't make hot cars, he took them. His rich father had cars to burn. Sadly, Moon had just burned the wrong one. His lovely mother's lovely new Ford convertible. A swooping set of rectangles, pale green. We'd spent recent weekends not scoring beautiful girls in automotive splendor. But without his glasses, which he never wore, Moon was legally blind and a terrible driver, and last week on the school bus I saw the Ford sitting in a cornfield.

At school Moon was in one of the johns, combing his carefully barbered hair. He radiated confidence and enthusiasm, no matter what. Were you watching his face but did not understand English you might have thought he was saying something like: "She was gorgeous and getting her in bed was a breeze," instead of, "Looks like you and I are in the same boat. I was brain-dead drunk and drove the goddamn thing right off the road." Though his mother's Ford looked pristine, the undercarriage had hit a stump and the car was declared a total.

Moon's plan: Go downtown and "drag the gut." Friday night every hot rodder in town would cruise the neon corridor of Broadway. You could see a '57 Chevy with candy apple red paint that looked three feet deep, a '32 Ford whose skeletal frame cradled a motor apparently sculpted from solid chrome—and even better, Broadway was one-stop shopping for girls and fights. But dragging the gut carless was like trying to have sex without genitals.

So where to get a ride? "What about Scary Larry?" Moon asked. No. Scary was out with a tall and very attractive minister's daughter who said she'd get serious if Scary got serious.

"How about Scherzer?"

Normally, Steve Scherzer was a good bet. A tall, hawk-nosed, gangly boy who had a killer golf swing—he'd hit a ball and it was gone— Scherzer was a great guy, and his dad had a new, long, low, blue Buick—fender skirts and plush black upholstery, an Episcopalian low-rider. Unfortunately, I was on Steve's shit list. He had a beautiful girlfriend, "the Mole," who had a *Playboy* foldout figure and English toffee-colored skin. Last week, however, I had convinced Scherzer to use his father's new sexy Buick to squire two cute fifteen-year-old girls who promised us a case of beer and "snacks."

The evening started with promise. Meaning, the little vixens weren't lying about the beer. But the snacks? The snacks weren't caviar. The snacks weren't even Triscuits. The snacks were Fruit Loops and Cap'n Crunch and the vixens got drunk and began heaving cereal all over inside Steve's dad's immaculate new, long, low, blue Buick and . . . "Scherzer's out with the Mole," I explained, staring through the Hudson's dirty windshield into the dark of our garage. "I think we'll have to walk."

If only. A little body putty, a factory crate V-8 fresh from a Chevy dealership, $2,000 in parts and labor could make the old blue paint-brushed junker '49 Ford the new Sudden Death, and Moon and I would be riding in style. Or maybe not. My friend Eric Horner had appraised my work on the chromeless and body putty–scarred Hudson, appraised the engineless Ford, and advised, "forget about it." Eric was burly, worked construction during the summer and was in Mensa, the Society of Geniuses. Eric rebelled against everything, including rebellion. I was growing shaggy hair that made me resemble if not a rock star surf god, at least an Irish Setter. Eric got a banker's haircut, locks cut and combed to a millimeter, and could be intimidating. He picked up tidbits of Shakespeare from Mr. Dietsche and would walk up to a teacher he didn't like, point in the guy's face and command, "Put your courage in the sticking place"—which had the feel of an insult but, magically, wasn't. Eric was in my creative writing class, taught by the leggy, intellectually provocative Miss Stephens. In the race to impress her, I came in a distant second. His initial short story: worldwide war between men and women—women who burned down the local sperm bank, "slaughtering the young male pre-fish"—leaving Eric's teenage army captain hero to lead his men under the banner MOPPING UP IS LOCAL GOVERNMENT on a suicidal charge against black radical lesbians—Martha and the Vendettas—holed up in the services bays of a Texaco station. How to compete with that? Then Eric unveiled a new protagonist for Miss Stephens' approval, the five-hundred-pound Blessed Reverend Organ Morgan, who preached the gospel of "feelin' fine." The Reverend lived for barbeque, and his answer to everything was "ribs." Happiness? "Ribs." World peace? "Ribs." Salvation of the immortal soul? "Ribs." His congregation included a gospel choir, a rainbow coalition of babe voluptuaries way beyond my best imaginings, and I figured, well, if you can't beat 'em, why not produce 'em? I'd become Eric Horner's Colonel Parker. I pitched him on an Organ Morgan TV show, Organ Morgan comic books, T-shirts, even a real Organ Morgan Church and rib joint. All Eric had to do was write an Organ Morgan novel, then we'd find a dirigible Jonathan Winters to play the Blessed Reverend and—wouldn't that be incredible? No. Why not? Because, Eric said, it won't work.

Okay, then we'd subcontract Organ Morgan to sunny, athletic Steve Lonie. Another far better writer than I was—Lonie's definition of nerve was "a guy who dives off a diving board, sees there's no water in the swimming pool, but does a half-gainer anyway," and though his definition for my enthusiasm for Organ Morgan was that of "somebody trying to vomit through a straw," Steve respected me. He'd asked for my help when his '53 Chevy wouldn't start—no surprise, he shifted gears without using the clutch—and he wasn't that pissed even after I tore his engine down to reveal a piston blown to metal gravel at the bottom of his oil pan before realizing the needle on his gas gauge leaned firmly to the left of *E*. Steve could write *Organ Morgan, the Novel*, we'd work a three-way split. No, Eric replied. Why not? Because it wouldn't work. I said, don't worry about plot, we can have Organ Morgan sample the babes in his Gospel Choir, have him run for pope, have him—no, Eric repeated, it'll just be a big waste of time because it won't work.

Also, and this was really off the wall, he said, never mind my cool drawings, I had no talent for hot cars and should lay off before I did any more damage. But I loved hot cars. Love and talent are not the same thing, he insisted. Right. Well, maybe I should consider the source. Though Eric had an IQ of maybe 185, he planned to buy a 1932 Ford three-window coupe and restore it. Crazy. The 1932 Ford three-window coupe is the sacred wellspring of hot-rodding; it not only begs but demands hot-rod reinvention, beginning with, say, a new supercharged Chevy big-block V-8. Restore? What kind of blasphemy was that?

Meanwhile, how many ways can you spell *This stinks?* It wasn't just having to trudge the streets like some upper-middle-class hobo, I needed a powerful machine to express myself. I wasn't adding up. My brother and sister were athletes. Daring, too. At the golf club swimming pool Scott would stand perched backward over the end of the diving board with only his toes still on the edge, *boing* to the sky, twist to a blur and, his arms stretched above his head, drop from the sky, a boy arrow, his nose missing the diving board by a hair. Little Laurie rode a horse big enough to have Greek soldiers hiding inside over high jumps that were videotaped for critique by her instructor, and the word at the stable was that she was headed for the Olympics. I had been third-string quarterback on the Raleigh Hills grade school flag football team and defensive left toothpick on the freshman B squad here at Beaverton High. You do the math.

Moon and I had set off across the shaggy grasses of Golfland, the pitch and putt course behind my house, walked down Beaverton Hillsdale Highway, over on the gravel, headlights swelling up and cars whapping past. Passing the 76 station by the Fred Meyer shopping center, in a service bay I saw the green Thunderbird, hoisted high in the air on a hydraulic lift. It belonged to Reno; born Ron MacCrae. His father ran all the Safeway stores in the Northwest and had recently given the T-Bird to his boy as a sixteenth birthday present. I'd seen it first screaming past the school bus I was still stuck riding, gone in a diminishing howl of an unmuffled 352-cubic-inch Ford V-8.

"Reno," Moon said, lighting a cigar.

MacCrae, wrench in hand, head tipped up into the oily mess of his undercarriage, looked at us and said, "Guys."

Reno had a sleepy, carnivorous Donald Trump look that said: "I'm here for dinner and I'm not in a hurry but I'm here to eat and I'm going to eat a lot." Girls thought Reno had "bedroom eyes." I know because he told me. Rich kid Reno had proven a generous black hole of a pal, constantly spewing off dollars but implosive in his interests; himself and his Thunderbird.

"Reno," Moon said, "how about a ride downtown?"

"No can do," my new friend replied, as his T-Bird sunk toward the concrete floor, then stood between us in the air, vivid as a great idea. What I saw inside the T-Bird knocked me out. Using a hack saw, Reno had cut a square hole in his transmission console to accommodate the chrome arc of his brand-new Hurst transmission linkage. Exactly what my father should have done. Reno had used his money to do to his Thunderbird what I had wanted my father to do with his: He had punched out the 352-cubic-inch V-8 to 390 and replaced the car's automatic transmission with a three speed. I was dry throated with envy. Here was a seventeen-year-old who could do what he'd dreamed about. All he needed was cash.

"Your dad's not going to do anything drastic about your mom's car, is he?" Moon asked, as we walked into a shopping center parking lot, oily black from recent rain. I could see my breath, and see also my new mother's wiped-out coupe, and replied that I wasn't sure yet. Normally when my dad got mad it was the way people got mad on TV, it was like he was just acting and I didn't worry too much. But this time, it was frightening. Because he didn't seem mad at all. In fact, pretty much, he remained as quiet as an unexploded bomb.

Moon and I walked into Fred Meyer's shopping center, traipsing down avenues of food, clothes, records and toys. Time to, in Moon's words, "stud down." Which meant Moon auditioning Jade East cologne, potato chips, doughnuts—he was fingering up a green clod of lime sherbet from a gallon tub when a skinny, balding clerk trotted up to ask what he was doing. "Testing your merchandise. It's not up to my standards," Moon assessed, striding down the aisle. As the sliding glass front doors hummed apart to let him pass, Moon rubbed his hands together and said, "Minisnakes. Salvation."

Then I saw. Miniskirts spilling from a battleship of a Plymouth station wagon. The vixens. Curvy little girls wearing makeup that, under the lights of the parking lot, looked like house paint. I dreaded this. I knew it was bound to be a nightmare, or at least jail. And that would mean military school for sure.

"Hello everybody," Moon said.

"Oh you," a girl with pumpkin-colored hair replied.

"Now, now," he put up a hand. "All we need is a ride downtown."

"We were going to the dance," she said, her eyes ghoulish with mascara. "Do you have any beer?"

"I can get some," Moon affirmed. "Downtown. Don't look at me like that. We're good for gas."

The driver, a tiny blonde boss of a girl, said, "Okay," and we were off.

This was not going to be good mayhem, it was going to be bad mayhem, though there was one plus: with the two bubbleheads was a girl from my typing class. We sat scrunched together, hip to hip, knee to knee. She was almost as tall as I was, I liked her, but the two years between us made her a kid. "Finger watchers flunk," she reminded me as the station wagon sighed up over Portland Heights and down into the constellation that was the city at night. We talked about school—how my typing in typing class stunk due to my inability to spell (in English class: "Mr. Dietsche, does 'Question Authority' begin with a 'C' or a 'K'?") and the little blonde girl driving was just beginning to explain how the reason she was driving when she wasn't old enough to even have a driver's license was that she had snuck her parents' station wagon out and—*wham!* A car flew by. Farrel Cron, a seventeen-year-old aspiring stumblebum whose dotty grandma had lost enough of her mind to have bought him a gorgeous Chevy Rat-motored 1940 Ford convertible, ripped by—headed, it looked like, for either hell or the Promised Land.

Now high up in the West Hills, we were approaching the scene of my crime. My father had gotten remarried to a very smart, lively young woman, a photographer, who did not understand a house where the only rules were the kind you found on the back of a Ouija board.

She had a nice way of imposing order—"Please, don't ad lib your way through the groceries"—an actress's expressive face and could convey most any emotion in a glance. I liked watching TV with her. She'd explain movies in a voice no louder than thought. During *Mrs. Miniver* I got the story on Greer Garson, Lend-Lease and the Battle of Britain and, in any event, my new mother also had a neat 1958 Ford coupe and, driving it one night, some guys in an old pickup gave me the finger and, chasing them into the hills here above the city, the Ford slid off the road into a tree. My father drove by the wreckage, slowed to say, "Call a tow truck" and was gone. And I knew that I would be too—

gone to some private penitentiary where I'd be learning hup two, three, four years before my time—if I screwed up again.

"All right," I heard Moon instruct, "let us out."

Out. Okay. But where were we? Downtown, on Broadway.

"Where's our beer?" the blonde boss vixen demanded.

"In my stomach," Moon replied. Then to me, "Nothing but mini-snakes. Better fishing ahead."

I guess. We stood on the sidewalk below the neon splay of the big theaters, hot rods and cars full of girls easing by. Though blind as a cave newt, Moon had an eye for this. "*Vogue* material," he nodded toward two young women in an Edsel. "Watch." As the light changed, he strode out and fell under their front wheels, then sprang up and was, in a motion, leaning into the driver's window, claiming they'd "hit" him.

The young woman driving, who was older and very pretty, looked both disbelieving and scared. Next, we were in their backseat. Moon introduced himself as Jake Barnes and suggested a movie. "*A Mad, Mad, Mad, Mad, Mad, Mad, Mad, Mad, Mad, Mad, Mad World* is playing at the Orpheum."

"I thought you were hurt," the girl in the passenger side said. She looked anorexic enough to be a fashion model.

"I am. But," he lit another cigar, took an exploratory puff, a tart tendril of smoke rising between us, "maybe if we went someplace dark then I won't . . . have to sue anybody."

"Hold on," the girl driving said. "You're the Martian."

"Moon," Moon corrected. The tart tendril was becoming a smelly river.

"You vomited on Sally Dent and then fell through the plate glass window at the Sigma Chi function. You're not even in college yet. You and Mick Jagger beat it or I call the cops."

"Now, now," Moon said.

She opened her door. "Beat it or I start screaming."

We started walking, thumbs in the air. For some reason, no one stopped to give us a ride. Six miles on foot. Almost all up hill. No way around it, no matter what it took, it was time to get a car of my own. All I needed was the cash.

16

First Things First

A whole new life is about to be mine, a life of less thinking and more doing, a *real* life that occurs outside my head minus fictions and phantasms, a life I get paid well for, a life promoted from journalist and novelist to kick-ass bureaucrat, a hot car life, a life where my wife won't have to be half scared to death wondering where the money is going to come from if Mrs. So-and-So doesn't pop for that 18th century Chinese armoire this week, a life where, sure, I'll still be writing: checks.

With luck, we've found the guy to build the Xeno. All we need is more money. So first things first.

"Start a company," Steve Scherzer says, covering his long face with tan hands. "Scary Larry says start a company."

"Steve," I say, "the kid's a new design Messiah, he's got the Midas touch."

"Yeah, okay. So . . . what do the investors get out of the profits. Half?"

"That's what I suggested to Nick. Does that seem right?"

"About. On these wild speculative deals, investors tend to want to spend a buck to make a buck. One hundred percent return."

I am at Scherzer's law office high above Wilshire Boulevard. Scherzer is tall, exercised and has precisely cut bushy blond hair, a craggy face, big white teeth. "There's a big difference," he says, "between long-term investors opposed to one Joe Schmoe who just wants to drive the thing around so he can get laid."

A poker player at the caddie shack at the Portland Golf Club when we were both fourteen, Steve once literally took my shirt and was a player in college too. A sign DRUGS: USE NOT ABUSE hung on his dorm room wall. He was almost a judge at thirty when vodka caught up with him. "First," he told me, "you forget the tonic, then the ice, finally the glass. At the end, I'd twirl the top off the pint, throw it on the liquor store parking lot and have half the bottle down before I got to my car."

Now Steve's drink is Diet Coke. "The problem is, you're selling a security," he says, "an interest in something that doesn't exit. If you keep the offering under a million to twenty-five investors or less, you can do it without a Security and Exchange Commission full-blown prospectus—those can take years. Who'd you say Nick's granddad was—"

"The guy," I reply, "who was the model for the boss patriarch in *Peyton Place*. I think his telephone company is the biggest one in New England."

"Then why not just get Nick's parents to pay for the car?"

"Not likely," I reveal. "Nick's mother and her boyfriend think he's going to lose his shirt."

A little something I'm going to have to deal with.

Stars still in the sky, I'm headed from my house to Nick's freshly rented studio, driving beneath vast unconnected swoops of new overpasses that look oddly ruined in their incompleteness, as if to suggest that one day L.A. will be an irradiated ghost town, leaving these overpasses to be the pyramids of Gaza to the mutants of 4000 A.D.

Gideon says there will be no money until we produce a plan "that, at least remotely, makes sense." So . . . last week I went to see CadZZilla, *Hot Rod* magazine's hot rod of the decade. The dark blue 1949 Cadillac—a Cadillac like my mother's—had been stretched, lowered, chopped, channeled and suaved to perfection. Created for ZZ Top, CadZZilla was a promotional engine for *Hot Rod* magazine's "Person of the Year," Boyd Coddington. His meal ticket: wheels. Boyd turned out seven thousand a year to fit everything from Chevy trucks to Dino Ferraris. They sold for $400 to $2,000 apiece and stood in long shining rows outside his office, fifteen minutes from my home, like Godzilla's coin collection.

Dream car products. Why not? I called Nick in Miami. He and Henrietta had jetted to Florida to yacht around with Henrietta's dad Wolfgang and I asked: "Why limit ourselves to just the car? Henrietta's dad is the biggest fashion guy in Germany. You can design that stuff. Jackets and accessories. Wheels. Hot rod wheel makers have made a fortune in wheels you could design in your sleep." Nick said cool, and when he returned I met Wolfgang. Boyishly handsome, fair-haired, blue eyed. According to Nick: "He's happy, sad, angry, modest, boastful, your best friend and the biggest prick ever, all in a second, a triple-edged sword."

Poolside at the Beverly Wilshire, Wolfgang resembled more a twenty-five-year-old lifeguard than a forty-five-year-old German fashion king. He has made a fortune in Europe, marketing everything from designer jeans to couture perfume. Floating up off a lounge chair beside another blonde man who had a scar the size of a candy bar down one cheek, Wolfgang let a hand hang out, and I was surprised that when our palms crossed it was like shaking hands with a pair of pliers. " 'Ello," he said.

And at a round white table under an umbrella here at the pool, fresh-faced Henrietta, in a bathing suit revealing her in lunging swoops, said her father had just spent $50,000 to have Herb Ritts photograph him and his male companion.

Nick sipped a purple drink. "Wolfgang bought tons of stuff. Dude, he put the Beverly Center in a shopping cart."

Nick says that though Henrietta loves her father, they can't live on the same side of the planet because Wolfgang, "takes over wherever he goes. In Europe he's everywhere. That's why Henrietta had to come here. So she could be herself and not just his daughter. If he comes to America he'll take over. Completely." Nick snaps his fingers. "Turn on the TV and he's on *Good Morning America*. Drive down the highway and he's on a billboard. Pick up a *Vanity Fair* and he's there on the page."

Nick ordered a chicken sandwich from a white-coated waiter. On Wolfgang. Water, water everywhere, but—Wolfgang could sign for the Xeno as easily as he signed for Nick's sandwich.

Dawn. I pull into the parking lot in front of Nick's vast new studio. Nick has built an apartment upstairs, Henrietta fast asleep, he shows me a picture of a cylinder covered with cowhide. When I ask what it is, he replies, "A coffee pot. A friend designed it. Killer, huh?"

"Why is it covered with cowhide?"

"To symbolize man's inhumanity to cattle. He got the leather from a slaughterhouse. They weren't hip to what he was up to so they let him have it for free."

Then Nick hands me a new clay ray gun he's invented. He's design-ing a fantasy world, "Future Zone," for Steven Spielberg. You walk into a lifesize "computer screen" and battle robots with laser guns. Good money. Tradition dictates that when young you have to eat at least one can of pork and beans, but Nick doesn't buy it. "Henrietta and I want homes in Los Angeles, Hamburg, New York, Paris, Monte Carlo. When we have kids we'll have a nanny so we'll be there for the good stuff and the nanny'll be there when the bad stuff hangs out."

Carefully, the rough edges of its plywood base cutting lines across my palms, Nick and I lift the model of the Xeno into the back of my rented white Chevy station wagon. The model, sleek and shiny, is made of clay—which is heavy—and is about as easy to cart around as a dead man.

Nick and I drive north, the Xeno in the back, to see Sam Foose. With luck, our salvation. Sam is Nick's friend Chip Foose's father, a hot rod and prototype builder who has conjured movie cars for *Blade Runner* and *Robo Cop*. Around Ventura, Nick says Henrietta fears his success, that it might lead to megalomania and—this was a new one on me—homosexuality. Also, Henrietta found one of his old sex tapes. "I tape *Wild Kingdom*. I thought she had one of my nature shows." No. She picked up a video of Nick doing a nature show with an old girl-friend.

On the plus side, Nick says Henrietta now has $250 million in her bank account, though her father really isn't aware of it. "Wolfgang's got an attorney he totally trusts—the guy's great, he's like Henrietta's father's father—anyway, this kindly old German is a total shark, he built the money side of Henrietta's dad's empire. The lawyer had Wolfgang sign these papers when he was like half asleep—if he knew what he'd signed, he'd freak! It gave his company to Henrietta."

"So Henrietta could finance the Xeno—"

"All she has to do is call the attorney and get the number to her Swiss bank account."

Sam Foose greets us in his driveway in gray sweats, glasses hanging from a string around his neck. He is maybe fifty, has shaggy gray-blond hair and looks like someone who, at one time or another, knew his way around a football field. Right away he amends our plans. "No polished aluminum body. You'd need a million dies and stamps and you can't cobble something that perfect, you're talking about a *lifetime* of body work."

Sam's garage is as big as a house. Inside, a 1946 Ford delivery wagon, brown with primer and its nose about an inch off Sam's concrete floor. Next to it, an old, full-fendered Ford Victoria.

Sam Foose is among the last of the great California customizers, a dynasty that, just for the record, was begun by teenager George DuVall in the early 1930s. DuVall, a tall, thin beyond precious kid, had already been groomed as an executive for Safeway grocery stores when he went to work for an outfit called SoCal Chrome Plating in Los Angeles. Influenced by the designs of Harley Earl—who had also grown up in L.A.—DuVall began creating custom bumpers and grilles, mostly for Depression-era Fords. It was a relatively inexpensive way to give his clients Cadillac style when a Cadillac was a luxury few people could still afford. The swept-back "speed boat" DuVall windshield is still a prized hot rod accessory, and George DuVall went on to inform the work of more famous custom car greats George Barris, Ed "Big Daddy" Roth and Gene Winfield.

In the early 1950s, Barris created "lead sleds," long and low custom Ford and Mercuries that took their styling cues from Hudson's step-down construction. He draped bodies over frames, removed insignias and smoothed away whatever edges there were and chopped the tops. Barris's precision anarchy was a cool counterpoint to the conformist Organization Man 1950s. He graduated to the dream car business, conjuring extravagances like his 1953 Lincoln "Golden Sahara"—a convertible an inch or two off the ground that, with a telephone, tape recorder, bar and TV, had every accessory short of a swimming pool. Barris even included, for some reason, a complete set of barber tools in one of his customs.

Ed "Big Daddy" Roth was more flamboyant. How to describe Big Daddy? Words are weakest in this realm. I have a friend who was invited to bearded Big Daddy's house for a spaghetti dinner. Big Daddy served it from his dog's dish because, he explained, "It tastes better that way." For Roth a 600-horsepower metallic red flame-painted Corvette would be too conservative. Abetted by his henchmen Dirty Doug, Robert Williams—whose hot rod art now commands six-figure sums—Jake Jacobs and Goober, Roth created otherworldly steel cartoons—drag racing hearses, cars like the Beatnik Bandit and the Mysterion—designed less, it seemed, to be driven by humans than the pop-eyed monsters and pot-bellied leering rats that festooned the T-shirts Roth sold by the thousands.

Gene Winfield, conversely, made his reputation creating custom cars smoothed by classic European design gestures, but also made a killing supplying fantasy cars to Hollywood. Sam Foose, who worked for Winfield in the 1960s, built the *Man from U.N.C.L.E* car, the *Get Smart* car, the *Star Trek* car, created or helped create the swoopy, fiberglass Ala Kart, the "Reactor" car for *Bewitched*, trendsetting cars for *Blade Runner* and *Robo Cop*. Like his mentor Winfield, he also builds exquisite hot rods whose delicate spearlike bumpers and understated reshaping take their cues more from Ghia and Ferrari than Plymouth or Ford. It would be nice to impress him.

The Xeno model rests on Sam's desk, projecting its rude, jabbed beauty—Venus with a hairlip. Sam says, "To build a chassis, I'll need a 'true.'" A flat-as-glass metal surface on which to begin construction. "And that costs money." Sam lights a cigarette. "But what I'm thinking, build it around a Pantera. Pull the body off—just put together something rough to start out with."

Nick cracks a knuckle. "No way. The car must be right from the beginning."

Sam looks at us. "That'll be expensive. Take that center steering. You'll need custom universal joints. Custom safety glass costs a fortune. You want air conditioning—how much is it gonna cost to tube that shit? And I suppose you want antilock brakes and four-wheel disks. Boys." Smoke from Sam's cigarette rivers up around him. "This'll cost a fortune."

Nick cracks another knuckle, two more. "We can't compromise."

Sam nods. "Think of just the interior. You'll need jams, power window assembly, locks, latches handles, hinges, seals. And I'm not for free. I got a forty-one Ford convertible I've been planning to rebuild since 1979. The problem is, I can't afford me."

At dusk, he shows us a trophy one of his cars won at the Oakland Roadster Show. "You know what it costs to build a hot rod to win at Oakland these days? Three hundred fifty thousand. I'm not working on daydreams guys, get me some money."

I call Moon. After high school he majored in going berserk at the University of Oregon—the two guys who wrote *Animal House* stayed at Moon's fraternity to do their research and it is Portland lore that *all* of the top lunacy parts were based on Moon. Then he went on to become one of the key "Just Do It" marketing guys at Nike. Over the phone I give him the news. That exotics cars are popping up all over. The $450,000 Koenig Ferrari, the $350,000 RUF Porsche, the $500,000 Lamborghini Diablo. The V-16 560 Cizeta Moroder. The Moroder people claim one-hundred orders at $450,000 apiece—a car that can't even meet U.S. import standards. Amazing machines, some with every luxury except a spare tire and a trunk. George Harrison just bought a million-dollar 1,000-horsepower McLaren F1 and had it decorated with three-dimensional elephants. The Sultan of Brunei had bought over 150 exotics so far. He spent $900,000 to have one of his Ferraris gold plated, and his personal stock of exotics was worth more than $100 million. "Moon," I say, staying on message, "the kid's the new design Messiah, he's got the Midas touch. Help me plan this thing and we can kill."

"I like to kill," he admits. Moon has helped run three of the fastest-growing corporations in the Pacific Northwest. But how to invent a car company? "You need a pro forma source and application of funds, income statement and balance sheet. Plus a CPA to offer an opinion of value. You'll have to incorporate. But don't worry, Marko, an empire will soon be ours."

Saddam Hussien, a recalcitrant numbskull with only enough savvy to have amassed the fourth-largest army in the world, has failed to chicken out. Bombs are falling on Baghdad and Nick, staring at my TV, his knuckles going off like a string of ladyfingers, says, "I'm totally against war but totally for killing this guy."

Nick has made an appointment with a securities attorney. "He's not a car guy, but he's cool. Conservative, dresses *GQ*. I walked down this hall past this door, that door; I'm thinking, Nooooooooooo, but there it is, the corner office. Way, way above the ocean, and a golf course."

He also got a quote from Paul Batista to do the interior. "Paul says he can do it for thirty thousand to fifty thousand dollars."

When I say, *"Just for the interior?"* Nick gets upset: "We should abandon the whole project if we can't do it right. It's our vision against all odds. We can't plan for compromise."

"We can't?"

"Mark, I've asked around. Nobody's said we're insane."

"What's our vision against all odds going to cost?"

"Three hundred fifty thousand dollars. We're going after people who have two hundred fifty million dollars."

"Nick, I wanted to build a high-tech hot rod, not a pimpmobile for the Shah of Iran."

Nick looks punched, and I see him on the phone to Jerry Palmer at General Motors, asking about the GM dental plan.

"We are building an ultimate," he says. "We're offering a lot of fun, art and bitchin'ness. It will enrich their lives! But we must do the best job creating something greater than anyone ever has, ever. We cannot scrimp!"

17

HOT ROD

Fall 1965. Nighttime rain smashing the stolen VW's windshield, the freeway flying under us, I stare at the speedometer counting out loud, "eighty-six . . . eighty-seven . . . eighty-nine," when the car begins to skid and spin, slowly as if in a bad dream, guardrail looming, swung by, loomed and swung by as we twirl down the asphalt, magically not hitting anything, sliding to a stop, the Volkswagen facing the wrong way down the freeway, my big, bearish pal Mike M.—just out of reform school for driving his father's Chevy Corvair into the surf at Cannon Beach—noting, "Eighty-nine. I didn't think a Volks'd go so fast."

Why was I riding around in a stolen VW? Because when Mike arrived at my house that night I didn't realize that *borrowed* was his word for *hot wired*.

This stunk. I was sixteen, had grown eight inches in the last year and had to have a car so that: A) I wouldn't go to jail for grand theft auto; and B) I could make art—if I had the right car it would be as if I could take Ernest Hemingway's novel, *The Sun Also Rises*, chop out the Jew baiting, bolt on a Lolita . . .

My younger brother Scott already had his art. A master of fuzz tone and wa-wa pedal, chords flew out of his Epiphone electric guitar in booming riffs and shards as—a Lark filter hanging at the side of his mouth—he'd howl: *Come on baby, pleeeeeze. Ah'mmm down on my kneeeeez. Ah gave you a d-i-i-i-mond, you gave me diseeeze.* It was like having a thirteen-year-old Jimmy Page in our living room; soon his name would be in lights above Shea Stadium and he'd be heaving TVs out of hotel rooms and how could I top that?

By building a great car. Like Reno. True, he'd had problems. The day after he finished rebuilding his engine, he gave me a ride to school. Reno's T-Bird was a rocket. Actually. When I looked back, both rear exhaust pipes were corkscrewing great Saturn C plumes. Smoke so pro-found the cars behind us were gone in a roiling gray fog. The next day Reno was at my locker with news he'd gone through four quarts of oil in twenty-four hours. I said, "Maybe it's your gaskets."

"Gaskets," he asked, "what are gaskets?"

But my other friends were creating miracles. Like Bill Winfree's '55 Chevy coupe. White, elegant and so simple. Hot rodders were falling all over themselves slapping on every kind of geegaw, jacking bodies up and down, painting their rides as many colors as you'd find in an oil slick. Winfree had done the opposite. His car was the first time I'd seen art made by someone my age. Not because of what he'd done but what he hadn't. His Chevy coupe was spare as a knife. The car had its orig-inal chrome and from the outside looked almost stock. Even his hubcaps were standard Chevrolet wheel covers. The only hint this coupe was any different from its factory brothers—aside from its cleanliness—were the dual exhausts that protruded from either side in front of the rear tires, the large black tires all the way around, the white-knobbed Hurst shifter and the Sun tach mounted on the dash. But under the hood rested a fuel-injected 283-cubic-inch V-8 constructed with the care I would have associated with brain surgery. Simply by what he'd chosen not to do, Winfree made me reconsider everything I'd ever thought about hot cars.

Then there was Dick Donaca's '54 Ford, a car as garish as Winfree's was conservative. Lowered to the ground, fluorescent blue, chrome bulging and gleaming, it looked like a Transylvanian pimpmobile but was quick as light. Dick's older brothers had taken a 364-cubic-inch Buick V-8, bored it out until its cylinder walls were about as thin as a traffic ticket, slipped in pistons big as paint cans, installed a racing cam and three two-barrel carburetors and shaved tolerances between to the molecule. The result: 360 real horsepower. A cool joke to be played at somebody else's expense.

One night we were riding around and Dick slowed for a light and pulled alongside Heinrich Himmler's own Pontiac GTO. Jet black, jacked high off the ground, monster tires, Mickey Thompson mags, capped dump tubes standing like cannon below the front wheel wells. Dick, built like a tough pixie, had a sense of the ridiculous. "Watch this," he said and booted his accelerator. His exhaust pipes crackled.

The guy in the GTO looked over. "Pussy wagon," he said.

"Wa-wa-would you la-like ta-ta-ta race?" Donaca stuttered.

"Hardy-har-har." Rock jawed, crew cut, maybe twenty, maybe thirty or forty, he peered at Donaca's blue Ford as if it were just off the bottom of his shoe.

"Aw, ca-come on," Dick said, "I ju-just ba-bought it from a gy-gy-gypsy and want ta-ta-ta see how it goes."

"Twenty bucks," the crew cut replied.

"Okey-doke," Donaca nodded. The light changed and the Ford exploded off the line with enough force to snap my neck. The GTO was lost in a billowing cloud of burning rubber by the time Dick stood on the brakes for the light by the Fred Meyer shopping center down the road. The guy followed us into the parking lot at the McDonald's across the street from Taco Time.

Stepping from the GTO, he reached into his wallet, forked over a ten, a five and a fan of ones. "What on God's green earth kinda engine you got in that thing, anyway?"

Donaca shrugged. "Beats me. I can't get the hood up to find out."

I had to have a car. Because there was more. One night I rode to a teenage nightclub with a friend and his girlfriend and ran into a pretty, bookish girl who had smooth hair the color of cut wood and who was short enough to still be growing—the friend of a friend of a friend. Over the racket of "Wooly Bully," she said she "liked" me. Later we went out and climbed into the backseat of my friend's empty four-door Dodge. He and his girlfriend had tottered off into the night and left the car parked in front of my parents' tall hedge. In my past, romance had plateaued at the word *no*. But now there were no noes. One door opened up after another and soon I was in a room I knew nothing about.

I could see a pattern here, one I wanted to firmly establish. But in a machine of my own. I got a job at a car wash. Fired for snapping towels, I was hired to wave a big red flag atop a Sizzler steak house. I'd begin after school and wave until nine when I'd trudge home to catch the last minutes of Ryan O'Neal's sex problems on *Peyton Place*.

Within months I had two things in my corner: $350 and no common sense. The want ads were a garden of earthy delights and I quickly fell in love with every other tarted-up piece of motorized rubbish in the county.

I begged my father to let me buy a rust-gutted yellow-and-white '55 Chevy four door with sheets of oil oozing from the blown soft plugs of its huge Ford truck engine and nearly cried when I couldn't find an extra $100 for a '56 Ford coupe that was a steal, even though apparently a hand grenade had gone off on the front seat. After all, what were STP and seat covers for?

Then I lucked into the metallic blue 1953 Chevy. Green-gray leatherette seats, a little six-cylinder engine, dual carburetors, a polished aluminum Offenhauser valve cover, an Iskenderian track cam, a split manifold with dual exhaust and dump tubes, a Sun tach, big 8:20/15 tires on the back, a Corvette shifter and a 3,200 heavy-duty clutch mated to a balanced aluminum flywheel. It was gorgeous and it took me only $1,000 and a year to turn it into a howling piece of thundering junk.

The big problem I had with the car was I couldn't drive it. Not without a B average. That wasn't happening. So I couldn't drive the Chevy outside of my parents' driveway. I'd remove the caps on the dump tubes so that the exhaust would shoot straight out of the manifold, back the car up to the street, rev the screaming engine up to 4,000 RPM, dump the clutch and send the Chevy hurtling through the breezeway and into the asphalt cul-de-sac in back. Then I'd slam on the brakes, bang the shift into reverse, back up and—the rear tires screeching—do it over again. Until I broke the rear axle.

I jacked the Chevy up, pulled off the rear wheel, removed the brake, slid a greasy, busted shaft from the dark hole of the axle housing. Awful. I wanted sex, not gynecology.

Briefly, my dad relented. I could drive the car, but couldn't have anybody else ride in it with me. I was walking again when he discovered I'd let friends ride *on* the car, rather than *in* it, driving around with pals standing on the rear bumper clinging to the rear window post to avoid falling off the back.

I had to face facts: The car was jinxed. After having the valves ground, my pals Dave Mills and long, tall Loog and I were torquing the head back on when Dave slipped into the car to light a cigarette. I was using a study lamp for a trouble light and, holding the unhooked fuel line over the socket, Loog said, "I'll bet you got an electric fuel pump. Start 'er up, Dave."

I said, "Are you crazy!" just as Mills hit the ignition. Gas shot from the fuel line onto the light socket and, *whoosh*, fire everywhere. The engine compartment was blazing, flames were licking at the frame around the garage door. The three of us pushed the car out to the driveway and I began squirting it with a garden hose.

"That's not gonna do anything with gas!" Mills said.

"Then," I replied, "let it blow up." I was sure the gas tank would go any second.

Instead Mills ran inside my house, dashed back out and began heaving rooster tails of flour all over the engine and, I was astounded, in minutes the fire was out.

But water and flour and heat had made a bread that coated everything. The metallic blue paint was fried. The hood looked like the face of the moon. The end was near. Somehow we got the head torqued back down and the car running again. Shortly thereafter a friend had a problem in it drag racing a Corvette ("Sorry, man, but when I hit second gear your hood ripped off. Lucky it didn't smash through the windshield"), and now my dream machine looked like it had been eaten by a bear and shit off a cliff.

The car was immobilized completely after Dick Donaca borrowed some long-sleeved shirts from me and returned them short-sleeved. In a rage, I told my brother I was driving over to Dick's house to kill him and my brother told my dad.

Out in the garage, I hit the Chevy's ignition and all I got was the sound of the starter motor. I popped the hood, everything seemed in place, then went back inside where my father held up a piece of plastic. "You know what this is?" he asked.

I said, "No."

"It's a rotor. It passes electricity from your distributor to your spark plugs. You're not driving anywhere, buster." I went ape. I chased Scott around the house. He locked himself into our bathroom and I knocked the bathroom door off its frame. This wasn't some hollow fiberboard tract home door, this was a heavy wooded doctor's door and, my, I'd knocked the frame from the wall. Wood splintered, a row of big nails all curved. Weird. I set out walking to Donaca's, amazed to be angry as ever. It gave me confidence. *That* would be my career: psycho. But when I got to Dick's house he wasn't home to kill and I woke up the next morning disturbed at my own calm. Long sleeve to short sleeve, so what? At breakfast, however, my father said the Chevy was in the garage for good.

Okay, if I couldn't drive it, I could still change it. What to do? Rip out my motor. Because my '53 Chevy's minuscule six-cylinder racing engine wouldn't be blowing any Nazi GTOs off the road, that was a for sure. I needed V-8 power against the day, month, year, decade, millennium I'd be on the loose again.

So, a plan. By now I knew that while a hot rod is a good place to get drunk, fucked and possibly killed, a great hot rod is created within a highly defined format—success goes to he who makes the fewest mistakes. For all its bows to anarchy, a successful hot rod is a device whose body, engine and interior is organized around a series of dramatic and enduring design headlines à la "JFK Shot in Dallas, Lee Harvey Oswald Nabbed as Suspect, LBJ Sworn In," a confluence of taste, money, craft and gall. Building one is an endlessly self-referring business; every new best hot rod is about the new best ones preceding it.

So, picture this, it'll make you nuts: a brand-new big block Chevy Rat-motor 409, like Patty's boyfriend Dick had but better. Bored and stroked, balanced and blueprinted and threaded with a big, fat Iskenderian roller cam, one that makes the nice *lubba-lubba-lubba* sound at the stoplights. For carburation, dual Holley four barrels on an aluminum high-rise manifold. Around the edges, Mallory ignition and a brand-new Sun tachometer. Plus an aluminum flywheel and truck clutch bolted to a T-85 four-speed transmission and—wait!—I almost forgot. Back to the engine. Tuned Hooker headers and polished aluminum valve covers. What else? Hurst shift linkage and Chevy factory Positraction, plus Traction-Masters. As for the exterior, why go overboard? I'd settle for American Mag wheels mounted on brand-new Firestone Tiger Paw tires. Big 8:20s in back and less-big 8:00s up front.

All that separated me from my goal was about $2,000. At $1.10 an hour at the Sizzler steak house I'd be flag waving up on the roof into the next century before I saw that kind of money. Then—salvation. My friend Jimmy Huygens had a 322-cubic-inch Buick V-8 he said he'd sell me for $40. Unbelievable. Dick Donaca's engine right there. Or at least it would be as soon as I did all the things Dick's brother's had. Forty bucks was nothing. I slipped Jimmy two twenties, knowing I was home free at last.

Smoke erupted from Loog's wide mouth in a stony white cloud, popped back in, then began leaking in two sibilant streams up his nose. "You're fucked," he informed.

Loog was even taller than I was and as skinny, mantislike, he had fists as big as boxing gloves and a voice that sounded shot through an empty oil drum. Loog's hobbies ranged from cat burglary to interior decoration. At dinner, plates were bureaucracy. Loog ate from the pan and knew few car problems that could not be solved with a crescent wrench, case of beer, a ball peen hammer and the words *Reef on it*.

Thus, I'd been shocked when, slumped in a corner of my dad's garage, gazing at the six-cylinder engine hanging above the Chevy on a chain like a side of beef in a meat locker, Loog—an acrobat with Pall Malls—blew one smoke ring through another and said, "Dig it, dog: Fifty bucks says that car never runs again."

Getting the little six out had been easy, he said, but getting the Buick V-8 in was gonna be not. The Chevy transmission, enclosed driveline and rear end was not built to handle the torque of a V-8. So surgery was required. Like a whole new drive train. A chore I could do like an ape does algebra. A cool, competent-looking local mechanic who owned a pink Lincoln Continental with tail fins to rival the one on a 707 agreed to install a '57 Chevy rear end and axle in exchange for my Chevy six. Jimmy Huygens and I towed the engineless hulk six miles to the guy's shop where he revealed complications in our bargain. $350 in extra labor.

I got a better job, at Taco Time, making burritos and pouring tomato puree and oatmeal into the raw hamburger to stretch the meat, and hope sprung eternal.

Huygens and I—well, Huygens mostly, with advice from the Loog: "Reef on it, dogs"—conjured a primordial mechanical swamp under the hood of the Chevy that nourished the rudimentary life of an engine.

I'll never forget push-starting the Chevy in the rain at night in front of my parents' house and hearing the Buick V-8 pop, hiss and explode to life, my eyes tearing with the smoke that filled the car's recently perfect interior.

The Chevy lurched forward. My new Hurst shifter wouldn't hit second gear and it was soon apparent the V-8 needed a little work. Like new rings and valves. But so what? Who cared if the clutch slipped and would not adjust, and if the Buick three speed had a shifting pattern as tricky as a combination lock and if the V-8 caused the little Chevy radiator to turn into a boiling tea kettle after three miles.

I had achieved V-8 power. Or would have if I'd had more than eighty-five pounds of compression in any of the cylinders. I remained, however, optimistic. For, after all, there was Jimmy Huygens. He was a smart mechanic, a smooth-faced boy with a neat haystack of straight blond hair who when walking held his arms slightly bent at the sides as if he were wearing guns. He was possessed of a Cotton Mather-ish rectitude and real will. He'd already built a great little junker '32 Ford roadster here in the garage. It was metallic red and ran a stock Chevy 265-cubic-inch V-8. Nothing fancy, just chassis + body + motor =

hot rod, and he was about to start another. Months ago he'd been like me, just one more inmate of bonehead classes designed for boys whose idea of promise was boot camp. Then Jimmy's banker dad offered to finance the hot rod of his dreams if he, Jimmy, would improve his grades. A's everywhere in one term. So I was confident. With Jimmy's help I'd have the car cherried out and beautiful girls would want to ride around in this, the first of my many four-wheeled *Mona Lisa*s.

Well, not many girls qualified. Like just two. For one thing, I had an exhaust leak so bad blue clouds hung above the driver's seat in strata. Romance within the Chevy was out. It was like trying to neck inside a gas chamber.

A bigger problem was the brakes. There was only an inch of play before the brake lever hit the Buick engine's fat steel bellhousing. So the brakes had to be constantly pumped or I could die at any stop sign. Thus, just two girls in the Chevy. The first was my actual girlfriend. Yeah, now I had one. A swimsuit model who was in the gifted program at our suburban prison of a high school. I'd met her at a dance and the next day she walked up to me while I was stuffing books into my locker. She had a big smile on her little face, as if I were a really good joke she'd never heard before.

An animist, I remember her putting her hands around her eyes to peek at the Chevy through the garage door window. "It ticks and groans and makes noises even when it isn't running," she said. "Have you ever wondered why?"

"Yeah," I replied, "because it's fucked up."

"No," she said, "because it's alive."

Girl two wasn't as kind. Blonde, hot tempered, for her one ride did it. She flew out of the Chevy, coughing, waving her arms. She hit me. "You're nuts. That car is suicide."

Well . . . so? I was not, on principal, against that. Because at Beaverton High in 1966 it was hip to be dead. Boys who got killed crashing cars got big rewards. Classmates held candle vigils on their front yards and many of the best-looking girls mourned openly after their ghosts. It had occurred to me, in fact, that I'd be lots more popular at school if I were six feet under.

Jimmy Huygens in his suit of lights, worn Levi's and a white Penney's Towncraft crewneck T-shirt, came to the garage to get things done. He saw the world in simple terms. Right was right, wrong was wrong.

Climb into Jimmy's new roadster, dump the clutch in first gear and you got two lines of scorched rubber a block and a half long.

Climb into my Chevy, dump the clutch in first gear and you got pistons all over three counties. Assuming it ever ran again. Afternoon after afternoon, Huygens and I were beneath the Chevy, down in the grease pit, typically pulling the transmission. From a radio above, Barry McGuire's gravelly baritone:

> The eastern world, it is explodin',
> Violence flarin', bullets loadin' . . .
> And even the Jordan River has bodies floatin' . . .
> You don't believe, we're on the eve of destruction."

I was glad for Huygens's help, assembling as I was oatmeal tacos thirty hours a week to support a car I couldn't drive without a B average I couldn't get because I was working thirty hours a week. More and more, I found myself playing Igor to somebody else's Dr. Frankenstein. I held the sun of the trouble light while my pals did the work. Huygens approached a car as a series of problems that could be solved by reason, skill and hard work. I approached a car as a series of problems that, pray to Christ, could be solved by jumper cables. Too, there was my swimsuit model girlfriend (after all, that was what the Chevy was supposed to help me *get*, wasn't it?). Frankly, it was more fun being twined together on a sofa in her parents' basement listening to "California Dreamin'" and her dreamy tales of crazy relatives than being crouched down in a concrete coffin under a filthy ceiling of rusty mufflers and dripping oil pan, and Jimmy Huygens could only do so much. At this point the Chevy didn't need a mechanic, it needed an exorcist. Oh, I'd made improvements. I'd gone to Radke's Auto Supply out in the heart of industrial nowhere in East County. Radke's was a ground zero of desire, a galaxy of chrome and speed. Christmas morning every morning. Except no present was yours unless you had money from all your flag waving, towel snapping or taco bending to pay for it and half my hours after school were spent clawing my way up the executive ladder at Taco Time, just to keep gas in the tank. And for what? It was like owning a hot rod built by Dr. Seuss.

And the truth was, the Chevy was dragging me down. Though on no one's short list for prom king, I was not a very alienated kid. A photo ID from the time shows me staring out at the camera, long haired, more pretty than handsome, smug. Still, I was six three, built like a dandelion and I didn't need any smoke-belching, crazy boy's car as ad for the fact I was—as my girlfriend had remarked—"from Planet X."

I had driven the Chevy to the service station where Bill Winfree worked—his perfect white '55 Chevy a trophy in front of the service bays—and his review of my efforts, "Christ, Mark," stung.

Meanwhile my friends were getting cars that made sense. Dave Mills, who was a tall, clean-cut boy who resembled me, except that he had a brain and a chest, bought a beautiful 1957 Ford, with a six tricked out deftly as the Chevy's had been—and proceeded to do the smart thing: nothing.

So how had I gotten myself into this mess? To make art. I'd already tried to write a novel, *Catch 22 II*—Yossarian flies off in his B-26 to firebomb Japan—but what sounded hilarious in my head wasn't on paper, and I had to do something. I had too much to lose. Like my girlfriend; brains, charm, a figure to stop a clock—the sweaty-palmed crowd at school was dogging her heels. One guy even slipped her a James Dickey poem about a stewardess who fell from an airliner and disrobed to meet the earth. How could I compete with that?

Maybe, just maybe—perhaps I should forget hot rods, go upscale. My father had bought the car of his dreams, a new Oldsmobile Toronado. A knife-sided mothership with a 385-horsepower motor as big as a doghouse mounted *beside* the transmission—power was transferred by chains, like a lawn mower, to the front wheels. The Toronado was General Motors chief designer Bill Mitchell's greatest hit. It was also the last, best passionate design to come out of Detroit before bumper safety standards and the gas crunch turned American cars into tin barges and gutless wonders. And it was a blast—hit the gas and the front tires would go insane. The hitch was the Toronado was a car of my father's dreams, not mine. When I asked him to let me drive it, he said: "That's what your hot rod is for."

Right, I forgot.

That the Chevy saw the road again at all was thanks to Jack, the owner of Jack's Shell station, which sat across from the pitch and putt golf course behind our house. Jack was a wiry man with a graying crew cut and veins that stood up on his forearms. He was direct, rugged. The kind of man who had helped win World War II. I bought two heavy-duty shock absorbers from him and he adjusted my leaking four-barrel carburetor for free.

And thereafter, he spent hours working on the car for almost no money. I was very flattered. For Jack was a big success. His gas station was avant-garde—built not like a traditional station, but more like an excellent suburban house, with a peaked and sweeping shingle roof and inside wall-to-wall computer "diagnostic" devices. Jack was as smooth as my father, a man for whom little could go wrong, and if something ever did, he could take care of it in a snap. The exact kind of guy I wanted to grow up to be.

No matter how busy the station was, Jack always had time for me. My Chevy would roll in smoking like the ruins of a burned-down house and he'd say, "Give me a half hour" and fifteen minutes later it would be back on the road. One afternoon I watched, handing him tools, as he replaced the spark plugs, belts and almost every gasket on the engine. This time it took hours. He charged me eight dollars for labor. When I said something (fearing he meant eighty dollars but had dropped an *O*), he said one day I'd discover the difference between my ass and my elbow and help somebody out myself. I could not believe my good fortune and, in some ways, Jack's death put the end to my hot rodding career. One morning when the Chevy wouldn't start I jumped-started it off my dad's Toronado and wheeled the smoking hulk in front of Jack's pumps, where I saw a chubby new face through his office windows. I got out, went inside. "Where's Jack?"

"He hung himself." The guy wiped his fingers on a red rag. "He got in a fight in a bar. His wife heard him come in late, went out to the garage in the morning and found him twisting from a rope."

18

Skies and Limits

The upper ups dropped us into a landing zone in the middle of a dug-in NVA company, the copters coming in on elephant grass six feet high. Before we'd even strung out our circle-the-wagons concertina wire Alpha Company started to scout out their side of the perimeter and their point man was blown to memoryville. I'd played pool the night before with one of the men my idiot Captain sent out to set up an all night listening post. It was about two in the morning when the L.P.s started signalling on the radio, then screaming outloud. "Fuck! They're all around us! We're coming in!" There was a scramble for rifles. We put in a call for artillery, to put up luminous rounds. They obliged by lighting up the jungle ten miles away.

The three L.P.s were rushing for the wire but couldn't find the opening. One had his legs blown off and the other two were dragging him in. A bunker down from me. First Squad opened up on what they thought was the gooks. It wasn't. My pool shooting buddy lay twenty feet in front of me, legs gone, whimpering, "Oh my God, oh my God, our own men have shot us."

As the sun rose, smoke was pressed to ground a deadly fog. I started to cry when I saw how close the L.P.s were to the bunker. I looked down at the guy I'd been playing pool with. I picked up his legs and carried them over and dropped them in my poncho and trudged back for his torso.

—Kit Bowen, from his journal

My phone rings. It is Kit Bowen calling from Portland with news. "Marko, a great salesman doesn't listen to you, doesn't take a no. He doesn't know your name ten minutes after you're off the lot. I put' em in a bubble. I can turn cars ten million ways, four square 'em, hit 'em at point of payment—better be ready to pick up the second pencil. Torture the pricks."

Kit Bowen sells cars, lots of cars. He could sell Torahs at the Vatican. I have sent him Nick's drawing of the Xeno, and Bowen, impressed, already has two potential clients. Number one, Bruce Stevenson, a timber baron. "He's car crazy: 'I've got a gullwing in the loop, but I've gotta finish this other Mercedes first.' He can be our man, one look at Nick's car and Katie, bar the door." Kit Bowen sells Fords, gives 10 percent of everything he makes to charity and on Thanksgiving he puts together a big dinner for Portland's winos and bums, but he is not a traditional do-gooder.

I'd known Bowen since seventh grade. One night at my parents' house, not long before I graduated from high school, we got in a fight after I told him to stop monkeying around with the Hudson's rearview mirror. Two beery, stick boys swinging under the moon, I hit Bowen in the eye. He got up, tackled me and would have beaten me into the asphalt had I not grabbed his ear and shrieked, "I know karate, let me up or I'll rip it off." His cheek cut open, Bowen left in a rage and the next morning I was in the garage in the grease pit under the dripping Chevy holding the trouble light for Jimmy Huygens when I heard the door open and the word *Christensen*.

I figured *shit*, but no, he had a Polaroid. Of his face—his eye and cheek all scabby, black, mottled and iridescent as a pigeon's chest. A "souvenir."

I went to college; Bowen drank beer one afternoon, joined the army and went to Vietnam as a medic for one of the First Infantry Division's endlessly beat-up, shot-up, blown-up combat companies. A war hero who saved many lives, Bowen was wounded badly several times and was profiled in *Newsweek*, in Peter Goldman's book *Charlie Company* and on a Bill Moyer's special *Charlie Company: The Reunion*. Back home he got a job selling weight-training machines and became a muscle man. Now he sells cars.

If he sells this one, I explained, he'd make $35,000, and over the phone I go through the Midas the Messiah business about Nick, and tell Kit I just read about this guy named Gerry Weigert who has a little $350,000 exotic car factory located not a half hour from where I'm sitting right now. Weigert builds a 600-horsepower dab of steel and Kevlar known as the Vector and has more orders, I read, than he can handle.

As for buyers, I suggested Tiger Warren, a friend who looks like James Dean—if James had lived another ten years. Tiger has got to be the luckiest man in the universe. He established the award-winning Macheesmo Mouse Mexican restaurants and, not incidently, just inherited $50 million from his grandma.

Kit is enthusiastic. "Macheesmo Mouse could go in the shitter and Tiger'd sit there grinning on his bed, flipping cards into his hat. Marko, picture this: I'm out at this big fat cat's estate on the Wilsonville River where all the local blue bloods are raising money for the opera—this huge mansion, tinkling glass, the sound of thoroughbreds *naa*-ing yonder in the paddock, when suddenly I hear this *rrrrrrrrrrrrrrrrrrrrrrrrrrrrr* coming down out of the trees. There's Tiger, landing his biplane seaplane *kersplat* on the river. Thirty-five grand. Consider it sold."

Kit calls back. "*Tell no man. Tell no man.* That zipperhead Gideon Bosker is stealing my juju. He's already seen Tiger Warren. Do me a favor: Hoover Doc back to Jupiter while I sew this up."

Shit, as the old saying goes. As zipperheads go, Gideon is fairly well evolved, up for a professorship in medicine at Yale, and I can feel this getting out of hand. Best to act fast. Businessman Moon will know what to do, and on the phone to Moon in Portland, I report, "Just so you know, something called the Lotec C 1,000 is going on the market for nine hundred fifty-thousand bucks. *Road & Track* reports three-hundred cash customers," and Moon, one of Nike's original "Just Do It" executives, replies, "Get a securities lawyer or a tort guy to write up a voluntary release of liability, so you're called harmless, so that no matter what you guys build you can't be thrown in jail for it. Do that, then get up here as soon as you can."

"The first thing we do," Jim Lance told us, "is try to set up a corporate screen no one can pierce." Nick and I had gone to see a securities attorney in Century City. A pleasant, square-faced man with a nice office. Little ducks and hunters on his wallpaper, the halls of silver-sidedness. "Because," Lance said, "if someone commissions you to create a car and then crashes that car, they'll start suing their way up the food chain." He also said that any investors we acquire, from Gideon

Bosker on down, "may logically try to own Nick Pugh." Why? I asked. "Because he's the goose that lays the golden eggs."

Food for thought. Nick said thanks, and handed Lance a check for $4,000.

"Dad," my beginning-to-be-long-and-lanky daughter says, handing me the phone. Morning in our white kitchen. I say, "Hello."

"Okay, we never had this conversation, not if you want to keep Scary for a friend."

"Kit?"

"Is my pencil ever sharpened. I stayed up all night thinking about what I want to do. Offer Bruce Stevenson a right of first refusal for three hundred thousand dollars. The guy's timber. Stevenson, Washington. That's his *town*. He just bought this 1920s Mercedes Manheim for two hundred and fifty thousand, took it to Manny, Moe and Jack's, then sold it for a million five."

"So," I say, "if Stevenson puts up the three hundred thousand dollars, he can buy out everybody else?"

"Hey, it's if, if, if, if, if. Just air."

"Yeah, right. Kit, I can't authorize that."

"Then I'll get frozen out. Which, right now, would mean big, bad hurt." Kit, an actor as well as a car salesman, has just done a Miller beer commercial—he looks like a big robust beer guy, though beer nearly killed him—but it's local and all he got was $350. Meanwhile, the minister who holds the note on Kit's house is threatening to foreclose. "Thirty-five thousand bucks is real money, Scary's not going to want me horning in. He's already seen Tiger."

"Wait a sec," I say, "I thought you said it was Gideon who went to see Tiger."

"They both went to see him! Everybody's going crazy for the car and Scary'll lock up Tiger and—"

"Scary is not doing this for money, he's going because he's my friend."

"Mark, you got another forty years to make friends. For thirty-five grand, *I'll* be your friend."

"Kit," I say, "I worry if we get tied up with some guy who I don't even know, that guy could end up owning Nick."

Kit sighs. " 'Van Gogh. I bought you the paint. I bought you the pallette, so what about those clouds? They look hostile to me, *angry*, Van Gogh. Let's clean up those clouds.' No, we won't play that game.

The car is the ad-on, the car is the bonus. *Nick* is what I'm selling. But they'll be no decision partners, or it'll be: 'Hello Mahk, this is Mahty callin' from New Yawk. I showed my wife Alice da pikchas you sent a da upholstery an' she don't like the culla.' No. With the Xeno we're just going to walk down the hallway slamming doors, *boom, boom, boom*."

I'm not off the phone five minutes when Gideon calls to say: "Car, chronicle, canonization, cash. This isn't about high finance, it's about high art. Don't let's make it complicated. Just do the prospectus. It'll be the equivalent of printing your own thousand-dollar bills."

19

VECTOR

Start a company. Yes. At 130 miles per hour buildings snap by—a warehouse, wrecking yard, a Mexican pipe fitter's—Vector engineer Mark Bailey, wiry, thirty-four, an ex-Lola Can-Am race car driver and a former program manager for Northrup Aircraft, says, "It's the safest car the feds have ever tested. They drove it into a wall at thirty miles per hour, slammed a four-thousand-pound sled into the back. Four thousand pounds would blow out the windows on a regular car, we took it to five thousand and didn't even crack the gel coat."

Bailey is tipped back in his seat as if in a dentist's chair on a rocket ship. Hurtling toward the swelling octagon of a stop sign, the red Vector's wastegates pop off pressure from the car's turbochargers with a sharp sigh as he nods to the "electroluminescent" screen to the left of his steering wheel. "We topped out at three thousand RPM. Three grand is just high idle."

Here is Gerry Weigert's dream car on the back of a cocktail napkin. Engine: a 366-cubic-inch aluminum block twin-turbo 600-horsepower V-8 (which Weigert says "can jump to one thousand by cranking up the boost on the turbocharger"). Body: six-layered "crash-proof" Kevlar-based steel. You enter a Vector in sections—right leg first, then drop, swivel, pull up the left leg. Inside, moon shot decor. The speedometer goes from zero to 999. Video-faced fuel, manifold and oil pressure, water temperature and exhaust heat displays are built into a dashboard billet machined out of solid aluminum. Wilton wool carpets, a $10,000 sound system, a rearview camera with three-inch diagonal monitor and heads-up display. Onboard computers allow you to tune a Vector while driving it. Basic performance: zero to sixty in 3.9 seconds. Top speed two hundred miles per hour plus. Price, well, what day is it? This minute, the Vector is tagged at $332,000. Speculators are buying "first positions" on the cars and offering them for sale at nearly $500,000 before they've even rolled off the assembly line. If Nick and I simply followed in Weigert's footsteps—

"Damn," Bailey says. A police car is in our side mirrors and we have only a star-spangled BUY AMERICAN for a license plate. For the Vector—this Vector, any Vector—is not street legal, despite the fact that it ran cleaner than a new Honda or that Vector Inc. had spent "hundreds of thousands of dollars" on government safety and emissions tests. A worry. What's good for the goose may end up cooking ours. We don't have "hundreds of thousands of dollars" to put in anything.

Bailey floors it. We pop to the horizon, fly over asphalt rivered with a tarred crazy quilt of cracks and across two chrome bright lines of railroad tracks, whip up onto the Harbor Freeway and are boxed between a moving van and an old Volkswagen. With a tick of Bailey's wrist, the Vector swings left and background is foreground.

Secure in the walled Vector compound, young guys with big hair and tattoos who invite the idea that this is what Mötley Crew and Guns 'N Roses do during the day wipe off the car.

Vector Assembly. Where Nick and I may need to be. Gerry Weigert runs this dream of his life near the Port of Los Angeles, next to a former whorehouse and a chop shop—a stolen car stripping operation where hot automobiles were cut up and sold for their parts—Weigert's building, blockish, clean and gray, faces a falling down two-story house-made-hotel whose sign reads: $75.00—UNA SEMANA. Next to Weigert's chained-off parking lot two gay junkyard dogs fight, make love. Inside, a main office jungled sparingly with potted palms to the assembly bays and there, under an American flag as big as a garage door and a sign that reads NEVER FORGET YOU'RE BUILDING THE FINEST, six Vector W8s in stages of construction. Angular sharks, they exude a cool, dangerous WASPy allure.

Not since John Z. DeLorean started a car company as a beard for a cocaine deal has an American attempted production of a wholly new automobile on a scale like this. Bailey takes me upstairs to where Vector components are all filed in neat rows like new books on bookshelves. Aisle after aisle of precise and gleaming metal gizmos—perfect gauges, perfect pistons, perfect little nuts and bolts. I feel like I'm in heaven's library of mechanical exactitude. Too bad I don't have a sleeping bag, jug of water and a pile of Power Bars, I could stay up here for a week.

———

Gerry Weigert, big, in jeans and worn cowboy boots, is droll. He signals hilarity when one side of his mouth lifts a quarter inch. "A car ought to last as long as the man who buys it. People need to know they are getting something better than what they thought was the best. This isn't a car spot welded together by robots. It's not built by committee, a bureaucracy or product planners or accountants who don't know a goddamn thing about what a great car should be. The Vector's got better bearings, a better engine, better switches, better wiring, better paint than a Ferrari."

With an engine three times as powerful as a conventional V-8 and aluminum brake discs big as serving dishes, the Vector W8 can accelerate faster and stop quicker than any American production car ever built. According to *Road and Track*, the Vector is "a supercar with unmatched performance, quality and durability . . . the fastest, most sophisticated automobile made in the United States."

The Vector could be our true north. All we have to do is do what Weigert has already done. Vectors are being sold quicker than they can be assembled. Buyers—there are now thirty-two—number three Saudi princes and Andre Agassi. At the Los Angeles Auto Show, exotic car dealer James "Jimmy" Glynn, a natty moustached possum, stood before a purplish Vector and put it this way: "The Vector is what Rolls-Royce would be building if it still had any testosterone. The Lamborghini Diablo doesn't even compare."

It is a great time to be making a car like this. Opulent, overpriced automobiles have been around since the century's early Rolls-Royces, Hispano-Suizas, Duesenburgs and Auburn Boattail Speedsters, but there has never been anything like the craze for 1990s exotics—a craze set off, by the introduction in 1987 of the Ferrari F40. Designed to replace the Porsche 959 as the fastest production car in the world, the F40 had a $305,000 sticker. Today, F40s go for five times that used. The Vector W8 looks better, is made better and goes faster. All we have to do, it would seem, is follow in Gerry's visionary footsteps.

Though one thing that worries me is that Weigert has had a very hard time blazing this trail. Like Nick, he graduated from the Art Center College of Design in Pasadena and shortly thereafter began his quest. "I built a life-size urethane foam model of the Vector—a push car. All materials—wood, foam, fiberglass, wheels, tires, were donated. That resulted in a mock-up that premiered at Auto Expo '76, which gave me the exposure to attract the two million dollars in cash, labor and donations it took to finish a running prototype. All I'd need was three million dollars to get into production. I figured it would be easy. It wasn't. I found myself landlocked: no credit cards, no money. Just a telephone."

Well, at least Nick and I have several of those.

"I bought in twenty-five to thirty investors," Weigert continues, "but they were small, and to make things worse, I was running technologically way ahead of myself—designing a car for tires that didn't even exist. It was like building *her*," he says, making a sweeping gesture toward his slender, miniskirted assistant.

But by 1988 he had raised $5 million on a $6 million stock offering, and got an order for his first Vector from the late Malcolm Forbes.

"This is a very tough business," Weigert allows. "It takes, for example, one hundred times as long to build a Vector as it does a Lexus, Cadillac and BMW. Want to make a fortune in computers? Borrow one hundred thousand dollars from your grandma, jump on a jet to Hong Kong with a marketing plan and you're in business. Want to make a fortune in stereos? Design a logo, fly to Taiwan and you're in business. But what we've done is akin to the Boy Scouts putting a man on the moon."

On the other hand, he says. "Ferrari sells four thousand cars a year; all we need to do to stay profitable is sell two hundred and fifty Vectors. If we capture just three percent of an already very small market, we're fine."

I show him Nick's drawings. Weigert is perceptive. "This kid has really got it. I'm going to completely redesign the Vector, and I'd like to talk to him before I do." Then he flips a bound document across his desk.

When I ask him what it is, he says, "The Vector business prospectus. It cost me a fortune to have drawn up, but you can use it to help make your own."

I am stunned. I say thank you and Weigert shrugs. "Just remember this. The car has to be everything. Be willing to sacrifice your friends, sacrifice your health, sacrifice it all."

20

RELATIVITY

The thousand-dollar bills should be on their way to the printer soon.

Nick has made drawings of the main chance, the perfect crime, the winning ten-million-dollar Lotto ticket, that is to say transcendent drawings of wheels, leather jackets and sunglasses. We get an engine builder to build a first-rate V-8 for $25,000, a fabricator to build our chassis and suspension for $75,000, a body builder to build a body for $75,000. $75,000 for interior, paint and everything else; unless I've got a major leak in my pituitary manifold, this really should not be that difficult. My $E=MC^2$: Our first car costs $250,000 to build, the second, third, fourth and fifth $150,000. Our total hard cost $900,000. Five cars sold at $400,000 apiece—two million dollars. A profit of over 100 percent. We'll use Vector components, Weigert's machined more original top-quality hardware than anybody.

But Nick says, "We need to totally disclude Vector. Vector is mass production, we're individual craftsmanship."

Weigert hasn't built ten cars. That's mass production? "Nick," I say, "Weigert's got the best parts anywhere. We'll need parts, because I don't think we'll be making our own."

Nick, who has eaten two pounds of pizza as fast as he can chew and swallow, says, "I'm noting a serious lacking of palm trees. What is this, Nazi Disneyland?" No. Solvang, California. Storefronts with gingerbread and faux castle fronts, Anytown USA if the Germans had won the war. We have driven up to see Sam Foose. Nick is reinventing our car, via "muscle car things. Make it elemental, boiled down, even a little hot roddy. I used to look down on hot rodders due to the snobilization of Art Center." But live and learn. "Five years ago I didn't even know Chevrolet was made by General Motors."

———

In a gray sweatshirt and sweatpants, Sam Foose says, "You're building a monster." We're in his garage beside a purple '40 Ford with painted flames licking its front fenders and hood, six-way electric seats and a supercharged Chevy V-8 engine.

We go into Sam's office. He lights a cigarette. "I started figuring materials—chassis, door jambs, motor, interior—I got up to a half million bucks and said, 'Well, hey, they don't want to see that,' and threw it in the trash can."

Nick looks at me, then to Sam. "We've simplified it. We had a lot of hydraulic experimental, complicated stuff we eliminated—the front skirts and the center steering."

The model sits beside Sam's desk. A crooked weed of a crack has grown up the side. The Xeno is collapsing under it's own weight. Sam does a quick drum roll with his pencil on his desktop. "It could take me sixty hours to get the hood to shut right, one hundred and sixty hours to make the door jambs. You gotta figure compression rate of the rubber." He suggests we make the car out of fiberglass. "But you fuckin' itch like crazy afterward. You gotta take a cold shower—a hot one opens your pores and the fiberglass goes right in. A cold shower and use dog shampoo." Sam puffs on his cigarette and sighs smoke. "There's such a thing as time, you can do it quick and dirty—"

"No way," Nick says.

"—or you do it right. But right takes fuckin' time, if you'll pardon my French." Sam looks at the model of the Xeno. "Like I said, you're building a monster."

"Look," I say, "except for the body, this is just a hot rod, right?"

"If you build it without all the bells and whistles."

"Just more stuff to break," Nicks says. "Let's go with existing systems."

Sam nods. "Sure, get a GM steering column with all the trips, dimmers and tilt. Simplify. Dump a cowl vent below your windshield and forget air conditioning."

"Yeah," Nick says, "but I want to plan everything—draw it out—before we begin."

"You can draw till your butt falls off, then you go to full size and see, hey, it's better this way." Sam stubs his cigarette out and says he doesn't want to do the car.

"Mark, raising a hundred grand, is fun, raising two hundred and fifty grand is work. Are you and Nick aware of that?"

A clean, well-lit West LA place. California cuisine weighing at about $40 per entrée—not including salad, wine or dessert. Nick and I are having dinner with Gideon who—a plane flight from Portland ago—has just had lunch with Tiger Warren. Gideon fans through my just-completed prospectus. "What is this, a *dream prospectus?* Where's the car? All I see is a corporation." He points to a page. "What do *sunglasses* have to do with building the greatest car of all time?"

I say, "Porsche. Monkey see, monkey do. All the top companies make fortunes selling accessories—leather jackets, sunglasses, whatever, off the image of their cars."

"This cost of the car has gone from *one hundred and eighty thousand dollars to three hundred and fifty thousand dollars.*"

Not a great week. It looks as though the roof may fall in even before we've had a chance to build it. Scary called to say he can't represent us. "Creation of your company represents a security," he said. "I looked at my malpractice insurance. 'We will not cover you if you look at, smell or touch a security.' Be careful or you'll get nailed under the blue-sky laws—you must disclose to investors all material risks. Fuck up and investors'll want complete recision, plus attorney fees for the pleasure of sueing you, plus lost opportunity for the money."

When the dinner bill arrives I reach for my wallet and Gideon smiles. "Pay for all of it or none of it." I look at a bill that somehow totals $430. "Put your money away," Gideon instructs. Then to the basics: "Forget sunglasses, forget lawyers, forget corporate shields. Just figure out how to build the goddamn car."

"Avoid the razzle dazzle of *R and D.* Avoid custom parts. Say you sell the car to some gal who curbs it, it breaks and she's on the phone asking who's going to fix it. You have to make that part all over again." Overall, Bill Noirs says it's linear. "Determine basic configuration then figure where to put the lump for the engine and transmission. We can chalk it out on the floor," Noirs concludes, and quotes us $70,000 for the chassis.

Off a jet in San Francisco, Nick, Henrietta and I drive south in a rented Ford to Salinas. Where, in a shopping market parking lot, Nick empties his pockets for a snaggle-toothed beggar then assures him that the pickles that he—Nick—was offering him weren't poison. When he gets back in the Ford, Henrietta announces, "Nick, I will build your car."

Nick replies, "Killer, *lasmie*," which I think is Nick German for "Fantastic, my love," but later, at a roadside Mexican grocery, after Henrietta has guided a meat sandwich down the throat of a Nick Pugh biting and swallowing as if he were a starved crocodile, Nick wipes his mouth and says, "Fine, you build the second one."

We were at the base of, in Nick's words, "Them thar hills." Long, shadowy, green mountains above a flood plain whose dark soil has been tilled in mile-long rectangles. Now we've driven up to a ranch house with a huge garage attached surrounded by chunks of McLaren race cars. One with the words BEEHIVE BAIL BONDS GARCO, UTAH painted across the nose.

Bill Noirs's place. Noirs has been recommended by every other top race car company I've contacted. Fifty-ish, graying, a well-known race car builder, he has the car Bruce McLaren took first place in at Watkins Glen and another that "burned down" at Riverside in 1970. I say the car is beautiful and he says, "Actually, it's a piece of shit."

In his immaculate, barn-size shop, he takes cleaner to a four-foot-by-four-foot piece of sheet steel he uses for a tabletop and sets Nick's specs on the now shining surface. "There's not a panel on this thing that's not a compound curve."

"I'll build," Nick replies, "a full-size push car—a foam car coated with fiberglass, like a plug, give it to a composite shop, have them take off the molds and make the body panels. I can shape surfaces very well. From the push car, we can make the molds to make the body for the real car. While you make the chassis."

Noirs puts a finger on the finned front end. "This is a very abrupt treatment. You'll have to channel air around the nose and out—because if this," he points to the front of the Xeno— "becomes a shovel driving air underneath the car, the car will pick itself off the ground."

He nods to a photo of a McLaren on his wall. "They *fly* at one eighty. We took that one to Le Mans—it flew right off the ground at one eighty-three." He shuffles through papers, takes out a photograph of a McLaren flying upright through the air and says, "Jim Hall at Stardust running over an M6 McLaren."

Nick asks, "Did he live?"

"Yeah, but his back and legs weren't one hundred percent."

"*This is not your car, Mark*—and that's what we have to get back to," Nick exclaims. "You wanted to make the ultimate hot car, but it's got awesomely away from that. Raw! Aluminum floors. Super, tough, powerful and totally fun but low toxic so you don't feel like shit when you're out there ripping it up. Boil it down to the bones. I lived in Paris and London, I also lived with New Hampshire rednecks. I know about *simple*. I know how to do this. We are in my world!"

Also lost. It is night. Rain is slamming into my windshield, I'm driving north back toward Berkeley and his dad's house, while Nick remembers being a kid. "My dad was like an original hippie and my folks gave me an incredible freedom," he says. "When I was little they'd let me get on a bus and go to school all the way across town. I'd make my own transfers, no sweat. But when they got divorced, I went half crazy. To this day, I have no memory of them together, just apart. I was afraid I'd turn into Hitler, I wanted to kill people for no reason. In shop class I'd be next to somebody and I'd want, not because I didn't like them or anything, to jam their hand in a spinning lathe."

At sixteen, Nick says he lost a job at Domino's pizza after three days. "Work started at six and it'd be five and I was still at the beach. I just wanted to surf and leech off my parents."

About the same time he was in a terrible wreck. "My friend's parents bought him a beautiful old Mercedes. We hit a power pole and it cut the front of the car off. I ended up upside down with my hand broken in half. Across the back of my hand was a new set of knuckles." The hand he draws with.

Lost to his story, Nick forgets to tell me the exit. "Where we're going is right over there." He points into the rainy night. "We're only separated from it by a hundred billion gallons of water."

The San Francisco Bay. Angry, Henrietta tells Nick, "You are a bird of prey, Piggie."

"That's because I know how to escape. So are you."

"I am not a bird of prey, I am not afraid of anything."

We drive most of the rest of the way in silence, me thinking: Where are we going to get the money to pay a Noirs or anybody like him? Gerry Weigert's business plan was all about selling stock. But unless we invent the antigravity machine along with the Xeno, I'm afraid we'll practically have to sell ourselves out of our own company.

These are things that I don't understand in this world: Nick's mathematician father's careful explanation to me that night, how he demonstrated that it's possible to turn a sphere inside out without breaking its surface, and things that I do: "Europe is full of guys who look like you who drive Ferraris and have twenty-year-old girlfriends," Henrietta observes the next morning at breakfast. I say something about European culture and Henrietta laughs. "Europe is even more crude than America. In America a woman meets a man and asks, 'Where did you go to college, what do you do?' In Europe she asks, 'How much do you make and where is your wife?' In Monaco, I tell men I am a car designer and they think I am a whore."

Reality is sinking in. Henrietta is not hog wild to move to Steinbeck country, nor Nick dying to live in San Francisco: "There's not enough energy, industry and panic."

I slept on Nick's father's couch. This is where, sort of, Nick had grown up. Born in Paris, raised in England, Brazil, Massachusetts, New Hampshire, but mostly here in this tall, stately old house in Berkeley. Nick's little half brother Harrison woke me up. He is the biggest, healthiest four-year-old ever, twice as big as my own boy Matthew. His wrists are almost as thick as mine and he seems to have invented a private language. He shouts, "Jew-goo! Jew-goo! Jew-goo! Jew-goo!"— hitting a crazed cousin of high C.

Nick's dad takes Harrison to nursery school in his little old Datsun roadster. The car has never had the top up. Why? "My dad's a little eccentric," Nick explains. It is raining and the two take off down the street, the Datsun farting up through its gears, father and son wearing hats.

21

BEGIN THE BEGUINE

"Jackpot!" Nick exclaims, "We are so lucky. These dudes are the top of the top, the highest tech in the world. Aero Vironment, they built the hottest electric car ever, built the airplane somebody pedaled across the English Channel. Awesome. The only thing is: I'm afraid they'll think we're idiots."

Nick, sitting on our green leather couch, papers and drawings all around, says the guy Bill Noirs recommended, John Mason, "sounded annoyed, a little agro, on the phone."

"Send him pictures of the car."

Nick shakes his head. "To an engineer pictures are froufrou and designers are airheads. To an engineer a real car is one that steers best, goes quickest, wins races. This 'end-of-aero high design' we talk about; our design may be so aerodynamically wacky it's useless. But with an exotic we have to deliver two hundred miles per hour or nobody will pay what we're asking. Who'd want to go that fast? It's nutty. Like superbig cocks. Girls don't even like 'em, but every guy'd die to have one."

John Mason's shop is in a wood building under big, thick-leaved trees beside his two-story house, which resembles a ski chalet. Here in the wooded foothills above Simi Valley, elaborate gardens on one side of the street, rusted-out jalopies on the other, a neighborhood for bikers and hobbits.

Mason built two chassis for the eight-million-dollar General Motors solar Sunraycer, the most sophisticated electric automobile ever made. The goal was to devise the lightest car possible—one, thus, that could run most efficiently on the least amount of power—and the chassis

Mason fabricated weighed only thirteen pounds. The Sunraycer won the two thousand-mile trans-Australia solar-powered race in 1987, beating the nearest of its twenty-four competitors by six hundred miles.

I read his résumé. Mason has built race cars and race car components for Indy drivers Gary Bettehhauser and Dirk Dergurson, Porsche, Danny Sullivan, GTU National Championship driver Dave White, Trans-Am National Championship driver John Baur, Paul Newman, Johnny Rutherford and Mario Andretti.

John, who with his moustache and gold-rimmed glasses looks scholarly in his sweater and jeans, points to a flatbed metal floor that rises above the cement floor of his shop and says, "It all starts here. The point of your car's origin will be this centerline. You want corners?"

"Suspension?" I say, "Yeah."

"I can provide an engine as well. You can crank twelve hundred horsepower out of a V-six. No reason to lug around a lot of weight." And when I ask about the possible use of a supercharger—which would add at least another 100 horsepower—he shrugs, "It's quick power, because it is run directly off a belt. But a supercharger consumes horsepower to turn it. The trend is to turbochargers."

As for our chassis. "In a racing car you want it as strong and rigid as possible. They go to monocoque honeycomb. They don't want flex. That's what suspension is for. Also tube is heavier, by maybe fifty percent, but easier to repair." He points to a chassis on his stand. "This is monocoque. No tubing. Just aluminum boxes."

"What is it?" I ask.

"What is what?"

"The chassis."

"An old Lola."

My. What a gorgeous relic—streamlined, bare metal laid out the same way the Xeno should be: front suspension/driver/motor/transaxle/rear suspension. Moncoque is an attractive option—very tried and very true—it goes back to the 1915 Indy 500 when Howard Blood entered a monocoque racer, the Camelian. The Camelian broke down, but shortly thereafter French aircraft designers developed monocoque airframes for fighters and coined the term—combining the Greek *mono*, meaning "single" with the French *coque*, meaning "egg."

The principle was simple. Say you want to present a sheet of cardboard on its strongest yet largest form. All you'd have to do is make a cardboard box whose six sides resist twisting, the overall torsion resolved as shear load in your box's six surfaces. That's basically what a monocoque chassis is, a bunch of hollow boxes in which you stuff the driver and drive train.

During the 1950s, Jaguar D-type racers used semi-monocoque chassis supplemented by tubular subframes, and Colin Chapman's 1962 monocoque Lotus 24 and 25 enjoyed success in Formula I, but it was the Lola that brought monocoque to full flower. Created by British race car designer Eric Broadly—who had the idea to put a V-8 in the rear—the compact, lightweight Lola Mark 6 chassis was constructed of sheet steel and light alloy, and was a lightning success after it made its debut in 1963. Its successor, the Lola T70, soon became dominant in Can-Am racing. During Lola's heyday in the late 1960s, featherweight 1,300-pound Lolas were running monster 494-cubic-inch Chevy Rat motors and burning up racetracks all over the world.

"What did you have in mind?" Mason asks.

Nick unrolls his specs, big vellum sheets, and warns, "It's a strange-looking car."

John puts a finger on the Xeno's tail. "That's the front."

"No," Nick says, "the rear."

"Are you going to wind tunnel this? Flow it?"

Nick says, "Definitely."

John is still staring at the drawing. "Is this the back?"

Nick says, "That's the front."

"Logically it looks like the rear."

Nick says, "We're trying to make a whole new statement in environmental high-performance vehicles, a revolutionary end to planned obsolescence."

John tells us the Sunraycer was built in two months with four people and when I ask why it cost $8 million, he replies, "The solar cells. Galium arsenite plates. Each cost a hundred seventy-five dollars apiece. And they needed seven thousand of them. It'd burn rubber. Didn't even have a tranny. Just a step-down. No clutch."

I ask how he liked Australia.

"Didn't get to go. I did my job too well. Nothing broke. But I'm pretty busy right now. I've got the Lola to finish and an Indy car coming up. I don't know if I can squeeze you guys in."

At this point, Nick makes his pitch. "I'm dyslexic. I failed math in high school, I've failed all kinds of engineering things, but not because I wasn't good at putting things together."

John ponders that for a moment, then says he'll build our car like a race car, steel tube on top of monocoque, in six months to a year. He suggests we use a Porsche transaxle. "Mate that up to independent rear suspension and I'll make everything else."

Nick says he can build a push car in ninety days and on the way home declares that he knows too many "people who'd sell themselves out in just the time it takes to have the thought. I'd suffer for years to achieve the right great thing."

A feral cat has given birth to kittens behind the seats of Nick's little old dead sports car. Nick is worried about them, afraid that if he gives the kitties milk it will spook their mother and she'll pluck her kittens from the safety of his ruined Austin-Healey Sprite.

"Which would be very not good. 'Cause it's a dangerous world out there, dude."

Yeah. An expensive one too. Could be we face an extra added expense. To the tune of $300,000.

Nick has designed a "sail house" that looks like an airplane's wing set on end. Four stories high, it is to be mounted on an axle so that it could be pushed whichever way the wind blows and could serve as our corporate headquarters.

He's just tacked it up on his wall when John Mason, in jeans and a T-shirt, slightly puddle-gutted below his friendly dignified face, comes up the stairs to Nick and Henrietta's cavernous loft, a slim, sunburned Herman Drees walking up behind.

"You have conflicting inputs," Mason says. "You want exotic high speed and relatively low price, but also durability, drivability, tractability, dependability. These things don't necessarily go hand in hand."

Evidently not, for it looks as though we may have to build two cars instead of just one.

Herman's idea. He works for Aero Vironment, the prototype company that built the *Gossamer Explorer*, the bicycle-powered airplane that flew across the English Channel, as well as a flying mechanical pterodactyl. Aero Vironment is also reported to be developing fifteen-pound pilotless jet drones armed to their little teeth with God-knows-what and able to shoot any modern fighter out of the sky. Herman, who is a graduate of MIT and Dutch by the way of Texas—his father designed the Huey gunship—is also the former president of the American Windmill Society and is, among apparently many other things, out nation's formost expert on wind-generated electricity.

About forty, Herman designed and fabricated the chassis, suspension and drive train of the Sunraycer, he also designed the main drive components for General Motors' one hundred-million-dollar electric car, the Impact, as well as components to the Freedom space station.

He is slender, bearded, tan, wears a white shirt, tie, new Levi's and a sport coat and running shoes—and is not in Nick's new loft ten minutes before he proposes we build not one but two prototypes. "One is sold, you keep the other as a demo, as a test vehicle."

"*Two cars?*" I ask. "One we can't even sell?"

Outside, I can hear a tiny hiss. Nick has rigged up a grid of watering hoses that runs off an electric pump just below the ceiling of his truly cavernous studio, so that plants can hang from the ceiling—wall to far apart wall.

"Once you've sold the first car," Herman says, "what have you got? What can you do? Call the guy up and say, 'Can we borrow your car Sunday so we can go show it to so and so?"

"Yeah." Nick gets up off his streamlined couch, stretches. "But won't the costs go up a lot?"

"You'll get a better product," Herman says. "The first car won't have to be as finely finished. It'll establish suspension characteristics which are difficult to change. If you build just one car, there'll be mistakes; you'd put a thousand miles on it test driving. It'll be worn, a used car. The second car'll only take fifty miles of testing. No scuff marks, no worn pedals." Herman's right fist strikes the flat of his left hand. "A prototype, damn, it's got understeer we gotta change it, or the shocks are weak let's put new ones in, tear out this bracket and put it up here."

Air seems to be leaving the room. I say, "It leaves us with a static investment of three hundred thousand dollars. All that money tied up gathering interest while investors on the sidelines are saying, 'Hey, when are you going to sell this thing? Where's our money?"

Nick asks, "How much can we cut costs from the first prototype to the second?"

Herman says, "We designed and built Sunraycer in three months and tested it for a month and then built the second one in three weeks. Because we had all the molds and patterns from the first aluminum frame. We had all our sourcing done, knew where all the parts would come from. So we could just bang it together. The fiberglass shells you'll make will be the major portion of the cost. The rest is just parts and labor, which you will have already done once—so you'll be way down on the learning curve. The second Sunraycer took us only twenty-five percent of the time we spent on the first."

Herman says we need a wind tunnel study to determine the shape. "Because you have a surround body you're like the Sunraycer, the shape delivers lift, there was enough lift to take the Sunraycer off the road, so we added fins to spoil that flow. I have access to Cal Tech. We used that one for the Sunraycer and the Impact. With a wind tunnel study we can also determine the drag coefficient and with your shape I think it will be extremely low."

I ask, "What's the tunnel testing going to cost?"

"Twenty thousand at the most. Two days in the tunnel will cost you under eight. Everything is done on site. You change it there. You get clay and knives. You do a quick modification. It's all computerized. I worry about pressure distribution fluctuation in the car in crosswinds and the resulting handling problems. It could cause crashes, it could cause spinouts. On a turntable we can test for crosswinds, for lift forces, ground forces. It gives you data telling you your suspension design will work, very important because every doubling of wind speed increases the aerodynamic forces four times. It's exponential."

Herman says he's got a team to build a body. "They built the Impact. They're the best. The timing is perfect. All of them laid off from Aero Vironment. The body can be flawless for three hundred thousand dollars."

A strict meatitarian, Nick eats cheeseburgers like bon bons and has just downed a big tortilla-clothed bag of beans and chopped beef before the Taco Bell cashier could give him his change back. Patting his chin with a napkin, my partner reads aloud, *The chassis consists of four basic sections. One, the nose box, which is crushable in a frontal impact, affording protection for the driver by absorbing load-through crushing. Two, the 'tub,' which comprises the main portion of the structure housing the driver and passenger. Three, the fuel tank enclosure housing the fuel cell or bag and, four, the aft section, which provides structure for the trunk space and storage.* This is Herman's technical plan for construction of the Xeno, which calls for a semimonocoque construction using *"an aluminum honeycomb interior epoxy bonded to zero-point-oh-five-oh to zero-point-oh-six-three-inch-thick corrosion resistant seven-oh-seventy-five aircraft aluminum face sheets."*

Getting back in my wife's Volvo, I ask how he likes our two thousand dollar, thirty-page document. Nick jerks a thumb in the air. "It's great, but dry. Could you put jokes in to liven things up in case we have an investor who doesn't like technical, fiddly stuff?"

I tell Nick he'd better get Henrietta's help. He says, "I can't. Not anymore. I should of, but I didn't. Now it's too late. We're not getting along. She wants to kick men's asses." Nick is getting $8,000 for designing a hot rod for Universal Television. Four days work. He's whipped out a flying muscle car. "She dying to make it with movie people like that. But it's a man's world in the biggest way. Those movie offices? It's the guy his secretary, the guy his secretary, the guy his secretary on and on. She'll smash into that, get more pissed." He looks back at Herman's report, reads on: "*The front end will be stiffened using a foot bulkhead and a dash bulkhead. These bulkheads are to be the attachment points for the front suspension. The engine is mounted on the rear bulkhead behind the fuel tank enclosure. A seat back box inclination in the monocoque of thirty-seven and forty-five degrees is specified in the preliminary design.* It says what it says, but doesn't grab you."

We're driving in downtown Long Beach. "Nick, we may have to take a loan."

"No, I must be invisible to the system." He cracks a knuckle. "I didn't even get a Social Security card until I was twenty, I didn't get a checking account until last year. I pay cash. You give me the thing, I give you the money. No loans. No monthly payments."

I say I'm concerned we've bitten off more than we can chew, and he says, "Don't worry, we have. What we've planned may be irresponsibly impossible, but the only way I can work is if I'm overconfident. If I'm overconfident I never fail. The only thing that would make me back out is if you did. You gotta tell me you'll never bail, never give up."

I promise Nick that I never will.

PART TWO

BIG PROBLEMS

22

UNDER THE VOLCANO

So stupid. I knew I was going to ditch the cop before he even stopped me. All he had to do is do what he did. I was eighteen, home from college and had been downtown exchanging Christmas presents. I saw the red lights flashing in the rearview mirror of my dad's Thunderbird, then heard the squad car's siren behind me as I was racing up the twisting lane of Burnside Boulevard into the hills above Portland toward my mother's grave.

I pulled onto the gravel shoulder of the road beside Calvary Cemetery and watched in the rearview mirror as the cop got out of the squad car. He looked alone and, sure enough, he didn't even glance at the Thunderbird's license plate as he walked to the car. I waited until he was to my open driver's side window, then floored it.

The cop didn't have a chance, he had to run back to his car, climb in, take off—and the way I was driving no way he could catch me. So why was I scared witless? The T-Bird was rocketing through the cemetery over the top of whatever the name of the hill I was on, and flying down toward the Regal House of Mystery, a big estate that loomed above an ivy-hided wall at the bend of the road. I'd always wondered who lived in there, somebody superrich, maybe they had a knockout, naive protected-from-reality-by-convent-schools daughter who—Jesus! Where were the brakes? I was sliding into the turn, the T-Bird was off the road, onto gravel, skidding into dirt. I hit lawn that felt like ice, the T-Bird spun and I found myself facing the road the other way. I could hear a siren. In the headlights I saw that my dad's tires had cut a dirt J J across the grass, and the back of the T-Bird had slid so close to the wall of the Regal House of Mystery that it blushed the white stucco with its taillights. Lucky the motor was still running.

I hit the gas and squirreled the T-Bird back onto the road. Now I was dead. The T-Bird careened down the winding road right up onto somebody's taillights—my cousin Jerry said never pass on a blind curve except at night when you could see headlights coming the other way. I couldn't see anything at all, so I whipped around the taillights and hit straight road for about a quarter mile and at the end of that quarter mile, as I squealed into the turn, I saw in the rearview mirror the cop car's flashing lights as it hit the straightaway. Down the twisting Scholls Ferry Road, I could see the light where Scholls Ferry crossed the Beaverton-Hillsdale Highway, could see that the light was green, but then yellow and red. This was it or not. Oh well, I was never going to die, and so what if I did? I shot into the intersection—horns honked, headlights flashed on the T-Bird's windows, but I was still flying. I snapped off my lights. The night was nothing but shapes, the Thunderbird flew past the ghostly bulk of Raleigh Hills grade school, I slid off Schools Ferry onto Lauralwood, past the white barn that had held the *Faux Pas*, then left onto Homewood, right onto the long arc of Woodside Drive and onto my parents' driveway and through the breezeway. I parked the T-Bird behind the garage, got out shaking, ran into the house and into the first bedroom I could find, my brother's, and locked the door, waiting for a siren in the driveway, a bang on the door, five minutes, ten minutes, a half hour. Nothing. Home free. I began to feel the orgasmic thrill of escape, then felt something else, not something heroic, but something rabbity, cowardly, dumb. What if there had been kids in a car at the intersection and that car had been going quicker? Also, think about it, maybe I hadn't escaped after all. Neighbors had heard the Thunderbird roar by, maybe a couple looked out and saw it had its lights out. You'd remember that, especially with a squad car flying by right behind, and if the cop retraced his steps and started asking around I'd be eating mashed potatoes and fish sticks at the Oregon Correctional Institute in no time, and who would care? The world wouldn't mind if I sat in a box for six months, the world needed a break. Then I heard something. Me, sort of swearing in tongues. I had often wondered what a babbling psychotic was like inside, but I never thought I'd inhabit one.

It was Christmas vacation. The first night, the usual. Somebody was getting married and Moon and I went to a bachelor party in Lake Oswego. Girls from a local topless bar and a movie projector projecting a porn flick starring a hairy-backed ape and his skeleton girlfriend. The auteur's art was extreme close-ups and I found myself sitting out on an enclosed porch playing go fish with a motherly young stripper, already thinking: courtship, marriage, two or three kids, an amicable divorce, when Moon stepped in to say, "This isn't happening. Let's beat feet." He wanted to go to a pajama party populated by "a Whitman sampler of rich nymphomaniacs."

So we grabbed as many beers as our parkas had pockets, got in Moon's mom's latest car, a Volkswagen. Dark green with its fenders painted black, but supernew and virginal and, Moon, where exactly is the party?

Over there, he waved, as we zipped down the road. Over there, was a fir tree-shrouded hill, really steep. "On the other side," Moon said as we wheeled down an avenue that ended in a cul-de-sac in front of a nice suburban ranch house. Rasping, "Northwest Passage," Moon drove across the lawn, down a flight of concrete steps beside the house, across the backyard and onto what was a dirt road for two seconds before it turned into brambles. Moon floored the Volkswagen into the trees, its tires beginning to spin until the car stopped. "What do we do now?" I asked.

Moon shrugged. "I don't know about you, but I'm going to sleep."

I will say this for Moon, he had the best bad luck. In the morning we walked back from the stag party house and found one of Moon's fraternity brothers whose Jeep had a power winch. It took hours to drag the Volks out but the man who owned the house didn't even care that the Jeep's tires ploughed two slit trenches across his backyard. He thought it was funny.

I did too. But, you know what, we had nearly wrecked Moon's mother's car. Why? And that ditching the cop. God damn. Now I was at the Donacas. I'd stayed away from my parents house for days. Go home now, and I could see the squad car sitting in their driveway. It was so unfair. I wasn't a criminal. I was—what was I?

This was the last minute of 1967 and there were explosions in the trees and among the drunks running around the backyard. New Year's Eve. One hundred and fifty-one-proof rum punch and fireworks bombing the stars.

Ahhsayhey! You! Get! Offa! My! Cloud! whumping out of speakers on the back porch where I kissed, at the instant of 1968, the girl I'd been dancing with. Her boyfriend popped from the chaos and hit me in the mouth. I looked down at him. His face was as bright as the moon. I hit him in the eye. He fell over a low hedge that divided the porch from the backyard.

Best to go upstairs to the garage. Chunks of cars and motorcycles. Forget Homer, Shakespeare, all the tinny rumors of civilization, this is where I should be, not at a pencil-neck university in Eugene. Someone told me that Jimmy Huygens had just become or was about to become, at nineteen, the youngest guy to win Best of Show at the Portland Roadster Show. For a V-8-powered 1923 Bucket-T he constructed without, annoyingly, the help he should have had from me.

Distracted, I went back inside and saw John Donaca, big brother of my friend Dick. The same sculpted surf of greasy tan hair, the same muscular, baby-faced Elvis Presley. Our last time together we'd driven across town in Huygens's father's high pro Mustang during a race riot. At an intersection black men called us honkie muthafukkas. John gave them the finger. I said: Why do that, we're outnumbered ten to one. No we're not, John replied, pulling a .45 from under Huygens's seat.

And I knew when I saw the moon-faced guy that I'd hit at 12:00.01 bound up the stairs, shirtless, blood tentacle-ing his chest that I was in trouble. The guy was so wild-eyed he didn't see me as he hurtled through the Donaca's kitchen, but John, gracious host in charge of party justice, sighed to me, "Now I'll have to kick your ass."

Suddenly, the bare-chested guy was in my face, screaming. Panicked, I swung, saw my fist whiz past his bloody face and into my friend Steve Lonie's mouth. Steve had been, until that instant, a very nice-looking kid. Sun-bleached hair, clear blue eyes. Now those eyes looked scrambled. He reached in, plucked out a front tooth and held it up, its root between us, the tip of a bloody iceberg.

John was officious. Put it back in, he said. Lonie did. John, gently, pulled up Lonie's upper lip and said, "Fuck." Then he said to me: "You idiot, get him to a hospital."

Steve and I weaved into the abandoned traffic jam on the Donaca's long driveway. We got in his once beautiful '57 Ford he drove like a bumper car. Want to go to the hospital? I asked. No, he replied. We still had, in the Ford's backseat, beer.

Hours later I wandered into my parent's garage and stared at my blue '53 Chevy coupe, a hammered-up burned-out hulk. No more girlfriend, she'd lost interest in loving vapor. Moon and I had gone off to the University of Oregon and at least, thank God, my problems paled next to his. He'd so enraged his girlfriend she had him arrested for "fornication," under an obscure Oregon law that made sexual intercourse out of wedlock a crime. But she hadn't had him arrested for screwing somebody else, she had him arrested for screwing her (they got married three years later, but that's another story). I'd bailed him out. We had decided once again a car was a must.

"I've got just the rig," Moon said, "twenty bucks and half of it's yours." A 1952 Chrysler with paint the color of a stab wound. Moon couldn't believe our luck. The car's seller was a "sucker." Driving the first time, the temperature gauge leaned to hot. "False alarm," Moonman explained. So a champagne flight to Portland. Minutes out of Eugene the Chrysler began to smoke like the rear fenders were on fire. Moon accelerated. "We'll shoot right through this phase," he insisted. Then the engine blew up. Not in dramatic hold-onto-your-hat-space-shuttle style but in sad bucks, sighs, thumps and chortles. He pumped the gas, furious, then eased the Chrysler off the road. Gravel crackled under us.

We hitchhiked to a gas station. The motor, the gas station guy said, had so overheated that it had welded itself together. Give him the car and he wouldn't charge us for towing.

The life of a flying saucer. I'd been admitted to the university's Honors College on the basis of my short stories and artwork. Declaring myself a journalism major, I had been assigned the head of the journalism department as an advisor. He looked at my academic record and made a big fat fucking point out of refusing to advise me. "You do not belong in our program," he said. "I don't know what else you want me to say."

Okay, then I'd make art. Make my dad happy by becoming either an architect or a car designer. I enrolled in a sketching class run by a long-haired Marxist-Leninist art teacher who could not have cared less about my cars of the future and then some cute girls wanted me to go to Hawaii with them and when I told my dad about all this he said: If you give up design you may give up the most important opportunity you'll ever have, because it is the only important talent you have.

Finishing the dishwatery dregs of my beer and gazing at what had been the focus of so much hope, work and money, I began laminating over my wrecked Chevy the things that might redeem it. A Rat motor was the obvious answer. Why not just rip the car apart, drop in a 409-cubic-inch V-8 and top it with a GMC blower to stand skyscraper tall in front of the windshield and get a new, even sexier girlfriend? Even as a daydreamer I was losing my touch.

The next day I put an ad in the paper and saw my dream machine towed out of our garage by the father of a boy who was tall and skinny and moony with hope as I had been when I was his age, three years before. Seeing the car go, I comprehended, if just for a millisecond, the cost of giving up.

— 23 —

OUR WAYS

Adam, my first customer, was on his knees bent over his old tattered sleeper sofa praying to the good Lord the car I had just sold him wouldn't turn into a ton of blue smoke the minute he drove it off the lot. We had gone to his house for his checkbook. It was in the northeast section of Portland. Black, poor and bitter. The only picture on Adam's wall was of the Last Supper, all twelve apostles staring at me as if to say, "Kit, we do have our ways."

—from Kit Bowen's journal

"Bowen's ready. The iron is hot," Moon promises. "Grab a cheapo flight, don't forget the business plan and leave the rest to Kit and me."

Kit Bowen says, as a bonus if I come up to Portland, he'll lease me a new Ford Explorer to drive back to California. All I'll have to do is pay for it. When I ask him to quote me a price, he seems surprised. "Christensen, did we grow up together or what? Lemme paint the stage: Just fly on up to Portland and come out to the lot."

So I do.

At the huge Ford dealership where he works, golden-haired Kit, big, hail and hearty as the happiest pro wrestler ever, puts a bearlike arm around my shoulder and sweeps me out among the trucks. "We're gonna get you bought." He leads me to a big blue 4 x 4 Explorer. When I stick my head inside and say it smells funny he agrees. "Yeah. We just gave it a douche."

Bowen is wearing a gold shirt open at the collar, and I can see his scars. Shrapnel, and the ripping gouge left by the shaft of a '49 Ford's steering column spearing into his chest—the result of Vietnam and a night drinking after he got home from Vietnam.

Bowen ploughed the Ford through a parked truck and into a house and, though he was declared DOA at the hospital, surgeons were able to untangle heart, lungs, stomach and spleen and get everything going well enough to leave him still on his feet here twenty years later at Landmark Ford.

In high school, we could have been brothers—two tall, skinny boys with big mouths and no problems. Then Kit went to war, and I didn't. I figured: terrible haircuts, getting up too early in the morning and no hippie chicks. Bowen figured: I'll impress my dad. Two days in the country and Kit was loading the freshly dead into body bags.

Now this. "A guy comes into the agency looking for an Explorer truck. He was a medic in Nam, like me," Bowen says as we walk back to the big Ford showroom. "A brother in blood. He's got a beautiful Vietnamese wife, a wonderful Amerasian daughter. We're an honest outfit. Not one of those liner-closer places where you're lucky to get a twenty-two-year-old salesman with *love* and *hate* tattooed across his knuckles. I am ready to deal in absolute good faith here, to give as well as get. But before I can say, 'Kemo sabe, this is not a tube of toothpaste. This thing is called a car. You need to bargain with me,' he offered straight sticker on an Explorer."

"What'd you do?"

"Ripped his face off. Accepted his offer. Hit him full bore. The only reasonable money I made all month. Selling cars, you can't make any money unless you're selling to the elderly or the stupid. You want to know the future of car sales? You hire two college kids to sit at a computer in front of a warehouse."

Kit says Portland has more car dealers per capita than anywhere. "We get everybody. One minute it's a Yuppie from hell, the next grandma and grandpa come in, spread their legs and we ram it home for full gross. I just did a great deal for my mom. Two hundred dollars on her trade-in."

"You only gave your own mother two hundred dollars?"

"Her car was only worth one hundred dollars. A shitbox. Believe me, she was treated right." But re: the Portland car freak whose father owned a town. "I gave Stevenson the Xeno prospectus in a restaurant. He was at the bar with his sexy little wife, and he just gave me this 'my dick, your mouth' look. I felt the power shoot right out of my veins."

And a little problem with that $4,000 securities attorney. He charged $325 an hour and used up our $4,000 having me explain to his assistant what the car business was all about. Scary Larry had to threaten to sue him to get our money back and my father says forget $325-an-hour security attorneys, get a broker, incorporate and issue stock. I inquire: How does that work?

I am sitting in the living room at my parents' ranch, three hundred acres—mostly fir trees and grazing land—draped around a hillside about forty miles from Mount Saint Helens.

"You divide the profit," my dad says, "by the total number of shares to determine the amount of profit per share. Then you pay out according to the number of shares you have outstanding. If there is ten cents worth of profit per share, a guy with one hundred shares gets ten bucks."

I ask, "How long do these investors get to participate in the profits?"

My father looks at me. He is so thin. I can see too clearly the shape of his skull. Years playing golf in the sun have left his cheeks streaked with ocre marks that resemble Indian war paint. "As long as the company exists. Forever," he says.

"Just for putting in money one time, investors get to share in the profits forever?"

The man who raised me sounds calmly incredulous. "You are asking your investors to take a large risk, to invest nearly a million dollars in a company that will produce, what, just twenty cars?"

Well, yeah, that's what I've just heard myself say. Twenty cars. At $600,000 apiece, shouldn't that be enough?

I choose this moment to unveil the Xeno renderings Nick made at the Art Center, renderings that will show my father that his son did not grow up to be just a watcher or a propagandist, but someone who was about to get something done, something wonderful, something he would have loved to have done himself, something even better than the *Faux Pas. See Dad, I'm doing what you always wanted me to do.*

"The guy that designed the car," I say, "is the hottest young designer in the country." When that doesn't get a rise, I add. "Maybe even the world."

I show my father the prospectus. He looks at Nick's renderings again, says, "Streamlined" and sets the drawings aside.

My brother Scott and I shoot pool in the garage. The last time we really hung out together was long ago, the summer the West Coast traffic courts got computerized, all my tickets from Hawaii, California, Oregon and Colorado came together in the office of one Oregon judge who, after telling me that he prayed I'd kill myself before I killed somebody else, informed me that I was one more moving violation away from walking for the rest of my life. My brother was then a tall, long-haired teenage lady's man with a pink 1962 Rambler four door, a machine at the cutting edge of throw-away culture. With Scott's WHO CARES ABOUT APATHY? bumper sticker hanging off the rear bumper, the "Midday Rambler" was a great car to drive around in and drink Spinada, the wine you'd get if you mixed grain alcohol and pancake syrup. A right-wing hippie guitar player who wrote songs about lost love and union busting, Scott would take off on dexidrine in the morning, fly up, up and away to the friendly neighborhood highway-side Golden Garter Tavern at noon and spend balmy hours at the bar coming in for a landing on twenty-five-cent beers with his feisty little monkeylike pal, Smacko. This went on all summer until one afternoon Scott saw Smacko turn into different shapes and, realizing Smacko had inexplicably poisoned his beer, swung at his friend the very moment Smacko passed out. Smacko hit the Garter's orange shag carpet before my younger brother could even finish his punch. Which wigged Scott out. "I didn't touch him! I didn't touch him!" he shouted, convinced that poor Smacko was somehow miraculously dead. Scott jumped into the Midday Rambler, wheeled out of the parking lot, was quickly the cause of a hit-and-run accident up by the medical school, drove his freshly obliterated pink sedan to Raleigh Hills, rammed it through my parents'-ten-foot-high arbor vitae hedge, locked himself in his room for thirty-six hours, then moved to Kansas, finished college and got married. His wife was a voluptuous cocktail waitress and Scott, disguised as a barfly, would sit drinking in a corner during her shift and wait for some guy to come on to her—then boom, Hiroshima. The next thing I knew Scott had quit drinking, got himself a slimmer wife and a job teaching the type of students he had once been: kids who were fairly seriously unhinged.

That afternoon, through binoculars, through my parents' big living room window, I count thirty-five elk across the road, standing on a tilting pasture before a curtain of second-growth fir. Bad news about my Explorer. Kit Bowen's manager told him he couldn't sell a car to a Californian, for tax reasons.

My father and I walk down to the big metal outbuilding where he stores the Hudson. I open one of the old car's heavy doors and smell my cousin Jerry's aftershave, its scent at least twenty five years old, inside.

My mother has told me that she is worried that something is very wrong with my dad. Retirement, would be my guess.

Now he has become very quiet, like a ghost of himself. I grew up thinking my father should be president of the United States but now that he is old, I wonder what he will do. He used to hunt, but no longer likes to kill. Golf? How many rounds can you play? His old Thunderbird and Toronado sit on rotting tires sinking to their rims. Swallows nest above and the cars look as if Jackson Pollock had painted them in bird shit. I say he should restore them. He says that will be my job.

I drive down to Portland, where Gideon works at the emergency room at Good Samaritan Hospital a few days a month. "I do it so I can wear my lab coat and not feel like it's Halloween."

Gideon says if he buys a car he wants stock too. "There's tremendous risk. Nick's still an unproven designer." He says he hasn't got time to raise money and walking me out of the hospital, laughs and says, "Mark, you're Tucker."

Without Tucker's millions. Or even tens of thousands.

Nick and Henrietta have flown to Monte Carlo to furnish Henrietta's apartment and to raise money for the Xeno. Nick called just before I left. "There's no energy here. I went to a classic car auction but no one bought most of the cars. Wolfgang got a bed for one hundred and fifty thousand dollars that would have normally gone for a million. I talked to some famous fat cat who really liked the idea but said, 'See me next year.' I said, 'Dude, I don't need money next year, I need it *now*.'" Nick added that "fifty feet away from me probably, hanging out" is a famous race car driver whose name he can't remember, but can I FedEx his big drawing of the Xeno immediately so he can show it to the guy? "To get into the studio you have to lift the whole door up to turn the lock. You'll see how to do it on the glass in the shape of my arm in old sun lotion." Then I get a glimpse of the-other-half living. Though Henrietta pays $6,500 a month for her four-bedroom, five-bathroom Monte Carlo apartment, Nick says, "We don't have a *pot*, we don't have a *fork*, we don't even have *salt*. No curtains, no curtain *rods*. I woke up to the biggest sun in my eyes I've ever seen. We don't even have lights. Just wires dangling from the ceiling. Dude, we had to sleep in the towels." They've got to spend "like fifty thousand dollars" furnishing the place and it is awful work. "In America you go to a store and say you wanta buy this thing and they say, 'Why not buy five of them?' Here, you go to a store, say you want to buy this thing and they say, 'Sorry, it's the last one we have, come back in nine weeks.' "

I sent him the drawing. Which he showed to no one.

Time to resort to Moon. The Xeno prospectus and Herman's engineering report beside me on the seat of my rental car, I drive out to a new housing development. Moon is a realtor now. New houses stand on a grassy hill, dark firs fence the horizon. His pickup is parked outside a model split-level. When I walk in he's alone at the new kitchen counter reading, so engrossed I have to say, "Moon" three times before he looks up. It's the Moon of twenty years ago. The same smooth, bright features and careful cap of sandy hair. Tan sport coat, khakis and saddle shoes.

By the time he was twenty-five, Moon, short of shopping crematoriums, had his whole future planned and I was surprised when his life exploded. His wife, a pianist, left him to become "the next Linda Ronstadt." He got a new girlfriend, a tall, busty blonde who'd witnessed a Mob slaying in Boston and fled to Portland, convinced the murderers were tracking her down. She had a temper, took her fists to Moon, then a knife and finally a gun. Now he's selling real estate.

A young couple arrives. The guy is big, wears a baseball jacket and Levi's, and instructs, "No sales jive." Moon flushes. He is thorough with his spiel, schoolboy polite, but when the big guy turns away Moon mimes whipping and strangling.

"You got a floor plan?" the guy asks.

"No," Moon says, "I can get you one."

"You expect to sell me a house without a floor plan?"

"I said," Moon repeats, a wintery smile sliding across his face, "I'll get you one."

The guy turns to his wife. "With no floor plan we can't even tell how big the place is."

Moon says, "Then call the cops."

The guy's brow descends. "What did you say?"

"Then call the cops." That freezing grin. The original Yuppie, Moon is, nevertheless, tough, and this could be fun. But they leave, no problem, and I show Moon the prospectus. "Cost estimates are only general. That's where you come in."

Moon's orderly face blooms with the old mix of idealism and greed. He picks up one of Nick's drawings and declares, "Da Vinci from Jupiter. This is the motherload," then dabs his lip with the cuff of his sport coat. He is, just a bit, foaming at the mouth.

24

ROUTE 666

Nick says, "We need to completely redesign the car, otherwise it'll be a joke, a tank, a slug. The Xeno isn't sexy enough. The front is like the front of the White House. A regal arch. It doesn't say sex, it says authority. It's completely wrong. You can't make stately awesome. Also! People can't even tell between the back and front. They look at it and just go, huh? What we have now isn't a real car. But this is." A sketch is on my coffee table in my living room. The Xeno, but with open wheels and its needle tail high in the air, wasplike. "It's like a massive killer whale," Nick says, "versus a rippy little shark. This is about cars as art. At that level we're invincible. Most art just sits on the wall or a big pile of junk in a corner, but this art goes one hundred and seventy miles an hour."

Nick is buying a gun with a laser sight. Debbie asks why. Nick describes an ambush. "If somebody broke in at the bottom of the stairs Henrietta and I'd be ready at the top, lying down, looking over the ledge waiting."

My wife suggests, Why not just call the police?

"Ten minutes after Henrietta is raped and my throat is slit, the cops get there. A psychopath in your house needs thirty seconds, with a knife. With a gun," Nick raises an invisible one and goes: "*Puooo, puoo, pooo.* They're histo."

Good news. Once again, Henrietta offers to finance the car. Nick reports she looked in her bank account just to check and, yeah, there it was, the two hundred and fifty million dollars. Just sitting there. Cool. Now I won't have to sell all my Eye-dentify stock or our house in Portland now—

"But I don't want her to do it," Nick concludes. "My dad says if Henrietta pays for the car I could end up like an egg in a bag with a rock." So where are we going to get the money for this? Maybe all we need is just one thirty-year-old 1980s-style I'd-sell-my-mother-for-a-nickel guy in a white shirt and red suspenders. Under any rock during the Reagan years. Now they've all been lost to Christ or recovery and I am thinking we may have to settle for a simple con man when I hear Nick say: "Ralph Lauren. The famous clothing designer. He's got a car collection—a Porsche Spyder, a Ferrari P-4, Bugattis—he could finance the whole thing. Henrietta can get his most personalized personal address. The one his junk mail doesn't even come to."

Nick's TV is on. He's on tape in Monaco going through Henrietta's echoey apartment, it's all angles, like a big luxury prison cell. Henrietta—if you add what she pays for this place and her apartment in Monte Carlo—spends as much in rent every year as the mayor of Los Angeles makes in salary.

We're upstairs. The remodeling, which Nick began with such energy and inspiration two months ago, has stopped. Nick made a bathroom at one end of the balcony. The shower works, but just stands there, a big white shell, a big white box. No curtain. No *wall*. So that if you are in the shower or sitting on the toilet you enjoy a grand vista to the studio space below.

Nick hunched above the wreckage of his breakfast, scraps of toast, smears of jam on a plate, asks if I can write "killer promo." Though the only promo I can remember writing was for an underground newspaper ("Whether it's the Second Coming or just a new wing on the County Methadone Clinic, read about your alternative interests first in the *Portland Scribe*") where, at age twenty-four, I was the Marxist paper's top necessary evil. Though I sold enough ads to fill a phone book it was quickly made clear to me there would be no ad sales people in the socialist paradise. "Yeah Nick," I say, "sure."

My opus begins:

The goal of Xeno Automotive will be the creation of an American ultimate road car. The Xeno, timeless and alluring, will debut a revolutionary "high-information" design that translates the subliminal

```
forms of nature into a new concept of automotive
style.
    Xeno AfterMarket will manufacture wheels,
steering wheels, seats and other automotive after
market products . . .
```

And after he has finished reading, Steve Scherzer, his craggy face tan, says, "What's the sticker for one of these babies?"

"Nick said something about six hundred thousand dollars."

We are at a big new Wolfgang Puck restaurant heavy on red slate and brass. "Ferrari F40s are going for one-point-two million," I say. "These cars are the new diamond pinky rings for the superrich. Even Bugatti's going back in business, somebody bought the name and they're building a car that'll go for six hundred and fifty thousand dollars."

"What'd you say Nick's last name was?" Scherzer's brows become opposing diagonals. "Nick Ferrari? Nick Bugatti? Nick Porsche?" A waiter appears with salads. "Six hundred thousand dollars for a car," Steve peers into a riot of colorful plants. "Come on."

Why do I feel as if I had convinced, say, the twenty-two-year-old Dan Marino to not sign with the NFL but to instead start the Dan Marino and Mark Christensen Football League?

At the Art Center College of Design in Pasadena, classroom walls look covered with Nick Pugh wallpaper, new car of the future after new car of the future designed in the bladed Nick Pugh style done by what is a whole school of Nick Pugh apostles. One of the instructors tells me no student here at what amounts to the Harvard/Yale/MIT of automobile design has ever had such an influence, and what is Nick doing, by the way? Wasn't he offered a big job at Chevrolet or Ford or BMW or—did he turn it down or what? "He would have been a design chief by now."

This will be the key to our whole project. At Nick's huge studio, here amid the industrial ruins of Los Angeles, Nick has made a crucifix in chalk. Two white lines on his concrete that define the length and width of the car we will make.

We are down to our last $3,000—the table scrap left after I paid for a table saw at Tool City. Kiss $2,421.30 good-bye. Nick can no longer use Art Center equipment because "I think they've finally figured out I don't go there anymore."

We must have tools to build the model. The model is vital. It will reveal and define the new "real" Xeno, the Xeno we can actually build. It would be crazy to build the real car without working the design through in model form first—still, why didn't we just rent the damn saw? We won't make it at this rate. "We're just minimum guys," Nick assures me. "All you are is a salesman for me, a designer who a lot of people will hate for making designs they think are completely insane."

Nick augments the crucifix to present a plan view of the Xeno drawn the way the police would silhouette a murder victim. In new white high-top basketball shoes, knee-length black-and-white Hawaiian-style surfer jams, barechested and still tan from Monaco, Nick points his new Heckler and Koch SP89—the same gun used by the German Secret Service—at Rooter, his Vietnamese pot-bellied pig. "Die, piggie," he instructs. A red dot flashes across the pig's bristly swayback. Perhaps Nick, who is as big as a gangly middleweight boxer, could have spent his money better on karate lessons from his pal Dean Robinson, but—

Nick points the barrel at his forehead, flicks on the laser so the red dot stands above his eyes like the third eye on a Hindu. I say once the gun has been loaded he can never do that again. Nick says he's hip, then pops the laser off and on, blasts bricks off the wall, shoots the band saw, blows away the table saw. Nick tells me Henrietta is buying a stun gun and he reaches out, stabs my shoulder with a finger and says, "Zzzzzzzzzzzz."

Then back to business. I'm excited; when it comes to made-from-nothing car models there are those at the Art Center who believe Nick is the best in the world. He'll make the model of the Xeno out of clay. Three hundred dollars worth of oil, sulphur and dirt that will define the design of the car. In the very early days of automobile styling, coach builders often made models in wood, and much later some cars—the original model of my father's Hudson, for example—were created in plaster. But plaster and wood are hard and tough to reshape and since the 1920s when the young Los Angeles designer Harley Earl began using modeling clay borrowed from movies sets, clay has been the car designer's medium of choice.

"The first side will take a week," Nick says, "the second side more because everything has to be matched exactly." But first he has to finish the baseboard—the wood box and aluminum slab on which the model will sit. Basically, it's just a box two inches deep made out of plywood and chipboard he found at a JCPenney street sale. John Mason gave him a quarter-inch aluminum plate to mount on top of that. It has been mounted on the top, attached to the wood base by countersunk screws. Straight aluminum rails are mounted on the plate, to surround the model. It's a frame. "If it's not accurate in quarter scale—this is a quarter-scale plate—when you blow it up to full scale any mistake will blow up four times. A thirty-second of an inch wrong in this scale equals an eighth of an inch wrong in real life. Which will screw a door, wreck any fitting. If I had a machined surface to work off of, I'd make it perfect. But I can't. Because I am not a mill."

The full-size Xeno will be 190 inches long and 80 inches wide so Nick has made 380 marks across and 160 down, each one eighth of an inch apart. The model car will be sculpted inside that rectangular rail frame.

"But first," Nick says, "we have to build a buck. It's the model's skeleton—pack the clay on the buck, pound it down, sculpt it, make the design decisions, first on just one side of the car—this is what I'm best at, most experienced at—then transfer the points exactly accurate." He picks up his surface gauge. A scribe attached to an adjustable arm. At the end of the arm is a point. After the point is set against a surface it can be locked in place, then he can move it over to the other side and it indicates that same point exactly. "Once the clay is done," he concludes, "a fiberglass guy will lay fiberglass into the clay model, and pop out a fiberglass part. That will be the mold."

The buck is just a wood frame. "You could make the buck out of garbage if it was put together okay," he says. "It just displaces clay." He has sawed wood wheels out of jelutong modeling wood, blond and light, resembling a hard balsa. "It's from a rain forest, bad, but it's all that we have."

He cuts fiberboard into sides, hood and top, and has nailed it together. I take an electric drill and put holes in its side and top so that clay will have something to hang onto. "We can finish it in a week," Nick assures me, "but let's clean up. I'll start you out on precise, accurate prep work."

Vacuuming.

"Where's an open outlet?"

Nick says, "Just find one."

With banks of floodlights on stands, the new saws and other power tools plugged in, I can see no open outlets. So I unplug a line from a tangled ganglia of other lines. No lights go out so I figure no problem and, pushing the vacuum forward, begin sucking swathes of clean across a gauze of sawdust and grunge.

The next day Nick in white tank top and khaki shorts, Henrietta in zebra tights, go see their landlord, Richard, about installing $3,500 worth of skylights. Richard is wiry and cowboylike. He has a Brooklyn accent, a red Ferrari and lives in a palatial loft. A man from a TV detective show checks it out as a potential set as Nick lays out the plan: skylights all across the ceiling of their studio and Richard says fine. As we walk back Henrietta says, "Nick was magnificent." That the skylights will do nothing but add to the value of Richard's property and that the $3,500 comes all out of Henrietta's pocket wasn't an issue.

Back to work. The holes we drill in the plywood frame of the buck make it look like a picture I once saw of an old streamlined Italian armored car shot up by Ethiopians. "You can't put on clay in blobs and balls," Nick says, "but in thin layers like plywood, pack it on at about one hundred and five degrees. At room temperature the clay becomes hard and waxy so you can carve it. It's not like a sculpture where the surface you make with your hands becomes final. You use tools, a rake and a steel to get surfaces accurate down to a hundredth of an inch."

But when he opens the clay oven, the clay is cold.

"Goddamnit!" he says. "Yesterday, when you were vacuuming. You must have unplugged the oven!" He begins cursing me with respect, at a distance, backward, his face to the wall of his studio. "Shit! A whole day lost!" To make sure, he strides back to the clay oven, yanks open its shiny aluminum door and jams his thumb into one of the long, brown clay sausages. "Cold as the dead. It'll take eight hours to warm up again." He grabs his head in his hands. "The *one thing* that can stop everything." Cold and hard, the clay can't be applied to the buck.

"The wires were tangled up," I say. "Nothing happened when I unplugged it. I figured it was just a power tool."

"Nothing we can do now. You might as well just go home."

I go out the front door and Henrietta slips out behind.

I say, "I should have traced the cord. It was my fault."

"*Ja, ja,*" she says and waves a hand. "It was your fault he wouldn't show you. He gets an obsession and won't listen or tell you what you need to know. It's my fault all the time too."

———

"Skinny knees." Nick makes a circumference from his thumbs and fore-fingers. "A waist like that." He makes an O with his thumb and fore-finger. "Breasts that point." They took a trip across country and Laurel expressed her love at every border. "The West was cool, but New En-gland. Those states are small, about an hour drive apiece. The roof of my car got all dented up."

Nick's old girlfriend Laurel has called the studio and wants to come over. Laurel, a former Art Center student, is now writing country and western songs in Memphis or Nashville, and has a reunion in mind. Nick was firm: No way. And why not? "I can handle Laurel on the phone. But in person—she's totally *Playboy* and *Penthouse*, Mark. If she met you, you'd be doomed. If she walks through that door and likes what she sees, your marriage is over."

But he tells me it would make him "sick" to cheat on Henrietta. "I used to go to parties just to try and find a cute girl I could get drunk enough to go home and have sex with, but now that I have Henrietta parties are useless. I love her that much."

Standing over the buck, waiting for Laurel not to show up, we apply the clay in Xs, smears and stars. I reach into the bin. It is hot. I pull off one of my plastic gloves. My hand is bright pink, poached by my own sweat.

Henrietta is mad because Nick bought a porn magazine—nothing kinky Nick insists, "Just some majorly nasty babes"—and when she gets home, Nick races up the stairs making machine gun sounds but then, waving the Heckler and Koch, sees her foot up on a chair. "*Lasme*, shit! That chair'll cost two hundred dollars to get cleaned."

I am not paying much attention, packing clay onto the model a gob at a time, something cut into my palm. A dime-size piece of skin has skidded off the flesh beneath it and a blister has risen in a half moon— but I hear Henrietta say, "Mark would never get angry over something so petty."

"If not for Debbie," Nick says, "Mark would live in a junkyard."

"Mark and I would have fun." Henrietta's foot glides back up to the seat of the chair again, hovers, eases back down. "Not just live in a crazy studio waving around a machine gun."

———

A new world. Nick is holding a copy of the prospectus. Which he has not, for some reason, read until now. "This is so goofy. 'The Xeno will be for the individual who would, comma, given the chance, comma,' I can't hardly even read and I know that's badly written."

I say, "But you wrote it."

"I'm not the writer. You're the writer."

"Nick, I can't reinvent everything you say."

"My mother does."

"Does what?"

"When I was in school she'd take my ideas and put them into her words and that's how I'd get good grades in English." He looks back at the paper, reads, " 'Each Xeno will be constructed in the tradition of the old coach builders. Each Xeno will be signed by the designer, builder and engine builder.' What's the engine builder have to do with anything?"

"Nick, the engine is the soul of the machine."

"Then say that in a way that's both more ethereal and more clear. To me that's loopy and glompy. Too blunt yet confusing. It's not romantic sounding at all."

Nick points to the manuscript. "You started a sentence with *and*. I learned in second grade nobody starts a sentence with *and*."

I say, "Not if they're in second grade."

"You're bitchin' at the clever stuff, at the punch lines. But there's no analysis that leads to a sale. It's like making an egg. You're good at the yolk, good at the white, but you don't know anything about supplying the shell that holds everything together. We need a superhard shell nobody can break. You write novels and books so you must have some idea how to do this."

I swallow a fuck you. "Read them and see for yourself."

"I don't have *time* to read. Look, what we'll do is just give this to my mom. The points are all there, we just need my mom to put the salesmanly light in the right place."

"Nick," I say, "the prospectus is supposed to very soberly and accurately give the potential investor the facts. With no hoopla. It's not supposed to be a sales pitch."

Nick whacks the booklet. "That's what you don't understand! *Everything we do is a sales pitch*." He drops the prospectus on the coffee table. "This is the assignment: figure out what I'm doing, write it down and get it to my mom. Clear?"

No. And when, in a daze, I say we can get Nick's instructors to endorse him, Nick is appalled. "That's *nothing* to a Ralph Lauren. If you have a hundred fifty-million-dollar company as the most successful fashion designer maybe ever I'd say, 'Who cares what his teacher thinks? What does Giugiaro think, what does Gondini think? What does Ferrari think?' But my *teachers*? You cite Tom Matano. A lot of car guys will say: 'His Miata's cute but the Lotus Elan is a lot nicer.' But the President of the United States endorses Nick Pugh, whoa! Madonna orders a Xeno! That talks to Ralph Lauren. We're designing extraordinary, eccentric cars for extraordinary, eccentric people. Clear? Do you agree or not?"

Maybe twenty minutes have passed, another sea change. Nick is saying, "I'm nothing. I'm twenty-four, Herman and John are the foundation. I'm just the concept, the pinnacle, the cutting edge, just a guy with a lot of ideas. But I've got the right people to build those ideas. Do you agree or not? We are selling incredible design, incredible engineering and incredible people to execute it."

There are spills and fjords of quarters, dimes, nickels and pennies around Nick's pens and brushes and X-acto knifes on his design table, enough to have the spirit of treasure or the cartoon troves of Scrooge McDuck. He picks through the coins, looking for change to buy a Coke. "Ralph Lauren. He's hot on history, hot on timelessness, hot on quality. What all his cars have is a name and a history, a racing history, a personal history, a financial history." He picks up the prospectus, points to where I have noted the Xeno's roots in cars like the Phantom Corsair and the Alfa Bat. "Out. Out, out, out. Those are cars only designers know about. Meaningless, if we're going to be the Ferrari of the future.

"Our lack of history is scary. What if Ralph Lauren says, 'How do I know you guys won't just build one car?' It's risky as hell for me to spend this much money on a car that could turn out to be nothing. What's our overall argument against that?"

What's my overall argument against walking out of here? I say the Xeno is a flagship car. "A completely fresh look at design. It allows somebody to be the first to buy—"

Nick chops an arm through the air. "Yes! It won't be just one car— that this is my passion, my love, and it's risky, but it'll work. So when the guy says, 'Your car has no history,' I can say, 'We are presenting the history of the future.' The car as a pure art piece, a signed sculpture that goes two hundred miles an hour. That's the future!" He looks at the prospectus again. "We say it here but we say it badly." He reads, " 'Untethered' . . . Don't say *untethered*." He slaps the paper. "Just say it, quick! fast! mean! and there! So they say, 'Fuck, man! That's the best idea I ever read in my life! It's so fuckin' awesome! These guys have got a great idea! A great team! And all I need to do is sign a check.' "

At night, in bed, I tell my wife, "He can barely read and he's telling me how to write. He looks at words and tells me they look like 'equations.' He scoffs at the idea of reading a newspaper."

"You were assisting him." Deb's small face appears from behind a *New Yorker* magazine. "You get him lunches. Vacuum. Maybe he thinks you're becoming his underling. Maybe you started out as a big flashy *Playboy–Rolling Stone* writer and now he sees you as just some guy living in a duplex."

"The thing is," I say, "he has to be ruthless in the pursuit of his ambitions, otherwise—"

"What?"

He'll end up like me? Just some guy living in a duplex. "Otherwise," I say, "he'll get lost in the shuffle. I talked him out of taking a job in Detroit and he is so far ahead of every other designer it's pathetic."

Debbie says, "Sounds like it." She has worked her perfect butt off to make money to keep this going, would eat bird food if it meant having steak for Katie, Matt and me, and I do not want my situation to sound worse than it is. "Nick's an incredibly good guy, actually," I say.

"He is?"

"He's just desperate and scared."

Thanks to me. I'm responsible for him. Had it not been for me, "America's best young car designer" would be in Michigan designing, if not the twenty-first century's first supercar, at least the twenty-first century's first supercar's hubcaps. Instead of laboring away at a utopian wet dream that after however many months has still not produced a dollar.

"Don't worry," I say. "The tail will not wag the dog. Teenage lunkheads build cars all the time, and if I can't get the best young car designer in America to create just one car, what does that make me?"

"Stepin Fetchit." Debbie grins and turns out the light.

25

Clear

Tick of the time bomb. I drop my sliver-armed daughter Katie off at school. A gray summer morning. Katie has been fitted for braces. She's got a big overbite, she brought home a cast of her mouth resembling the fossil jaws of a prehistoric bird and I worry kids may make fun of her.

I drive to Nick's lux bus garage of a studio, where Rooter the pig has learned a new trick. Chewing gum. Nick is in a good mood. "You missed it. I freaked out. It got gnarly. I flipped the model over and cut it apart."

What?

Deep slashes run over the front of the model, clay bashed off—glass all over the floor. Nick plays the video he made of wrecking it. He introduced his drink. A glass swimming pool of chablis fills the screen as he narrates. "Gnarly living room, gnarly some other room. Wharzzz the pig?" Jimi Hendrix plays in the background as on the TV Nick destroys the car.

This "in the meantime of yesterday" after he came home to find one of the workmen putting in the skylights had unplugged the clay oven again. Nick had taken out his frustration on the model.

"No big deal, it was trash. It was too controlled, too analyzed and lacked the insanity, the lunacy it needed."

"It did?" Jesus. "Well, you're the doctor."

"Doctor! Mark! If I was a doctor I'da been sued for malpractice. It lacked guts. So I cut it into pieces, smashed glass all over it—clobbered it with Henrietta's chair, I was even going to shoot it." He loaded the Heckler and Koch, then ran upstairs on the roof and took a shot at L.A. instead.

"He! Is! A! Spoiled! Child!" My wife is playing the pots, pans, cabinet doors, spoons, knives, forks and anything else she can slam around in our kitchen in the explosive way Charlie Watts drummed at the end of "You Can't Always Get What You Want." "He's been fawned over by his mother, his teachers, everybody else and it's great that he's the best car designer in the universe but we! Can't! Afford! Him! You cannot make his dreamworld real."

We'll see about that. I'm maybe twenty minutes and a Coors and a half into the Yankees vs. Atlanta when the phone rings. It's Gideon, upset. "This has gone from Dream Car to Dream Car, Inc. A month ago we needed four hundred seventy-nine thousand dollars, now it is eight hundred sixty-seven thousand dollars."

I have to admit it takes the breath away. "But that figure represents construction of two cars, not one, and of molds to build twenty more. This should be the high watermark."

"Twenty more cars? What planet are you on? You've got more lawyers than engineers. This started out as—"

"—one hot rod for one hundred thousand dollars. But exotic cars are going nuts. Let me read you—" I'd made a list—"about the heavy hitters. The six hundred-horsepower BMW V-12-powered MacLaren Super Car. A million plus. The Schuppan Porsche 962 twin-turbo one-point-sixty-two million dollars. In this market, we could sell Xenos like party favors."

Gideon's not impressed. "At what, five hundred fifty thousand dollars? Six hundred thousand dollars?"

"Try seven hundred thousand dollars." I amend.

"Then try this: Find your money elsewhere."

"She's seeing another guy," my wife confides after Nick, Henrietta and I get back from Vector Assembly. "She was telling me about somebody she met and you could see it in her face."

Gerry Weigert invited us to the unveiling of a latest Vector and Nick and Henrietta and I arrived just as, with press people milling around, Gerry got a ticket for reckless driving right in front of his own front door.

He's had to lay off most of his employees because of the licensing problem and time is not on his side. The Vector is a car of the future, but from a 1980s future, its hard, cold "fighter jet" design is beginning to date and in an Italian restaurant near my house, I conclude that the Vector is more about power than sex. Nick replies, "Dude, exactly. Wouldn't you say, Henrietta?"

Her eyes go to the ceiling. "I do not find the car sexy."

Nick says our car will be very sexy and asks Henrietta what the Xeno seems more like, a man or a woman, a he or a she?

Henrietta puts her hands beside her eyes. "You are a horse with blinders. I don't give a fuck."

"Yetta," Nick says, reaching across the table to take her hand, "please" and the next morning when I arrive at Nick's, he opens the door in drab olive pajamas looking like a prison camp inmate from *The Bridge on the River Kwai*. "Henrietta and I fought all night." He yawns. "After she didn't come home until three in the morning.

"She wants me to worship her and I won't. I worship—" he turns and throws a hand toward the model—"this."

The fifth of July. I have just talked to Dave Stollery, formerly Marty of Spin and Marty, the Disney duo who courted Annette Funicello on TV by way of the first hot rod I had ever seen. Dave is not encouraging. He left television to become a successful designer for American and Japanese car companies and his latest creation, the 385-horsepower Arex, is all over the car magazines. "We have corporate funding, but we're held back by licensing," he told me over the phone. "Styling, engineering and product planning are relatively easy. Licensing is the hard part. You must pass Federal Manufacturer's Vehicle Safety Standards. And the Environmental Protection Agency. It's not just a knock and CO particulate test, they really put you through the ringer, lots of endurance tests. You can go bribe a judge and license in Alabama or cut the cross member off a junkyard Chevy, take the VIN numbers—" That would be the vehicle identification numbers. "—and call it a radically modified Chevrolet, but if I were you I'd get a certification engineer."

"Where?" I ask.

"I'm not going to tell you."

"Why not?"

"Because you're a competitor."

Okay. I wondered: How was Annette?

Unwilling to kiss the by now remote promise of Gideon's $100,000 good-bye, I've asked Herman to create a "New Testament," making clear how costs will drop as we build five, ten or twenty Xenos—facilitating an annual return of 12 to 20 percent. "New Testament" in hand, I meet Nick up on the patio at the white cafe behind his studio, where he is staring at a slender photographer's model with an intent that shoots beyond sex to dinner. Nick follows her walk across the parking lot, his eyes fixed like a tracker on the African veldt. I almost say, "I'll help you gut her."

Nick says we shouldn't show "the Gid Monster" Herman's new numbers "before they're more polished and ready. It's like if he came into your restaurant to order your special roast mallard, you don't walk by his table with the beheaded bloody duck."

We walk back to his cavernous studio. He is about to transfer his design from the "raw" established left side of the model to the unrealized right. "Duplicating the best moves I have on the first impressionistic, unhinged, whacked-out left side and then refining on the right side. The first side is worked as a sculptor would work a form, to get the right proportion. There's a pattern to get good proportion and another pattern to get good surfaces. You must establish the perfect proportion on one side before you can do the surfaces on the other. Even if that perfect proportion is wrong."

But why make it perfect if the proportion isn't right?

"Come on." He waves me up the stairs. "Let's look at it from above." I follow him up to the balcony. "See the roof line? It has to dip down just right, if it dips down too far it looks—"

"—swaybacked."

"Exactly. But if it doesn't dip enough it looks too flat, too parallel with a main style line that defines the flank. I couldn't see that until I had done it very carefully wrong."

Nick trots back downstairs, pulls the oven door open. Inside, a brown sewery jumble of warm clay. "People aren't invited to be smart, they're invited to go for stupid TV, stupid movies and stupid songs. So it may help to have details not too smart or subtle but cartoonish in model form. A model is little, so important details have to stick out more, so I may accent things—exaggerate—for the fiberglass model, then tone them back down when we create the full-size car."

Nick scrubs balls of clay into the area above the rear vent then indicates the style line defining the flank of the Xeno. "The line dies, doesn't unwind and accelerate the way it should."

He puts a finger on the side near the rear haunch of the car. "This is weight. This is a woman who is too fat." He puts a finger on the main style line. "This is a woman whose bones aren't straight. This is not solving problems like a mathematician. The solution is emotional and visual versus numeric and formulaic."

The studio is so big and bright with the new skylights that I can see smog in the air. Nick works on the "last bastion of completely undefined area on the car," the front quarter panels. There are no front wheel wells, just the bladed shape of the slab side. He lines up the angle and mouse on the "raw" established side, then lines the angle up on the "new" side and uses the mouse on the same coordinate station. "This way," he says, "I can make half of the car—front to back—then duplicate that half exactly front to back on the other side." He lines up the surface gauge on the established side of the model, then transfers it to the new side. The point of the surface gauge eases into the clay. He fills the hole that the point of the gauge has made with white gouache. Using the feeler gauge Nick makes "tiny volcanoes" then builds up around them. He takes the flat steel and strokes the surface into shiny smoothness.

Above, from his pen on the second floor landing, Rooter the pig makes sounds that announce his alimentary canal works in two directions. It's hot in the studio. Uncomfortable. Nick wipes at his forehead with the top of his wrist. "Pretty soon, you'll do one side then a computer-directed mill will cut the other side in exact duplicate. You can already design a car by cross coordinates fed into a milling machine that cuts it out in foam. I don't like it. It's the difference between watching porn and really having sex."

Henrietta cut a heart in the front of the clay Xeno model before she left for the Art Center this morning and Nick uses a big nail to cut it larger. He will labor over a surface for days, exercising a microsurgeon's precision then, once he considers the surface resolved, use it for a scratch pad.

Before she left, Henrietta worried that the car looked "blodi."

But Nick, his confidence rekindled, assured her, "It won't be 'blodi' for long."

He has to spend his fjord of nickels, dimes and quarters to pay the

Mexican maid, has no money left, so I buy him two hamburger burritos from the tavern across the parking lot. After lunch I make an air intake atop the roof that is divided by a low, rectangular fin right down the middle, and when I'm done Nick circles the car, bonks his head with his hand head as if trying to shake water from his ear and says, "Let me finish it."

He carves and shapes the intake and then says, "It's got to be smaller or it'll be like a brick on the back of a cheetah. The car is almost overloaded already. Like if you have a pretty girl, then give her a really striking hat. The point should be the girl, not the hat. This," he points to the intake, "is the hat."

A beautiful car is emerging. The smooth plane of the windshield works as backbeat to the spiky action in the front quarter panel. Accelerating curving lines wind up off the back of the car and sweep forward with explosive grace. Nick describes these final shapings. "Some are measured to the fraction of an inch, others purely by intuition and even accident. It's like being both the cook who doesn't measure spice—he just tastes what's right, and the chemist who works by formula—one-point-zero-eight-five-three milligrams of pepper."

He's made the complex surfaces of the front fenders essentially two curved surfaces converging like the front of a plow. Simplicity makes it stranger. More imposing, and the most striking car I've ever seen.

26

BERSERK

Those twenty thousand shares of Eye-dentify stock. You'd think if you
invented a light allowing you to walk into a bank naked and cash a
check without ID because that light could identify you by your retinas,
you'd have it made. But I guess not. The company thought it would be
so successful so fast it went on a hiring binge and, long story short, I
just sold my twenty thousand shares for one cent a share: $200. The
good news is, though, the clay model is done. We drove it out to the
desert to a mold maker's shop. Patched asphalt, a little Japanese pickup
truck with HEY MON fingered across its veil of dirt, the dusted, darted
shapes of drag boats among big long old shacks. The owner had a red
beard, gorilla arms and a big belly above short-pantsed legs. He charged
us only $400 to make the fiberglass shell. The idea was simple: You
have the clay model, then you apply a coat of mold release, then apply
the fiberglass over the model to create the mold. Once the fiberglass
shell, known as the "part," is "kicked out" a layering of fiberglass is
begun inside the newly created fiberglass mold and soon, or at least
within days, you have it, a tough shell from which you finish your
fiberglass model car.

And that's what we've got. So forget Eye-dentify, a major investment
broker, Jim Hansberger—a friend of a friend—has expressed interest
in developing our company, and, Nick says, "Mark, with your ideas and
my ideas, I am going to have a great empire and I want you to be my
partner. You'll end up incredibly rich."

But this second he needs Glycerite-catalyzed urethane primer filler
and Evercoat ultrasmooth finishing putty and wants me to go get it
right now, forget that I'm thirty miles away in Long Beach and that
it's nine o'clock at night.

At dawn Nick's best friend at the Art Center, Dean Robinson, enlisted to paint the model, calls. "Nick wanted me to shoot paint at three in the morning. He's fanaticking out. He wants the look of mercury for the windows—to stretch Mylar over the canopy and then paint it. The lacquer will eat the Mylar, but you can't tell Nick that. It's like, if he *wants* it to work, it *will* work."

I meet Nick in Pasadena for breakfast before we go to Dean's, and suggest we make Herman president of our company because of his experience and reputation. I expect to make a long, ticklish spiel the message of which is *Herman should be president because he is competent and knows what he is doing, while we aren't and don't*, but Nick says, "Cool, just so he doesn't have all the power."

Then when I say I'd sell my house in Portland to get the company going, he looks confused. "But you're not even in the company."

"*I'm not?*"

"Not according to my mom."

What about our empire? "Nick," I say, "I came up with the plan, found most of the people, including you. Jim Hansberger controls a hundred-million-dollar investment portfolio. If he decides we're his cup of whatever, our problems could be over."

Nick's eyes narrow. "My mom says Hansberger just wants to make money off us." And as for planning the company: "You could have just been some guy who told me the plan in a bar."

To prepare for final paint, Dean fogs the fiberglass shell with green primer ghost coat, a mist of paint applied to be sanded away to reveal irregularities—highs and lows—on the surface. Nick and Dean fix warps, waves and declivities in the fiberglass, fill them with Bondo and catalyzed glazing putty. Taking Nick's plastic template, I pencil the shape of the rear light on Nick's last piece of expensive design wood and, using a band saw, cut the shape of two rear lights. Nick looks at the result and says, "Fuck, dude! We're in too deep for me to correct any of your mistakes."

I say, "What's wrong? I cut it to match your template."

He looks at me as if I am a Coke machine that has taken his quarter and needs to be kicked, then circles the car, gazing at it as if it were alternately a diamond and a turd. "That's the problem, you cut it too close for me to correct. It's either perfect or it's shit."

———

Upstairs in the loft of Nick's apartment—which looks out over his vast and increasingly messy studio like a watchtower above a prison yard—Herman sits on a fading purple couch and advises we hit up Henrietta's family, and Nick, in white high-top basketball shoes and plaid boxer shorts and scratching at his tan boy's chest, shakes his head. "Wolfgang's completely unanalytical. Do you know how far he'd get reading this?" Nick holds up our prospectus and puts a finger to the bottom of the title page. "There. Wolfgang couldn't add ten and ten. He fell asleep during the meeting that sold his company. But he's like the old lion who still has lots of power in his claws. One swoop." Nick lashes the air. "Everything we had would be ruined."

I say, "What if we got a loan?"

Herman shrugs. "I took a loan to finance my windmill company that cost me proceeds of a buyout from an oil company."

Nick is sympathetic. "Bummer."

Herman says, "Yeah, I lost a lot of money."

"No, I mean, to sell out to an oil company."

"Why?" Herman asks.

"I have morals. I'd never sell to an oil company."

Herman puts a hand to his forehead, rakes copper hair back. "By that time I was living in a place with no hot water, bathing my sons in a metal tub."

Nick is jetting to Germany with the model in four days and the model is nowhere near finished. But he is determined to get the car in front of German investors right now. At Dean Robinson's, out back in his detached garage, we wear respirators while Dean jets more clouds of green primer over the model. Nick wants the body pure silver. Dean and I have tried to convince him to hit the silver with a tincture of blue, 5 percent in solution—just a ghost of a blue. "The silver by itself," Dean says, stepping outside, "is not very interesting."

Nick yanks off his mask. "It's interesting enough for Porsche to use on all their prototypes."

Dean smiles. "Tell me what you want and I'll do it."

Nick replies. "I want a look that's hard, cold, mechanical. I want to go to Santa Rosa and have it electroplated."

I say, "Where do we get the time and five hundred dollars for that?"

Nick scowls. "If it's not right, why do it?"

Dean and I go into Dean's little kitchen. On the counter rests the latest issue of *Road and Track's Exotic Quarterly*. Dean painted the Corvette on the cover. Dean says Nick once wanted him to make a car look like solid gold. "Like the back of your grandfather's watch. You can't do that. Not without real gold plate." Nick strides in. "Remember when you wanted me to make your gold car?" Dean asks.

"Yesssssss, Dean." Nick jerks open Dean's refrigerator and plucks out a Coke.

"But you know what you're doing, Nick."

Nick walks back outside. "I don't know what I'm doing. I just know what I want."

Dean tints it blue anyway. Everything is getting done too fast, but nothing fast enough. Henrietta has flown to Germany and in the studio there is water in lakes across the uneven red concrete floor. Nick had been running an "airborne" irrigation system for the grid of plants that hang suspended beneath his skylights and he went to bed, forgetting to turn it off.

On the TV hanging from Nick's ceiling, a table of clay-faced morticians announce Gorbachev is out, that they are the government now. Nick is outraged, would like—if he had time and airline tickets—to face the tanks gunning for the Russian Parliament, and wants George Bush to declare "this is way bogus."

I am six three, 195 pounds and though I have had it playing aide de camp, I worry that recently I have intimidated my partner. But no. Waiting to talk to Luftansa reservations, Nick mouths, "Bring me a chair." Wiggling a finger, he points to the floor under his butt. I bring that chair, push it toward him. Once he's off the phone, "A little bad news. The bank says one thousand dollars we didn't even have has disappeared." He stacks his returned checks in a deck on his drawing table, deals himself a hand and says, "Herman. He must have cashed his check."

"What check?"

"One I forgot I gave him three weeks ago."

Nick occasionally balances his memory of checks he's written, then goes on to other things. He's been working since dawn. Now it's midnight. Paul Curley, a designer even more adventurous than Nick, has come to help. John Mason has finished a beautiful aluminum box in which to carry the model and Nick's brother Dave is here. A charming, slightly chunky college kid, Dave is Nick relaxed. He fingers DEVO across the dust on the Xeno's blue windshield, scratches it a little and Nick gets angry, then isn't. "These are glorious times," he says. "Besides, he's my brother and I love him."

I light a cigarette, ask Nick for an ashtray and he says, "The floor's the ashtray."

The next morning he and Paul complete the undercarriage for the model. During their forty straight hours of work, the Ukraine declares independence, the Soviet interior minister commits suicide, *Pravda* closes, KGB headquarters is attacked amid rumors Gorbachev is dissolving the Communist Party. Paul's thin face is bright with fatigue, his eyes red. He says this is nothing, at Art Center he did twenty-two all-nighters in one semester.

All that is left is to mount the model in its aluminum box. Nick's friend Errol, a photographer, shows up to take pictures. The model is gorgeous. Errol shoots late, we orbit the Xeno under the moon and by morning the studio is a grimy wreck, I'm filthy. Nick has lost his passport and is at his desk, banging through his files. I am making the cardboard box to cover the aluminum box, Nick rips the bathroom door off its hinges. It cartwheels through the air and lands with a crack on the cement floor. "My unbelievable stupidity," he shouts, "is ruining our chances to achieve our dreams."

"Doughnuts, he wants doughnuts," my wife murmurs, ghostly in her white nightgown and looking like a kid in the dim light, her eyes lines, still in her dreams and standing at the door to our living room. "Who'd call at six in the morning after doughnuts?"

"He worked all night." I pick up a phone. "Nick."

Nick says, "What's up? Don't get the Safeway or Vons or grocery store kind, get a bakery kind, okay?"

I'm thirty miles away.

At the studio, the broken bathroom door is face down on the floor and there is a confetti of ripped-open mail by the front door. Nick has torn the studio apart looking for his passport. He's labeling the box with a felt-tip pen, writing instructions on how to move it. "Mark— 'wheel,' one *E* or two?"

We mount the model on its mirror platform. He lost the chuck key used to attach the drill bits and Nick cuts his fingers attacking the drill head with wrenches. We put the model in the aluminum box. I cut the stems of the two bolts that secure the front of the model to its platform. Then say, "Let's be ultrasafe and crank these down. I can see the bolts vibrating loose on the airliner and the model crashing upside down inside its box."

Nick says, "Hand me the Zap. It's the superest of superglues." He squirts it where each nut is twined to the stalk of its bolt. "This is a weld. No way these bolts'll ever come off now."

Turning the box over we hear a cracking sound inside.

"What's that?" Nick asks.

"Just the model settling down on itself," I reply. "Let's go or you'll miss the plane."

Driving downtown, Nick crosses his bloody fingers. At the Federal Building, magically, they give him a new passport in minutes. He has no luggage except for the car, no clothes, no toothbrush. Sweat blobs through his green silk shirt, his face—big slash of a smile—looms over the airport crowd, his thumb shoots in the air and he's gone.

I'm stuck with Rooter the Vietnamese pig. Nick got Dean to agree to take him and then Nick got in an argument with Dean's girlfriend and so now he's mine. Rooter, his sage old-man's eyes notwithstanding, is a numbskull and whereever Rooter is is where Rooter wants to be. I carry him out to the pickup truck I've borrowed to take him back to Long Beach. Eighty pounds. I could be carrying a screaming sack of soft cement. His bleating draws students from the trade school across the street. Black boys with patterns cut into their short haircuts led by a big redheaded kid with what looks like gold cufflinks hanging off his ears. He rubs big chalk-white hands together and says, "Lunchtime" as I set Rooter's furiously peddling hooves on the metal bed of the pickup. I'm afraid he'll leap out of the truck on the freeway, but in minutes the whorling panorama of the 710 is his home and he won't leave the bed of the pickup truck when we get to my friend John Case's, who has agreed to board Rooter outside by his garage.

Nick calls from Europe. "When I got on the plane I was so wired I took a tranquilizer, and had a drink. Some kids saw my drawings and flipped out. The last thing I remember is all my drawings floating up and down the aisle. When the plane landed and I woke up and saw Germany, I threw up—and you know that cracking sound we heard was the rear wheel breaking up. We cranked the car to the ground and we'll never get those bolts off. They're Zapped on forever. I don't know what to tell potential investors."

"I'm not a major automotive collector or an expert in auto design," Jim Hansberger says, "but I've never seen a more beautiful car and I'd like to help Nick find financing." Outside on a leafy-walled patio at the Beverly Hills Hotel, broker Hansberger, thin, dark, good-looking, says, however, that "typical forecasted earnings in high-risk investments like yours run between forty to fifty percent from the first year on. You need a seed money partner, a driving force inves-tor. You've valued this—eight hundred and fifty thousand shares of-fered at about a dollar twenty-five apiece—at one-point-two million dollars, which is not a lot."

He asks Herman, "Would you put two million dollars into this?" When Herman shrugs, Hansberger says, "You're not selling an earn-ings story here, you're selling a trophy."

Nick calls. He put Henrietta on a plane from Paris to L.A. but now, back at his family farm in New Hampshire, he can't find her by phone. Could I drive to the studio and see what's up? Just a sixty-mile round trip, so why not? The studio is empty, the wreckage untouched. I phone home. Debbie says Henrietta just called from the studio. I say, "I'm *at* the studio."

"She said she'd just been 'asleep.' " My wife's voice changes to mimic Henrietta's: " 'Oh zos stuuu-pid boys, zay get upset ofer nahzing.' Asleep where, Henrietta?"

"I don't get it," I say.

"She's with a guy. I almost said: 'Henrietta, why not just tell me the truth?' "

Yes. Nick calls with news: "Just some dude. She's screwy." Due, Nick says, to her upbringing. "It was like growing up on a luxury liner during a hurricane. My aunt says I should learn to meditate, to focus on one."

"One what?"

"The number. To focus on the most basic thing."

His aunt also wants Nick to take Henrietta to Hawaii to visit "a New Age healer named Nehru or Behru and stare at crystals for two weeks." Nick's prognosis: "Henrietta's forcing me to give her the shittiest kind of love there is, jealousy."

Henrietta calls. "It's like having a nice hot bath and then the water is getting hotter but that is okay, more intense, but then oh no, you can't turn off the water, the tub is overflowing. My friend says the night Nick came looking for me he had the gun."

What night? What friend? No matter, I say we can get rid of the gun. "Was he stalking you?"

"Stalking? No. But it's not just the gun. He asks me for a watch. I say, 'Okay, we get you a watch.' But he wants one that costs a thousand dollars. In a restaurant he orders not the most expensive things on the menu, but the *three* most expensive things on the menu. He just wants, wants, wants. This summer when you two were working I had no privacy but was always alone."

I'm thinking, I'd better get the gun, but first I have to return the pig, John Case is tired of hosting this Vietnamese manure machine and I go ask John's friend Jeff Wright to borrow his truck. A "doolie," it is as long as a limousine with double tires in back.

At John Case's handsome Spanish house, Rooter is in his outdoor cell by the garage, standing among his orbs of shit, each with its whizzing electron shield of flies. Rooter, seeing me, makes a farting sound with his throat. I whack the bristles on top of his head and say, "You idiot," then grab Rooter and sling him across my chest. He goes crazy, braying so loud and convulsively that I think, What if he has a heart attack? Yet the moment I set his bite-size hooves on the bed of the pickup he calms, begins sniffing the steel. As if he lives only in the now, as if what is happening to him is all that has ever happened to him.

I wonder: Maybe I should rope him down. Then again, why? All Rooter has ever done is eat, shit and stand there. But on the 710 north I have a foreboding strong enough to make me wonder if Neil Armstrong had felt better atop the bomb that shot him to the moon. But why get so worried? A pig, big deal. Farmboys the world over drive pigs around in pickup trucks every day of the week. Swinging off the 710 and down the ramp that slips me onto Interstate 5 north, I begin to feel the unweighting delight of an impending success, the rich heat of accomplishment, when a Jeep pulls beside me and a grizzled blond kid makes parentheses around his mouth with his hands and shouts,

"Your pig is gone!" Right. Bitchin' joke. Funny though, no Rooter there in the rearview mirror.

He has surely flopped down under the back window where I can't see him. But when I pull off at Nick's exit, no Rooter. All that is left in that pickup is a dozen lonely little turds. The pickup's bed is deep. How'd he do it? Suddenly I can see Rooter bouncing down the freeway like a fumbled football. *Shit*.

I drive up and down Interstate 5. On the radio an announcer intones, "We have a wreck caused by an unidentified object near Florence Street," Florence Street? What if Rooter killed somebody? I pull off the freeway, spot a squad car at an intersection, try to wave it down. The cops look at me and drive away. I drive back down the freeway but can see nothing. No pileups, thank God, but no piggy either. I drive back to Long Beach, to Jeff Wright's ripped-down mansion. "He's *carnitas* by now," Jeff says. He bought a house as big as a little hotel, is remodeling, and now all that is left standing is the wall in front. Jeff has his tool belt on and is sipping pop out of a big wax paper cup. "I wonder if anybody got my license plate."

I say, "You couldn't be liable."

"If the pig caused a wreck, everybody'll get credit."

I call the police and talk to four cops on a party line. A woman says, "The pig is in an animal shelter." An old timer says, "Heh heh, go figure how he survived. What were you going sixty? Seventy?" Another cop says I was breaking a city ordinance. A wise-ass, when I ask what happened to Rooter, says, "Severe rugburn."

For the first time, I like Rooter. Falling out of the truck is the most audacious thing he's ever done. But that night Nick calls to inform me that an animal shelter is not the best place for Rooter and that I should have "removed" him.

"Remove him where?"

"If Katie or Matt jumped out of the pickup, wouldn't you get them to a good hospital?"

"You're comparing my children to the pig?"

"No, I just don't think you acted very responsibly."

"I am not your butler."

Silence. Then. "Could you have designed the Xeno?"

"Designing the Xeno has nothing to do with it."

"You need me, Mark. Your future is tied to me and if I get too much shit, I'll walk."

I say: "Be my guest," and hang up, then lie down on my bed. Best to plan for a new future. I pick up a copy of my novel *Mortal Belladaywic* to see how much talent I have. The story is actually getting pretty good when the phone rings.

It's Nick. He says, "Sorry, dude, I was reactionary." I try to explain about the accident, but he replies, "I don't have a million years to talk about the pig."

Okay, why not just beat him up? Just punch his lights out and get it over with? For one thing, at age forty, beating people up doesn't seem to me the be-all to end-all it once did. For another, beneath the hubris, Nick Pugh really is a very good guy. For another, I'm in too deep. At this point, we're like Siamese twins—if Nick gets cut, I bleed.

Nick is home. No investors invested in Germany and all is not well. "The telephone machine is broken, the compressor's broken, the toilet's broken, the fax is broken, my stereo's broken, the TV is broken, the band saw's broken, the clay oven is broken, the pig is broken, Henrietta and I are broken."

Henrietta has taken his gun. "She says due to my ripping the door off and going up on the roof to shoot the city—way stupid, I admit—I could go crazy and shoot her. Which is insane."

We are driving downtown. I say that he's big enough to defend himself without a gun.

"Mark, you've had fistfights. But I'm defenseless from a three hundred and eighty-pound psycho with a knife who'll rape Henrietta after he kicks my balls in. That gun made me feel a thousand percent safer. At night I hear every sound and Henrietta never locks anything and isn't afraid of anything so I have to be afraid for both of us."

Henrietta had also been busy, seeing not one guy but two—the second a TV producer. "She says she loves him even though he's boring and I'll bet she's porked him—gnarly, but which I totally deserve—I just hope she had him wear protection. Just what I need to be, dead in a bed two years from now." Though Nick sees a bright side. "The guy's a good musician—he left one of his tapes in the car and even I'll admit it was excellent, and, get this: He's got a pit bull that's completely chicken shit, but when two black guys from the school across the street saw it they ran across the parking lot yelling, 'There's a fuckin' pit bull in there!' so I do feel, in a weird way, a little more secure."

We drive back to the studio, the Xeno in the back of Debbie's Volvo station wagon. Nick's got a $250 ticket for lack of registration, his insurance has lapsed and he has no money to pay for either. "I've proved with my arguments that I love her and am not an asshole," he says, "that what I'm doing is best for us, not just me. I feel like I'm defending my soul at the gates of heaven." He vows reform. "So far my priorities have been art, work, life in that order. Now it's gotta be life, work, art." I tell him we have a $2,800 bill for the latest revision of Herman's engineering report and suggest, "Now that Herman's president maybe Herman could be persuaded to help raise the money to pay Herman."

"Herman is *president*? President of what? Our company?"

"Nick, didn't we work that out before you left?"

He says no big deal, he just forgot, and back at his studio he says oh shit, he gave his key to the maid. We wait outside, and an hour later Henrietta comes home from school. Inside something new. She has made models of satyrs for a movie, little naked clay men prance around her worktable, two with erections as long as their legs, one spinning on his hard-on like a top.

27

Via Dolorosa

A "design team leader" for Ferrari who Nick met at the Art Center comes to the studio to see the Xeno, and declaring it "the most significant new car design I have seen in years," asks Nick if he would like a job. Nick declines.

Had he accepted I would have been finished, so why am I not jumping for joy? Why does some part of me consider it my fault that he will not be a designer for Ferrari?

Our future, our path: a $4,000 Xeno five-year business plan fresh from Xeno president-to-be, Herman Drees. It begins:

GENERAL *Referring to the attached five year pro forma, the XENO business plan is based on an initial investment of $850,000. Over the five years, one prototype car is to be designed, fabricated and tested and five more cars are to be fabricated, promoted and sold. The sales price for the cars is assumed to be $500,000 each. Should these and the assumptions described in the following hold true, the plan will yield a 67.3 percent gain over the initial investment.*

I hope so. Because our other alternatives look shaky. On my phone machine at dawn, a cheery nasal voice: "You're asleep but this is my best idea ever. We buy a Russian fighter plane, a MiG-23. For ten thousand dollars. No shit. It was on CNN. I'll sell my car, my stereo, everything. Can you scare up five grand? We'll go halves. Call you tomorrow with the details."

Nick does and the details are he heard the newscast wrong, it was not $10,000 for the plane but $10,000 for a ride in the plane. He's just returned from Berkeley. A big fire. His friend Eric's parents' million-dollar home, constructed of imported Australian eucalyptus, has burned down. Nick and Eric hosed the roof until the water pressure went away and the fire was spilling down the hills and houses around them were exploding and pieces of homes were flying through the air like "burning kites."

"Whole neighborhoods burned to glowing coals. Water mains were geysering, broken gas lines were shooting flames everywhere." They climbed up the flaming hills, helicopters flying above, hearing people screaming. "It was like a combination of StairMaster and the Vietnam War. There were charred animals all over, the taillights on a Porsche we passed had turned into runny red-eye mucous, it's tires were charred away and its aluminum engine had melted and trickled down the street."

Home, Nick is worried because Herman, when asked by Jim Hansberger if he—Herman—would put a million of his own money into the Xeno, shrugged. "That'll kill us," Nick concludes.

"Herman," I say, "will shrug for us, but not lie for us."

Later he calls back. "I've got a new fuel. Hydrogen." For some reason I hear Led Zeppelin music and see a dirigible, swastikas on its tail fins, going up in a billowing ball of flame. Nick says he still can't drive and can I give him a ride to the Art Center? Neither he nor Henrietta have current licenses on their cars—in fact, Henrietta has never had any license at all.

Hydrogen. My dictionary says, "A colorless, highly flammable gaseous element, the lightest of all gases and the most abundant element in the universe. Atomic number one."

My future tied to the simplest element in the universe. It has a nice, if explosive, feel.

Nick, who has solved his license problem by forgetting about it, drives over and shows me a thank-you note to a former Swedish fighter pilot and broker, Finn Hedland, who has zoomed him around in a new commuter jet during the weekend of the Berkeley fire. Nick has written: *It was a pleasure meating you and flying on the Avanti. It is a very beutifull plain*, and when I ask how can a genius pass through a university system and spell like that, he tells me, "Slackademics—at the Art Center English was a joke. You don't have to be able to write a book to design a Chrysler, dude."

Nick has offered a new master plan. Having learned many attorneys bill by the quarter hour, he suggests we log everything we do every fifteen minutes. When I ask, Why?, he throws up his hands. "All I am is order trying to control chaos. I have to force myself into systems and schedules or I'll just blow up."

We've been invited to join an exhibition, "The Car, the Art" at The Citadel, a shopping mall museum in Los Angeles. We bill the Xeno as "a muscle car for the new millennia." Perhaps the Citadel will yield a benefactor. Who knows?

We walk down Second Street and go upstairs to Murphy's pub. We sit on the balcony above Belmont Shore four blocks from my house, where Nick spends his last dimes buying us beer. We are celebrating the fact that he may soon be homeless. While that fits in with his hippie heaven *weltanschauung*—to own nothing and use everything—it's spooky. Earlier today I was standing under a bright November sky by a bank when I heard, "This is way bogus" and saw Nick in a muraled shirt, purple jeans and the new $175 basketball shoes Henrietta bought him in Germany, gazing at a statement from the bank's cash machine as if it were a Dear John letter. "This festers. It says I'm broke."

"How much money does it say you have?"

"Minus sixty-seven cents."

Now, two pitchers history, Nick predicts he and Yetta will part agreeably and that as a bouquet to throw on the burning pyre of their dying love, Henrietta will agree to complete his lifelong romantic dream—a threesome. Nick has a "major babe" lined up. I wonder if Henrietta still has the gun.

Katie swan lakes into the kitchen, legs scissoring, her toes barely touching the linoleum. My daughter, with her sleek brown lines for legs and long tree branch feet, is in her black ballet costume. The old kitchen in our new rented house is little and she has to concentrate not to hit walls as she twirls. She has my features but as she spins, her mother's look of concentration flicks across her face. She's bringing her new best friend, the seventh grade's president of popularity, home this afternoon and Katie, I think, is auditioning for chief of staff.

I'm grazing the financial page of the *L.A. Times*. We've got to build our car before the roof caves in. It is fall 1991 and across the country forty auto dealerships a month are closing.

Nick strides through the front door and flops down on my green leather sofa and flips the pages of Herman's prospectus and says, "Four thousand dollars for something that might as well be written in Chinese." Nick then, out of nowhere, there on the couch, becomes host of a game show called *Nick's Fate* in which I am the only contestant. The questions are: *What should I do with my life? How can I get rich? How can I pay my rent? How can I be happy?* "I've been trying to love Herman's plan for a big company but I hate it. I'm an artist; a businessperson isn't who I am."

A midlife crisis at twenty-four. "People like Dean think I'm a user." Nick's eyes narrow. "Dean's great. He just wants to help. He's a momly guy. But I can't work with him. We each have too-fixed ideas."

I get up. A photograph is on the dining room table. Me at Nick's age, sitting in the driver's seat of Ken Kesey's famous bus at Kesey's house, my hair in wings touching my shoulders, a towering rag. "I can recruit a businessman," I say.

"I'm not a businessman," Nick amends, "I could sell you the *Queen Mary*. I'd hit all the *Queen Mary's* good bitchin' fun points so no matter who you were, you'd have to have the *Queen Mary*. The problem is I'd sell you the *Queen Mary* for a dollar."

Let's, I suggest, go back to Plan A: Just build one car first. "It's easier to sell a bar of soap when you have a bar of soap. Instead of just plans for a bar of soap."

Nick jerks an affirming thumb up in the air. Then says he wants to move in with us.

I say, "In with us? Debbie? Me? Katie and Matt—here?"

"In your garage. It'll be fantastic if I just act now."

Nick sees departure from the lap of Henrietta's luxury as a plus. "We were paying four hundred dollars a month for electricity and there wasn't even a heater. It was decadent. Living in your garage will be shitty at first, but I'll fix it up. Don't worry. I'm not one of—" he makes a whipping motion over his shoulders to either side of his back "—those guys."

He stands in my yard as Gideon drives up in a boxy new Volvo. Gideon's wearing a nice double-breasted Italian undertaker's suit and a tie that's a phantasmagoria. Sun and time have put lines under his eyes. He tells us he's made a new deal. Pharmatecture: "Mao's *Little Red Book* for doctors." A Unified Field Theory for Drugs, so that once a doctor has figured out what is wrong with his patient he just punches into

Gideon's Pharmatecture software program to the doses for all the needed medications.

On the way to The Citadel, on the freeway, I say, "We had to change the car because the original speed form presented big problems— money problems, aesthetic problems."

"Gid," Nick says, "to operate the covered front wheelwells could have cost one hundred thousand dollars. And that low to the ground, one bump, and the rear end would have been histo."

"Also," I say, "it would've been a rich spaceman's car—a car for Elvis to return to earth in. It was too wacky. We need to be part of an established market—racing."

Gideon frowns. "If you think you're in love with one girl, then the next day you think you're in love with another, chances are you're not in love with either one."

But at the exhibit hall, his face goes bright when he sees, mounted on a pedestal beside a Vector chassis, our slinky new model. "If I were to buy this," Gideon says, "I'd want the right to be able to drive it out of the builder's garage and smash into forty Ford Pintos as a performance arts piece."

A shadow crosses Nick's face. "I suppose you could."

"All I want to know is that I own the car free and clear."

At my front window watching Gideon ease away down the street in the rented Volvo, Nick says, "Do you believe it?"

I say, "I think."

"Gid's perfect," he exclaims. "Great taste and a huge ego. The dream come true."

We walk to the beach to buy beer. "This is the movie." Nick points out to the street. "The camera's right there."

When he leaves I eat pizza, go to bed, wake up at 3:00 A.M. thinking this is how football players must feel when they make the Super Bowl. I drink more beer, cough once, then again, then there's beer and pizza all over the floor.

The next night I pick up compact, spiffy Gideon at the Hotel Bel-Air, a white mansion tucked in the wooded hills above Sunset Boulevard. Gideon brings Laurel, a beautiful woman who is funny and has curves of pale yellow hair to the shoulders of her ankle-to-wrist-to-neck skintight black velvet cat suit. She is a saleswoman for the drug company sponsoring his antidrug campaign.

At Genghis Cohen, a dark, colorful Chinese restaurant, Nick is smitten. "A skintight cat suit," he murmurs to me. "Fuckin' A." Gideon sets the menu aside and instructs the waitress, "Just ask the chef to make us the best of what he has," and Laurel tells Nick if we need a bimbo to pose with the car, she's our girl.

Thick curls of spiced shrimp appear with a catfish in a candy sauce. Gideon says he wants Nick and me to "blow the stamp right off the envelope."

Nick, spooning up shrimp, agrees. "Yeah! We're going to power the car with hydrogen."

Gideon puts a napkin to his mouth. "Isn't hydrogen incredibly dangerous?"

"Dude!" Nick says. "It's totally the hippest, most abundant thing in the universe. Superpowerful and if we harness it, all the world's energy problems will be over," and on our way out, he confides, "A Laurel. I've always had great luck with Laurels."

Gideon flies north to confer with his attorney, his accountant, his God. Finally, an assessment: "Laurel said Nick stared deep inside her, pierced her very soul." Then: "Nick's a paper tiger—he hasn't put anything through space. If we do this, I don't want Nick designing cars under any other name and if you guys get cash off this thing, it goes to me."

"I don't blame him!" Nick exclaims. "If I were the Gid Monster I could probably make more money buying stocks blind than investing in two of the biggest risks in the world."

That would be us.

But good news, Nick definitely wants to move into my house. As a bonus, he'll bring Rooter. Nick, who won't be spending $500 a week in restaurants anymore, is shoveling down bowls of Great Grains, a cereal I have bought that per pound costs the price of T-bone steak.

"Nick," I say, as he pours dollars' worth of more cereal, "forget staring into souls. It makes people nervous."

"She said she would be my bimbo. Do you think Gideon would give me her address?"

He has downed four bowls of cereal. In the past Nick's appetite has struck me—at worst—as eerie. But now if he moves in here, I foresee him literally eating us out of house and home.

———

Debbie says she will celebrate turning forty by saying no to Rooter. "When I was twenty, I would have said yes. When I was thirty, I would have said maybe. But now, forget it."

Nick says, "I didn't say in your house, I said *at* your house. It's not like Rooter would be hanging out watching TV or anything."

When I say I agree with my wife, Nick replies that is because I don't like Rooter. Which is not true. I do like Rooter. I have grown to like him a lot. In fact, I'd like to eat him. Smack Rooter in the butt and what you feel is nothing but ham. He must be a hundred pork chops.

Kit Bowen calls. "Gideon Bosker's popping? He's going to pay for the car? Geez, Mark, I feel like a goose, every time I blink it's a whole new world."

Yes, and even more good news. A Hollywood agent has seen pictures of the car in a magazine and wants to broker the entire project. Maybe whoever this is and Gideon can become partners. Meanwhile, my friend John Case has hired Nick to design a "bike station" for Long Beach, so that cyclists can more conveniently bike to shopping and work. Nick's drawings were so good that John says he'd like to raise money for the Xeno, even though the only thing I know that he knows about cars is that I wrecked his Mercedes when we were in college.

Too, Nick has a new girlfriend. He met her in Berkeley. He shows me a picture. Tall, pretty. Her father is rich and has a polar bear mounted in their living room. "It's so big they had to cut a hole in the ceiling to make room for its head." Then he tells me, "Henrietta and I went out to eat and she said what I needed was a business major who worked in a daycare center. That's who she is, Michelle. I started crying, right there in the restaurant."

Gideon wants to talk to Portland exotic car dealer Monte Shelton, "to see if I need a back door." I tell Nick, "I can see Monte holding up a fist and saying, 'Doc, guess how many cars like this make money—this many.' See, Nick?" None of my fingers pop up.

The Hollywood agent calls back. He seems excited, in fact, panting. "I compare this car to the U.S. space program. Dynamic, beautiful, dangerous, like a spaceship."

"You want to represent the car, so—"

"No. What I'm saying is I can't help you. It's like the space program—too risky. What if I sell the car to one of my clients and it blows up, or he crashes it?"

The sound he is making, I realize, is that of a man miles into a hard ride on an Exercycle. Thank God we've still got Gideon.

"Monte did not like the look of the car. He said it's Buck Rogers. He said movie people make cars like this all the time."

I am astounded. "Gideon," I say, holding my phone to my ear, "how could you follow this for two years and then one hour with a Portland car dealer and you're ready to change your mind?"

"I'm trying to find people who think this is a good idea and don't know where they are. I'm not an auto fetishist who needs another trophy to slip inside his six-car garage. This'll take two-thirds of my real dollars. Cash is worth a lot right now."

"Gid, I have money problems too. I forgot to be a journalist last year."

"I realize you're desperate."

I hang up. Henrietta calls. "Gideon finally realized it is time to do it. He has come to the toilet and does not have the courage to take a shit."

28

WATER BOYS

The chance to propel the Xeno with a 700-horsepower engine fueled by tap water presents itself after Nick and I drive the model in its shiny aluminum box from his new tiny apartment by our house to an American Hydrogen Association meeting at Riverside Junior College. Maybe fifty people are there, a handheld calculator crowd, mostly either old or young, aging professor types or guys with smooth, pasty, student skin—and the essential message is: Hydrogen is the best fuel ever, but nobody really knows how to use it yet.

Holding a handout that reads: "Take part in the most important transformation in history . . . to a renewable solar-hydrogen economy that will last forever. The time to stand and be counted is rapidly slipping away." I am introduced to a tall, round-stomached, golf-shirted, black scientist, Harrison A. McCoy, and his colleague, a wiry Australian engineer Spiro "Ross" Spiros. With wild dark hair, jug ears and an eagle's beak for a nose, he wears a starched collarless blue-striped shirt and blue suit coat like a minister, and the first thing he says to me is, "You Americans are ten ye-ahs behind."

Ross invites Nick and me—with the Xeno model still hidden in its coffin-size box—to their laboratory.

When? I ask. Now, Ross replies. It's late, but . . .

Under stars, I sink into a mammoth, gray, disco-era Lincoln Town Car. Wheeling onto the freeway, Harrison A. McCoy, who has introduced himself as an expert in thermal waste processing systems, industrial waste water treatment, hazardous waste management, sewage waste management and recovery, the land farming of compost, biomass waste reduction management, i.e., garbage, explains, "We want power."

Before I can ask what kind, Ross says he's developed a secret way of propelling an automobile on hydrogen. I say we'd like to fuel our car with hydrogen as well. Ross peers at me over the top of the big leather passenger seat. "A'ent you afraid if you're successful the oil companies would do away with you?"

Headlights from oncoming lanes stream by us. "You mean Nick and I could end up dead on the bottom of a river somewhere?"

Ross nods solemnly. "You have no idea."

Harrison drives us to an industrial park and in a small office under liverish light, he introduces Alex DeCuir, a pale little black man in a baseball hat. Around us in his office are posters of Ferraris attended by beautiful, bikinied young women.

A year ago I might have found this scene bizarre or even vaguely scary. Now I just cut to the chase, present Nick as the top young car designer in America, recite his bona fides like the endlessly repeated lines of some ancient, oral poem and then Nick and I lug in our big aluminum box and unveil the Xeno. Ross is wowed—"My Gawd. It's almost as cool as the Vectah!"—and instantly wants all of us to be partners. He says we can fuel the Xeno not on regular hydrogen, but a "hydroxy" hydrogen. "We'll make it onboard. From watah. That's all. Watah in a fuel tank. It will be cracked and injected straight into the piston."

Wizened little Alex DeCuir tells me to follow him to his garage next door so I can see his race car. Nick and I trail Ross and back inside Alex says, "I use a five-speed Taurus motor."

"What kind of engine?" I ask, not sure how the "race car" connects with the "hydroxy."

Alex says the initials loud. It sounds like a sneeze. "Esss-aaaaaitch-OHHH!." SHO. He peers into a door-size hole in the rear end of his slab-shaped Kazara race car and says he's bought the whole Kazara company for $8,000.

The Kazara is familiar. I have, if memory serves, seen several Kazaras whizzing through the pages of various sports car magazines and—the whole company for $8,000?

"You wanta see strong? I'll show you strong." Alex, monkeylike, gets up on top of the Kazara, jumps up and down on the roof. Then he demonstrates his "revolutionary" lubricating oil—jamming the oiled tip of a screwdriver into a spinning and oiled gear to show that, thanks to the oil, nothing happens. Ross endures Alex DeCuir's spiel stoically for thirty seconds before beginning a demonstration of hydroxy gas. Two feet of flame in a bright translucent needle shoots from the stubby nozzle of a welder's torch. He heats a white hot blob on a dull white brick until it is bright as the sun.

This superheating process, he explains, is the cornerstone to his water power system, one that will change the world. We watch as the flame cuts through the high-heat resistant ceramic used to line potter's kilns. I have no idea how all this adds up, but Nick speaks for both of us when he says, "Fuckin' A."

Back in the office, I am assessing the bikinied Ferrari women when Ross takes me aside to confide, "You've come at the right time because we're raising money. We only want up to about one hundred and fifty thousand dollars seed capital to produce the prototypes and the thermal processes." He says the Xeno can become "the world's first watah-powered supahcar. It will have a range of two thousand five hundred miles."

Spiro "Ross" Spiros, among many other things on his "Air Duke Limited of Australia" vita, lists "in-depth private tuition over five years from Professor Yule Brown on the theoretical and technical constructs of Brown's gas technology." So what is Brown's gas? Hydroxy gas, I guess. But once again I can't understand half of what I read: "Remaining off-gases exit the Thermalairolator chamber into a quench chamber/scrubber where it is cooled and 'weighted' with atomized water generated by spray nozzles. This weighted effluent is drawn into the Thermal-clone wet dynamic separator and centrifuged at fifteen thousand to twenty thousand FPM."

Ross seems to think Nick and I have money and we spent the rest of the evening trying to pick each other's pockets. The next day we return to Alex DeCuir's office where the Ferrari women on the walls bathe in the light of a noontime sun.

Ross explains that Air Duke is run by Frank Spinks, the youngest man to have commanded American troops in World War II—as a seventeen-year-old lieutenant in the Australian Army, and also "the bloke who invented underpants with no seams on the sides."

I ask what happened to Yule Brown. "Is he still alive?"

Ross says, "Sort of."

Nick says, "What was his trip?"

Ross puts a hand missing fingers to his curly brow. "Brown made the first watah-powered cah. Overheated so badly it melted the cah-buretor and sucked it right out the exhaust pipe."

I ask if overheating is the only problem.

Ross says, "Only a gray area in the law of thermodynamics."

I ask, "What is it?"

"I can't tell you. It's proprietary."

Ross says their financing is on its way. I ask: When? and he looks at his watch. "Two weeks. Within three months we will have a cah that runs on watah." He then offers us 1 percent of the company for $10,000. "Because you believe, we ah giving you an opportunity. You'll be millionaires. In the history books. It'll be like being with Edison before he turned on the light. But if you want to come in, you gotta give."

"How can this foul up?" Nick asks. "Worst case?"

Ross says, "World War Three."

Minutes later, out here in the middle of industrial desert hell and gone, sitting in his Honda in front of Alex DeCuir's engine shop, Nick's head is at a diagonal, his pupils halved by his lowered brows. "Dude, this is unreal."

I have just read the Air Duke vita. The company maintains corporate offices both in San Bernardino and Sydney, Australia. It describes its chief product as a "thermal processor" that "runs on hydrogen gas and oxygen derived from water." A mix that burns so hot that it reduces all carbon-based waste to a "noncontaminated silicant."

That would be, I think, glass. The vita further claims that Air Duke's superheated "hydroxy gas" has the ability to weld aluminum. If true, that would represent a monumental technological breakthrough allow-ing, among a world of other things, John Mason to build our tube chassis from aluminum instead of steel at a weight savings of 30 percent. The vita concludes that Air Duke forecasts a $400 million return on its hydrogen patents over the next five years.

I ask Nick, "Who do we call—Shearson Lehman or the police?"

Days later I watch Ross demonstrate the power of hydroxy gas at his "lab" at Balboa Pacific, a construction company situated among a hodgepodge of old buildings across from the great long lawn of a state mental institution. He cuts through every kind of metal and even a superheat-resistant Space Shuttle tile, he finally shoots a flame through water and it cuts just as well. I invited my friend John Case along, because John is great at figuring out the essence of things. Like, when we were in college, the Vietnam War: "They don't want us there. We're going to lose."

We meet Frank Spinks. Quiet, friendly, Spinks doesn't look like a shyster. He explains that Air Duke has teamed with Grano, a huge waste management company. Grano has given Ross lab space. Spinks is in the United States to meet investors. Air Duke's meal ticket is superheated hydrogen able to cook polluted soil clean at the rate of $40 a ton. Evidently Ross's hydroxy burners are able to break almost all waste—including nuclear and medical "red bag" waste—down to little more than carbon or glass.

Ross gave me a copy of the Grano annual report. A "waste management" company, their list of clients reads like the top half of the Fortune 500: Boeing, General Electric, McDonnell Douglas, Union 76. Yesterday I called Grano and had "Spiro Spiros" paged. "Mr. Spiros will be right with you," the receptionist trilled. I offered to pick Ross up after work—he still worries about driving on "the wrong side" of the street—and when I got to the big Grano building he was clearly ensconced in a lab, where prototypical engineering types in short-sleeved white shirts and narrow ties bantered with him like he was a long lost pal. Grano is dead-center corporate America, and it has been my experience that corporate America doesn't kiss up to con men. Ross vows he can finance our car by cooking garbage. "Forty dollars a ton, fifty tons an hour. Two thousand dollars times eight equals sixteen thousand dollars a day."

After his show-and-tell, Ross takes off with Frank Spinks and driving home I ask John Case, "Do you think this is for real?" John's face gets the look of pain it takes just before he addresses a dicey issue. "Off center as he looks, Ross is onto something, but I bet there are problems. Maybe patent problems. Otherwise they wouldn't be trying to beat money out of the bushes."

"What bushes?"

"You and Nick."

29

THE BRIGHT SIDE

Sitting outside at Hamburger Henry's restaurant down the street from my house, Harrison A. McCoy shows me news clippings documenting that he is descended from the original "real McCoy," Elijah McCoy, Harrison's great-great-grandfather, the son of a slave and an inventor who patented (patent number 646,126) the automatic lubricator cup, allowing machinery to be lubricated automatically for the first time. Such a success that it lead to a demand for the device as "the real McCoy."

Here at breakfast, Ross has offered us his biography: He was born on a banana ranch among poisonous snakes in northern Australia. He grew up, enlisted seventy of his relatives in a hydrogen gas scheme orchestrated by his mentor, the brilliant but diabolically short-sighted Yule Brown, who blew all their money on lawyers to protect his patents. Now Ross laments, "I'm ovah here trying to get my family's money back."

When I ask him to begin at the beginning, he says the banana ranch stood before a long cliff fifteen stories high. He remembers flying foxes, wombats, blowflies, chickens, the snakes all over, his "barracks" bedroom where he slept with his two brothers and three sisters under a veil of mosquito netting. He remembers his dad cutting a lamb's throat, slitting the lamb's skin above a hoof and putting his mouth to the wound. His father blew into it, the lamb's skin ballooned away from its muscle, making the animal easy to skin. He remembers the muscle cut to chunks, marinated in lemon, oregano and salt, and nailed through on rods as thick as a finger and a yard long and barbecued over open fires. He remembers the time a poisonous brown snake slithered through the kitchen window and his mother hit it so hard with a broom that "its vertebrae jumped out of its skin." He remembers too their neighbor Mr. Lee, who "carried around auto parts in a coffee bag and then suddenly there was a motor."

Ross grew up, became a Rev Head. His first car was a 1964 EJ Holden panel truck with a mattress in the back, his second a 1973 Tarana Holden, an Australian Chevrolet equipped with a 202-cubic-inch straight six. Ross installed triple Weber carburetors and bigger valves for more air and gas, he ported and shaved the heads for more compression, installed a racing cam shaft, dual exhausts, a one-ton truck clutch, an Alfa Romeo five-speed transmission and a K-Max suspension system. Then at work at a bank safe factory, he lost all but the little finger on his left hand feeding a waxy bar of lubricant into a metal saw. The saw's teeth caught the bar, yanked it forward and Ross's fingers were gone.

When his hand healed, he drag raced. His Chevy would kangaroo—it's rear tires jumping as they lost traction and spun—but beat Fords. He lost engines. One blew a bearing, the crankshaft seized, a piston blew out. He overrevved another and same story. The car was stolen after engine number three.

Ross was driving a cab when his old "bikie" pal Colin Freckleton burbled up beside him on his Harley Davidson and suggested the two open a bar in Knights Cross. It was constructed with low-cost bikie labor, the Double D. But when it was complete, the bikies didn't want to leave. They wanted to stay and drink up the profits. So Ross dressed the bikies up in black waistcoats, black hats (each with a feather in it) and made them bartenders and bouncers. Pimps, prostitutes, American sailors and $600 in the back pocket every night. When the authorities threatened to shut him down, Ross sold out, met Yule Brown, who claimed he could weld brick through the miracle of hydroxy hydrogen, aka Brown's gas, and Ross shot from cabdriver/drag racer/bar owner to investment counselor. To investors Ross counseled: Invest a bundle. "This was back ten years ago in the boom days when you could sell a million shares in a cockroach crawling up a wall. We had three million dollars right there in our hot little hands, when Brown, who'd been jailed in his native Bulgaria for his reactionary political views, refused to issue a prospectus. On grounds of sublimation versus vaporization of tungsten. He refused to change one word . . . the ratbag!"

Sublimation or vaporization? Before I can ask, Ross is on with his story: Brown flew to Japan. No word for a year, then the Bulgarian mastermind phoned Ross up, suggesting they try again. The waters "now muddy" in Australia, Ross decided to "float the whole thing off the Tasmanian stock exchange. A million dollars worth of stock." Enter ruddy Frank Spinks. The youngest man to command American troops in World War II, inventor of those underpants. Frank bought thirty thousand shares. The rest, as they say, is history.

Ross says he likes my beach neighborhood, and, in fact, is going to live here. Dressed in denim and seated under a warm winter sun he— wallet flopped open—tries and tries to give Henrietta money after she paid for his omelette, then reveals friction in their partnership with Alex DeCuir. Alex, Ross claims, is a loose cannon. For example, embarrassed about his lack of formal education, Alex, Ross says, compensates by telling people he's in the Mafia.

After breakfast, Ross and Harrison and I go apartment hunting. It appears Ross has been living out of the Lincoln. "This is getting a bit difficult," he says. I notice that he has walked off the sides of the heels on his old brown wingtips.

"Ross," I say, "we've only been looking twenty minutes."

Ross says that to make the Xeno "run on watah" he'll "crack" the water into hydrogen and oxygen, pump it into the combustion chambers and fire it with spark plugs. But how to crack the water? Electrolysis, using an onboard electrical system? That would—by some recollection I have from high school chemistry—take as much energy as it produced. What, then, is his formula? Ross says he can't say. "That's the billion-dollah secret, lad."

Down by the ocean we spot, across the street from the huge tavern called Yankee Doodles, a two-story apartment building. The owner, an old cigarette-smoking woman named Ernie, whose father started Best Western hotels, takes Ross upstairs to a studio. Seeing a floor, four walls, a ceiling, he says, "I'll take it." Ernie likes her new tenant so much she cuts $100 off his rent.

My friend and ex-private detective Chuck, who is now in the drug detection business and wants to hire Nick to lend "curb appeal" to his new line of urinalysis machines, says, "It's a scam. Trace the black guy, McCoy. If he's been around the environmental world for twenty years he's left tracks. Call the California Air Resources Board, the South Coast Air Quality Management District, Cal Edison, the EPA's Office of Technology Assessment. Ask 'em: Who the hell is Harrison A. McCoy?"

But I don't. Why not? I spent years off and on as an investigative reporter, going after heroin dealers and bad politicians, and I do not mind tracking people down. But Harrison A. McCoy is the picture of straight, and it would seem like a shameful and even risky betrayal—I call Joe Blow at the EPA and the first thing he does when he gets off the phone is to call Harrison and say, "Guess what, McCoy, some guy named Christensen just asked me if you were a con man." On the other hand, perhaps I just don't want to know that these people are a mirage, because without the mirage, what have we got? Air Duke is the only game in town.

Or maybe not. Gideon calls with news he's made a killing in the stock market and claims he can finance us after all. Fine. But John Mason wants to start right now. He's building two Indy 500 cars soon that could delay the building of our chassis until spring. I tell Gideon we can do little else until the chassis is completed and he replies $250,000 is a lot of money and he cannot be rushed.

Meanwhile, the exotic market is crashing of its own weightlessness. Cars that went for $500,000 last year suddenly beg for half that now. Christmas morning. Downtown Long Beach. I am looking for earache medicine for Matt. A black man with the Rosetta stone shaved on the back of his head is making a complicated condom deal with an old lady pharmacist who has hair spun up above her narrow face like white cotton candy. When I get home I see that Matt's bedroom is a wrecking yard of new cars, his haul: a fleet of tiny exotics. Debbie bought two dozen Ferraris, Lamborghinis and Porsches in a blister pack on sale for $4.99.

The new year. Harrison took me by his house over the weekend and if he's a con man, I'm a girl. Harrison dresses like Andy Williams: sweater, golf shirt, slacks. His house is neat as a scalpel, he has a beautiful wholesome-as-fresh-milk wife. It was just too black *Ozzie and Harriet* for words.

But a car that runs on water?

Harrison, Nick, Ross and I drive the model to Palm Springs to the home of an ancient Hollywood playboy—pal to the Sinatras, Howard Hughes and Harrison. Very old, tan and handsome—Don Juan from the crypt—and married to an ex-model half his age, he declares, "Nick could be the new Raymond Loewy." He's seeing Lee Iacocca this weekend and suggests Chrysler can foot our bill. Good, because Gideon just found out he's going to have to pay $78,000 in income taxes and can I find another investor to go halves on the car? I say that this is unbelievable. He replies, "I can't let your considerations get in the way."

Nick says, "Look at the bright side, if Gideon bails we've still got Ross."

No money from the old Palm Springs playboy and Nick's family farm is in jeopardy: "Grace Metalious wrote about my family in *Peyton Place* and forty years later they're all still doing the same wacky shit." Namely, battling each other over lovers and property rights. And here in a tavern by his tiny new apartment, Nick worries he's a meaningless speck in a godless universe and if we can't start building the car by April—a month from now—he "just can't do this." He makes a gun of his fingers, sticks it to his head and wags his thumb. "I've thought about killing myself."

"Over building the Xeno?"

"Mark, you have other things. No unqueer guy in a million wouldn't want Debbie for a wife. But all I've got is this." He taps his head. "One hundred and fifty designs for cars just as good as the Xeno are trapped inside there. But they can't get out until the Xeno gets out, and meanwhile all I see is the progress from me to you to that rotting old man."

At Yankee Doodles, seated above a green felt grid of pool tables in a tavern bigger than a gymnasium, Spiro "Ross" Spiros in a Levi's jacket worn over his THE GREENHOUSE EFFECT—THE HEAT IS ON T-shirt says, "The secret is that I'm simple. Do you think I could have designed that game oveah there?" He waves toward a *Terminator II* pinball game. His mouth drops in incredulity. "Nevah! My genius is I only see the obvious. The watah-powered car is as simple as, why is a wheel round?"

"But what is it?" I ask. A tiny waitress in shorts tight as a second skin sets down beers. Ross, his brow furrowed above his nose as if one side of his mind were battling the other, replies, "I cahn't tell you. There's too much at stake," then adds that what we need to spearhead our plan to build a race car that runs on tap water is the "perfect Jew."

Why? "Because, Jews control the politics, the media and the money." He shows me a dollar bill. "Before 1977, there were stars from the flag up there, now it's the Star of David."

I say I grew up with Jews and never noticed a conspiracy or that they are bad.

"My God, Mahk! I don't say they're bad, just in control." The solution? A stitch in time. "Arabs, Israelis. Get rid of the lot. Nuke 'em all. Turn the sand to glass."

"You mean obliterate the entire Middle East?" I ask. "Nuke little kids, women?"

Ross lifts his beer glass, drinks. "Mahk, I don't mean it puhrrsonally. I would hate to kill a fly! But if we don't do something the Arabs and Israelis will be the flash point to apocalypse, the end of us all."

Nick, sick, burning with fever, his brain cooking in the frying pan of his skull, says, "I know the secret." I go see him in his new tiny apartment down the street from my house above Dodd's Bookstore. He's rebuilt the place. It looks great, like the inside of a polished wooden submarine, and now his life is at arm's reach: bed, studio, kitchen, bathroom. A stack of French bread, a block of cheese and a jar of Ragu spaghetti sauce has been breakfast, lunch and dinner for a week. He eats oranges so he won't get scurvy.

"Ross told me the equation so I can do the patent drawings. I could tell you the whole formula in three sentences. Three." He raises three fingers. "It's more like *cooking* than chemistry but it's going to change the world."

"She's Wendy," Ross tells me, his eyes filling up. He has just met my wife. "Same curls, same angel face. She's the spittin' image of the love of my life, my Wendy. Yah Deborah's even bought the same cahpet." He points to an Indian rug on our living room floor.

"What happened?" I ask.

"To what?" Ross replies, still staring at our rug.

"To the love of your life, Wendy."

Ross blinks, as if waking from a trance. "Mahk, I spent my whole life trying to impress her and, finally, she said enough. 'Ah'm taking ahr cat and going someplace else. Ah can't live on yah dreams anymore.' Ah've never been so crushed. My hand." He holds it up. "Those fingahs were nothin'. Don't evah lose yah Deborah, you won't find anothah."

Ross says we must hide his technology before it's too late. I feel bad for him. In his spacious 1974 Lincoln Town Car—it has less a dash-

THE BRIGHT SIDE / 211

board than a wall in front of the driver that is embedded with gauges—
Ross tells me about his new American social life. Dial-a-date. So far
he's had two. "A black one, and a blonde one. The blonde was a stone
overweight but, oh, what eyes." Then he tells me Yule Brown is in
league with the Red Chinese. That the People's Republic has five hundred engineers working to steal the secret of Ross's water cell.

Before Ross and I left this morning, my Ross-adored wife asked me:
What if Ross is crazy? "Not babbly crazy or seeing-Jesus crazy, but just
deluded crazy?" Possibly, but as John Case says, "There are a lot of
deluded crazy people in the movie and computer business who are making money hand over fist. Ross has got to show his real hand sooner
or later, why not just wait him out?"

So, I figure, why not tag along. At Suppose U Drive, we rent a truck
with a bed as big as my living room and head to Ross's lab across from
the beautiful long green lawns of the state mental institution at Balboa
Pacific, an old garage with red diamonds with the word DANGER written
in foot-tall letters posted on every wall. Grano has moved Ross here
because of the "hydrogen detonation possibility." On a big old table
are fat brown bottles marked ALUMINUM SULFIDE, POTASSIUM PER-
MAGENATE, and a strew of dirty test tubes.

He has a last experiment before we go, to do with his brand-new
pyramid-shaped "Mini-Mega-Furnace." Ross asks me to step back in
case of an explosion. Designed to create superheat, the pyramid was
constructed by Ross and a truck driver pal, it is made out of steel plates,
filled with "poured refractory material," weighs sixty pounds and cost
$27. It has been designed by Ross to be the hottest hydrogen furnace
ever built and is hooked to an ignition transformer. The glow is too
bright to watch. Ross has got the sun on the side of a brick. "Look
out," he warns, "water dissociates at a hundred degree Celsius," he says.
"You get a back burn—the flame shoots back off brick."

The pyramid looks like a real version of a fake invention from some
old late-night horror movie on channel 666. Worried that he might be
nabbed by a supposedly-in-the-United-States Yule Brown, Ross built it
on the run, mostly out of the back of the Lincoln. All it appears to be,
essentially, is four triangular plates of steel welded together around a
heat-absorbing brick hollowed at the center.

Suddenly, *bang! Whooooosh, buuuuzzz.* Its triangular surfaces insulated
and still cool, Ross lifts the pyramid up. It looks like a little rocket
engine. "It's two thousand degrees in there," he says. "It exploded the
first time, I thought I'd blown the whole guts of it out."

His goal is to "kill molecules." The hotter the pyramid gets, the better. Were it to destroy itself, by Ross's lights that would be great news. "I want to achieve meltdown, so carbon and water will be the ultimate and only end products."

It is Friday the thirteenth. We've loaded nine very heavy "Brown's gas" electrolysis machines into the truck. Each is as big as an office safe and doubtless weighs as much. Pulling them across the bed of the truck, one after another, I feel like a new Sisyphus. High above the road, I drive us toward Henrietta's. Though she and Nick are, as Nick puts it, "histo," she has agreed to let Ross "hide" the electrolysis equipment at her new apartment.

Ross says Yule Brown's Chinese Communist pals may be trying to track us down. "Brown's already found me by phone—though he doesn't know exactly where I am—and has demanded a meeting. I refused so he's got his Commie minions looking all ovah fah me." The secret, he says, is to get out of the waste stream and into the art stream. "Everybody knows everybody in waste, all over the world. But nobody in waste knows anybody in art."

I say, "You mean Chi-Coms could be tailing us right now?"

Ross looks over his shoulder. "Would be a bit rude, wooden it?" He adds that he has just had a nightmare in which the water-cracking fuel cell we are about to construct blew up, and he, Nick and I all were staggering around with shards of cast iron hanging off our faces. "I woke up screamin'."

I park the truck in Nick's old parking lot. We're walking four flights up exterior stairs made out of steel mesh to Henrietta's new apartment when Ross sags against the brick wall and says, "Oh mah Gawd." I ask what's wrong and he says, "It's me fear of heights," and he scoots around the corner and in the door.

Ten minutes later we slide Ross's big, boxy iron hydrogen-making machines off the back of the truck. I push the first one but gravity welds it to the sidewalk. Ross shoves the metal tongue of the dolly we've trucked along under a corner of each machine, and we push-pull them across the sidewalk, through the front door of Henrietta's building and to the industrial elevator that serves her new fifth-floor studio. By the time we haul them all up Ross looks as if he has climbed, clothed, out of a swimming pool. "Ya think the ancient Egyptians coulda moved stones this way, you're barmie."

"Well," I say, "then who built the Pyramids?"

"Aliens."

Ross says Nick and I are the only "honest Yanks" he knows, that all he really wants is to go home to his girlfriend Wendy a hero, but that if he's killed first he'll make sure the secret ends up safe with us. "Then all the glory can be yours."

30

LOST

I love Spiro "Ross" Spiros like a brother but *what exactly is going on here?* This much is obvious: *If you have a method to fuel the world's automobiles on water, as these people apparently believe Spiro "Ross" Spiros does, you and yours will end up making Bill Gates look like a paper boy.*

But is that even remotely possible? Or is Ross, if not crazy, a figment of his own imagination?

I don't think so. He's just too *literal* for that. Are these people fools? Unlikely. One of the engineers at the end of the table went to Annapolis and has commanded a destroyer—and he seems to enjoy a rather *junior* position here—and if Ross is a hallucination, steely Frank Spinks looks as real as a colostomy bag.

Not far from Hollywood at Sam's Hoffbrau, a *manque* of a German beer hall, at a table long enough to seat the Last Supper, Ross announces the results of a vital test. "My solution stayed in reaction for fifteen hours." That is, his "secret formula" produced hydrogen and oxygen from water for over half a day. Meaning hydrogen and oxygen can be shot straight into the combustion chamber of an engine and ignited. "Twenty gallons of watah in your cah! You can drive across the country for twenty-five cents."

Nick has been put on the Air Duke payroll at $400 a week, plus promised $20,000 of free Air Duke stock, to do patent drawings for the hydroxy burners Air Duke is marketing to the waste industry and Ross says my about-to-be-bequeathed Air Duke stock could put my kids through college.

When Nick asked, "What if Dow Corning discovered wireless hydroxy cell technology in 1956 and put it in a box?" Ross grinned.

"The multiple plate patents are held by Yule Brown, not Dow Corning." So nobody has ever done this before? "Nobody in this solar system," he replied. "Why lads? Everybody's afraid of hydrogen. Brown took his machines to NASA and when he told them how he made hydrogen they booted him off the premises."

Evidently, a pattern. Now Balboa Pacific, like Grano before it, has given Ross and his experiments the heave-ho. "We've had to be gypsies, people are terrified of the hydrogen oxygen cocktail!"

Here at the beer hall, Ross declares that we must immediately build the Xeno II. He brings out diagrams he has drawn up, showing his water fuel system would provide the Xeno a range of thirty-five hundred miles while generating almost 300 horsepower.

In what context outside Southern California could you make a spiel like that and not clear the room? But these people are engineers and businessmen who had filled a part of the parking lot outside with their Mercedes and BMWs and, to one degree or another, they all defer to Spiro "Ross" Spiros.

I say that what we want is for Air Duke to contract Nick and me to build the Xeno at a cost not to exceed $250,000, not including the Air Duke water propulsion system.

Frank, bearish and casual, says, "We'll do the water fuel cell as soon as we can. My job is to ensure profit; the worst thing we could do now is press forward with something fantastic and fall flat on our face. Right now we must do waste. We must get the burner up and running, have a sure formula for making money."

Nick, in baggy purple pants and a T-shirt advertising a Mexican bar and grill, his fists clenched on either side of his cornbeef sandwich, exclaims, "But you could just *wipe out* the oil companies!" The thrill of this thought has made Nick look fourteen.

"I'm not sure we want to," Frank says, rubbing his nose. "The car is essential but the question is, What do we do and when. The car represents a tremendous cost."

I can see us through Frank Spinks's eyes. We have reverted to type. Nick the kid, Ross the curly-haired Greek UFO whackologist and me— the tall, angry-looking stranger in the corner. He says, "Finish the fuel cell and prove it, then we'll give you a letter of intent."

"There is nothing," Ross insists, "on this device that Jules Verne could not have constructed one hundred years ago. Any fool could build one of these."

But he's worried back voltage created during the reaction could ignite the hydrogen as it is being created and blow us up. When Nick suggests we use Kevlar to create the cell walls, Ross replies, "Forget that. I don't want chunks of plastic hanging out the side of my head. We'll give it a chance to blow up in steel first."

At R. G. Dunbar Enterprises, Machine Shop, Welding Shop, Welding & Repair, the smog is so bad the sky is a screen. Inside are big dim machines. A Shibaura Horizontal Boring machine, a World War II–vintage Boye & Emmes lathe—one part weighs thirty-five thousand pounds. There, Ross builds the water cell out of thick pipe. Its basic structure appears simple. Aluminum plates, spaced a fraction of an inch apart, will be set in a stack in a cylinder. Water, in a solution with a secret third ingredient, will run through this cylinder, react with the aluminum and separate into hydrogen and oxygen that will fuel the car.

Construction eats the day. Driving home, Ross tries to decide whether or not we should stop at a topless bar while, as well, handicapping his chances of winning a Nobel Prize.

Ross tells me the secret while shooting pool at Yankee Doodles. It's water plus aluminum in reaction with caustic soda.

"The same," Nick enthuses, "formula I used to make hydrogen in high school! Ross just went the absolute obvious way, that's all. Kids learn about it every day in chemistry class."

Oh. So every halfway awake sixteen-year-old chemistry student knows how to create endless free energy? It seems implausible but, bottom line, I suppose it'll either work or it won't. Jesus either rises from the dead and we start Christianity or he doesn't and we don't. The idea is to test the cell in the new Air Duke shop in Fontana and see if it works or explodes.

We go to Suppose U Drive to get a truck to move the fuel cell equipment and Frank Spinks's credit card doesn't work. Nick whispers, "This really scares me."

"So what?" I say, "I've blown up plenty of credit cards."

"That's why," he says, climbing into the backseat of the Lincoln, "I wouldn't want somebody like you running our business."

Ross slides behind the driver's seat, looks in his rearview mirror and says to Nick's reflection, "Ooooh, that's rude."

Nick reaches over the seat and whacks me on the shoulder, "No offense. But Ross: Mark and I are artists. Not businessmen!"

Ross grips the steering wheel with his hand and a half. "If you were rich you wouldn't put up money to build your own cah?"

Nick wags his head. "I don't care how much money I had, I wouldn't want me to fund a project like this."

"You mean if you had five hundred thousand dollars and you asked you to loan yourself what you needed, you wouldn't give yourself the money?"

Ross says when we "activate" the cell it may explode and, "Just a warning, lads, we could all be killed."

"We'll end up dead or in jail," Nick says. "Ross doesn't understand that every goddamn community in the United States requires permits to use hydrogen. Air Duke is so mixed up, like a Mr. Potato Head with the mouth, noses and eyes in all the wrong places."

At the new Air Duke lab in Fontana—a big garage, basically—Ross fires up the pyramid. It hits 1,700 degrees in thirty-seconds. A flower of flame shooting out the bottom. Full throttle. Flame rolls up the side in a puff of smoke. "Twenty-one hundred and climbing," he cackles. "Nobody does this. Too dangerous. They haven't got the nerve. Tomorrow, lads, if you've got the guts, we test the cell."

31

BOOM

Zooming the 605 Freeway in his Lincoln, Ross takes his chin in his wrecked hand and allows, "I need a billion, no more." He's angry at Harrison, who has told me that General Motors is building a water fuel cell and that if Ross doesn't get his butt in gear all will be lost.

Ross says the furnace may hit 3,000 degrees. "Once you reach two thousand seven hundred thirty-two Fahrenheit, you break the bonding electron, no compound can survive. A hydrocarbon becomes hydrogen and carbon. I've got a funny feeling the temperature may go to fusion."

"Meaning what?" I ask.

"Fusion is the sun, my friend, the ultimate force. We can get a flame so hot we'll burn water. It'll either work today or we'll both be blown to Kingdom Come."

We're headed to the new "refurbished" lab in Fontana. Driving too fast over desert mountains, Ross recalls his buddy Tom King, a bikie married to a prostitute who gathered $500 worth of aluminum cans to buy stock in Air Duke. "You're a might scared, I imagine?" Ross grins.

"Oh no," I reply, "not me."

Perhaps in an effort to stabilize my pulse, he reflects on the evolution of his gene pool. "Greeks marrying Greeks. My father's sister married Mr. Hedger, Mr. Hedger's brother had a son that married my sister. Eventually I noticed all my aunties were a little silly, inbreds!"

If I didn't know better, I'd say the new lab's "refurbishing" has revolved mostly around a lot of sweeping and the tacking up of DANGER signs everywhere. I look at the cell. It appears no more complex than a flush toilet, a simple maze of pumps and chambers. But something is wrong. Ross is getting energy through the Voltameter, the needle quivers upward when he attaches it to the aluminum discs at the heart of the fuel cell. At first he thinks it's "fielding" not a short, but creating its own magnetic field because of leaks. The seals are metric, the holes made to accommodate them in the plate, Imperial.

Nick drives up. It turns out the short was caused by caustic soda on Ross's hands and Ross, after inspecting the cell one last time, announces, "Lads, we're ready to rock and roll. She's all tight. The plates are off a bit but the gas won't know."

Ross turns on the hydroxy machine, touches wires together, the wires throw sparks and there is a big loud rag of light. "Well, I've got powah!" he nods.

He says he wants to go for a 10 percent solution, "Ta maximize production, but minimize heat—if that doesn't work I'll go all the way up to a twenty-five percent, whatever it takes."

I tell Ross to be careful with the caustic.

Ross says, "Ah, you *are* frightened."

I reply if it gets in your eye, you can lose it.

"Where'd you hear that? It's just glorified salt."

Unglorified Drano would be more like it.

We put a blue plastic bucket on a scale and measure in twenty pounds of water, two pounds of caustic. Ross screws a regulator into the cell to control back pressure and a pressure gauge into the cell as well, then cuts, for some reason, into the fat electric wire from the pump that will keep water circulating through the cylinders. "What's the positive color in this country?"

Nick and I shrug. And Ross says, "Let's assume black, it's the most dramatic." He splices wires together.

I call Debbie; she says my Uncle Bert, who not only has a Ph.D. in chemistry but who *taught* Ph.D.s in chemistry, says the fuel cell is "lethal," that making free hydrogen is insane—and that she's keeping the recording I left on our phone answering machine when I called earlier and said that I loved her.

"Could you and Nick please just come home?" she asks. "Your uncle said what you guys are going to do is completely, stupidly dangerous."

I tell her we'll be fine and that we'll be home soon, and not to worry.

Nick and Ross screw in the "view tube," a clear plastic cylinder that will allow us to see the solution moving through the cell. Ross says, "I've had these tubes to a thousand psi, they swell like balloons but don't blow up."

I find a funnel and pour water into the cell. Ross pumps hydrogen in from a Brown's gas Hydroxy machine to check for leaks, water pees out the top of a view chamber. I notice, standing near Ross, that there is fabric under the curling hairs at the crown of his head and realize he's wearing a wig.

The regulator won't work and Ross, for the first time, looks worried. "You can make as many errors as you want with watah, but not with caustic." He plugs in the pumps and his knifed-together juncture of wires skyrockets in sparks and, *whump*, a blinding flash.

Nick says, "Fuck!"

"We just blew a breaker," Ross says and sighs. "That's all."

Down the street, I get carded at a 7-Eleven. I think the chubby cashier is making a joke. I say, "Lady, I'm forty-three years old."

"Honey," she says and smiles to show tank-trap teeth, "beer is beer and you look young to me." Outside in the parking lot, Nick is not happy. "This festers. Ross shorts out another wire with free hydrogen in the room and, dude, good-bye us."

"Well," I say.

He pulls the ring tab on a Coors. Foam rolls over the top of his hand. "Want to just bolt? Your uncle's probably right, and Ross is obsessed, he'll do it whether he kills us or not."

"I don't know," I reply, looking up at the stars. No answer there. "I guess, in for a penny, in for a pound."

Or more than that. I've got to see if this works, or not. Otherwise, I'll be hostage to whatever story Ross chooses to tell, if he manages to survive.

Back at the lab, Ross runs a line off the fuel cell to a blowtorch: if hydrogen is created from the water within the cell, it will fuel the torch. Declining Coors, in gloves, he pours caustic into the cell and plugs in the pump. Nick says, "The pressure's increasing."

Ross peers at the gauge. "By God, we've got a reaction. There's watah backing up, feel this line, it's heavy as a snake."

"Why don't we have face shields?" Nick asks.

Ross frowns, shrugs. Inside the cell something is making a noise, like fine faraway radio static. The hand on the pressure gauge is ticking up a pound a minute. Ross touches the side of the cell, says, "No heat."

Nick says, "Light the torch."

Ross says, "Wait," then kneels in front of the cell, touches wires from the Voltameter to both terminals. "No current."

The pressure gauge ticks to 31 psi. I touch the belly of the cell. Ross grins when I say it feels as warm as a girl. The gauge goes to 41 psi.

Nick says, "Something's happening in there. We're cruisin'. Forty-two, forty-four."

I suggest, "Light it."

Ross's good hand stabs into his front pocket, he pulls out a Bic, snaps the lighter's flint. He sets a drop of flame against the needle nose of the torch, twists the valve and there is a flowery flame. Nick says, "Holy shit."

Ross says, "This cure your doubts, lads?"

He leans over, gazes into the flame. "This is a straight hydrogen flame. This is ideal. This is what we need. *The ideal*."

Nick looks at the pressure gauge, says, "Forty-seven pounds, foooorteee-nine!"

Ross says, "Pressure means fuck all, Nick."

The needle on the gauge quivers up to sixty pounds per square inch. I read the temperature gauge, say, "Nine hundred fifty-eight."

Nick says, "This is more fun than ten blonde babes being in love with you all at once."

Ross, holding the torch, says, "Well, more fun than six."

The flame pops with little stars. The flame turns blue.

I say, "One thousand seven hundred fifteen."

Ross says, "It's too hot. We're makin' too much gas too quick." Ross kills the flame, looks down to his creation, takes a wrench, pops the bolts securing the horizontal stack of plates to the fuel cell, twirls them free one by one. Steam pours out around the gasket in thick white strings.

Then Ross gets down on his hands and knees before the cell, instructs, "Stand back." I ask why and his eyes go round. "Good God. We have no idea what's actually in there. This soup could be deadly, lads."

Nick puts his hands on his hips. "I thought you said it wasn't poisonous."

Ross looks up. "How the hell would I know?"

Ross slides the plates from the cell. A dirty steam pours up around us. I take a screwdriver and touch the edges, they are still sharp, look only sooty. Ross says, "Put this in the cah—just two hundred pounds of these cells and we'll do a thousand miles on one fuel tank of watah! We've severed the cord to the UFOs!"

I say, "Huh?"

"We've done it, lads!" Ross exclaims. "Free hydrogen!" He grabs a yellow cylinder of Coors and finally begins to drink.

32

SOCIAL DISTORTION

On our TV, Daffy Duck is giving Porky Pig the business, and Ross declares he loves cartoons because of the way they break the mass inertia laws. Air Duke has made a deal with the Queen of Tahiti—her island will energize itself burning its garbage with hydroxy gas at superheats Ross is determined to achieve. I ask how it's going. He grimaces, "So-so. We got to twenty-eight hundred degrees Fahrenheit."

"But isn't," I ask, "twenty-eight hundred over the threshold that breaks all compounds to their base elements?"

"That's right!" Ross's eyes are saucers. "I'm so tired I missed that. Mahwk, you're going to make me rich."

"You gave away the secret?" Nick, in my kitchen, is livid. "That's like breaking the law." Nick has turned down a "lucratively huge" job to design a rocket mural for the Johnson Space Center in Houston to work for Air Duke. Who have nothing for him to do. Driving back from the lab in Fontana, Nick said it bugged him getting paid $400 a week just to stand around. It bugs me worse not getting paid $400 a week just to stand around. People who have southern accents and names like Mrs. Fairchild and Mr. Hooks leave summons on my phone machine to "call about an important business matter." Yesterday, I did. American Express wants their $7,000 back.

The other day Nick said he feared someone will build a waterpowered car before we do. "The Japanese built one in 1928 that drove six hundred miles using the same technology."

"What kind of car was it?" I asked.

"No kind," Nick replied. "They just built it on paper."

"And drove it the six hundred miles in their minds."

"Yeah," he agreed, "but it's the same formula. Ross says if anybody just reads the standard academic book he read about it in, they could do it because it's all there in black and white."

"So Ross'd have to snatch the book out of every college library in the country to return our formula to secrecy?"

I got a quick, hooded, diagonal glance that says: Fool, you refuse to buy the dream, and today when I say that I told my uncle the water + aluminum + claustic formula because we have to know what's going on, he barks, "We're artists! Not scientists. Let Ross fuck up or not. It's his secret."

"Nick," I say, "you told your mom."

Nick appears incredulous. "Because that's who she is."

"My uncle is a highly respected chemist."

Nick hits our kitchen counter. "Who'll see that formula and know he's hit the jackpot."

"He's an eighty-year-old man, he's not gonna—"

"I don't care how old he is. He takes one look at the formula, sees how to solve the whole world's energy problem and Ross is histo. You betrayed his trust. I can't believe it."

Nick's mother's boyfriend Ed, a scientist at the brink of discovering a cure for scar tissue, says Ross's formula may have great promise, but last week my Uncle Bert, the former head of the chemistry department at Oregon State, showed up at my door with my cousin Jerry. White hair brushed back off his high forehead, smiling, his old eyes long and narrow, his cheeks wide and tan, Uncle Bert could have been a Scandinavian Chairman Mao. He looked at Ross's formula and laughed. "Markie, don't put your name on the prospectus and if they've agreed to pay you, take nothing but cash."

Ross booms into my house in denim head to foot, his big eyes owlish and his complete hand on his nylon curls. "Bit of a dust up with the Queen of Tahiti, she's not really the queen, but the crown princess—twenty-two and gorgeous, gorgeous, gorgeous. The pyramid blew up in her face. Worst hydrogen accident I've had in years. No need to get alarmed! She wasn't harmed."

I say that we need $200 to make a new quarter-scale model and Ross says I've got to learn to be patient. I ask him to follow me outside. We walk to the back of my house, where I kick open the garage door. "Do you know what this is?"

"A very nice Porsche." Ross blinks. "Ooooh. You're not suggesting we rip out the engine and—"

"No, you numbskull, it was a wedding present from my parents— I've had it for thirteen years but I'll have to sell it if you don't get off the dime and get us some money quick."

At Hamburger Henry's, Nick declares he needs a lot of power to affect global change, but is paranoid that oil companies will find out about the water cell and rip it off. I say I'm paranoid journalists will find out about the water cell and expose us as cold fusion junior. My Uncle Bert says the cell will produce enough poisonous waste to create a little rolling Chernobyl. Nick's face darkens. "What if the cold fusion guys punked out not because they were full of shit, but from being silenced by the oil companies?"

Across the street sexy hairdressers from Shear Pleasure stand looking like they can't decide whether to hook or smoke cigarettes. "It's *Penthouse* over there," Nick says, "it'd be worth it to save the world just to get the babes."

"He's building an ICBM in his living room," Nick says, his face managing to show skepticism and awe in a glance.

"It's a wondah," Ross says. "The bloke, Ron Milford is his name, has had to push back his couch, move his TV a bit, but the rocket's all there—the nose shoots through the dining room. Hard now to have a sit-down dinner for twelve, I'd say."

Ross and Nick are in my living room just back from the hydrogen lab in Fontana, where, thank God, they have once again failed to kill themselves. "When it's done," Ross says, "it'll make it to Japan. Maybe even into orbit."

The Air Dukes, it appears, are diversifying. Investing, for some reason, in this missile enterprise. I am worried about their commitment to us. Air Duke's fund-raiser Hy Weisman told me yesterday, "I'm sweating at the bank. The money's coming in in dribs and drabs. Nothing but thousands. Gimmie two weeks and then we'll sit down." So I called my father about getting a second mortgage to finance the chassis. He can't conceive of a car capable of driving twenty-five hundred miles on a tank of tap water and was not convinced by Ross's formula: Water + Aluminum + OxyChem caustic soda. The secret, my Uncle Bert said,

$$2\ Al(s) + 6NaOH(aq) \rightarrow 2Na_3AlO_3(aq) + 3H_2(g)$$

would not produce enough hydrogen to make the cell useful. "The Law of Conservation of Mass says that for every two moles of aluminum you get three moles of hydrogen. So fifty four grams of aluminum will yield six grams of hydrogen. That works out to one pound of aluminum for eight gallons of gasoline equivalent."

Thus informed, my dad referred to the creation of the Xeno as "pounding sand down a rat hole" and told me if I wanted $20,000 I'd have to borrow it from him and, if I did, he'd be wanting it back. Fast. How to do that, given my $00.00 monthly earnings from Xeno Automotive? Sell our Oregon house. Our beautiful hillside Portland home. Moon can do the job. We talked about the possibility earlier. "I guess we better get going," he says on the phone from Portland, "because I already pounded a FOR SALE sign in your front yard."

Ross and I are on my tile front porch. Matt is riding his bike on the sidewalk. A straw-haired five-year-old in black shorts, white stick arms stretched to grip the handle bars, white stick legs pumping, his red T-shirt on backward, its square pocket hanging off his shoulder. Hurtling past us, he screams that he can't stop. I bolt after him, he starts to fall and I sweep him away from the sidewalk like an inch-off-the-grass touchdown pass.

The mailman hands me a white envelope. I rip into it. There it is, $20,000. My father's signature on the bottom of the check. Ross peers over my shoulder. "My God! Congratulations, we're on our way."

33

JOHN'S IDEA

"Realistically," John Case says, "Nick is worth an incredible amount of money."

We are playing chess at John's beach house in St. Malo, a gated neighborhood north of San Diego. My prospects in this match are excellent, proof that it is only an unhappy accident that, over twenty-five years, my batting average playing John is about .090.

John is our new partner, to seal the deal he gave—loaned me, technically—$3,000 last week after we played tennis. I have an almost fast serve, but am so uncontrollably accurate that the ball always goes the same place, right off centerline, so I was delighted when John blurped my first serve into the net. This happens about once every Olympiad. John's great at sports and the key to his success is that it looks as though he doesn't have a clue. He has no serve. Just a *boink*. But almost nothing gets past him. Hit John a blooper, he returns a blooper. Hit him a rocket, he returns a rocket. Once I showed him a tennis book I'd bought, and he shrugged, "Here's my book: Return the ball." John just stands there like a guy waiting for a light at a crosswalk, then hits whatever you hit right back. It makes people crazy. Once at a tournament John was matched against a hot dog who laughed at John's serve and asked the line judge, "Has he been seeded right?" and when John beat the hot dog into the ground, the guy claimed John was a ringer. "Nobody that bad plays that good."

John destroyed me in straight sets, and wrote me a check for $3,000. This could be unreal. I met him at the University of Denver, a very nice college where there were often more Porsches than Volkswagens in the student union parking lot, where guys wore sweaters as shawls, where I dropped acid, ate dog food and saw God and where I impressed John with my ability to find profitable talent. John was in charge of the university May Day dance—the big spring moneymaker or breaker for the student body—and I got him to book a guy who in the spring of 1970 nobody had ever heard of: Alice Cooper, and—what else can I say?

John is not car crazy, but has great taste, and at DU John's car made me question whether hot rods were truly the staff of life. I'd just spent a year surfing in Hawaii and, with no money over there for anything but an old beer can of a Hillman Minx, was amazed that I could have Miss Young Hawaii for a girlfriend—I didn't need a hot car, I just needed to always agree with her about what rotten parents it sounded like she had, and when I saw John Case's modest smooth, blue, round-shouldered Mercedes sedan, it made me think. Not at all flashy, a sane car, a responsible car. For the first time—looking at the little Mercedes—such a vehicle made sense.

John was the Elway of campus touch football, the only quarterback I have seen *daydream* during a blitz. In a huddle John's plan was always the same: Everybody he saw on one side blocked, everybody he saw on the other went long. A pass thrown by John floated across the sky but, in case your hands weren't that good, the ball gained enough magic acceleration on descent to bury it safely in your guts. If you were on John's team you never lost and in the time since, we've never had a cross word. He's the original fair-haired boy. Last year an elderly Orange County farmer sold John his avocado orchard for half the price he was offered by the railroad, just because he liked John so much and John turned around and sold the property shortly thereafter for about a million-dollar profit.

"I have an idea," John says, staring at the chess board. "You know Raymond Floyd?"

"No," I admit.

"He's a famous golfer most people have never even heard of," John clarifies. "Cadillac pays Raymond Floyd a million dollars a year just to be a symbol for their car. All Floyd has to do for his million is have the Cadillac logo on his golf hat. Floyd doesn't have to talk about Cadillacs, he doesn't even have to drive a Cadillac, all Floyd has to do is *wear* the Cadillac."

I lift my bishop to pop away a pawn in the fence of pawns around his king.

"Goooooooood moooooooove," John says. Brown from surfing and, his pale hair thinning a little in front, he could be a recently retired Padres pitcher here to sun at the shore.

He moves a bishop to the center of the board. Interesting. A similar push set up a fatal feeding frenzy on my left flank during the last game. "How are your funds?"

"Not good," I reply. I discovered I'd borrowed $6,500 more from my parents than I'd written them a receipt for. My mother said not to worry—everybody makes bookkeeping errors—but this was stupid enough to be embezzlement. "The Air Dukes haven't come across."

"No big deal," John says. "But you know Sleepy?"

Now I do.

"Forget nickel-and-dime investors. If Floyd can pull a million dollars a year out of Cadillac just for being Raymond Floyd," John asks, "what could Nick's cars do?"

Staring down at the board, I consider that. I am up a rook for a knight. Great, except for a hole leading to my king big enough to drive a Xeno through.

"Nick's cars," John says, "are not just cars, they're art. The one you're trying to build could become a symbol for a car company or a big fuel." John advances a pawn. "Think about it."

I move my remaining knight forward and am surprised to hear John say, "You win." Not understanding, I watch as he says, "See?" and quickly moves both his pieces and mine, revealing to me his doom only as he plays it.

As if he were a rabbit popped from a hat, Demetri Wagner of the American Hydrogen Association has appeared almost magically from nowhere. I'm not asking questions though, because he is wild about the water-power fuel cell, wild about the Xeno and wants to break the hydrogen-power land speed record. Our car mated to their "revolutionary direct injection" hydrogen engine. I write Gideon:

> The key is just getting everyone aimed in the same direction. Imagine, you're on the plains of ancient Germany. You see a mob of blond Neanderthals swinging stone axes, raping their cousins and setting fire to any village that isn't theirs, and you realize: organize these folk and you can become Attila the Hun.

John Case flies Nick and me to Phoenix. What a relief to have somebody else take charge. John is great at handling things. When

Debbie, Katie and I moved to California so that I could write a book about television, John put us up at his house and built an office behind his garage for me and my muse. When the city complained the office violated code, he tore it down and built me another one. Anyway, Phoenix. Just another godforsaken sunbelt boomtown. A smiling Demetri Wagner greets us in front of an new industrial park. Phoenix is made of them.

Maybe forty, in boots, jeans, a checked shirt and with a thick moustache, Demetri is little. He could be a miniature cowboy. He shows us his hydrogen-fueled Oldsmobile Quad 4 that stands on an engine stand. Using a direct injection system, it will, Demetri says, develop 15 percent more power than gas and that, mated with the Xeno, we can break the land speed record for hydrogen. Which at 120 miles an hour, Demetri beams, is a juicy apple waiting to be plucked.

The facility is beautiful. We check out their new race car trailer. Tall, metal and sparkly, like a walk-in refrigerator on wheels. Nick whispers. "Talk about infrastructure, I counted seven computers in there." John leaves, "pumped." He says that he sees a big future and that he may donate two helicopter ski trips worth of his vacation time to our project.

Nick's new girlfriend is buoyant, cute. I met her down the street from my house at Nick's dark, wooden submarine of an apartment. We shook hands and a pink ball shot out of her mouth. Bubble gum. Nick says, "She's a sorority girl. Way nice but sort of too satisfied. Like, she'll ask how, but never why." He reveals he may have to "rebuild" her as he did Henrietta ("Though that sure got out of hand, didn't it!"). "I know I can take her apart, it's getting her back together again that I worry about. What I need is a Debbie who is twenty-four. A girl supercute, smart, honest, who'll put up with anything."

Deb has a big remodeling job. A twelve-foot-deep hole has been dug beneath a wealthy client's home high on a hill in Palos Verdes—ground scooped out to create a playroom in the basement. I was up there last night. The house rests on four I-beams. Thick hairs of rebar curled beneath sheared-away foundation. I'm proud she is in charge of the colossus. Among other things, it is paying the bills.

I need to sell another book. I am working every day on a novel, *Aloha*. It is set in Hawaii in the early twenty-first century. I do not buy the sexy dooms of the *Blade Runner, Escape from New York* future; I'd bet a near future of few-rules prosperity, when guys less smart than Nick or me will have access to terrifying technology. *Aloha* is about an heir to a Honolulu construction fortune who decides to create a new Hawaiian island by blasting a hole to the earth's magma with a hydrogen bomb. I'm at my desk in my office that is also my tiny bedroom, staring at a computer screen. I've had to reposition the nuclear blast that kills a quarter million people three times. A pain. Last year I made as much as a good teacher or a bad dentist. This year I have made $30—ghostwriting Ross's preamble to a lawsuit he plans against Air Duke if they try to boot him out of the company. Across the hall, the sound of "Suck My Kiss," endlessly. My deerlike Katie has been grounded. She got straight As then snuck out of a girlfriend's house and, at midnight, got picked up outside her middle school by the police. Her friend's dad called a boy they were with "a little fucker" so the boy, "Damien," has threatened to kill the girl. Katie is holed up in her room with the Red Hot Chili Peppers.

Debbie calls me from the living room. "Unbelievable," she says, "they let them off." The cops who beat up Rodney King.

Nick and I are taking $5,000 to John Mason so he can start building the car. We drive through burning-down Los Angeles to Simi Valley but we can't see the smoke, let alone the fires, due to the smog. The whole dirty sky stands on my windshield. Nick is appalled. "I never got racism. I always wanted to say, 'I'm better than you, because you're a nigger,' but never could. Even when I was a kid and black guys beat me up. I just figured they were assholes."

At his shop, Mason, a graying boy banker in T-shirt and shorts, says he's finishing three "Indy Lites" and building parts for the secret Aurora space plane but that he can start on our car in two weeks and finish in two months. Our chassis: suspension, wheels, tires, steering, footbox, for $15,000. He'll build out of Chromaly aircraft steel tubing. Nick asks if we can cram into our fifteen grand Indy 500 brakes. John says, "Too heavy, too big and way too expensive. Indy cars go into corners at two hundred and twenty miles an hour and four Gs. You won't have to scrub off that kind of speed."

Nick has sketches for the Xeno's frame on tracing paper laid out before us. A breeze lifts and glides the paper across the picnic table. Nick chases the paper, grabs it and says, "It's got to be so that when *Road & Track* gets in and tests it—" plans in hand, his arms make the motion of a steering wheel going violently this way and that "—they say it blows off a Porsche."

John pulls on a corner of his moustache. "Guess how many millions Porsche has invested so that you can't go do that?"

Nick slaps the back of one hand against the palm of the other. "But it can't just go great straight—we've get to build the ultimate high-performance car. That's our vision!"

John smiles. "On fifteen thousand dollars? You can't make chicken soup out of chicken shit."

The next day Nick drives toward mountains we cannot see, on our way to confront the Dukes of Air. The sky is gauze. Surprise. The Dukes may fire Nick for "incompetence." They claim that his patent drawings were unacceptable. So, a showdown.

Nick is in a bad mood. Last night he drove through a series of roadblocks to get home to the beach. "The cops know where the rich people live," he says with grinning disgust. "They could care less if the rest of Long Beach burns to the ground."

Already, I am getting bored by the fires. There are evidently thirty-seven hundred of them. People who don't know anything about Rodney King but everything about free Budweiser, Nikes and Cheez Whiz are torching anything that—

Nick's engine suddenly dies. He slams his fists on the steering wheel. We push the car off the freeway, a feathery knife cuts floating curves around my lower spine. Result of pushing Nick's old Austin-Healey Sprite back and forth across the street each week to avoid the street sweepers. The Sprite has a flat but Nick says, "It'd be crazy to fix it until I can do a complete restoration." Anyway, we push the Honda down some little city's street, push it across an intersection to a garage. A mechanic smiles, says, "We don't work on Hondas."

Nick, sweat pouring down his face, snarls, "Don't be fuckin' with me, dude."

Then the Honda starts. On to the staff meeting. Under the DANGER signs and in their shirtsleeves, the Air Dukes could be the Israeli cabinet. Frank Spinks says their patent lawyer says Nick's patent drawings for the hydrogen furnace were unusable and that the entire company is frozen in place until they can be redone. "The drawings," Frank says, "should have been done on computer."

"You didn't hire a computer, you hired these," Nick says and holds out his hands. "I told you that in the beginning."

I say, "This is ridiculous. Nick agreed to work with the assurance that Air Duke would underwrite the construction of the car. We were led to expect a letter of commitment by May first. It's time Air Duke honored their commitment."

The "youngest commander of U.S. troops in World War Two" rests a thick arm on the table. "You want us to put money into something that may not work. I'm afraid Nick may have to go."

"You have the best automobile designer in the country busting his tail for you for four hundred dollars a week," I say, "and you're going to can him?"

As a matter of fact.

Driving home, Nick whacks me hard on the shoulder. "You defended me! You should have seen your face. It was incredibly mean. It had 'Don't fuck with us' written all over it."

Yeah, well. I had looked at Frank Spinks's face. He had "These two sinkholes are gone" written all over his.

"Nick, this has got to go from art to steel." At this house in front of his computer and under a model of his "dope blimp"—a thirty-foot-long government airship he designed to detect narcotics smugglers—Herman Drees says, "I need to know the geometry of the uprights, so I can put the A-arms where they have to be."

Nick is quizzical. "The upright is?"

"What the axle and wheel bolts onto."

We are in the high desert flatlands of Simi Valley. The safest community in California, according to a TV newscast I heard the other night. But I'm not sure Nick is impressed. Pretty much, Nick's unasked question to a lot of people over thirty is, "If you're so smart, why aren't you rich?" And Herman isn't. Aero Vironment is one of the most prestigious high-tech development companies in the world, but it has never been among the highest paying.

Herman lives with his two teenage sons in a small ranch house with a small swimming pool in back. He runs fifty miles a week and aside from his computer, and a couple of his guitars, the running shoes on the floor may be the most expensive item in his living room.

Staring at a schematic of the Xeno chassis he has drawn on his computer, he says, "First, we'll decide where bulkheads will be. The front, the pedal, the dash, the firewall/roll cage. Everything on the chassis has to follow contours defined by the body design. Nick, you need to give contour lines, for reference, and stations." He indicates the space between the dash bulkhead and the footbox bulkhead. He points to the area over the nose. "I'll work using dimensions given by the body shape." He points to the firewall. "It's just cut and paste, but I need direction. It's just slobbered together, but from this I'll put all the node locations in my computer and establish finite element structural code, that'll tell me the stresses."

He shows us the model he has just made. "I went through the cross sections, triangulated everything to make it stiff." Usually a chassis resembles just the necessary spaghetti that holds body and drivetrain together, but this is V-tailed, made of slender pieces of wood, like a crystalline teardrop turned sideways.

The chassis is spined by "beams"—chromoly tubing—that anchor the bulkheads and, in case of a head-on crash, "distribute and disperse" the "loads" from impact front to the back. Complicated because the car is broken up by the cavity of the cockpit and because the car's chassis is shaped like a pod with curving flanks. The first time he tried, "It all tweaked."

Herman discovered this defect, as a child might, by twisting the wood "Popcicle model" in his hands, establishing a "sound structure" even before he put the design into his computer. "It's fully triangulated, there's no weakening, no bending anywhere in the system. The computer just tells me how big to make the numbers." That is, how thick to make the metal tubing.

The engine will be suspended like a race car's, hammocked between the beams behind the roll hoop—instead of off the bottom of the frame like a regular passenger car.

"I'll figure sheer modulus, connect all nodes—tube steel, square steel, plate steel—give it mass and weights, mass for the fuel tanks, mass for the man, subject it to six Gs, six times the force of gravity on the model, then I get a printout. For every node, the computer gives you every stress; axial stress, sheer stress, moments in all directions, torsion, sheer, et cetera."

I ask, "What's a moment?"

"Torque. A twisting action." Shown on the computer in a percentage of a maximum stress Herman is allowing. He points to the screen. "Look at number five: ninety-two percent, almost failing. Only eight percent yield strength remaining. So I had to correct that."

He shows us on his computer a schematic of the "dope blimp's" pod hanging from a helium bag. "I gave the computer the material I wanted to make the pod out of, aluminum, gave it the information it needed to see that the pod could take a three hundred-feet-per-second drop and still survive."

In the mirrored cavern of Yankee Doodle's, Ross and I play eight ball, best of twelve for ownership of the universe. Up two games, I hear tales of hydrogen schemes gone bad. Ross's curly black nylon hair gleaming in the light above the pool table, he sights down his cue. "Once we got six hundred thousand dollars from an investor and spent it all on law-yahs when he sued us to get it back." Which gives him an idea: "Ring up your dad, Mahk, and flog him for some stock."

I say, *What?*

Ross taps the cue ball. It clicks into the seven, the seven rolls to a side pocket. "He's a mucky-muck, president of the eye doctors or some-such, and loaning you twenty thousand dollars for the car, right? He must have a quarter mil stuffed in a sock for his retirement. We could do very well with that."

I say Air Duke just fired Nick, they don't care two cents about us, why should I, Christ forbid, "flog my father for stock"?

A voluptuous waitress presents us beer, Ross insists on paying. "You're so wrong, Mahk, so, so wrong. They do care about you. They said, 'Nick! Nick's just a kid, but Christensen's no kid. He's angry and he may smack us with a lawsuit.' Believe me, they care about you a lot."

When I say I have no idea what he is talking about, Ross lifts his glass, sips, is left with a grin of foam at the corners of his mouth. "Mahk, they're scared of you, so now you've got the initiative, you hit 'em where they least expect it. With money! Give 'em a quartah million and—" Ross makes a claw of his good hand and holds it up between us "—you'll have 'em by the balls, right where you want 'em, in your powah!" The claw congeals to a half a fist.

I win the universe seven games to five.

Standing in front of the old white mansion barbecuing spiced beef, the Mexican family—burley dad, chubby mom, a million kids—is so happy to see John Case that you might think he was Santa Claus, not the landlord there to collect the rent.

The mansion has been divided into maybe a dozen units and we are invited inside a dark apartment that smells like a restaurant. A brown toddler in a pink jumpsuit, a remote control gripped in her tiny hand, is zorking the TV between professional wrestling, *Jeopardy* and *NBC Nightly News*. I sit down on a noisy couch. Tacos appear, cookies appear. Would I like beans or rice? John is talking to the dad in Spanish. Money appears. John pockets some twenties.

By the time we leave I realize why everybody is so happy. John has made many apartment improvements, and even though the dad didn't have all the rent, no big deal. As for that rent, Debbie and I pay more for laundry every month.

"Those people have it hard," John says driving back toward his house. "I got the property for nothing. It's appreciating like crazy and I just charge enough to make my monthlies with the bank."

John has been helping with the car. The Hydrogen Association "letter of intent" has arrived. It states that at "the natural end" of the project, the Xeno will become their property. Demetri Wagner promises if they don't meet construction expenses, "You'll have the right to take the car back." I, Repo Man. He says I should raise most of the money because there is more in Los Angeles than in Arizona. "Just put on a suit and go talk to the tree huggers."

Okay. Still, their revolutionary direct-injection system could make raising money worthwhile. But my friend Pierre Ouellette, here from Oregon, asks an interesting question: "Does it work?" John Case calls Demetri and the answer is no. "It's not finished. That's why they need you to raise the money."

34

NORMAN

Norman D. Hackett says he's got a way for us to break the hydrogen speed record on the Fourth of July. "But hydrogen is an expensive date. Natural gas is the answer. There's a hundred million dollars out there in natural gas money in Southern California alone and I can smoke 'em out."

Grayish yellow hair combed back in a smoky sheet and wearing a green workshirt, moccasins and jeans, Norman, who with his reddish tan and V-shaped smile reminds me only slightly of the devil, beams and says he's flying to Dallas to meet with T. Boone Pickens, the famous takeover artist and natural gas magnate, and will present to T. Boone a plan in which the Xeno serves as flagship for the entire natural gas industry. "It'll leave you jokers riding tall in the saddle, your fuckin' dream car bought and paid for." Nick and I are in Norman's perfect white block of a building in a nearly new Long Beach industrial park— no bootleg hydrogen lab, that's for sure. "Ford's using it to power thousands of their Crown Victorias. My crude grand plan is: Put ten million natural gas-powered cars on the road, put two hundred thousand people to work over the next two years. You two," he looks at Nick and me, "what can I say? Some days you just get lucky."

It's June and I'm forty-four. It's my birthday and I guess Norman is a present. I met him at a barbecue at my knock-out next-door neighbor Patti's pretty cottage, where Norm took one look at a rendering of the Xeno, got an expression on his face to suggest that maybe Pamela Anderson had just revealed to him the meaning of life and said, "Let me build your car."

Henrietta's $250 million is gone, my $20,000 is going. John Case is not about to write a $250,000 check, it would be easier to land Moby Dick with a fly rod and twenty-pound test than Gideon Bosker's

$100,000, which he says he's got parked in a new condominium in Cabo San Lucas "until I see an at least halfway rational plan." So what else could I say besides, "Sure, Norm, why not?"

"He's rude, brilliant, honest and very successful," Patti told me and I'll buy the last part. The model of the Xeno in its bright aluminum coffin case is at Norm's headquarters, the lap of corporate lux, revealed to Nick and me in a white conference room decorated with pictures of members of the 1976 Mount Everest expedition using Norman's oxygen tanks to sustain them up white slopes that appear steep as walls. The nation's leader in the development of "glass-fiber composite reinforcement for pressure vessel and piping application," Norman has a million-dollar house on the beach, a million-dollar ranch in the mountains, a Mercedes-Benz blacker than oil and as clean as a vacuum. His current girlfriend is a former Miss Port of Long Beach and Norman is into cars. Among many other things, he provided Ford the fuel cylinders for America's first compressed natural gas production vehicles—Ranger pickup trucks.

Norman shows us videos of engineers blowing up pipe as big as a locomotive. The pipes explode with great force but each time the blast is contained by Norm's garters. His huge springlike garter belts that wrap themselves around the world's largest natural gas lines, so that if a line blows up, the damage will be stopped at the garters. The National Bureau of Standards states that were the United States to implement Norman's gas pipe technologies, total energy savings could average around 40 percent . . . "about twenty-five million barrels of oil saved per year" and "savings of four times this would not be surprising."

Now Norman has turned his light on us. He asks, "How soon we can have a body and chassis complete?" and I reply, "Three months." Rick Pot, a composite expert Nick knows, says for the body all he needed were drawings: "Dead front, dead side, dead rear, plan view, connect the dots and build it out of foam, finish it like a surfboard by September first." For twenty-five grand.

Norm replies, "Cool," and then he says, "Let's go see my pal Carmen Pisano," of Pisano Racing Engines fame. We walk a broad avenue of big, clean block-shaped buildings, each as white as virgin snow and each with a bold logo of Norm's Hackett Industries, Inc. American flags stand on tall flagpoles all around. The smell of enfranchisement is thick in the air.

Nick says we could become the "Ferrari of America."

Norman replies, "That's okay, I was twenty-five once too."

We walk past what could be a race car wrecking yard, the arrowlike hulks of funny cars tipped up in several directions, to a big, pinkish building that reminds me of a mausoleum gone totally to seed. There we meet drag race legend Carmen Pisano. Thick curly black hair, thick black moustache, short and maybe sixty but with a linebacker's forearms, Carmen shows us his sleek world-record-breaking Studebaker, a mid-1950s model with a ton of cement in the trunk so that at high speeds it would not fly off the ground. A kitten sleeps on an old green Maserati. Beside clutch plates stacked like pancakes rest gleaning JP-1 racing engines. Nick asks for Carmen's resumé and Carmen says, "This is my résumé," and opens a wallet stacked with hundred-dollar bills.

John Mason says, "This is an aircraft layout fabrication table. It's as flat as pee on a plate. It retains tolerances within a thousandth of an inch, the degree of accuracy is the width of a scratch—which is five- or seven-thousandths of an inch. I believe Detroit relies on thirty-thousandths. It'll be very flat, which feeds back to driver controllability, so that it will steer absolutely neutral."

John is building our car on this table, working in "stations" fore to aft. The first station is for nose bulkheads and the footbox, already done. A trapezoid in square steel. I feel like I am seeing a baby, my baby, for the first time.

He has made patterns in the same length and width as the steel tubing—so he can transfer each pattern onto round steel to make usable pieces. The patterns are made of scrap aluminum, one pattern serves both the right and left side of the chassis.

A big change, actually. With a speed record in mind, the car has evolved to an aluminum-skinned single seater, the best-looking bullet ever.

"This is a prototype," John says, "so you can't finish welding until pretty much the whole car is tacked together." Then he asks if we want to see "the nine inch"—our Ford "nine-inch" rear end. Cro-Magnon wizardry cheap and tough as a railroad spike. We go behind his shop to where the grungy, crud-caked axle hangs from a wire over a bucket of oil. "Oh, shit," Nick says. He lifts the bill of his baseball hat. It has the image of an eight ball stitched across the front. "To settle for *Ford* parts is ridiculous."

"It's the strongest rear end anywhere," John corrects. "You're confusing perfection with price."

"I haven't sunk my life into this to compromise," Nick replies. "How can we have an ultimate car without ultimate parts?" Driving home, Nick asks how stupid I think Herman and John think we are and I say I think Herman and John think we're smart but "selectively uninformed."

Carmen Pisano became a hot rod hero along with his friends Ed Iskenderian, Vic Edelbrock, and Parnelli Jones. The Pisano brothers drag raced the most dangerous 1950s and 1960s cars—front-engined top fuelers, their supercharged motors so tall that the driver could see nothing but the side of the track. Carmen straddled the back of a motor modified so far beyond factory tolerances that it was less an engine than a death threat. If the flywheel let go—that is, if it ripped loose from the end of the crankshaft, as dragster flywheels often did—it had the energy to blast through the steel bellhousing and cut off the driver's legs. Carmen is no shrinking violet, so I am concerned that he is so concerned about our fuel. "Hydrogen is spooky," he says. "Very dangerous."

"Carmen throws in a motor, we finish the car by Christmas, then use it as bait to get investors for a much bigger program. But hydrogen's a problem." Big Norman Hackett, tan and fit, stands beside Carmen in the hard light of his conference room and, books and papers spread around, clarifies: "The small molecule of hydrogen's very invasive, so its hard to control, hard to carburate, so—what'll happen if we blow the fucking thing up in somebody's face?"

Though the prospect of Carmen Pisano "throwing in" one of his $25,000 racing engines is attractive, I sit wondering: *Norm, how much money are you going to pony up?* as he recalls how he was going to break the natural gas speed record in the famous streamliner, the Mickey Thompson Special. "You had to push it to two hundred and fifty miles an hour just to start it. We'd've drawn it out for promotion purposes, gone four hundred and twenty-five miles an hour the first time, four hundred and fifty the second, four hundred and seventy-five the third, up to five hundred." Then, sadly, "Mickey Thompson's thugs" repossessed the car and, even worse, Mickey Thompson got murdered. "That put the kibosh on the whole deal."

Nick wants Norm's friend Luigi, a famous old race car builder, to craft our body in aluminum, and he'd like a free Pisano racing engine too. Carmen, who could provide that item, scratches his curly head with thick fingers. "I'm real eager, too eager. But the JP-One is a drag race engine. It don't have a starter, you start it with a handheld aircraft engine starter. You want a starter, we'd have to redo the mold. That could cost twenty-five thousand dollars."

Norm sighs loudly, taps his fingers on the table. "We need a quarter million. Trailer, truck, drivers. Let's say one hundred and ninety for you guys, sixty for Carmen and me. But first I need to know, how fast'll this thing be designed to go?"

Nick jabs a thumb in the air. "Two hundred miles an hour plus."

Carmen says, "I'm afraid it'll flip at seventy-five."

Norman says, "You guys gotta worry about this stuff."

Nick says, "I worry about it even when I sleep."

"I don't sleep," Norman replies. "We gotta talk in my office," he says to me.

Prints by Gauguin, elephant spears used by native African hunters in one corner. Norman says, "Let's forget Luigi, he's an old man. What if he died on us? Who knows, Carmen might croak as well. But the real questions is, can you control this kid?"

"Nick?"

"There is a hundred thousand dollars between one hundred and fifty miles per hour and two hundred miles per hour and I can't have your boy wonder Star Trekking me into bankruptcy. I'm fifty, and you guys'll cost me two thousand dollars worth of my attention every time I look around."

Sitting under a glassy morning sun among the pigeons at Polly's Coffee Shop, two blocks between my house and his, Nick reads: "Norman Hackett has been described as 'abrasive, abrupt, profane, egotistical, and impatient.' A former business associate says, 'he tends to rub people the wrong way.' Then it says, Hackett remained at Alcoa until last year when Alcoa fired him. 'We discovered inventors don't make good managers,' said Steve Murray. And Mark, that's his *promotion material*. Why's this sound so familiar?" Fortunately, Nick says, we have an alternative, "Mean Gene." A Hollywood art director Nick has met who is rich and who loves cars. "But there's good news and bad news."

I say, "Gimme the bad news first."

"The bad news is he's a complete piece of shit asshole but the good news is that everything he touches turns to gold."

Norman says he's going to raise a million dollars for the car and I'm at a huge gas station in my Porsche, preoccupied. A busy week. Debbie is off in Wisconsin supervising a basement to attic remodeling job—she's staying at the condominium of an actor just hired by Phillip Morris to portray a new kind of Malboro Man. A homely beekeeper. Evidently the tobacco company suddenly realized it had for a hundred years ignored a huge market—nerds—and, anyway, I'm taking care of Katie and Matt and Norman has given Nick a one hundred-dollar bill to finance color Xeroxes. The C-note is a "test," Norman has explained, of how we will handle his million and now he wants to know where his hundred-dollar bill is. At Kinko's, where it belongs. Selecting a hose from a zoo of color-coded fuel pumps, I walk to a pay phone to call Norm to inform him of his C-note's fate and on the way home, the Porsche backfires, begins to make crazy bangs and belches. I drive to my mechanic Dave's, exhaust flagging out the rear in furls as thick as cloth.

Short and generally round, Dave revs the engine, flames explode out the exhaust pipes. His diagnosis: "You put diesel in this thing. I hope you didn't fry the engine." My taxi ride home costs as much as a full tank of unleaded supreme. The fat driver tells me about Rodney King's big mistake. "Prone is not this," and he makes a peaked roof of one hand, his knuckles the beam. "Prone is this." His hand goes flat.

Ross, with no knock on my front door, dashes into my living room. "They took the Lincoln!" He says Air Duke has bought rocket guy Ron Milford's ICBM shop, locked Ross out and over cheeseburgers at Chuck's cafe down by the beach, Nick is sympathetic: "Face facts, they fucked you. Was it Milford's doing?"

"Naw." Ross takes a big bite of burger. "We get along like a house on fire." He wipes his mouth with the back of his half a hand. "It was the others."

Ross, sweating under his curly hair-hat, his brown eyes about to go to tears, hisses, "They said I have no knowledge." He says he's forced to return to Australia and when Ross leaves Chuck's, Nick predicts, "He'll be gone in the biggest way, dude. We'll never see his ass again."

"We've got a heat problem. This steel's harder than your *schmeckle* at love time. If I run the drill too slowly it can bind on the metal." John Mason marks the tube steel with a scratch awl—a metal rod that looks like a pencil with a very sharp point—and locks it in a sandwich between an L-shaped piece of ground angle steel and a miter gauge. Nick, observing this, gets an intense, skewered look of concentration that suggests all of God's reality is twelve inches off the tip of his nose. Mason completes the cut, then uses a mill to grind a "fish-mouth" arc at the end of the pipe so that this end can "mate" almost exactly flush against the side of another piece of identical tubing of exactly the same diameter. Because many of these joinings are not dead-on, but at angles peculiar only to Herman's chassis design, this is tricky.

Water from a pencil-thin plastic line pees on the drill bit that is cutting into the tubing. So it cools.

So nice. Our car—our real car, not just a model car—is getting made. Mario Andretti is giving us a steering rack, free. "It was the car he totalled at Indy this year and for some reason he doesn't want to use it anymore," John Mason reports. "I told him what unbelievable guys you were so Mario said, 'Let 'em have it, on me.' "

The front of the chassis looks strong as a jail cell yet weighs only 150 pounds and the rear of the chassis has been computer stressed to accept a 1,000-horsepower engine.

Beside this geometry of steel pipe, Nick's new model. It is made out of wood and skinned with paper, is about as big as a good-size salmon. Herman, in jeans and running shoes, cannot understand the "downforce" wheel shrouds Nick has created. These shrouds, pods that rest over the wheels, present a stack of fins in front of each wheel. "The key," Herman says, "is the ratio of the length of the wing and the width. That's why sail planes have long, slender wings to provide a lot of lift. Biplanes and triplanes don't gain that much lift. Because your penalty is drag. The best thing to do is one big wing, like an Indy wing."

Nick says Indy cars have lots of little wings.

"Naw, those are flaps. They generate a flow field around the car to create down force. But the flow field on this model is so dirty that it is impossible to determine the down force. Your model doesn't give us anything but the look. You can do the whole thing with body shape, but you have no idea of the aerodynamics and the less you have on the wheels the better."

Nick says he hates the Ford nine-inch rear end. "We've agreed as a team to go with independent rear suspension."

We did? From nowhere, a $7,000 change of plan.

Herman says, "Independent suspension is not easy. Why go to the complications when you don't need one?"

Nick says, "Aesthetics."

Herman is perturbed. "The goal was to set a speed record. This calls for redesign. I've been designing essentially for free. I'm not going to do that anymore."

I say, "The Ford rear end is completely adequate."

"Sure," Nick agrees, "and if I was blind I'd love it."

Herman begins to whistle, idly but expertly, John Lennon's "#9 Dream."

35

BAD THING

Norm goes to Long Beach Natural Gas to convince them to convince the Long Beach Grand Prix Association to make the Xeno this year's pace car. They don't say "yes" but they don't meet Norman at the door with their necks wrapped in garlic either. In the meantime, Green Motors, a hip "clean fuel" car dealership to the stars in Hollywood, wants to sell Xenos, *Kit Car* magazine has deemed Nick and me "visionaries" and I take Matt to swimming lessons at a pool behind a house in Seal Beach. It's a dollar a minute, but worth it. I love watching him get better. Moony skin, wide eyes and still baby-fine pale yellow hair, he's very game, and his bosomy young teacher loves him. After his lessons he hangs to the side of the pool, his legs ripped and jiggled apart in the refraction of the water. I say: Show me what you can do, and he tiptoes toward the deep end, then quickly frog paddles to an underwater chair at the middle of the pool, stands up, splashes off again but bobs under, then bobs back up again gasping. I leap up as one arm flails against the side of the pool and he pulls himself up, mashing water out of his eye with a fist. He looks at me, his mouth quivering before he smiles.

A so-so week. Moon hasn't sold our Portland house; in fact, true to his promise, he has not done jack shit. Nick and I have been invited to bring the car to the Specialty Equipment Manufacturer's Show (SEMA) in Las Vegas on November first. The biggest auto trade show in the world, "Nineteen miles of aisles." Potential sponsors galore.

Nick's brother Dave is in town. He's literate, thoughtful and he and Nick are very close—yesterday I watched them walk down to my house, Nick in front, Dave behind, both in bermudas, T-shirts and backward-billed baseball hats, like two guys in an invisible donkey suit. Dave is an English major and Nick said they will write a whole new business plan right now. When I said what a waste of time, Nick blurted, "We don't need excuses, we need leadership and systems."

Matt climbs out of the pool, shivering. I wrap him in a towel. "Daddy," he says as I strap him into the Volvo, "don't tell Mommy I was scared."

In Norman's long, black spotless luxury Mercedes, our air well conditioned, Norman and I drive up out of L.A. to the mountainous suburban veldt of Simi Valley, Norm recounting how he bamboozled Jacques Cousteau into endorsing his scuba tanks and how his oxygen tanks are aboard all U.S. Navy's nuclear submarines and George Bush's limo too, and at Mason's shop, he takes photographs like a cop at a crime scene and instructs John how to heat and bend the metal John uses to make his Indy 500 exhaust headers, though it appears that John knows a lot of this—perhaps even all of it—already.

The chassis, streamlined jungle gym that it is, is expanding, geometry by geometry, but when I get home I get a call from Nick. John Mason has a problem with Norman. "Mainly, he hates Norm's guts. We better keep Norman away from there."

In his conference room one hot afternoon in August, in green workshirt and jeans, genius Bluto Norman Hackett stares at photographs of the chassis in progress. Passing a hand through what's left of his hair, he says, "You guys gotta drive through the wall on this, you're way behind."

I say if he wants to speed things up he can write us a check for $25,000 and Norman looks at me as though I have stepped on his foot. "By the first of the year we've gotta have a car we can go like *fffzzzt* and fire it. Because my thought is to con—and when I say con, I don't mean con but promote—the city into an advanced technology program. Because Long Beach is on its ass."

Nick, who has talked so much he has lost his voice, croaks, "They're fucked, they are."

Norm agrees. "No more cold war means loss of aerospace jobs means the loss of peripheral jobs. The real estate market is tumbling. The *Queen Mary* is sinking, the *Spruce Goose* is going to Oregon. The city is beginning to flat-ass panic. What the city needs is a new symbol: The Xeno as the Spirit of Long Beach."

To promote Norm's inventions. "We're talking about the city de-

veloping an advanced technology program. Centered around my technology in natural gas vehicles. The city gas department can make
money selling gas. We'll lease the Xeno to these guys." He plans a
"copregnancy" between the local natural gas fleet office and one of the
big utility companies. "I'll chum the water with pictures of the fucking
car being built. That should do the trick."

Norman follows us out and walks down the wide road toward Carmen Pisano's. Nick, in his Honda, pulls up behind him. "What if I just
ran over him, wouldn't he be surprised?"

The SEMA show in Las Vegas, one-stop wheedling. Two million
square feet of performance auto parts. Free if their makers like your
project car. Hurst, Edelbrock, Moroso, Chevrolet Raceshop, all the big
names. Two months to get done. Just about the time the last of the
money I borrowed from my father will run out. But the chassis is complete only to the roll hoop behind the driver. The front suspension is
represented only by metal sticks, Nick tells John in the clear tones of
a grown man that we are worried that the chassis won't be finished in
time. I like that: a Nick Pugh fully able to state a problem, to handle
a crisis, a skill he'll need if he's to become "America's Ferrari."

John picks up a yellow legal pad, jots

QUICK   RIGHT

and says, "Circle the one you want."

Lollapalooza, seventy thousand people and there's Flea on the distant
stage, a millimeter tall, playing bass in his underpants. It's midnight at
an Orange County amphitheater. Katie and two of her friends are
catching the Red Hot Chili Peppers here at the "new Woodstock." Not
much has changed since the old one. Except freaks of the nineties seem
crazier and stronger than freaks of the sixties. We got caught next to a
mosh pit, fifty or sixty barechested goombahs whirling around in a human tornado, one guy swinging by, blood zigzagging like red cracks
across his face, me trying to keep the girls—who stood frozen in
fright—*away* from this tiresome shit.

A long day. Heavy metal mostly, as unchangeable and conservative
as the Catholic Church, all sin, doom and the devil. The geek show

was the saving grace, men piercing themselves with barbecue skewers. A cheek becomes a cone, a spike pushes through. Ex-ballerina Katie squealed, twirled and covered her eyes.

Carmen Pisano, who with his big moustache and thick black hair resembles the computer game hero Super Mario and who was racing cars between the fruit orchards of Southern California before I was born, has tried to find us a cheap, new 454-cubic-inch Rat motor V-8 but says they are so popular there are no bargains. "When the world has diarrhea," he concludes sagely, "everybody wants toilet paper. You need sponsors. Start with custom wheels and who you go after is Centerline. The best name in the business. You get them and everybody else'll fall in line."

Or maybe not. A friend of Nick's who is a designer at Ford told him that he found a complete design schematic of the Xeno in a Ford corporation computer and he is afraid his designs will get stolen. At Centerline Tool, Centerline manager Gary Ulrich, a big, clean-cut-looking man dressed collegiate casual, offers to make us $5,000 worth of wheels free. I say, "Nick, show him the drawing."

We are in the Centerline conference room, and Nick is holding onto his wheel designs as though they were made of platinum. He doesn't want to show them to anyone without getting a "nondisclosure agreement."

I say that the people who make the wheels have to see the wheels. "Show Gary the wheels," I say again. Nick hesitates, then does. The wheel is simple and elegant, a deep-set spun disk. Ulrich says it is lovely and will be easy to make. But afterward, outside in the parking lot, a veil of worry and concern. "We violated protocol!" Nick says, "We agreed as a team to follow the rules."

Booty! Tires stacked as high as fir trees, tires stretching almost as far as I can see. Not because they go to the horizon, but because, in this huge tire warehouse just off the 405 Freeway, there are so many tires they create a "tire mist" that makes the tires farthest away fade in a fog of their own rubber.

We've scored Toyo Proxes high-performance tires. Perfect cylinders of sculpted rubber. I stick a finger into the swooping grid that makes the tire's thumb-deep tread. Carmine called Toyo, said about ten words and told me to get over to the warehouse fast. There Nick showed a nice young man named Joe Jordan a picture of the Xeno. Joe said, "Wow. Done." We drive back to Carmen's but he's gone and when I get home Norm calls to say we better be more thankful to Carmen, or he'll abandon the project.

I may have to sell my Porsche because we've got, as Nick has described it, "a five-thousand-dollar boo-boo" to pay for.

John Mason has kept his word. Ninety percent of the welds are completed up to the tail section. The prototype-in-steel suspension is hung up front, on a little red jack, the wishbones parallel to the ground. Complicated three-axis geometries must be created here. The A-arms are too narrow by four inches on either side, because Nick was not around when Herman built it. Herman explains, "The angle changes may be small but are vitally important—the inside wheel turns more than the outside wheel—if we don't do it right, the steering will be squirrelly and dangerous."

How to pay for this? I go to John Case's office. His carpet is scattered with hundreds of papers, the confetti of apartment house deals. I say I'm flat broke and he says, "No problem" and loans me another $5,000 on the spot.

My phone rings. "Mark, Norm. I drive up to Mason's shop this morning and it's World War Three. That fuckin' chassis. Driss or Dress, the engineer Herman, I tried to talk sense to him and he looked up and said, 'I don't even *know* you.' "

Then a call from Nick. "Bad thing. You know how John Mason is always so calm? Big change, dude, he just went apeshit. He threw stuff at me, I thought he was going to kick my ass. He was screaming so loud I could barely understand the words."

"Why?"

"I was up at his shop and told him Norm was coming up to take pictures and did he mind if we sort of reassembled the suspension parts he had laid out so the car would look closer to complete and he just lost it, went berserk."

36

VISIBLE PROGRESS

Worse, the Xeno is too short to hold its engine and transmission, and it looks like construction is way behind schedule. But at his hillside shop, John Mason, in a white T-shirt and shorts, assured that he will never see Norman D. Hackett so long as he lives, speaks as an oracle: "Projects linger without visible progress. Visible progress is not relative to real progress, it's a mirage."

Nick rasps, "And the front end?" He caught a cold surfing and his voice is once more on its way out. The double A-arms are mocked up and John says, "Herman's working on the pull rods in his mind."

The rear axle has been suspended off six points at the rear of the chassis, four bars running front to back and two shock absorbers. I ask, "How long from the firewall to the tip of the third member there at the center of the axle?" I see a drivetrain problem. The engine is thirty inches long, the transmission is thirty inches long, the driveline will be at least seven inches long. And we have only fifty-five inches, firewall to axle. We're, what, twelve inches short?

"Well," John says, "you could lengthen the wheelbase."

"*A foot?* And make the car as long as a limousine?"

John shrugs. "Maybe you'll have to go to a transaxle."

Where does $5,000 for that come from? Nick and I drive to Burbank. I have an idea: Whack off the tail shaft on the transmission. We go to Darryl Young Transmissions and, sure enough, the solution is as easy as a "shorty kit."

Trying to get back on the freeway, we get lost. Marooned in Burbank. Nick bangs on the steering wheel. "We're so fucked up! We have no systems. We need maps," he croaks, "Plans!" His car is weaving all over the road. "Files! Schedules! Organization!"

I say. "But this is the Burbank airport. You said you came out here all the time."

"The other side," he says and points across the runway, "I always come to the other side."

My novel is finished. I reread it and suddenly the whole book seems nothing but tricks, mayhem and punchlines, and now Carmen Pisano— our connection to sponsors—says we have treated him like a "pigeon." Norman claimed that we don't give two shits about him. When I tell him this is absurd, Carmen, sitting on an oil drum, his short legs swinging back and forth like an agitated kid's, rubs a meaty hand across his dark face, and asks. "Then why'd he say it?"

Nick bends over, hands on his knees like a baseball umpire awaiting a pitch. "Because," Nick leans closer to the stocky Italian, "and I say this with total respect: Norm is a dick."

"I've got a surprise for you guys," John Case says. He has already scared up a cash sponsor who is dying to see the Xeno and John's new Isuzu Trooper is going sixty or seventy, headed north away from Long Beach to a greener place, when there is a noise on the roof. Nick squirts out of his seat, out of the window and is hanging out in the wind, grabbing at the thin ropes that lash the Xeno model in its aluminum box to the top of John's truck. John, wondering, Whaaaaa?, jerks the Isuzu off the highway.

Nick, John and I are driving: to Hexcel Composites in San Francisco. Big money. Maybe. But now this. Nick thought the model was falling off the top of John's truck. I examine tiny pieces of rubber, steel, glass, nuts and bolts that form a sort of car wreck gravel beside the highway while Nick cinches the aluminum coffin back down.

Twenty minutes later, the surprise. We ride an elevator up a Santa Monica high-rise to Charlie Risk's office, to see if Charlie can take Rooter the pig (currently ensconced at the animal "bed and breakfast" that, according to Nick, also houses "Michael Jackson's mid-size animals"). Charlie is John's pal and a movie producer.

His walls are covered with paintings; bright, sizzling surrealities. Charlie pops out of a bedroom office. Golf shirt, shorts, ruddy, oval face and high forehead. He says, "Sorry for making you wait but," raising a hand whose thumb and forefinger are close together, he says, "I'm this far from cutting a very big deal."

Then to me, "I want to show you just who I am so that I won't be wasting your time and you won't be wasting mine."

He shows me an article in the *L.A. Times* about how Charlie's girlfriend's ex-boyfriend was murdered by the Russian Mafia. "They blew him away and cut off his fingers and stuffed them in beer bottles." He says he is producing a film about a guy who kills himself and how just after completion of principle photography—stroke of awful fortune— the director himself committed suicide, which Charlie saw as a hot publicity hook. Before the director was embalmed, Charlie was on the horn to the media, pointing out this amazing life-imitates-art coincidence. "Mark," he concludes, "this is the kind of guy I am."

I have no idea what is going on. I say, "I thought we were here to talk about the pig."

Charlie is brisk. "I'll take him, but if he's a pain I'll get rid of him any way I see fit." Then he says this is more than a car, I have a movie. "John's pitched me. The high-concept American story: Boys build car. Money, speed, danger, chicks."

Charlie has set up a whole buffet for us. I say, "I don't know anything about this. Let's deal with the pig and—"

"Christian Slater is Nick. Jeff Bridges is John. No—" he points to me "—Jeff Bridges is you."

I suggest Jeff Bridges could play both of us.

Charlie says, "Mark, to be frank, you seem hostile."

At Charlie's dining table, Nick—with his hands, a knife, cheese, bread and his mouth—has got an assembly line going. "No," I reply, "I just don't think a movie means anything."

Charlie appears astounded. "What's wrong with you? Don't you want a hundred thousand dollars within ninety to one hundred and twenty days?"

I say, "My literary agent handles all this. Talk to him."

Charlie's round face takes additional color. "What the fuck does a literary agent know about the movies?"

I pour a glass of wine. "I don't know. Call him."

"And give away one hundred and fifty thousand dollars of free advice about how this town works so he can say, 'Thanks Charlie' and do the deal himself? No way. I haven't got all morning. I can get you a meeting with my agent, the legendary Jack Jalardi. Do you want one or not?"

When I say no, Charlie reaches across the table, pulls bread from a loaf, pops the tuft into his mouth, chews. "Anybody remotely involved with your project could claim the movie rights."

"And what," I ask, "do you plan on getting out of this?"

Charlie points to John. "Half of whatever *he* gets."

John's tan takes a quick, reddish hue.

We head north. Nick, who has budgeted two dollars (the contents of his wallet) for our three-day trip, has eaten enough hors d'oeuvres to last a week. The Salinas Valley whizzing by, I tell John my idea for Hexcel: We ask for $60,000 to skin the Xeno. We do the work, they provide the aluminum and the money.

John says, "Sounds good. Except we ask for seventy thousand dollars instead."

"Why seventy thousand dollars instead of sixty thousand dollars?" I ask.

"Because seventy thousand dollars is a rounder number."

Hexcel headquarters is in low, modern buildings below handsome hills south of San Francisco. Nick arrives in his green leprechaun suit with a metal lizard on the lapel. We set the model on a conference room table where it squats invitingly like a Thanksgiving turkey. No matter that it is not the same Xeno we are presently constructing. Hexcel executives assemble. John details our greatness, and at the proper moment—after their eyes have widened but before they begin to roll—I say we need seventy thousand dollars. The answer is no.

A spider with an abdomen as big as a thumbnail. Nick has a black widow perched on the end of a broomstick, caught in a slab of light falling into John Case's garage, where the chassis rests, about to go to the SEMA show in Vegas. Where, with luck, a bonanza. We've trailered the wheel-less chassis back to Long Beach, here to John's, who has thankfully become much more involved. In other words, he's paying for things—sort of magically, signing checks.

But problems. Herman dreamed the car "would shear a strut during a bending moment and tumble." He got out of bed, went to his computer, found his formula wanting and is rebuilding the suspension at his own expense. Then John Mason's wife Marie called, her voice as flat as a frozen lake. John Case's check to cover her husband's work bounced. Only a mix-up at the bank, but still.

We prep our chassis at John Case's cousin's house in San Pedro. With walls around him in a world he can control, Nick is confident, efficient. He paints and polishes, bathes the suspension parts in 1,1,1 techocholide, a cleanser designed to dissolve most anything but metal and him. We pop the grungy Ford rear end apart and to Nick's delight the gears are as fresh and sharp as new stiletto blades. "That's John Mason for you," he says, beaming. "Perfection where it counts."

Good news. An editor at Simon and Schuster says my novel is art, not garbage. It is Sunday morning. Last night was Halloween: Katie went out as a miniskirted, red-mouthed hooker and guys in cars whistled and screamed as she crossed the street. She has great legs.

I leave for Nevada in an hour. The SEMA show starts tomorrow. Matt is on my lap in the living room watching TV, using me for a chaise lounge. What could be better? The talc-y perfume of his skin, his feathery hair against my cheek. He joined a soccer team and scored his first goal. All these five-year-olds, they're like bees. They swarm around the ball kicking and screaming, the ball pops out and the hive dashes after it. Matt is poised and agile, his team won its first game and afterward Debbie made him lunch, a sandwich and an orange, crusts and rinds cut away, food for a prince.

But though Matt's teacher says he's a "sweetheart" and the woman who cuts his hair says she'd marry him if he were thirty-five, I worry. Every day I ask what he did at kindergarten, he answers, "Played." Everyday I ask, "Who with?" and he answers, "Nobody."

"He popped through the front door," Debbie says, " 'said, 'Where's Mark?' I said, 'Getting a taco' and he shouted, 'We'll be late! We're fucked! We're fucked!' Jumped back in his Honda and screeched off down the street."

I drive to John Case's cousin Bill's house, where Nick is frantically sorting parts on the driveway. All Nick will say is, "We're fucked, fucked, fucked," not the most detailed explanation in the world. I can't imagine what the problem is; what's the rush?

We tow the chassis back up to John Mason's. John is there with Herman. Both seem surprised to see us. We have to make Herman's rebuilt front spindles fit. They need to be remachined and that takes forty minutes. It's getting dark and Nick says we can assemble the car outside.

That makes no sense. The car has never even sat on the ground on all four wheels. In fact, it has yet to *have* all four wheels. But under a dimming sky we bolt the shocks and springs back on backwards. The fading light gives a confusing simplicity to the parts. I pick up two radius rods. In minutes they go from vague long flashes of metal to nothing but weight in my hands.

I say, "John has to at least let us do this in his shop."

"If I go in there he'll kill me."

"Why? Let me just go ask him."

"If you do, he'll go crazy." Nick clasps his hands below his throat, as if to strangle himself. "I plead with you, don't go back in there."

5:35 A.M. We are racing away from the rising sun toward Las Vegas. Herman got up before dawn to help us bolt the suspension together at first light, and we are driving into tan desert. The rub? Nick forgot to tell John Mason the car needed to be assembled, when John wanted to spend an evening with his wife and daughters. "His out-of-nowhere demands make me nuts," John explained, seething and, yes, it was best for Nick to wait outside in the dark.

In the afternoon we descend to a vast plain. Two riverboats are there in the desert. Huge hack fantasies, with signs out front advertising killer slots and cheap chicken dinners. Nevada.

Where Nick meets a beautiful young woman and falls in love head over heels.

37

Free World

We are in a convention hall big enough to house a small town. I've nailed sponsor after sponsor after sponsor. One guy, the young president of a composite company, comes up to me and simply asks, "What will it cost me to be invited to the party?"

What a light, what moths. I feel like my dad must have felt when his sleek sailboat, the *Faux Pas*, arrived at the Portland Yacht Club and knocked the old salts dead. Our streamlined chassis, with its big, wide tires and chalicelike aluminum wheels, is a smash here at the Concept Center, close by the Pontiac Portafino concept car, a lozenge the color of bubble gum, and a John Reed motorcycle that looks grown organically from its own engine block.

Around and above the chassis are Nick's drawings of the finished car, arranged like stations of the cross. In two days, thousands of people have beheld the Xeno. John Francis Marshall, the automobile illustrator, wants to *draw* the process of building the car. Even better, auto industry analyst Howard Koenig, short, wide, generally beige and trailing an entourage, declares that Nick is the most talented car designer ever and that by creating design icons for natural gas, we can revolutionize the world.

Natural gas, thanks to Norman, is the horse we will ride now. Why is it so good? I'm not sure. Mostly, I guess, because it's not hydrogen. Howard says Nick can "create the new energy paradigm." We are outside the convention center among auto executives, walking a gauntlet of pimps handing out pictures of naked women. Noting that "the equilibrium of disequilibrium is a force for stability," and that "self-similarity is a property that is ubiquitous," Howard instructs us that "this is the gag: design to context rather than content. You create a whole culture, the whole next world."

Money is talking to us, oil money. Castroil, Penzoil, Quaker State, Texaco. A sport-coated John Case flies in, a picture of fair-haired, sun-darkened, Kevin Costner-ish good health, and says, "All oil is is goo, it needs an image or it's nothing." We get names and numbers. John gets a poster of a big, beautiful lubricant promotion girl from the big, beautiful lubricant promotion girl herself. She gives John a smile to light a town. I suggest we could get cash commitments here like plucking $10,000 grapes and John shrugs, "I don't care about ten-thousand-dollar grapes."

"Hundred-thousand-dollar grapes then."

He shakes his head. "This project is worth millions."

This could be great because John, like Nick, could not lie, cheat or steal if his life depended on it. As a building contractor he is great with design—he could remodel the black hole of Calcutta and get it on the cover of *Architectural Digest*—and, best of all, he's does a lot of big deals. He's fair, generous—a few years ago, when he made a not-so-small fortune on some real estate, I heard that he gave his assistant $250,000 just for doing the paperwork.

John wastes no time. He informs oil company executives that the Xeno will be "on *Oprah*," that "Brian Gumball" will interview us on the *Today Show*. Parts fall from the sky. All I have to do is ask. Hurst shifters, Cyclone headers, Stewart-Warner gauges, Moroso performance parts. After midnight, John walks into the wrong hotel room and the president of a company gets out of bed and says he'll make us a custom steering wheel for free. Then General Motors appears in the person of Dave Hansen, director of Engineering and Product Development, Segment Planning and Engineering for Chevrolet Raceshop (I read this from his card, printed in both English and Japanese). Hansen, fit, slender and about forty, admires the chassis. A grin slants across his boyish face, and when Nick is done he says he may have a new-generation Rat motor for us.

SEMA is like an instant high school where we are immediately popular. People just plain like us. One especially likes Nick. Her name is Corina. A race director for Hyundai, John reports. "She's about up to here." He puts a hand to his nose. "Glasses, long blondish hair, like a sexy librarian."

"She's German!" Nick exclaims, striding out of the crowd to where I am standing in front of our display. "I'm in love. All these parts! Our luck has changed for sure."

———

Two hundred and eighty-eight crooked miles west by the odometer and not long after our drive home, next to John Case's garage, where we have returned the Xeno chassis, Gideon Bosker, just out of his rental car, puts a well-manicured hand to his well-trimmed head. "What impresses me, Mark, is your courage. When I didn't give you the quarter mil, you could have quit. Instead, you built this—" he gestures toward the chassis "—thing."

Gideon has been "writing songs with a fantastic woman." Driving to Case's, on his rent-a-car stereo, I heard a rousing, sibilant Madonna-gone-techno-industrial-country sound.

He offers to invest $15,000 and disappears in a puff of smoke.

"He's sort of a good-guy Dr. Strangelove," Nick says, as we stare at a glowing, roiling red-and-orange sky. The great arrow shape of an SR-71 spy plane appears, its delta wings divided by the long tubes of its huge jet motors. A voice intones, *"A revolution is underway that will lead to a new era of cleaner air and a reduced dependence on nonrenewable resources. California companies have lead the world in aerospace and other high-tech fields. Today a consortium of the best of these firms has taken a bold step. . . ."*

So begins the Calstart promotion video that Nick has inserted in my VCR. Nick has created quite a buzz for himself and Calstart executives have been very impressed with Nick's design work. We've been invited to join this consortium that includes Hughes, IBM, ITT, Cannon, electric utilities, labor unions and research institutions. Their collective goal: swords into ploughshares. The state plans, through this new umbrella agency, to save itself by hiring itself, through the creation of a $150 *billion* California transportation industry and Calstart needs a symbol for the twenty-first-century future. It looks as though the Xeno is going to be it.

The "good-guy Dr. Strangelove" is Lon Bell, who made a fortune adapting a guidance system he invented, arming nuclear missiles into an impact trigger for air bags. The Xeno is about to be a flagship for the clean, hip energy future. Southern California has suffered 80 percent of the state's job losses. In L.A. the office vacancy rate is 30 percent. Bell's Calstart, headquartered at the storied former secret Lockheed "Skunkworks" aircraft research facility in Burbank, plans to turn this around. We had just returned from the L.A. Auto Show. Nick's big rendering of a $14 million electric car created by Calstart dominated the lobby, above new model cars from the top students at the Art Center. More Nick clones. Demetri Wagner, from the American Hydrogen Association, was there, "Definitely unflaky as a schmoozer," Nick reported. Corina, the young woman he fell for at SEMA, was there too. I like her. Everything from her handshake to her wry contempt for the car show floozies Nick is so enamored of. I like it that people approach her before she approaches them. Nick is smitten: "She has rules. She will not leave a parking place unless everybody in the car has their seat belt on. She has a strict method. Corina knows to the last decimal point car talk etiquette. Like, say you're supposed to say *import*, if you say *foreign car* they know you're lame." Like Henrietta, Corina's parents were according to Nick, "Axis folks: A British bomb wiped out half their family, then the other half came here and made the American dream in the biggest way."

It looks as though this part of the American dream recently woke up to grim reality. The Skunkworks complex—essentially one huge building—is all but abandoned. Founded in the 1950s, the Skunkworks created the awesome—even though its motors overheated and its controls tended to reverse in a dive—P-38 fighter, the awesome—even though it become the definition of the term *cost overrun*—F-111, the awesome—even though it bled fuel through its fuselage—SR-71 spy plane, and the just plain awesome U-2 spy plane, programs that employed tens of thousands of people. But no more. The place looks like a ghost town.

It is January 15, 1993. On Nick's twenty-sixth birthday, a monsoon. Before we left, rain was whacking out of a shiny, white sky and pissing off the tiles of John Case's Spanish-style roof. A crazy man lived here and when John bought it the toilet bowl in the bathroom next to the man's bedroom was covered with his leavings. Stalactites. John and his young wife Georgia built a beautiful tile-floored porch in back and rolled out a carpet of grass and sod over the backyard, gutted and rebuilt the kitchen and today the only slight reminder of the previous owner are the black widows in John's garage, spiders surrounding the tubular, streamlined chassis of the Xeno.

Towing the chassis, we drove the fifty miles from Long Beach to Burbank, parked the trailer behind the wire-mesh fence that surrounds the tall, long block of the Lockheed building. A car races by on Empire Avenue and throws a splashing rooster tail of rainwater as big and long as a cresting wave. John wears a poncho, Nick and I wear L.A.'s idea of a raincoat—leather jackets. I pull snakes of cold chain that have secured the Xeno chassis to the trailer, they hang from my arms in cold, heavy loops and we wheel the chassis into a concrete-floored, concrete-walled, concrete-ceilinged room big as a football field. Here Lockheed assembled the "black boxes" for the F-111 fighter plane. Then the Soviet Union went away.

The building is massive, blockish, Eastern European. Steel-reinforced walls three-, five- and eight-feet thick designed to survive a ten-megaton nuclear explosion twenty-thousand feet directly overhead. The tolerances in concrete remain within one-sixteenth of an inch after fifty years. The empty belly of what used to be the beast. John and I walk through dark offices as big as basketball courts. Abandoned desks and more discarded swivel chairs than I can count. This is where they used to do the paperwork for the SR-71. John says, "Two hundred secretaries to keep track of a single plane."

At John Case's, Nick has declared, "We must take this opportunity to make the Xeno the most significant car of the century." I don't ask which one. According to Nick, Corina, director of the Hyundai race team that won last year's Pike's Peak Hill climb, says the cover of *Road & Track* will be a "slam dunk" if we follow her protocol.

More good news. Hexcel will provide materials plus $7,000 for the body, Chevy Raceshop is giving us an engine, transmission and Corvette independent rear suspension, my novel sold to Simon and Schuster and in John's pale-walled dining room—John not here but off skiing somewhere—Corina says we should debut the car at the Detroit Auto Show instead of the show in L.A. because the Detroit Auto Show attracts more international press. I ask, "Truck the car to Michigan?"

"You," an elegant finger is pointed across the table in my direction, "owe him," the elegant finger swings to Nick, "the widest exposure. Do you know who you have here?"

"Nick?"

The honey-haired young woman shakes her head. "No. The new Bugatti."

GM is rebuilding our transmission for racing purposes. I can only knock on wood and hope it arrives before my knuckles break.

In our new shop at Calstart, Nick uses thick pieces of paper as "mock aluminum" and says he's dressing the chassis "at one hundredth of the time and one thousandth of the cost that it would take and cost normally," i.e., two days and $27.50. John Mason comes by. "This place used to be absolutely huge," he says. "They had their own restaurants, their own hospital."

"How could we ask Lockheed for fifty thousand dollars?" Nick wonders.

"They poisoned the ground," John says. "People got sick and Lockheed just laid them off."

"Let's ask 'em for one hundred thousand dollars," Nick amends.

The car is big. The front tires are so wide that the space across them becomes a no-man's-land, stretched out. Hard to cover without the shroud looking like a big metal hat. The car is long and hippy in the middle. "What if we cut off the nose?" I ask.

Color leaves Nick's face. "Thousands of people have seen the plans for this car."

"Who cares?"

"My goal is to stick to process and procedure."

John Case says, "The nose looks like a long-billed duck."

Nick grabs his knife. "That's it. Off goes the nose."

"What about . . . ?" I draw an arc, so that the canopy and nose become a single shape.

"Go home," Nick says.

I describe a Nazi rocket plane with a blunt, chopped-off intake. "It had a cross like a crucifix up front that sent great gothic signals. Plus, it'd suck up lots of air for the radiators."

Nick cuts the nose off, says, "Maybe, maaay, heeee—naah."

"A wing up front would give us more down force."

"That would seal its fate as an F-One wannabe."

Nick tapes the nose back together, then cuts it off another way. It looks, after many whackings, like a cowcatcher. He is left to stare at a mosaic of taped-together paper shards.

I say, "What if you needled it, just made it more narrow?"

John says, "I don't think so, just let Nick do the—"

"You're right," Nick says, "it takes away the duck."

Going home, Nick says he can't be bothered by the "griefs and the beefs" of subcontractors and employees, so when the Xeno scores big he will hire an operations manager to replace me and then confides that a Calstart exec, seeing his portfolio, got down on his hands and knees and did the Wayne and Garth in front of Alice Cooper "We're not worthy" bit from *Wayne's World*.

Pete Wilson, the governor of California, is standing by the Xeno's chassis, informing several dozen news and industry people of his "determination to work together as Team California. We all share a single primary responsibility. We're here to create jobs."

"Here" is Burbank. Wilson is in the football field–sized "nuclear warhead–hardened" basement, and there our prototype sits beside the dais on a bright gray rectangle defined by the kind of bright yellow tape police use to isolate accident scenes. Outside, through the huge steel service doors, I see what is left of local aerospace. Nothing. Lockheed has bulldozed blocks of its former self down to huge carpet-flat fields of dirt so poisoned by years of toxins that it had to be carted off in dump trucks to be *burned* before being returned to the ground. Wilson, small, tan, dapper, addresses dozens of news and industry people: "What's right about California starts right here, in this abandoned hangar."

Last week the president of General Motors was to visit Calstart, and Nick spent two days in his suit here at his desk waiting, like a doll in a diorama, but the guy never showed.

I suggest we go to Calstart director Mike Gage and ask him to cover our costs. My time, Nick's time, John Case has invested time and money—it all adds up to . . . $437,050.

Governor Wilson introduces "Team California"—corporate executives stand by the Xeno—then promises to create "the great California comeback. We need to hear from you, the leaders of business in California." John informs me, "That's us."

38

LUCKY US

Moon has scored Debbie and me a very nice profit. The sale of our Portland house has jumped to a conclusion, one accelerated by the art director buddy I had living there who got drunk one night and called me up to say that, driving home, his windshield fogged up and he hit three trees. Then he called the next morning from jail to report he'd been mistaken about the trees, the three trees weren't three trees, they were three Mercedes, parked in a row, and that the police had practically broken our door down to get into the house to charge him with hit and run, but not to worry because Scary Larry was coming down to bail him out. "There was a huge scene up there, you would have thought the cops were busting the SLA." Moon said, "I own a gun now. If you want, I'll go shoot *You asshole* across his chest."

The neighbors made it very clear that they wanted us gone.

So, in about a day, Moon sold our house. For $40,000 more than we paid for it, $40,000 that was gone in the time it took me to write the checks to cover all the debts we'd run up in the meantime, but Moon had done a great, fast job and I thought it was time for him and John Case to join forces.

Because, for one thing, they already knew each other. From hippie days. Tet, screaming yellow zonkers and student riots. My mother sent me news clips sporting headlines like "Nine Drop LSD, Go Blind Staring at Sun." Fortunately at the University of Hawaii and then at the University of Denver, I'd smoked enough pot to realize that *love* was just *evol* spelled backward, and that nothing really mattered. The world could blow away for all I cared. Except for the beer and birth control factories, and McDonald's, so I could still eat. Soon whirl would be king, Janis Joplin president and Captain Beefheart secretary of state.

At college, nothing was ever a problem for John—whatever went wrong always worked out. During spring break we took off in John's Mercedes from Colorado to Tucson to pick up Moon at the airport. We drove at night across the desert, over two hundred miles getting lower on gas by the mile, no sign of civilization except the road in front of us, but John just shrugged. "Don't worry." Finally, at the top of a desert hill, the Mercedes died and I was thinking: Time to worry, John, but he was still slumped in his seat, like he wasn't even interested, and the Mercedes was rolling down the hill, its headlights pushing into the dark, onto some kind of building there on the side of the road, to illuminate a TEXACO sign.

I'd already discovered that John was good luck. On the weekends, for instance, unlike Moon, he didn't want the world to explode. We'd go to nightclubs, our mantra, "Wanna dance?" to girls from the telephone company (by this point I had whittled my linguistic ability down to the essential one-ness of "Far out" and "Fuck you" and the year before, at the University of Hawaii [*My daily schedule: 7:00 AM to noon, Surf. 12:00 AM to 8:00 PM, Dream the Impossible Dream. 8:00 PM to 8:20 PM, Walk to International Market place, tell tourist girls my entire life story, walk home. 8:20 PM to midnight, with two pencils, practice drum solo to In-A-Godda-Da-Vida. Sleep and repeat.*], I was informed that I was the only white kid ever to have flunked the "spoken English" part of the entrance exam), or drive around downtown Denver until John would spot cute girls in a car at a stoplight and ask, "Wanna go to a party?" Where? "At your house," he'd reply and next, I'd be off in the dark, say, conjoined with a girl who claimed her brother was the drummer in the band who did "The Bird, Bird, Bird, the Bird Is the Word."

The things I was good at, John was better. Chess. My senior year, I'd beaten the president of the Beaverton High Chess Club, but John would plough through my side of the board even faster than my dad. I thought I was a fast skier, John could ski as fast as I could backward. He was arguably even better than me at being my father's son. He spent part of the summer at my parents' house in Portland, where we had jobs working construction, and after about a week I got the feeling my mother and dad were thinking, Gee, if only . . .

Then I spent a week in L.A. at his house. John's parents were both excellent painters and had three paintings on their living room wall. One signed by John's mother, one signed by his dad and one signed by—I had to squint to make out the little signature—Picasso. An original. They were generous people. John's dad looked like Spencer Tracy and owned half of Case-Swane, a big fruit-packing company, and John and I went to Mexico with him once when he took his farmers out to dinner. There was confusion with the waiter about who John's dad was supposed to pay for, and with a shrug he indicated, why not make it simple, he'd just pick up the tab for half of the restaurant.

John's idea: We go straight to General Motors, our wheels greased by our new advisor, Howard Keonig. "Here's the gag: I'll use you to mate California aerotech with the capital A, capital I, Auto Industry. But right now you guys are just a bunch of arm wavers," auto industry analyst Howard says, his bulky face flush from the cold, his neck puddling over the collar of his white shirt. Detroit. An airport like a huge public library. Howard drives up over dirty ice in a new minivan.

Flat farmland, mottled with snow, slides around us. I am here for the SAE show. "This is a sitcom sell," Howard concedes. "Gray-suit bullshit. You'll meet every other pencil-protector geek in the Midwest."

Hexcel asked us to present the model at the SAE—Society of Automobile Engineers—convention in Detroit and John Mason gave me the fax number of the Wailing Wall in Jerusalem. So if we go broke again we can "plead for divine intervention at one of Judaism's holiest shrines. The Israeli national phone company will deliver your prayers for you. But beware, it's not a toll-free service."

Howard drives on. Detroit rises around us. Below tall buildings, ice floats in the river. The SAE gathering is big. In a huge bright room I see the flashy guts of American technology: spark plugs that last forever, tires that never go flat, natural gas tanks as light as hamburger buns and I wonder if our problem may be we've got a geegaw instead of a gizmo.

Nick, standing by the Xeno model like a wan carnival barker, introduces me to a garbageman "who is in racing and not really in garbage but actually in the Mafia" and over ham sandwiches in the media room, Howard says, "You don't present a product, you present a protagonist. The gag is: Nick Pugh is the star. We say: Not since Frank Lloyd Wright or Bugatti has there been a visionary like Nick Pugh."

The General Motors buildings are long, pastel. Outside the Chevrolet reception area, metal fish jump from a long rectangular pond.

Nick and I are there to ask for more Chevy support, and when public relations chief Ralph Kramer, big and gruff, says, "If we go to our dealers and replace a salable car with your car at car shows, we'll have a fight." I suggest, consider the opportunity. The engine General Motors is giving us is their latest-generation Rat motor. Chevy's biggest big block ever using clean, cheap, powerful natural gas. I say the Xeno will represent a sort of New Age Rat-motor ideal; an elevated, classic design for clean American kickass power that both construction guys and Yuppies will kill for, a design, so to speak, with a green, redneck, white-collar, blue-blooded twist. Ralph Kramer smiles again, laughs and then says he may have a use for us after all.

39

BOO-GOT-TEE

"The time is right. It won't be a car anymore, it'll be a national event," John Case vows. "A symbol for natural gas."

John wants to present the natural gas industry with a program with unprecedented depth. We'll make the original Xeno, then do a natural gas-powered truck and real-world car like a family sedan. A multimillion-dollar program. Wild.

Driving under the shadow of John's towering $32 million condominium complex on the beach of Long Beach—a venture financed by John with less than $25,000 up front—Nick, alarmed, asks, "How can we make three cars when we can't even make one?"

"John," I say, "is taking the project and turning it from a single thing into a phenomenon."

Risky, of course, but if John said the sun would explode tomorrow, I'd buy new Raybans, because he sees the future. John created a Gap/Banana Republic–style clothing store before there even was a Gap or Banana Republic. He has great timing. He was in Prague when the Czechs threw out the Communists, in Berlin when Germans tore down the wall. He mailed me a chunk. Also, he has great energy. Last year he biked across Ohio, border to border. Another time, he saw people about to run a marathon, parked his car and ran it too. In his street clothes. With no training. He was in bed for two days afterward, but I figured, like they say, it's the thought that counts.

Nick and I go talk to a chipper, chubby, honey-haired PR lady in Santa Monica whose office is her living room. Knocked out by Nick's designs, she asks Nick what his position is. "President. I run the company," he replies, and on the way home makes two requests: "Mark, when you call me the new Bugatti, it's Boo-*got*-tee not Bug-*ah*-tee, and when I'm talking please don't interrupt."

Days later, switching lanes in afternoon traffic, driving under graffiti-slashed underpasses to Calstart in his Isuzu SUV, John Case says, "The eight-ball baseball cap on backward, the bermuda shorts, the no shirt on, the no shoes. Investors don't like kids."

Kids Nick's age led battalions in Vietnam, but that's another conversation.

Back from skiing in New York, John is on his way to Calstart. We need money. Fortunately, Calstart's mandate, to quote it directly, is to: "*Coordinate . . . fund-raising activities for program participants and it further notes that Calstart's discretionary R & D program will provide funding for support (member) technologies.*" This "discretionary fund" holds $687,000.

Nick wants us to meet with Calstart President Mike Gage and has written me these instructions: "SPEEK THE RAP. SET UP MEETING NOW. GAGE IS NOTORIOUSLY BUISSY."

I tell John that if we are to become a "national event," he needs to create a master plan for our funding. He asks, "Why?"

"You are the financial officer."

"I am the financial officer?"

I hand him a promo pack with his job description on it. John sets it on his steering wheel, reads, says, "Okay, I am." Then he reaches into his backseat, grabs a magazine, flops it on my lap. "Read the article on financing, it'll give you a start."

"We're going to learn how to finance this whole thing out of a magazine article?"

"Why not?"

"John. You're a full partner in the project."

"I am?" Driving, he considers our promo pack there on his steering wheel. "Oh yeah, I am."

Nick is dubious. "We're running on angel hair. We must have rules, schedules, titles, strict organization and protocols. Who is John Case in this company?"

"The finance officer."

"No way! John is the host of our fine and mellow activities when he's not off skiing. Things—" Nick makes a chopping motion with his hand "—must be repetitious, methodical, plodding; it is time to create a highly efficient machine."

"That's what I'm talking about. That's why John should be president."

"You trust him with that much power?"

"What power?" I ask. "John is down to earth, and he's made a lot of very big deals. Superhonest, godfather to my son. He just wrote me another check for five grand. He's already loaned us thousands. The problem we've had is that he doesn't know who he should be: President of Xeno. We need a real businessman in charge or we'll be, as you'd say, histo."

Nick says, ". . . Okay," and, thus enfranchised, John immediately finds us a natural gas engine expert, Bruce Eikelberger. A former champion offroad racer, Eikelberger's shop is close by, in Huntington Beach. It is filled with beautiful, spotless classic cars—an early 1950s Allard, a DeTomaso coupe, a rotary engine–powered Austin-Healey and, anyway, Eikelberger took one look at Nick's drawing, said, "I get it, a green hot rod. No problem," and now John has us up in West L.A. at Dorf and Stanton Communications. The eighth-largest public relations agency in the United States owned by the largest public relations agency in the world. What clients—Eastman Kodak, Ford, Nabisco, Ralston Purina, Pepsi.

Their West L.A. office is populated by attractive, articulate women. John pitches Dorf and Stanton Director of Operations Peter Snyder this scenario: The Goliath natural gas industry has a great fuel—powerful, plentiful, clean and cheap—but is getting its butt kicked by the electrical and grain-fuel Davids and that our program, which John has now dubbed NGV/USA*, can, in one three-year fell swoop, reverse this.

"So," Peter says, "we'll represent the dumb natural gas Goliaths against the smart electric Davids."

"Ahhhhhm, yeah," John affirms. "But that's not bad."

He displays Nick's renderings and says, "Exciting cars to be shown off by *Sports Illustrated*–type people. Models. Long, blonde legged girls in bathing suits or whatever."

Peter Snyder, forty or so, built like a small college fullback, immediately likeable, funny and smooth, bites. He forecasts a "tremendous

*Natural Gas Vehicle

opportunity" and only smiles when John says we'll be partners, not paying clients, and smiles more as John concludes, "As long as we are fairly compensated you can make a million, five million, as much as you want. I couldn't care less."

One minor glitch. We meet with Calstart diretor Mike Gage to touch him for the $437,050. Gage is big and friendly, like an affable football coach. John put on a great show, explained how as a platform for "overt" technology, the Xeno will focus attention on L.A. as the center of the automobile's future and be a media bonanza, but when John asked for the $437,050 big, friendly Mike Gage said, "Sorry, the money had already been spent."

Gideon's $15,000 has yet to drop through the mail slot of the two-story home Debbie and I have just rented for a fortune a month and I find myself standing at the door to my daughter's new upstairs bedroom, reading a collage she has created to decorate her wall:

depression warning memory poetry
HATE   Trash   True Believers   LOVE
I was at the bottom
of a deep black hole   MYSELF
and couldn't climb out   TRUST
Parents   Black and White
and sex
            Kill
What is   *To do it or not that*
cool?   AIDS   *Is the question*
DEATH   !   LOVE

Matt and I walk to the park with a ball and a bat. He is playing Little League T-ball and I am assistant coach. I want my son to have a skill like a World Series superstar, not just to end up plunging around in middle age chasing sure-fire get-rich-quick schemes.

At the park I see my pitching arm for the first time in thirty years. Balls loop everywhere. Finally, he connects. A line drive to my nose. Knocked on my butt, I open my eyes and see my legs before me on the grass. I swear and get up. My little boy is squinting up at me like my face is the sun.

Stocky, casual, charming Peter Snyder says, "We must not think with skinny wallets," and that this may be Dorf and Stanton's biggest project yet: "We'll double consumer awareness of natural gas as 'the clean, powerful, safe, preferred fuel of the next century.' "

He begins to explain and Nick sighs, "Numbers. Oh, no."

"Nick's a genius," John says, "but he can barely add and subtract."

Peter draws a table that reads:

START	'93	'94	'95

"We need—" he says and scrawls:

	1.15 mil	1.15 mil	1.15 mil

"And you guys?" he asks.

"Ahhhhhmmmm," John replies, "put down a million."

Peter does. "So we're—us Dorf and Stanton are at one-fifteen per year and you—"

John says, "I'll be generous. Two and a quarter mil for you. One and a quarter mil for us. Five hundred thousand dollars for a promotional video."

"So," I say, "four million dollars in all."

"Sounds good," Peter replies. "A promoter's dream."

"Ahh, these two," John says and nods toward Nick and me, "will do great on TV. TV loves wacky artists."

I feel, oddly, about to be bumped down the food chain.

"With due respect to Mark and Nick," John says, "Peter, when you want to talk, talk to me, that'll be less confusing."

I say, "With due respect, I need to know who here is specifically answerable to us."

"With due respect," John says, "that's not a concern."

"Yes, it is. Will it be you, Peter?"

"I'll be riding point," Snyder says.

"Mark," John says. "These guys are committed."

"Okay. For how long?"

Peter claps his hands softly. "If, after four months, we're not getting anywhere, we may say this dog won't hunt. Get me a budget and we'll be on our way."

At John's house, sitting outside on his handsome Spanish-style veranda, I present a budget: three cars for $700,000 give or take, mark that up $150,000 and tack on $500,000 at $44,000 a year apiece to cover three years' worth of salaries. Nick frowns. "We won't make much money at that rate."

I say, "I doubt we can charge more than twenty percent over cost."

"Mark, we are artists not businessmen, how can your estimate let us both make a lot of money and do what we promised, how can we not violate our ethics if we want to make a profit?"

I suggest if we "violate our ethics" Nick may end up designing cars in the state pen, and John's wife Georgia's face lights up. Georgia is just a few years older than Nick and is still as lanky as a kid, but she has the natural gravity of a judge. "Nick, we are going to do nothing dishonest," she says.

"No." He looks at the ground. "But our goals to make a lot of money doing the best job won't fit into Mark's numbers."

"Then," Georgia says, "you may have to compromise."

"Ahhhhhhm, Georgia," John says, "Nick doesn't compromise."

"Then perhaps he'll have to settle for just doing the best job ever," Georgia suggests. "This has to be squeaky clean ethical, or we can't do it."

Good old Georgia. When John met her she was nineteen and already a manager at a department store, where her motto was "Know your product." When John is involved in a project, she is involved. She's tough. Once she a got a stomachache that would not go away. I took her to a local emergency room and she was so stoic describing her pain the doctors did not believe she was really sick until her appendix ruptured and destroyed an ovary.

Nick and I drive back to my house. "I don't think you should be throwing around dollar figures," he says. "That's not what you know about." I offer to call Peter Snyder but Nick says no. When I ask why, Nick retorts, "We are a *team*." He holds up a fist. "Me, you, John and Georgia." A finger pops from the fist with each name. "We can't make a budget phone call without the absolute agreement of the other members of the team."

"Why?"

"Because it's the corporate way of doing things."

"It's the Nazi way of doing things."

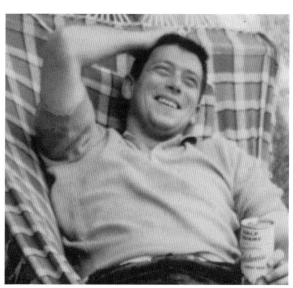

My father, Leonard Christensen, about sixteen.
Photo courtesy of Kathleen Christensen.

My cousin, Jerry Christensen, about twenty-four.
Photo courtesy of Jerry Christensen.

Portrait of the Artist as a Young Zipperhead. This photo, taken at twenty-four, was for my first professional feature story about a used car salesman, a guise I had no trouble assuming. Photo courtesy of Doreen Labby.

My friend Kit Bowen standing tall at the "Surf City" fire base in Vietnam. Photo courtesy of Kit Bowen.

Kit Bowen today. Photo courtesy of Kit Bowen.

Scary Larry Wobbrock, about eighteen, standing beside his first car, a very sanitary 1962 Chevy coupe. Metallic blue, chrome reverse rims, a small block V-8—what more can God give you? Photo courtesy of Mark Christensen.

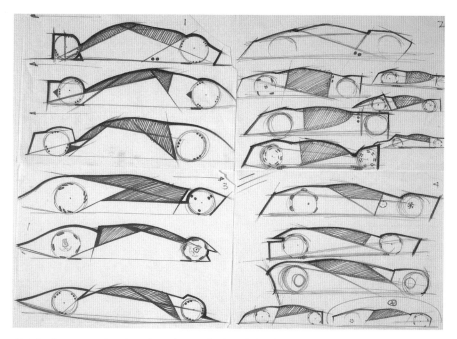

Original concept sketches done by Nick that defined car design language and became known as "new edge design." Renderings courtesy of Nick Pugh.

The first three-dimensional iteration of the design, dubbed the "Xeno." This is a fifth scale clay model done in April 1990 for a Mazda-sponsored project. Photo courtesy of Nick Pugh.

The author and Nick Pugh at the beginning, when it all looked so easy. Photo courtesy of Joanne Wilkins.

Front three-quarters view of the early Xeno. Rendering courtesy of Nick Pugh.

The rear three-quarters view of the Xeno that the author saw in 1990 and prompted him to ask Nick to do the "fast car" project. Rendering courtesy of Nick Pugh.

An early illustration of the third-generation Xeno. Rendering courtesy of Nick Pugh.

The concept art for the original Mazda "Xeno." Rendering courtesy of Nick Pugh.

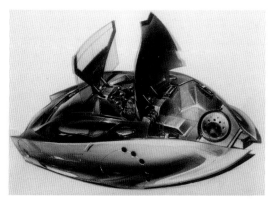

A modified top view of the Xeno showing off its hardware. Rendering courtesy of Nick Pugh.

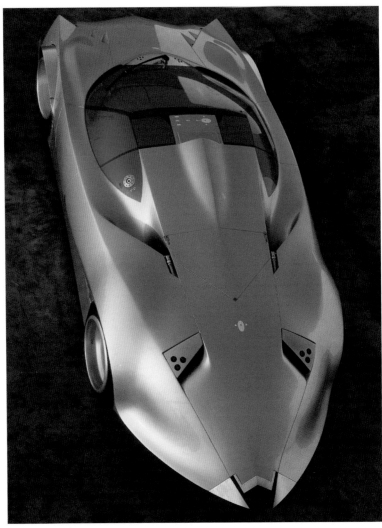

The second-generation Xeno that was unfortunately too expensive to build. Photos courtesy of Nick Pugh.

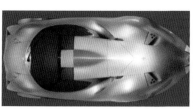

Top view of second-generation Xeno above and Ford Synergy below. Xeno photo courtesy of Nick Pugh. Synergy photo courtesy of G. Photo.

These images represent the influence of Nick's design language on the automotive industry. This is a comparison of the original Xeno design created by Nick in 1990 and 1991 with the Ford Synergy concept car released in 1995. Xeno photo courtesy of Nick Pugh. Synergy photo courtesy of G. Photo.

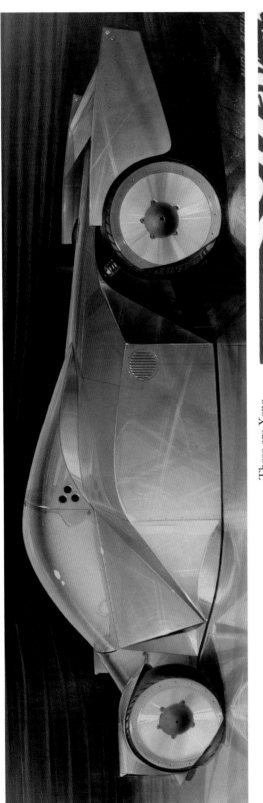

These are Xeno designs created as part of the project development process that were thrown out either because they were ugly, too expensive, or technologically impractical. Renderings courtesy of Nick Pugh.

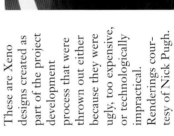

Ross Spiros with a hydroxy fuel cell prototype. Photo courtesy of Ross Spiros.

John Mason working on the first rolling chassis, which was eventually scrapped. Photo courtesy of Nick Pugh.

Above: Nick's original concept illustration of the fuel storage chassis. The vehicle illustrated here is composed of a composite sandwich frame that holds the natural gas cylinders within the structure and has a theoretical range of one thousand miles. Rendering courtesy of Nick Pugh.

Left: Gideon Bosker. Photo courtesy of Mark Christensen.

Catia computer model of the fuel storage chassis technology integrated in a Chrysler van frame. Model courtesy of Nick Pugh.

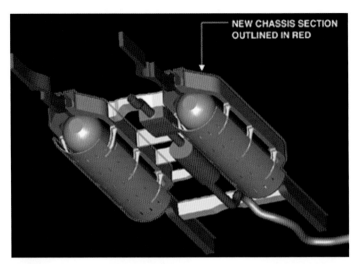

NEW CHASSIS SECTION OUTLINED IN RED

Matt Christensen. Photo courtesy of Mark Christensen.

John Case and Nick Pugh in front of the Longranger. Photo courtesy of Georgia Case.

The Longranger natural gas–powered prototype. Photo courtesy of Nick Pugh.

The final concept for the third generation Xeno backdropped by its charcoal cartoon. Rendering courtesy of Nick Pugh.

Katie Christensen.
Photo courtesy of Mark Christensen.

The crew tinkers with the natural gas fuel system. Photo courtesy of Tony Thacker.

My wife, Deb Wenner. Photo courtesy of Patti Gehrke.

Nick Pugh and Bryan Fuller in the Xeno. Photo courtesy of Eileen Pugh.

Nick's dad, Charles, with Nick's brother, Dave. Photo courtesy of Nick Pugh.

Jerry Forster. Photo courtesy of Tony Thacker.

Nick and Eileen.
Photo courtesy of Nick Pugh.

Nick and his mother.
Photo courtesy of Nick Pugh.

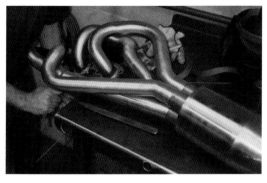

The exposed headers being built. Photo courtesy of Tony Thacker.

Robert Martinez machining the taillight blades. Photo courtesy of Nick Pugh.

Bryan Fuller welding the aluminum body panels. Photo courtesy of Tony Thacker.

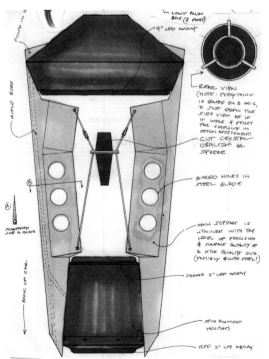

The sketched and then finished taillight. Rendering and photo courtesy of Nick Pugh.

Welding together the chassis. Photo courtesy of Nick Pugh.

The final Xeno III chassis. Photo courtesy of Tony Thacker.

The final phases of the Xeno III.
Photos courtesy of Tony Thacker.

The perfect beast. Well . . . almost.
Photo courtesy of Todd Johnson.

Nick's face goes from day to dusk. His hands become fists. "In the successful corporate environment that we must desperately have, creative freedom is perfectly balanced with rigorous corporate strictures."

"Guess what?" I reply, "I'm not going to live like that."

Beside smashed new cars—Fords, Volvos—sits a white Mercedes whose hood is covered with a hill of shattered glass where a crash dummy's head has slammed into the windshield. The Mercedes is parked by a new Honda Civic with a sign on its door that reads: NCAP 35 MPH FRONTAL IMPACT.

The Honda's hood looks like crumpled paper, its engine is litter and windshield a jigsaw puzzle. The Honda was towed to impact by a cable spooled to an old Chrysler engine that reeled the car into a plywood-faced, steel-backed wall at sixty-five miles per hour.

John Case and I are out by San Bernardino. Peter Snyder has declared our aim will be to double the public awareness of natural gas as a vehicular fuel by creating a *billion* new consumer impressions. The three-year budget is now up to $12 million. Using a huge tractor trailer emblazoned with a stylized American flag, we will tour the three cars to a hundred markets a year for three years.

John appears at least marginally rapt as Anil Khadilkar, a small, round-headed man who pioneered technology we may need to construct our "body glove" interior, explains how fourteen years ago he helped develop the Research Safety Vehicle, which could withstand, without the likelihood of fatality to its passengers, a fifty-miles-per-hour barrier impact. "Today's cars," he says, "are only certified for thirty miles an hour."

Great. But John thinks it's too much trouble. "The natural gas utilities have billions controlled by guys more interested in their golf scores than the bottom line," he says on the way home. "They don't care about safety interiors." He gives me a list of the annual revenues of the top fifty natural gas utilities. I see numbers followed by zero after zero after zero, proof of an industry making endless billions. John says that simply by giving us .0001 percent of their take, the industry can boost those endless billions by 33 percent. "The world is running out of oil. We are the gateway to the biggest new energy market in history."

"The director," Nick says, just back from Hollywood, "has eight su-percars, all white. He makes *fifteen thousand dollars a day*. The guy that guarded the Xeno drove a blacked-out Suburban truck with S-A-Y-T-A-N, for license plates—I asked why he didn't get S-A-T-A-N and he said Prince beat him to it."

Nick has been hired by General Motors to "dress" a make-believe GM design studio with his models for a TV spot showing how cutting edge Chevy design is. Our Xeno model—designed for and commissioned by Mazda—was the main prop to show off GM's hipness.

We are at my house. Peter Snyder calls from St. Louis, asks me why we even need GM Racing as a sponsor and when I remind him General Motors is the biggest corporation in the world and that they have already given us $15,000 worth of parts, he says, "That's only, what? One percent of our total budget."

"Yeah, also a bird in hand."

Matt is hungry. John Case picks up the phone. In the time it takes me to cut the crusts from the bread and smear it with peanut butter, our budget goes from $12 million to $16 million. Peter is commissioning the Gallup poll to do a natural gas market survey. When I ask who will pay for it, he says, "My treat."

My Uncle Bert has died. It is almost summer and at the old hotel where we are staying in San Diego, I read a mash note written to my daughter, *Katie: I'M STRICKEN But I love it*, under which there is a heart pierced by an arrow and below that: *CALL A DOCTOR*. This written by the handsome young bell captain who has scared my daughter with his flirting.

We are here for a memorial. At my cousin Jerry's condominium on the water, my father, looking delicate, gives a quiet account of how his older brother Bert kept him out of the lumber mills and got him into college. Afterward Jerry, my dad, Matt and I go for a cruise in Jerry's big speedboat. "You drive," Jerry says, tossing me the keys. I haven't driven three speedboats in my life, but Jerry says, "No sweat, ninety-five percent of seamanship is just aiming."

Crashing across the ocean, waves slamming against the bow of the boat, two aircraft carriers sitting high in the water to starboard and another speedboat heading straight at us, I remark, "Jerry, that guy's coming right at us, what's he going to do?"

"I don't know what he'll do," Jerry replies, "but I know what *you* won't do: Hit him."

Later, back at his condo, I ask what rank Jerry is now. Jerry moved out here to be a navy doctor. He no longer wears a crew cut, and his hair is grayer, but he is the same burley guy he always was. Reading a sports page, he says, "I dunno. What's just below admiral?" He wants to know how the project is going, and with my dad sitting beside me, I say that, chances are, I'll soon be filthy rich.

Before we left Long Beach, John Case said forget $44,000 a year, so I suggested $90,000, and he said forget that too, so I added a one to the $44,000—right after the dollar sign—feeling as I did so a queasy excitement that seemed like lust minus sex. Off hand, I'd say it was greed.

"The one thing that concerns me," my wife says, "is that John doesn't pay attention to details."

We learned that when we went in halves with John on a house, a fixer-upper in Long Beach. John was the contractor, Debbie the designer and they took the house from shack to perfection in about four months. Everything sanded down, repainted, rebuilt. A new lawn, sod rolled out like green carpet, flowers planted everywhere. The only problem was John didn't keep track of the construction bills and when he finally tallied everything up and Debbie saw that we were, how else to say it, wiped out, she became a tornado in our bedroom, stuff flying everywhere. Still, as soon as John realized his mistake, he wrote us a check to cover our loss and so I find myself listening indifferently in John's upstairs office, as Nick insists we become, "more diciplinarily businesslike."

John Case's house is beautiful, his office out back casual. His filing system is his floor. Surrounded by John's papers, Nick says, "In meetings, each of us must be in perfect sync and absolute agreement so that we form a seamless circle of each one of us backing the other one up relentlessly in precise unison. We must do our research militaristically in the most thorough, minute detail, so when we pitch a potential sponsor not only do we know everything about him, but everything about his daughter too. We must have absolute, uncompromised structure and organization."

Nick is suddenly impatient. "Every day I wake up and want everybody to say 'yes' right now. I'm just afraid that everything that has not happened before will not happen again."

John, sitting at his cluttered desk, says, "Your career is not a beauty contest where ninety-nine of one hundred people have to agree that you're the fairest in the land. All we need is one person."

Nick grabs his head in his hands. "All my life people said I'm maybe a genius. Then I ran into Mark and—" Nick makes a tumbling motion with his hand.

"Don't worry," John says, "this will make you stronger."

I say, "Here's an idea. We make a national natural gas marketing plan."

"Riiight," John says and smiles. "And charge them for it."

"If the natural gas industry doesn't know how to plan their future," I continue, "we plan it for them."

"Ig zackly," John says. "It's a package deal."

Nick is alarmed. "We had a plan. This is another plan."

Though John speaks softly, almost at a whisper, Nick has his fists planted in front of his ears as if enduring a roar. "Nick, listen," John says, "we must evolve to survive."

PART THREE

DAYS OF RAGE

T-BOONE

1970. The Days of Rage. Student demonstration time. Two helicopter gunships came wheeling out of the Colorado sky above me and my $90 Chevy station wagon. With luck, they'd machine-gun the whole student body. *Tin soldiers and Nixon drumming*, sang Neil Young from my staticky radio.

I was a film major. John Case and I had made a great one, too Andy Warhol for words: John walking around a paved circle in the middle of the park in a loop that could run continuously forever. So that if you had it projected on a wall in your house John would walk around that circle until the universe stopped expanding and began to collapse back in on itself. Also, I was making student commercials. Sample ad: Soft focus an attractive couple in bed. She: "Do you love me?" He: "Oh God, yes." Passion mounts, until—hard focus in the foreground—a woman's pretty hand sweeps an erupting bottle of Coca-Cola onto the screen. Foam all over, flash the kicker, COKE, IT'S THE REAL THING, and cut.

Of course, there might not be any Coke commercials after the revolution. Though John Case said, not to worry—the more things changed the more they would stay the same. Couldn't John see the obvious? Mick, Keith, John, Paul, George and Ringo, Bob, Joni, Grace, Jimi and with a little help from their friends Neil, David Crosby and the Doors (with, if need be, a goal-line assist by Country Joe and the Fish) were about to break on through to the other side. In the post–Rocky Raccoon universe, Zappa, Kesey or the Panthers would stuff Nixon back in his box, and the corrupt corporate criminal state would collapse to rule by Mick, Keith, John, Paul, George and Ringo, Bob, Grace, Joni and Jimi, who with a little help from their friends Neil,

David Crosby and the Doors (with, if need be, a goal-line assist by Country Joe and the Fish) would liberate Cape Kennedy's Saturn C moon rockets, blast the White House to Tranquility Base and record the superest of super sessions from outer space, a new hero guitar Constitution beamed back to earth and broadcast through the fillings in our teeth. "Meanwhile, here in Denver, John," I concluded, "you and I can liberate a bunch of Sizzler steak houses and eat forever for free."

"Never happen," John said.

At the time we were in downtown, standing on the sidewalk by a construction site. John, who was myopically less interested in the revolution than in how things worked, was trying to determine exactly how the steel beams of a new skyscraper were fitted to their concrete footings.

But who knew, maybe John didn't even like Sizzler, so I reminded him how—when the shit came down—there were probably twenty million single young women out there who neither one of us had slept with yet who—free at last, free at last—would, loosed from the chains of hypocritical bourgeois sexist morality, walk up and say, "My place? Your place? Or right here."

"Never happen," John repeated. He had a scrap of paper and was drawing the foundation. John's problem was that he was too conservative.

And here change was, the revolution. I was within a few blocks of the university and already I could see students and troops everywhere. A new world was at hand. The year before, I had seen a truncheon-waving conga line of Honolulu police make hippie goulash of a bunch of SDSers at the University of Hawaii and—though getting shot could be cool—I was in no hurry to get walloped. I hit the Chevy's accelerator, chasing the Army helicopter's tail as it sped through the sky toward campus. The revolution was at hand.

Revolution, indeed. Except this time, John Case is buying it. Twenty-two years after Kent state, Long Beach Natural Gas's T. Boone Pickens, who lost four hundred million dollars in the last five years and would dearly love to get it back, stands before a convocation of industry leaders and announces, "The natural-gas vehicle market is incredible. The mayor of Dallas is trying to get three hundred thousand vehicles within just four counties," and he predicts that "twenty million natural-gas–powered vehicles will be put on the road within ten years."

New-time religion: Our $65 billion annual trade deficit created by petroleum imports could be wiped out by the sixty years' worth of domestic natural gas reserves. Natural gas has 25 percent more octane than pump gas, is 40 percent cheaper and reduces overall polluting emissions by 20 percent. Car conversions now run $4,000, but as production reaches one million annually, that will drop to about $500 per car.

Peter Snyder—who has informed me that to propel him through work dawn to dark he drinks up to three *pots* of coffee a day—is not impressed. "Boone is thinking little. He's missing the awesome power of the consumer." Peter says we must "explode" in the public mind. "We will reach ninety-seven percent of the population by the end of year three or I'm hanging up my spurs." The program, he says, will run $6 million a year for three years—for a total of $18 million.

And the next day at a Thai restaurant, John declares we will ask only top money from the top people.

"That's not presumptuous?" I say. "We're not Madonna."

"But we *are* Madonna," John says. "And when Madonna goes on tour she says, 'Gimme Mike Ovitz'—'Mike, I'm touring. Get things ready.' We'll be the gas companies' Madonna, their star attraction, and that's how Madonna goes—straight for the top."

I make the drawing:

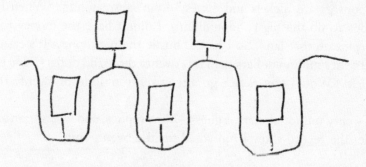

and ask John and Nick, "Do you know what this is?"

John looks pained. "Aaaaahm-eeeh, why is that important?"

"Because," I say, "the palooka with the Harvard MBA who runs the billion-dollar natural gas company may also have an engineering background and our unbelievable lack of simple knowledge of how an engine works may hit his bullshit meter."

"We're not motorheads," John says.

"We're asking five million dollars for three automobiles. If we're not motorheads, we've got a lot of explaining to do."

John regards me quizzically. "You have to be able to see the big picture. We have a visionary alternative to the status quo. This is not a car project anymore, it's a national event."

Peter Snyder is nonchalant. When I ask about the $500,000 tractor-trailer rig we will need to tow our circus around, he says, "Let's not get lost in half-million-dollar increments." He says we ask for $8 million the first year, five the next and five the last. "No singles, no doubles, we go for nothing but the big homerun."

I suggest this is getting out of hand, that we seek sponsorships at the $50,000 level and John tells me, "If you want fifty thousand dollars, why not just go borrow the money?"

"John, I don't have collateral to just go borrow it."

John looks mystified. "Has your dad gone broke?"

"My dad thinks this is nuts."

Now John looks worried. "You remind me of the salesmen in *Glengarry Glen Ross*. The movie. Angry guys just worried about their mortgage payments."

"A failed salesman didn't get our sponsors."

"Sponsors are nickels and dimes," John says, smiling. "When I got the idea to do the big condominiums, I didn't have the money to put a fourplex on that land. So I had to hustle the big money. It's easier to raise twenty million dollars than it is twenty thousand dollars." He turns to Nick, "Would you rather go after twenty million or twenty thousand?"

"Twenty million dollars, I guess," Nick replies, and when John asked me, let the record show I too voted for the twenty mil.

"Big power engines," Bruce Eikelberger says, considering our new Rat motor as if it might be good to eat, "are the cleanest because they burn every bit of fuel." But when I ask how much the easy power will cost, he smiles, shakes his graying head and says, "That's like asking, 'How long is a string?' This thing'll be hard to reengineer because it was built sooooooo right in the first place."

It is the Fourth of July. Chevrolet Racing's gift, the 502 V-8, has arrived at Bruce's shop in Huntington Beach. The result of $500 million in retooling, the biggest, newest, most powerful Rat motor ever, all ours, sitting in a big box surrounded by natural gas-powered police cars and a natural gas-powered meat wagon from the L.A. County Morgue.

Does that mean more expensive or less? I'm not sure.

A former semipro baseball player, offroad racer and magazine editor, Eikelberger has a nice shop. Cars all around: The old Austin-Healey, its body stripped down to metal and a new rotary engine, sits where the old inline six used to be. Eikelberger's own 700-horsepower propane-fueled Cadillac, a perfectly new-appearing 1920s-era milk truck and immaculate chassis to a 1938 Ford, bright red and cradling a factory-fresh Chevrolet 350 V-8.

With our block mounted on a stand that puts the Rat motor at waist level, he plucks it apart with the casualness of someone washing dinner dishes, and taking the engine down he talks about growing up in Kansas. "My mother's family was wealthy. They owned most of Riley County." He says he was raised in a hundred-year-old stone farmhouse and spent summers on his father's parents' farm in the western part of the states: "Butt ugly and so flat you could look out and see for three days." He drove combines and chased cows home with a pickup truck. His first mechanical experience was in a blacksmith's shop. "Firing a forge, heating metal and beating on it."

Bruce's first car was a 1929 Overland Whippet, "a bigger, nicer, prettier Model A." In that Whippet, the barely teenage Eikelberger installed a 1955 Pontiac V-8 and a "sluggomatic transmission." Then he built a 1934 Ford pickup graced with a DeSoto Hemi head. "You could smoke the tires at a hundred miles an hour. The problem was any time they got a bite of traction, they'd blow the driveline out. I'd go through two old Ford top-shifter transmissions a week."

He married early and had three kids by the time he was twenty-one. This cost him his chance to go to Vietnam. "Every time I'd get a notice from my draft board I'd just send them another birth certificate."

Meanwhile, he raced cars in Seattle. "I was just a motor nut. In those days, hang around the track long enough and somebody'd take pity on you and let you take a couple laps." He drove Top Fuel cars 170 to 185 mph quarter miles in Colorado and Texas. "I was braver than Dick Tracy and dumber than Sam Ketchem. I'd drive anything: 'Where do I sit and which way do I point it?' "

He crashed and was injured so badly he had to have a foot and a half of intestine removed, then moved to California, where he got a job with Bill Stroppe, Ford's top race promoter. There he got into off-road racing. *Car and Driver* credits him with at least 186 wins by 1983 and writer P. J. O'Rourke noted, re: Eikelberger's fabrication: "Every weld was like a row of dimes. Every bolt showed a dozen threads above its nut. Every edge of metal was filed smooth as a Gucci belt buckle and painted more carefully than a thing in the Louvre."

I like Bruce—he's given so much money to Long Beach State's women's basketball program his name is on the wall at their pyramid coliseum. And he seems to never not be working. His shop is like a Denny's, always open. He looks like an ad for tough, but fifty-three is fifty-three, and when Nick suggested he could have a heart attack, Bruce shrugged. "Nah. I take digitalis."

He slips off valve covers of the 502 and says, "Healthy stuff. These guide plates—things that guide the push rods—that's not standard. Killer valve seals—dual valve springs—good-lookin' productiony stuff— but big, strong, well designed."

He spins off head bolts, lifts off one of the cylinder heads, notes, "Giiiii-normous ports. We can dump a tremendous amount of fuel in here."

He says the block is going to his friend Yo. "I'll have it dialed in, make it straight, true, we'll bore it thirty-one thousands over—change the pistons—so it'll wind up about five hundred and fifteen cubic inches. That way we can create the piston top configuration that we want.

"We'll design pistons to wind up with between eleven and twelve point compression. Don Bass has a computer program that'll give us insight into what the configuration of the intake track should be, what we'll need in terms of piston configuration versus cam timing. Forged pistons," he says, lifting one. "This is not any kind of normal production motor. This is a gorgeous basic hot rod V-8."

Peter Snyder wants to give birth to NGV/USA through "ambassadors." He picks the editors of *Natural Gas Fuels* magazine to be first. John and Nick fly to Denver to see them. Returning, John says it was a "love-in." Nick made gorgeous new drawings of the car—one, diaphanous in a "luxury setting" outside a fancy restaurant, its mirrory aluminum body reflecting chandeliers and white table cloths. Another, a rendering of a huge natural gas-powered eighteen-wheeled truck resplendent in red, white and blue.

On the jet east they met, Nick reports, a fifteen-year-old "design freak," whose "dad has a disease that only like, seven other people have where God tells you to kill your family," and, as a dry run, John and Nick pitched the boy. The kid was bowled over, as were, next day, the editors. Nick sees clear sailing ahead and at the huge new postmodernist South Coast Air Quality Management District building—"the house that smog built" near Pomona—Georgia, Nick and I listen as John makes his case. We will market the clean fuel future through our cars and "good-looking *Sports Illustrated*-type people." The woman he addresses suggests we "modulize our request. Emphasize jobs created." What jobs would those be, I wonder. Well, Debbie and I need a maid. The Air Quality woman says, "Ask for four hundred thousand dollars and hope you get three hundred thousand dollars."

Afterward, Georgia says, "John, we have a problem. Tailor what you say to your audience. That woman doesn't care about glitz, or *Sports Illustrated*-type models. She cares about what we can do to help control air pollution."

John says forget $300,000, it's a waste of time chasing nickels and dimes. "But we do have a problem. The way Mark dresses. We've got to look like businessmen to be treated like businessmen."

I look down and see that while I am wearing slacks and a starched white shirt, John is resplendent in his suit: a timeless, if wrinkled, slab of gray.

We're going to Texas, center of the natural gas universe, to present our program to T. Boone Pickens. "How do you feel, John?" Nick asks, after John has finished booking all the meetings.

"I'm pumped."

"I'm superpumped," Nick says. "Georgia?"

Georgia, in tennis shoes and jeans, and looking about fifteen, surveys herself and says, "Yeah, I feel puffy and bloated too."

Nick says we need to go after big apples hanging off short trees and suggests GM as a money sponsor.

"Neat," I agree, "we could use another fifty thousand dollars and—"

"Three million dollars would be nothing to them," Nick says. "Mark, we're going to be rich."

Rich. What would that be like? I take Matt to "robot batting practice" at the Long Beach batting cages and watch all sixty pounds of him pop off balls thrown from a pitching machine, his bat cocked high above his bony shoulders and a big vein cording the side of his little neck. Driving home, we pass the mansion of the rich people who live up the street. A vivid, meaty family who have seven garbage cans and live in a new house that stretches, with its arches and bushes and flowers, across the block, and from this house pop new cars, new kids, new dogs, new—

I forage the Oscar De La Renta bin at Two Piece Warehouse, find a dark suit for $99.99 and John, Nick and I fly to Texas.

Austin. Hot. At our hotel room, Peter says he's readjusted our budget so that the three cars altogether are budgeted at $8 million. I ask, "How can I justify that cost?"

"Mark," Peter says, "writers live hand to mouth. They don't understand finance. When a prestige home builder sells you a mansion, do you question the cost of the bathroom fixtures?"

"People understand value," I say. "A CEO knows what a car should cost. Eight million dollars for three cars makes us look ridiculous."

John says, "The Calstart electric car cost millions."

"And it looks ridiculous."

John is getting aggravated. "We don't have just a car. We have Nick Pugh. If you hire Jack Nicholson to make a movie, nobody says, 'Why pay so much? He's just an actor.' If you buy a Picasso, nobody asks what Picasso's paint cost."

"Because," I say, "they have track records."

"So you don't think our program should cost eighteen million dollars?"

"We may be *lucky* to squeak by with *just* eighteen million dollars," I say. "To create *one billion* consumer impressions could cost a fortune. But eight million dollars for three cars' construction is insane."

"Mark," John says, "we are not charging for the fabrication, we are charging for the program. Eight million dollars is what the car part of the program costs, because that's what it's worth. We have a right to sell an idea for anything."

"An *idea* is worth what you can get for it," I admit, "but the cost of the cars will be seen as a real cost we'll called to account for. We'll look like idiots or worse."

John shakes his head. "The cost of the car has nothing to do with its price."

Nick, his eyes wide, says, "Mark, we're artists, not businessmen; why not just trust Peter and John on this?"

"Because," I reply, "there's no way I could convince people that these cars each cost two and a half million dollars."

"Then," John says, "we'll hire somebody else to be the project co-ordinator. You can go do something else."

Forget that. In the dark hotel room we are sharing, sitting on his bed, John says, "Me? Trying to get rid of you? No way. But this is a once in a lifetime opportunity. I've never had a chance like this to make a difference." He gets up, turns on a bathroom light and I see a slice of him in the doorway. "This time next year we may be sitting in the Oval Office talking to Al Gore."

The next morning we give our presentation to Austin natural gas executives and a PR lady gets salty at John's suggestion that the industry isn't doing enough to promote itself and suggests, "Take your foot out of your mouth before you try to talk to us." Then it's off to see T. Boone. We drive south in a rent-a-van, John and Nick high-fiving: "Are you pumped?" "I'm superpumped!" "Are you superpumped?" "I'm *hyperpumped!*"

"If I knew you two were gonna be this excited," Peter says, "I'd've brought a tongue suppressor."

Hours later, John pulls into a little old town, mostly just a street between clapboard shops, hotter than it is interesting. At Wild Bill's Not Quite Famous Bar-B-Que, I say that we better get ready for the long haul. This may take quite a while.

"I don't think so," John says. "Not at all."

Dallas. In Boone's office I am looking at a painting by G. Harvey inscribed "The heavens declare the glory of God and the firmament showth his handiwork.—Psalms 19:1," when T. Boone takes his place at the head of a conference table the length of a long room. A slender, gracious-seeming man who I have been told controls half of America's natural gas reserves and who reportedly lost $250,000 a day last year, he says, "Ah have only one question: How're yawl gonna make money?"

Peter offers a gentile version of buy low, sell high and Boone says, "You know why something like this has never happened?"

I say, "Lack of imagination?"

"Gas people are too shortsighted to know it is worth the effort. You got people who've said: 'We don't want to grow, cars are just a pain in the ass.' Utilicrats. But I like what you're showing me—nobody's come up with anything near this ambitious. Though to a lot of people eighteen million dollars still looks like a lot of money."

Boone's large, buff assistant Andrew Littlefield says, "We have to get the automakers pregnant. I think with Boone's muscle we can get them to go along with natural gas. But your budget scares the shit out of these guys, blows 'em right out of the tub."

"A pimple on the elephant's ass in the long run," Boone says. "This is a good idea."

Nick only brought deutsche marks, left over from Henrietta, and has to borrow money from John in order to eat. At a Houston natural gas company, John introduces Nick as "the Michael Jordan of car designers" and Peter Snyder as the "Michael Jordan of public relations," then gets lost. Nick takes over and does a stunning job. "It's today, it's now, it's happening, it's here!" He exclaims and booms through our entire program as if it were the Sermon on the Mount delivered by Lee Iacocca. A fresh-faced marketing woman says it is the best presentation she can remember, and that Nick makes her feel old. I ask her age and she replies, "Thirty."

John takes Nick to the wrong airport in Houston, we speed across town toward the other one, fly through an intersection, cop cars whiz by our van. Nick yells, "We're fucked!" and John, booting it, accelerating between a pizza truck and a taxi, laughs, "They're too busy for us."

He's right: Nick sprints to his flight without a minute to spare.

Home to Long Beach. I've just called Bruce Eikelberger. His main concern is to make sure our new motor delivers as much power running natural gas as it does pump gas. Pump gas is a liquid, natural gas a real gas. Though it is very high octane, because it is "dry" it causes normal pump gas engines to lose about 10 percent of their normal power, unless the combustion chambers are reworked correctly. Bruce says that's a cinch. Good. Looking out my upstairs office window I see my thirteen-year-old Katie, tall and tan and young and lovely and hanging onto the outside of a speeding city bus, hitching a ride down the street. I see a control issue here.

41

THE LIVING END

If I didn't know better, I'd say John was determined to make Nick Pugh America's favorite son. He and Nick just got back from Washington, D.C., where they had a "love-in" with rulers of two of the four "natural gas universes." John says our "Eighteen-million-dollar program is a done deal. It's just a matter of collecting the checks. It was big. It was really big. We walked through every door without a peep. We mesmerized the guy from the American Gas Association. We are creating a superstar."

"Who?"

"Nick. Our message is Nick Pugh's cars are rolling jewelry and Nick Pugh is the new Michael Jordan and he has embraced natural gas as clean, fresh, beautiful, sexy and real, and Nick has made the statement: All my cars will be natural gas cars. We'll put the car on Wall Street surrounded by not-a-lot-of-makeup, no-spike-heels, *Sports Illustrated*–type women passing out posters to people going into the Stock Exchange, putting the car right in their face, infiltrating the power structure. Then we go to Michael Ovitz. 'Michael,' we say, 'you've made a fortune in entertainment, now corral your superstars and throw us a party to change the world.' He'll say, 'If I could reduce air pollution by eighty-five percent just by throwing a party, I'll do that.' And what else will he do? A movie. He'll say, 'Mark, who shall I have star?' We stick the car in Disney World. Forget the Smithsonian. Six Flags, that's where the American consciousness hangs out. This is big. The way IBM got rocked by Apple, the way CDs replaced records, that's us. Things that would move in decades will move in years, we'll image this across America. It could destroy the oil companies. Home refueling. Gas stations will be the Laundromats of the twenty-first century. Nobody will buy gas unless they need to drive a really long way on one tank or can't afford the five hundred dollars for a natural gas home refueling station. Nobody will buy gasoline except the poor and traveling salesmen. Listen to me, Mark, this is the future. The American Gas Association has fifteen million dollars a year just for advertisements. We're selling too cheap."

This morning, Matt woke up with a cold, our rent check bounced and the gas company, from which we plan to extract millions, shut off our heat until Monday. Three days from now. Told we had a sick child who needed hot baths, they say, "Get a letter from a doctor."

Nick is broke and says he needs to borrow money from John, but that there's good news: "We're going to be bigger than Disney. Mark, my goal is to get you thirty million dollars by the time you're sixty-five. Because we are going to be rich beyond belief."

He has redesigned his head, had the hair around his ears cut way short. This has lopped years off his age, he looks like a Depression-era teenager who is, sitting on my couch in his shiny black suit, surviving the bad times well. He says he has cut out pictures of Michael Ovitz and pasted them in his notebook and that John is now talking about going "beyond *Sports Illustrated*-type people. We could get Claudia Schiffer for ten thousand dollars a day."

Nick reports: "John is a ferocious bulldog, you should see him meddle his way to the top. On the phone to Atlanta Gas, John got through all the secretaries until he was telling the top guy all about us and I don't even think the guy knew what John was talking about, but he said, 'Come see me in Atlanta' anyway."

Before I can ask for a clarification, Nick goes on, "We could go public within seven years with a two-billion dollar offering. Mark, Ferrari of America, it could be us."

Later, at John's house, I say we're drowning in our own hype. John replies that he wants Georgia "to meet all the builders and engineers, so that in case you're sick or on vacation or something she could take your place."

Buildings grown not built, all cars driverless, civil rights for machinery, new immune systems $1.99 off the rack at Wal-Mart, *Aloha* is set at the cusp of a new age, the tale of rogue trillionaire Frank Crawford who, as the lights go up, has just declined to buy the United States because the purchase "would involve too much paperwork" and ruffled feathers after he leased a Russian armored division, had it Fed-Exed to Honolulu to serve as his personal security and who, convinced that "whether you're Jesus Christ or just the Bitch of Buchenwald, all you need is one good idea," was determined to blow his own nation up out of the Pacific Ocean.

My beloved wife is impressed and my agent says *Aloha*'s black vision of twenty-first-century America may give me a shot at becoming if not the next F. Scott Fitzgerald at least the next Jay McInerney, and even though I remain ecstatic at having my entire life yoked to the likelihood of Nick Pugh becoming America's Ferrari, if John doesn't get me fired in the meantime, I'm delighted at *Aloha*'s prospects for movie money. I fly to Honolulu to literally make sure the islands in my imagination are those islands in reality and flying back from Hawaii I sit with a tall, charming, English world traveler who just got a call, unfortunately, from his girlfriend who suddenly had to leave L.A. and for some complex reason he can't stay at her house when she's gone and he's in a bit of a bind and—no problem, he can stay with Debbie and me. I give him my address and next, rapt to his technicolor tales of Africa, South America, the Antarctic, I realize he's insane.

What to do? Miraculously, when we get to baggage claim at the airport the Englishman simply disappears. Debbie rolls up outside in the Volvo. I really missed her. We've been together pretty much since we met at Portland's newest, hippiest steak house right after I got out of college. There Moon and I were nominal bosses of the waiting staff. I was supposed to "train" Deb. What eyes. I had never seen such a look of angelic, energetic intelligence. How to describe our romance? Basically, I was told to sit and stay. Implicit in that command was that I try to make something of myself. So now I'm a writer and there she is. My wife looks wonderful, her wild hair, her blinding smile, and she's very happy to see me until, the exit sign to Long Beach flying over us on the freeway, I tell her about the world traveler. "You gave a lunatic our address? To stay at our house? What if he kills Matt during the middle of the night?"

I say killer crazies are fairly rare birds and she veers onto the exit. "That's what my life has been with you, nuts. Nuts don't pay the rent. Neither do Nick or John. What do you want me to do, work until I'm ninety?"

I'm struck that this may be a sign that I had better circle the wagons. Though thank God the mad Englishman never shows.

Pierre Ouellette, who, as the original bass player for Paul Revere and the Raiders was booted out of the band for not learning the dance steps and whose ad agency grosses $30 million annually says, "Dorf and Stanton are the big boys. They do preventative press for heavy industry; who you go to when TV calls and it's not Katie and Bryant but Morley and Mike. But you have serious problems with your partners. Nick's the boy genius there to talk about his vision for the car. But this kid has a very rosy view of the wonders of corporate fascism. Nick is two people. One is a free soul who creates the fabulous but who also gets in trouble—loses passports, throws temper tantrums, humiliates himself. So he's created a second Nick: a narrow-minded, authoritarian cop to protect the free soul from himself."

Pierre, stocky and graying, has come to visit me recently in California and had met several times with John and Nick. His company takes up the twenty-first floor of his black, glass-sided building and now the two of us sit is his office high above Portland, the silver plate of the Willamette River far below.

"Look," he continues, "you guys do not even exist as a business, and if you submit inflated budgets to these utility people, you're finished."

Good to know. I met Pierre while editing *One Dollar* magazine, a Portland monthly I helped found that published articles like "Confessions of an American Glue Sniffer" and "Conspiracy Digest: How Aristotle Onassis Rigged World War II" and sold a lot of ads for stereo equipment, platform shoes and Aerosmith albums. My first real job. I drove to work in a 1967 Mustang convertible bought from a friend who lost his driver's license during an acid trip ("Mr. Virkus—do you know how fast you were going?" "No, Officer—seventy? eighty? ninety?" "Three miles an hour, Mr. Virkus. Could you step out of the car, please?"), a "suicide frog" whose tires were packed with marijuana in Mexico to be smuggled across the border. The Mustang had been crashed a lot and slabs of body putty—applied by the finest body shops in Tijuana—were falling off in chunks, and I got it for $400.

A simpler, more innocent era—that convertible would be worth twenty times $400 now. While at *One Dollar*, I published the first works of writers who went on to *Rolling Stone*, *Playboy*, *Esquire* and books. Pierre among them. The English rights to his first novel, *The Deus Machine*, just sold for $75,000, the screen rights for $150,000.

"You have John Case," he notes, "penciled in for a hundred forty-four thousand dollars a year as company finance director. If I'm the prospect, I'd think: finance director—that's just another word for sales-man, who's earning his money *by making the sale to me*. He sees your one hundred and forty-four thousand dollars and thinks: Okay, Chris-tensen created the team. Cool. But now Christensen's just a baby-sitter. Nick. Nick they gotta live with. Nick's still gotta *do* a lot. But what do *other* car designers make? One hundred and forty-four thousand dollars a year? Nah, I don't think so.

"Bottom line? I'd say John Case is doing the best he can the only way he knows how. It's about rescue," Pierre concludes. "Commerce must rescue art. The businessman proves his worth by saving the artists from themselves. John has made some sexy development deals. He's got a beautiful home, a beautiful wife, life's good, but he has no idea of the magnitude of what he's taking on."

I say, "I realize it's risky."

"No, it's not," Pierre assures me. "Risk implies a chance of success. This has no chance of success. These utilities will never hand over tens of millions of dollars to people who—do you guys even have a bank account yet—don't even exist."

"This is the Nike 'Just Do It' gone berserk. John Case has got boy genius Nick and the big PR corporation fighting the great fight to do right," Scary shouts over the scream of his engine, suburban Portland flying by in a woodsy blur. "And all that can stop them is you. The pea-brained ignoramus. They're wearing the white hats and you're the bad guy. Don't shift before redline, goddamnit."

Scary Larry is the only friend I've ever had who could get angry because I was not driving his car recklessly enough. We are in his hot rod Saleen Mustang. Recently charged with going the speed of light in a thirty-five mile an hour zone, Scary plans to have the Mustang's fuel system enriched by nitrous oxide to create explosions inside his cylinder heads so profound that those heads will have to be welded to the engine block, rather than simply bolted down. God knows how many horsepower he's coaxed out of it, but when I hit third gear, the rear tires break loose at what? Seventy? I'm afraid to look at the speedo-meter.

I am in Portland for my father's eightieth birthday, on my way to a 7-Eleven. When we get there, Scary Larry, who has just concluded his year as president of the Oregon Trial Lawyers Association, climbs out

THE LIVING END / 295

of his hot rod coupe and says: "You're screwed. This is a private stock offering. This isn't fee for service, you're soliciting funds to create your company. You're violating blue sky laws. The government will charge you all money paid back, dock you triple your profits, plus attorneys fees, that doesn't even include RICO."

"What's that?"

" 'R' stands for racketeering. It gets worse from there."

We drive back to Scary's house. Scary lives with his tall, model-lovely wife and his taller two sons. The younger one, Nick, is about to go swimming, the older one, Jake, is about to go to Stanford. Scary's house is big and, with its small-windowed dormers on the roof, looks as though it was designed to be defended against the Indians. In his basement he has a nuclear bomb shelter.

David Lindley howling "Your old lady sure looks good to me" on his stereo, he retreats to his patio, lies down on a deck lounge and rests a beer on his stomach. "Question: Why'd you make John Case president?"

"The big program was his idea. But it's not like he can order me around."

Scary drinks beer. "Of course he can. You made him boss. And if you don't go along with his plan, you're right, he won't order you around—he'll just fire you."

"No, he won't," I insist. "He can't."

"You don't get it!" Scary looks at me as if I'm a toddler. "You're too naive to realize they're too naive to realize you're the only one smart enough to know the promotion scheme is nuts. They're gonna get rich saving the world. How can you get in the way of *that*?"

I say, "I spent years having zero trouble editing people like John Shirley, an anarchist rock singer who founded cyber-punk science fiction, Katherine Dunn, who was nominated for a National Book Award, Mikal Gilmore, whose book about the execution of his brother Gary was—"

"Just geniuses," Scary barks, "not Midas-touch Messiahs. Face it. You've made monsters. Your partners don't care about the car anymore. The car's just an excuse for making the deal."

I left Oregon not long after I was married to the girl of my dreams by Judge Robert "Iceman" Jones during the recess of a local murder trial of a psychopath who had buried a hatchet in the forehead of a social worker who he believed to be an agent of the Antichrist from Mars. Scary was my best man.

As a wedding present my father bought Debbie and me a perfect 1964 Porsche 356C, and though I took the Porsche through hard times—crashing it once so badly that it looked like the reflection of itself in a fun house mirror—I am not looking forward to telling my father that I was just forced to sell it. Nice Italians in leather jackets and tassled loafers—looking like landed working stiffs—dealt eighty-seven one-hundred-dollar bills on our dining room table. I'd driven the car for almost fifteen years and it occurs to me that my ambition to create the Xeno at any cost will make about as much sense to my dad as if, twenty years from now, my son's son announced his driving ambition to become first oboe in the New York Philharmonic.

Trees. Big firs. Cut and stacked on log trucks that are sailing down the road in front of my father's ranch house, $10,000 a load. Loggers have punched a big dirt road through what was, until this week, a thick forest of second growth, a brown track that snakes up toward the blown-off top of Mount Saint Helens. Our great hill of blueberries has been cut in half to reveal an ancient shack, a sauna, its thick, rotted beams busted practically to dust. Behind the sauna is the raw, organized mayhem of a "thinning," a tree here, a stump there, there and there, that looks to me more like a clear cut. These are logs straight and round as pencils. They will go to make condominiums for the Japanese. A few truckloads' worth and my car could be built. My father is not happy to hear that my Porsche has been shipped to Italy and tells me I should have asked John Case for a guarantee he would finance construction of the Xeno as part of the partnership agreement. When he asks why I didn't I am frank: "Because he would not have agreed to that."

"Then," my father says, "for all his confidence, John has no confidence at all." We sit there. Me feeling, and my father looking, as frail as a couple of baby birds.

What if you were to develop an engine designed to run on natural gas, you would be—enfranchised. "Mark," Bruce Eikelberger says, "that may be the best idea you've ever had."

"You mean it would be possible?"

"Possible? It's lots better than possible, it'd be eeeeeeasy. And if you can build one, you could build a million."

Here's the gag, as Howard Koenig would say: If you want to convert your engine to run on natural gas, the conversion will cost you $4,000 and result in a 15 percent power loss. But what if we established a "critical path" toward eliminating the cost and power loss? Bruce says that by changing any standard engine's ignition timing and engine management system we can achieve much better power, drivability and much better—perhaps even ultra-low—tail pipe emissions. Bruce will reengineer an electronic fuel mixture control system to establish a standard for OEM mass production. We'll meet the very low ULEV standards and *still* have the high performance and drivability. Our engines will run thirty-five percent cheaper than an equivalent gasoline powerplant. We will have the first original blueprint for a V-8 engine "designed" to run on natural gas.

Georgia plans to write a government grant to cover the costs of engine development.

Visions of sugarplums. Leaving Bruce's we stop at Sam's Lounge in Sunset Beach. After the bartender insists Georgia show ID, I tell her the idea of making Nick more famous than Michael Jordan is nuts. "John used to be the most practical person I knew, but this, my God."

"John feels," Georgia replies, "that your forties are your peak earning years. Besides, if Peter—who runs one of the biggest PR firms anywhere—is confident, why shouldn't you be?"

I suggest resolving the securities issue is basic to our success and without it we may not have any, that Nick and John selling $8 million worth of cars without being able to tell a camshaft from a clothesline bodes poorly for our future.

Georgia says, "It's not our business to know that stuff."

"We're in the *car* business, Georgia."

"But they can just say we have the right people."

"I remember you saying way back when: 'Know your product.' "

"John does know the product, the product is Nick. He believes in Nick, don't you?"

"Sure." I do, don't I? "But Picasso didn't get a fortune for being Picasso until everybody figured out that he *was* Picasso. Nick can't get that kind of money without the recognition that commands it. We've got to get back to reality, stick to the facts."

"But too many facts can get in the way of the deal."

———

Two days later Katie, hopping up and down as if she is on a pogo stick, tells me, "Mom said Georgia said we're gonna be rich. Rich, rich, rich."

John and Nick are gone again, flying all over, pitching our program. Nick has designed several natural gas tank chassis to accommodate a range of at least three hundred miles and John thinks we can get it patented. Georgia is writing a grant proposal for the engine development program and Nick, when he returns from wherever he's been, flies into my house and says if we could make Bruce our employee we would own the engine development program outright. I reply that if Bruce develops it, he should own most of it. We should take, I pull a figure out of my hat, 20 percent.

"Mark, if we put up the money, we own the rights. After all, it was your idea."

Time to play to the cheap seats. "Do you remember the Bob Dylan saying, 'To live outside the law, you must be honest'?"

"I am honest!" Nick hoots.

"You want the key people to remember you as a friend."

"Business is not about friends! I really don't want to be in business with friends."

"So it is just a matter of cutting the next best deal with the new best guy?"

"I'm going to be tough! Honest! Trustworthy! Fair! Drive a hard bargain and make people stick to it." Nick's fist hits the thin wood arm of my Pier One African chair. "I want to be the guy who says that if you agree to do this, this and this and I put up the money and pay you, I get the profits. If the inventor gets fifty thousand dollars and I make seventy-five million—" he makes a signature motion in the air. "I say, 'You signed the contract, I took the risk.' "

"So what do you get out of all this?"

"When I'm your age I want fifty million dollars. Long term, five hundred million dollars."

"To do what?"

"Die having left the biggest mark. That's money, fame and progress. Making the world better for everybody. I want it all. That's the difference between you and me. I want to be the man. I want the lion's share."

42

DAZED AND REFUSED

A short note: Nick Pugh, who I admire and respect and pray will live long enough to be one of my pall bearers, is not now at thirty-three who he was then at twenty-four, a very young man lip-synching the war cries of the kick-ass 1990s entrepreneur. In fairness to Nick and others involved, I must admit that much of the following reflects my frustration over a project that I felt was now completely out of control.

Peter Snyder is hosting the Dalai Lama on behalf of his public relations company so he can't go to Atlanta to meet with David Jones, the president of Atlanta Gas. John and Nick go alone. Nick calls from Georgia. "Mark, Mark, Mark, Mark. This is Nick, we're in the big leagues now! Everybody loves it, just nobody is stepping forward. The key word is *nobody* can pay for it. It's like wringing water from the driest washcloth."

The next morning, John and I have breakfast at a hash house. He says Nick has finished his ground-up long-range natural gas chassis plan. And that no line item budget will be necessary because we're offering a package deal. For what is now a $21 million program. "We're in good shape," he says. "If one of us has a hissy fit and quits, the rest of us can continue on our own."

"Dad! Georgia told Mom that you might have two hundred and fifty thousand dollars by Christmas."

I am on my way out the front door to Matt's soccer game. Katie's in her jeans and her bikini top. She's surfing and taking tennis lessons, and is getting very good. She doesn't want me to watch her practice, but I do anyway—I hide behind a tree at the park and watch her on the court like some kind of sports pervert, as she smacks fast serves over the net. She is about to get her braces off. One of her friends has had her orthodontist engrave "Forget the waves, ride the surfers" into her bite plate. "Are we gonna get a new car or a new house or what?"

Or what, would be my guess.

But who knows. John and Nick have a point about the high cost of the three cars. The auto industry standard cost for the construction of a concept car is now about three million dollars. I've seen these vehicles. Gory welds, tinny construction, often the gauges do not even work and pop the hood and it is as if somebody just made a big steamer trunk of a streamlined body and threw the motor and everything else inside as an afterthought. Nick's three-million-dollar cars would be built, as he has promised, like Fabergé eggs. And John is doing everything he can. As usual. When Debbie and I first moved to Long Beach from Portland and stayed at John's house, I'd sometimes go out on his jobs as "construction conversationalist," keep him company while he did things like turn a falling down pee-soaked tenement into what—with its old Hollywood turrets—looked like Snow White's new castle in what to me seemed about five minutes. But still, the fact is, the best custom cars in the world are hot rod show cars and none I know about cost more than $500,000, and as for some of these other numbers, Jesus.

At a big park by our house, Matt runs across the grass toward his soccer team. A haircut has taken ten pounds off my son. When the game begins, he scampers and darts, popping the ball this way and that, aggressive. His coaches really like him.

"I do not see how this can work," I say to Debbie, "but what I can't understand is that Georgia buys into it. She is the most practical person I know."

Debbie says, "Maybe Georgia got hypnotized by the dream."

"Or maybe she knows something I don't."

An executive at The American Gas Association, who likes our program, tells me, never mind its zillions, the natural gas utility money is tightly regulated by the government and "the stockholders do not want their dividends jeopardized by any sudden cost of promotion."

When I suggest to John that we stress our "path to production" program and that we could raise tens of thousands of dollars just off sponsors, he says once again he doesn't have time "to run around raising bunches of tens of thousands of dollars." Then: "We need front. Good-looking offices. Something maybe in the World Trade Center."

And at John Mason's neat barn of a race car shop, the Xeno chassis, which we have trucked up from Calstart, now sits wrapped up in a blue tarp, leaves falling on the blue plastic, like a ditched or forgotten dream. Nick is talking about buying not one but two facilities "for my tax purposes," and says that once we succeed, "there will be a lot of celebrating, a lot of forgetting."

I tell Nick I'm worried that John considers the car just piffle necessary to get the deal done, and Nick agrees enthusiastically. "Absolutely! John doesn't even really *like* the car. To him it's a tree that's fucking up the forest, and too complicated. John's strength is he doesn't like to understand anything he doesn't have to. John is a hunter. He doesn't care about gutting the deer, cleaning the deer or dragging the deer out of the woods, he just wants to kill it."

Nick predicts NGV/USA could become "the new Chrysler," the result of a "four-billion-dollar public offering." If memory serves, that would equal the largest public offering in history—British TeleCom's stock sale to finance the European branch of the Information Highway.

Scary Larry voices a more earthly concern. Prison. We will be soliciting a security in violation of God knows how many security statutes and can all end up in jail if we do not modify our pitch.

"Look," I say, "Dorf and Stanton has done huge promotions. They organized the Arthur Daniel Midlands no-till approach to farming that saved billions in soil destruction. They—"

"I don't care," Scary shouts over my phone, "if they organized World War Two. They are going to organize your trip to jail if you idiots don't clear up this security mess, and fast."

Nick and John have just returned from Washington, D.C. They attended a natural gas conference to pitch our program, but were preempted by a blue-haired, New Age matron who, Nick says, "Got on stage and said we all must have love and if we wanted to we could all hug the CEO next to us. By the time we made our presentation, half the other CEOs had gone off to play golf."

Peter Snyder has flown out from St. Louis to L.A. for our meeting with Richard Furman, the head of Southern California Natural Gas. Pierre

Ouellette calls to say, "You'll never get him to bite without a line item budget, first the sun will fall out of the sky."

John has a barbecue and, on John's veranda by the light of the coals, Peter says, "How is your buddy—a medical malpractice attorney—going to know about securities? If we go to a securities attorney he'll just want to get us in the securities business. As for Pierre, he has a reputation as a high-tech visionary—but bluntly? Pierre is little, and we are big. Our parent company is the largest in the world. He bills millions, we bill billions. We've been down this road many times before. I own a house and a half, if you think I'd risk it over something like this—I just wouldn't."

I say the lack of a budget makes no sense.

"Mark, we provide an irresistible packaged service—they won't get down to that level."

At Southern California Natural Gas, CEO Richard Furman, trim and stylish, asks why are we doing this. John replies to do what's right, plus to make a profit. Furman says he wants a full budget and if he likes what he sees, perhaps we can talk again.

Sticker shock at Norjen, a prototype fabrication facility north of Simi Valley. They make gliders, thin, sleek aircraft that look as delicately evolved as prima ballerinas, as well as prototype cars for companies like BMW. One of the owners, Tor Jenson, worked as a Stealth executive and on his bid for our work, he says it will only cost them $330,000 to build the second car, and Nick calls from the road, worried that we'll "lose credibility" if our program doesn't cost enough. "The industry standard for a ground-up prototype is almost ten times that. Tor worked on Stealth fighters, he must know how to drive up a budget."

"You wanted a budget," John says, as he and Nick walk into my house, "here's a budget."

I sit down in the living room, read. "One hundred and twenty thousand dollars," I say, "just for Nick to design the car?"

"Don't you understand the number?" John asks.

"If anybody took a look at one hundred and twenty thousand dollars to design a car that basically already exists, it might raise a few eyebrows."

Nick says, "I'll need another full-time designer and a full-time modeler."

John frowns. "No one'll question these figures."

"You said no one would ask for a budget."

"I might like, need a runner," Nick says. "You know, like a messenger."

"What would that go for?"

"Minimal." Nick shrugs. "Forty grand a year including bennies."

43

Natural Disasters

Halloween. Fires have swept through the neighborhood south of us. Debbie and I pick through the rubble in Emerald Bay. A friends' house is cinders, the living room soot, except for a green glass rag that yesterday was a bottle of Heineken. All that survived was a barbecue, a can of lighter fluid, a box of charcoal briquettes and their two fireplaces. For days waves of flame made the bottom of the sky a sickening dull red. Ashes fall. "Like snow," Debbie told her mother, "just not as much fun."

"Know what this is?" Nick asks, sketching on the glass-topped coffee table in my living room. Cylinders have appeared at the end of his pencil, a box around them.

"A way to repackage natural gas cylinders in a chassis," I say.

Nick smiles. "You're right. It's so simple, it's completely dumb. Like why didn't an ape think of this?" Our dream, I have discovered, now includes the fortune-making possibilities from a long-range chassis. A simple raft of CNG* cylinders. John and Peter are paying for lawyers and a patent search, excited about the possibility of "packaging design" patents for natural gas fuel.

When Nick returns from a trip to Texas to see Bill Clinton's friend Gary Monroe, I get a big smile and a handshake—what I get from Nick now, first thing, every time I see him. He has bought a book on selling. "When we left, Gary's assistant said, 'We look forward to a long-term relationship.' Mark, do you realize what this means? We are in the presidential circle!"

*Compressed natural gas

At John's house I suggest we seek more sponsors, go to Mister Gasket, champion spark plugs, but John's mouth warps. "Auto stuff has a bad connotation. I'd go for Taco Bell." When I reply I won't see the car become a doodad for a marketing scheme, concern shapes John's face. Selecting his words carefully, as if he were a psychiatrist and I were a valued but volatile patient, he says, "You're an artist, and I'm not saying that just to be insulting. But you've got a lot of anger, you take things the wrong way."

"No he doesn't!" Nick declares, suddenly, "because I've seen you! I've heard you! You talk like Mark is anarchistic managerially. You make it sound like Mark's just the help."

"Would I have invested my whole future in what he created if I thought Mark was just—" John's face scrunches up "—the help?"

Again Nick and John fly east. Nick calls, worried. "In some meetings John hammers everything home, *boom, boom, boom*—like when he told these oil guys looking for new markets that natural gas could be the 'new American dream.' People see him as totally All-American. Which he is! Totally brilliant visionarily. Which he is! Totally a great guy. Which he is! Other times he's like a pit bull playing chess in a china shop. He has fantastic concentration on the ultimate goal: Everything he does is to go after the king, but he knocks over important pawns in the process. With women in the room, he talks about putting sexy models on Wall Street and I'm going to myself, No, no, no, didn't we talk about no bimbo promo stuff in front of women? After the meeting a woman came up and said, 'I like your program but you can't talk to women like that, we have power,' and I told her—because it's the truth!—that John is the least sexist guy I know, but in the next meeting with women he doesn't say *sexy model* but, 'Don't worry, ladies, we'll get articles about the car in *Ladies' Home Journal*.' I didn't say anything but inside my head I was shouting, 'Noooooooooooooooooo, John, nooooooooooooooooo!'

"My mom didn't say *fucked* but she said we'd be fucked if we don't have a partnership agreement and," Nick cracks four knuckles at once, "*incorporate*. But the problem is anything he doesn't want to do John says we don't have to do. Sometimes John says something and I think, 'No, no, no, no,' but I say, 'Yes, yes, yes,' because it's more valuable to keep his morale up than to disagree with him. John is totally tough but weirdly fragile. He works so hard!"

I ask Nick if he doesn't think that what started out to be about idealism is now about gluttony, and he replies that riches honestly earned, fame born of achievement and influence based on surpassing performance have nothing to do with gluttony at all.

At the L.A. offices of Dorf and Stanton, I insist that we incorporate and sign a partnership agreement.

"If you and Nick don't trust each other," John says, "you two sign one."

I reply, trust is not an issue. Complexity and lack of understanding is the issue. What if Nick comes up with a new fuel gauge for gaseous fuel applicable but not exclusive to natural gas? Does he owe me twenty-five cents of every dollar he makes off the patent?

I ask Peter to please check into the security issues, even if he's sure a violation is remote, as if it were a mammogram. A day later he calls. "You were right. I'm hiring lawyers."

Hearing this, Nick declares that he should be our president, not John. His mom's boyfriend, scientist Ed, told him so. "Ed says I have all the vision and should be in control."

Matt has a soccer game and his coaches don't show. So I'm coach. I've never played soccer. The best I can do is scream "No!" and "Go!" In the second half Matt gets broadsided by a boy a half foot taller. His nose is bloody and he tries, unsuccessfully, not to cry. They win eleven to one anyway. His team has won every game so far and my son has yet to know the meaning of defeat.

I figure, okay, I'll buy the dream: We present the natural gas vehicle solution as a complete package. We go to a Ford or Chevrolet or Chrysler with the idea of creating an NGV automobile plant at the Saturn level. Cars designed from the ground up to run on natural gas. We answer "all" the problems. You buy an NGV, you get a home refueling unit installed and "folded in" to the cost of the car. The NGV utility would make it's money back by surcharging the customer, say, twenty cents on the per-gallon equivalent, to underwrite the cost of the pump.

Nick and I are driving to John Mason's and he says, "Yeah, Tom Cruise buys an NGV, he gets a house refueling unit installed free."

I say, "Better yet, *you* get one free. The gas company charges twenty cents per gallon equivalent to pay off the cost of the fuel pump. That eliminates the necessity of gas stations—and guarantees the gas utility will be the car owner's only fuel source. You'd just fill up automatically in your garage—thus giving people a tremendous incentive to buy an NGV. It would guarantee the gas company a monopoly on the individual consumer."

"Then," Nick says, "the utilities combine with producers and pipeline companies to create a mega entity. This is not a bunch of greenies whacking off, Mark, this is us!"

A half hour later we drive up the narrow, woodsy lane to John Mason's, where God, and perhaps the California state lottery, permitting, we will soon have money to pay John to fabricate the aluminum body. John looks at Nick's drawing for a new independent rear suspension, and says, "I loved what you did, Nick, but you doubled or tripled the budget."

Nick says he's sick. It's flu season, but that's not what's making him ill. While John and Herman were talking, Nick went outside to look at the car, still clad in its poster board paper body, which John still had wrapped in a blue tarp. "All the hyperbolic surfaces are crushed, warped, wrecked. John wrapped the paper-bodied chassis like a present. It's fucked anyway. If it's not built right it'll look Robo Cop, like a klugged-together tin man. We're incompetent."

"Nick, when we were up here last time, I asked if you were worried about the car sitting out like that, and you said no."

Abruptly, a final solution: his girlfriend. "If Corina had your job every detail would be under constant scrutiny. Everybody would wear uniforms, everything would be measured exactly. She's so serene on the outside, but inside, it's frightening." He laughs, suddenly happy. "She's German!"

"He came down here and threw a temper tantrum about the paper," Bruce Eikelberger reports. "That kid's got to get real. I hear all these million-dollar plans from Nick and then he tells me you can't even handle a twenty-thousand-dollar bill to get the car up and running."

We've trucked the chassis down to Bruce's shop in Huntington Beach. Nick's paper template, crushed by John Mason, was no welcome addition. Nick says, "Three months of my work down the drain, Bruce threw out the patterns for the body."

"You said," I say, "they were ruined."

"There are two or three stages of ruinedness. The parabolic curves are gone, those got wrecked when John mounted the stuff, but the basic shapes were there. Now everything's useless or gone."

The Volvo has broken transmission mounts, and according to my towering mechanic Russ Knowles, "You can grab the driveshaft and shake it around like a chicken's neck." Oil is leaking everywhere, the front end is going and, given that I'm nearly penniless, I hope my command "Fix it well enough so it doesn't kill my wife" covers the bases.

I bought the Volvo to prove I wasn't crazy. Before Debbie and I moved to California I was a columnist for a Portland newspaper. The city was run by a bunch of Richard Nixons and one day I wrote that the mayor was a closet rocker who had penned Hendrix's famous line, "Roll over, Rover, and let Jimi take over." The mayor tried to sue, so next I wrote that the police chief was a dedicated hot rodder and author of a new novel, *Cars I Want*, that appeared to be just three hundred pages of classified used car ads but that had just been praised in *The New York Times* as an existential masterpiece. The police chief threatened to sue so, sensing a goldmine, I turned on my own newspaper, reporting that staff members had lured a horse upstairs to the editorial offices, tricked the horse into what the horse thought was cocaine but was actually laundry detergent, causing the terrified animal to leap from a window and fall to its death on the sidewalk six stories below.

Members of the staff insisted I be fired on the grounds that I was mentally unstable but the new editor, Mark Zusman, refused, and announced that if I was fired, he was fired too, and to remind my boss how mentally unstable I was I took him to the Volvo dealership where Debbie and I leased the sanest car ever—the four-cylinder, plain Jane green Volvo DL station wagon that stands above Russ and me on Russ's hydraulic hoist, plopping black oil onto his otherwise spotless concrete floor.

"I don't want to hear myself say this," Russ, who resembles a taller, craggier Bill Murray, says. "It needed an air meter valve. Five hundred and thirty dollars to you, four hundred and eighteen dollars to me." He points to what looks like a tin can with wires dangling off of it. "If I didn't do you right," he looks to the sky, "God can strike me down." He shrugs. "See, I'm still here. Though He may wait and strike me down on my way home."

"Peter may die," Nick reports over the phone. Ten days before Christmas, on the eve of their trip to hit up David Jones, president of Atlanta Gas, Peter Snyder has something go wrong with his heart. I call the hospital in St. Louis. No one can tell me what is going on. Nick calls me back, close to crying. John Case says that Nick will spearhead the pitch to Jones, because Jones "treats Nick like he was a son."

Peter's father died at what? Forty? Peter told me once, his dad was playing tennis in Mexico, I think. Keeled over of a heart attack right there on the court. This is not good.

And without Peter, the going has not gotten easier either. John: "Natural gas people are the most risk-aversive businessmen I've ever met." Nick: "It's like presenting a football team with a great plan to win the Super Bowl and having that team tell you they don't even want to belong to the NFL."

I thought Nick and John were asking Atlanta Gas for $400,000 but John says $30,000. Even that turns out to be too much. David Jones thinks our fund-raising plan is unrealistic.

John says that is the buyer's first bargaining tactic.

I call the hospital again. Peter's condition has been downgraded from a heart attack to simply "a highly irregular heartbeat." Perhaps because he drinks three pots of coffee a day. He's lucky his heart didn't rip its way out of his chest and go off running down the street.

Nick and John jet off to Texas and when they return, Nick reports they didn't get a standing O. "The Natural Gas Vehicle PR committee said we were just another money-making scheme." Christmas and no quarter mil. John allows the "windfall strategy didn't work" and asks me where we might find $20,000 seed money. Nick says—with eleven dollars in his pocket to buy gifts with—that he can't complain because John is paying all his bills.

Window shopping, John, Nick and I go to MetalCrafters, the fabricators who built the Chrysler Viper prototype as well as the most gorgeous concept cars in recent memory, Chrysler's recent 300 Series. One million dollars is their *average* price to construct an automobile. "This is the place," Nick says, "where the *real* people go," and the next day John calls me to say he and Nick want to "mothball" the Xeno chassis. I hear Nick in the background yelp, "I can't have my name on a hundred-thousand-dollar car!"

44

WE'RE DEAD

Winter on the freeway to San Diego, under pearling skies, John Case, his wife Georgia pregnant with their first child, drives while reading outloud: *"Take every objection, interpret it as a question requesting more information."* He reads on *"Mr. Prospect, I know how you feel. Just suppose that isn't a problem. You seem to be hesitant, Mr. Prospect, is it the money? What would it take to satisfy you?* Then the prospect says what that is," John tells Nick, who is sitting in the backseat of John's Isuzu Trooper in his black suit looking, with his widow's peak and hair slicked back, like Eddie Munster grown tall. "Then we say," John reads: *"That is exactly why, Mr. Prospect, you need to act now."*

We are meeting with the Natural Gas Vehicle Counsel in order to "close" a deal with the NGVC whereby the NGVC funds us to the tune of $120,000 in order for us to, basically, determine whether it is a good idea for them to give us the $21 million. As he drives, John is reading aloud from a "how-to" sales book.

In a beige hotel conference room on Coronado Island, Peter Synder, who has flown in from St. Louis, recites,

Whan that Aprille with his showres sote
The droughte of March hath perced to the roote,
And bathed ever veine in swich licour,
Of which vertu engendred is the flowr:
Whan Zephyrus eek with his swete breeth
Inspired hath in every holt and heeth
The tendre croppes, and the yonge sonne
Hath in the Ram his halve cours yroone

and so on and so on.

The prologue to *The Canterbury Tales*. Middle English was his specialty in graduate school. We've been left hanging an hour in a hotel meeting room. I asked John not to ask the NGVC to buy up our debts and then, thumbing through the formal proposal, read: *The monies contributed would go to . . . reimburse some of NGV/USA's cash expenses to date.*

We're dead. When our party is finally summoned I offer that the media will not come out for upfitted four-door Chevys, that it may be glamour or die, and when the dust settles NGVC head Jeff Seisler says the program represents "a tremendous opportunity" but, "it's a hugely expensive package. What if we started with just one vehicle to take to car shows?"

New York Union Gas Vice President Mo Shaw, a big, athletic but ill-looking man, says, "We have to do something. I go to the 7-Eleven and tell people my car runs on natural gas, they say, 'Isn't that just for cooking food?' They don't even know what it is."

A bearish Ford representative, Harvey Klein says, "This is a great idea for the green market. But I'd take a sharp pencil to these numbers."

Jim Moore, a gray-haired Texan, says, "Our chance of getting these kind of funds are no more than five percent at best."

Jeff Seizler says, "More like zero to five percent."

Afterward, in the bar at the hotel, Peter Snyder says, "My takeaway is that John will get a call from Mo Shaw. We'll get a go-ahead but probably lose the class-A transport, lose the video."

Nick says, "We floundered in closing. We have to reassert control, modulize the program, repitch it."

"Nick," Peter says, "there's no point running around in gastric circles trying to micromanage the future. Let them come back to us. I'm not giving up on the twenty-one million dollars."

John says, "I'm not either."

"Lots of luck. The natural gas industry motto is: 'Forget the gold, grab the brass,' " a natural gas attorney tells us at an NGVC party at the hotel, but during the ride home, in the dark, Nick, from the backseat of John's truck, says, "They must know it'll cost five hundred thousand dollars to build the Xeno. That's MetalCrafters' cost. *Minimum*."

"Didn't you listen to those people?" I ask. "Our program costs too much. We gotta start performing more and promising less."

"We must live up to the ideals we agreed upon," Nick barks. "Or the car won't be perfect, not the rolling jewelry we promised. I won't debut a car with my name in it that's not perfect."

Peter sits beside Nick, asleep, but upright, his head tipped forward, as if hanging by an invisible noose.

"What will we do next?" I ask John, Nick and Georgia at breakfast outside under umbrellas at Hamburger Henry's. "Patent how to get out of bed in the morning? This is ridiculous, there's no way the government will let us patent how to arrange natural gas pressure tanks in a row between the frame rails of a chassis. It's crazy, simpler than two plus two. How many years do we have to waste chasing hairbrained get-rich utopias? Meanwhile, we've blown every rational chance we've got to do something every other high school kid in the world does. Build a goddamned car."

John Case looks at me across the table. "Calm down," he advises. "I've talked to our patent attorney, he says we are right on. You're the one who's sounding nuts."

"The new Bugatti holds the natural gas land speed record," our engine builder Bruce Eikelberger says in his spotless Huntington Beach shop. "Two hundred and twenty miles an hour. We can break it."

Bruce's friend Woody Gilmore, the man who developed the modern drag race chassis, is building our independent rear suspension, but when Nick, enthusiastic, says we can get lots of natural gas pressure tank sponsor money, Bruce, wearing a sweatshirt and glasses that hang on a thin chain off his neck, says, "No. These companies spell conservative with a *K*. They won't whip out their checkbooks on a wish and a prayer. You have a great concept, but you've got gunboat mouths and rowboat asses. The industry has seen your program. If you don't start producing, you'll be dismissed as just more hustlers with suits and a line."

Bruce considers our chassis. "You could drop it off the Empire State Building and not leave a scratch, but the suspension is tissue paper. Not safe at high speed. We'll use Corvette front uprights, brakes. Use the full Chevy pull rod coil over suspension, create our own control arms and use the Corvette front steering rack. I'd like to—"

"Wait!" Nick says. "We're going to get rid of Herman and John's front end too?"

"We're talking about a car that could go three hundred miles an hour. It has got to be absolutely safe."

"Dude," Nick replies. "The front end is beautiful."

"We may have to change the tires too."

"Then we're screwed. The car won't work."

"The world doesn't stop over a set of tires," Bruce says. "The tires need to be narrower, taller."

"Then the wheels," Nick says, "they'll have to change, the hubs, this is my dream—"

"It's time to get serious. At one hundred and fifty miles an hour," Bruce says, "tiny, tiny things create enormous aerodynamic problems. If you want the car to be stable you need a front wing, a spoiler—"

"No spoiler," Nick says. "That is a total cliche."

"The canopy is way too high," Bruce says, as if unhearing. "If you want to go fast, it's got to be low and stable. At just two hundred miles an hour, we'll need one hundred horsepower just to overcome the extra turbulence, turbulence that works on every other surface on the car. There's been no wind tunnel work and we've got all kinds of stuff that wasn't thought through, doesn't match and doesn't make sense." Bruce looks at me. "The driver's positioned so if he's sitting up where Nick wants him, he couldn't push on the pedals—your knees'll be into the steering and he'd be sitting damn near a foot below the top of the roll hoop."

"Herman and John wouldn't have built something dumb," Nick says.

"Nick, they were just doing what you told them to do, build a fast concept car, but certainly not a car capable of speeds we're talking about. Look at your own drawing. The vent behind the driver will not take air, the air will hit the front of the canopy and shoot up, creating turbulence. I'd like to eliminate bulk and hippyness on the side pods. There's too much tubing in here, bulk that doesn't need to be."

"No," Nick says.

"No what?" Bruce asks.

"No, I don't want to chop up Herman's design."

"Nick," I say, "Bruce won't do that, he'll just make sure the car is safe at very high speed."

"Nick," Bruce says, "believe me, I've been to the city and I've seen the elephant. I want this thing to happen right and happen once." He tells Nick that to get air in the most efficient way into the radiators, we will need to use NACA-ducts, vents shaped like a sideways Y that are most commonly used by race cars.

"Dude!" Nick blurts. "I will not use a NACA-duct. They are total design cliches."

The muscles of Bruce's jaws knot. "We have to get air into the motor." He looks at me. "We can run up big numbers on a flat track but turn this thing and it'll pogo like there's no tomorrow. You get it upside down and that roll hoop will smash flatter than a fritter. It'll be cleaned off, and your driver beheaded. It's too much leverage, too *long*. We have to make it safe and properly gussetted, so nobody winds up dead."

"If Bruce is involved," Nick says behind the wheel of his Honda, ripping out of Eikelberger's lot into the night, "he'll control the project. If my standards are not upheld, everything will have been a total waste." Nick accelerates around a jacked-up house-high Chevy Suburban. " 'Hi, I'm a NACA-duct. I've been done a million times and now we're doing me again,' so the car'll lose its breakout design to become a bunch of cliches so we can break speed records I could give a fuck about. Another thing: I can't have Bruce lecturing me."

"He wasn't, Nick."

"Maybe not lecturing me to you, but lecturing me to me."

I say, "Bruce is just talking to you like a football coach who wants you to win."

Nick grips his steering wheel as if to strangle it. "*You* had football coaches, I *hate* football coaches. I realize Bruce is your new guru, but I need to have him speak to me in a way that is proactive, positive, corporate, managerial and salesmanlike."

"Salesmanlike?"

"I need to either boss or be bossed, I can't have it both ways."

It is almost spring and I am trying to buy the newest dream. Time has passed. Katie got nominated winter formal princess, her date was named winter formal king and she dumped him the next day.

We've got a dog, a monster puppy, New Yeller—he knocked Debbie down at the pound and, once home, ran right through a screen door. And Nick has been hired by Amerigon president Lon Bell to design the body for the most ambitious and expensive electric car ever, Amerigon's second prototype. He has been instructed to dumb down, to do nothing audacious but rather to design what looks like a 1980 Toyota of the future. Still. Electric power people may not be big on style, but they keep plugging, developing better batteries, better engines, pushing range to over 150 miles with recharge time under five minutes. They've focused on the big market future.

And, I guess, so have we. At a Long Beach Dodge dealership, Nick and I are lying on our backs on asphalt, staring at what we hope will save our lives: All the wasted fuel space underneath a utility van. There is a lot of it. Room for huge natural gas tanks, or hydrogen tanks or just plain old-fashioned gas tanks.

Nick has applied for fourteen patent iterations of a chassis designed to give natural gas-fueled automobiles up to an eight-hundred-mile range. Here is how it works: The metal chassis is a load-bearing platform that houses four roughly one-foot-by-five-foot cylinders, which will store about thirty-five gallons of gasoline equivalent. Tanks that will fit between the frame rails. The modified chassis can be adapted to a minivan, pickup truck, full-size van and box van, maybe half the motorized vehicles in the world.

If these patents go through, our attorney in Washington, D.C., a friend of a friend of John Case's—Mike Stone—has suggested that anybody who wants to make a truly efficient dedicated natural gas vehicle will have to grease our collective palm.

"It could be the ceiling of the Sistine Chapel up there," I say, dying to be optimistic.

"If this works," Nick replies, snaking back out from underneath the Dodge Ram van, dusting himself off. "I don't know. Forrest Gump could have patented this. It's the easiest, dumbest idea I've ever had. All you gotta do is say, 'There's a tremendous amount of space nobody is using under half the cars in the world, so let's patent all the ways we realize that.' "

"Patents are strange animals," Bruce Eikelberger says. "I hold a bunch. If Nick has lucked onto essential design configurations, no matter how simple, you guys may have hit paydirt."

Let's hope. Bruce got us $2,000 worth of pressure tanks with a phone call, and can get the independent rear suspension built for $5,000. Add

$6,000 to get the car running. Not a fortune for people floating a $21 million promotion program. John Case has agreed to pay for the rear end but says, as for everything else, "We need to get the big money first."

"How long will that take?"

John shrugs. "Maybe a year."

A year? Even though I've got unfinished novels piling up inside my computer like cord wood, I've staked everything else on this. "John, Nick, let's stop dreaming dreamy dreams of world conquest, let's get some fifty-thousand-dollar 'nickel and dime' sponsors and build the goddamned car. We're borrowing fantasy sums against tomorrow so we don't have to pay the small real sums now."

John looks at me. "What do you mean?"

"We talk about raising twenty-one million dollars. We could stoop to conquer by raising one one-thousandth of that." I suggest a $500,000 one-car "pocket tour" program to get us in actual business with the gas industry. "We'd provide the car, the displays, and a three- to six-city tour to show we can perform."

"If you don't believe in the program," he says, "if you don't believe in changing the country's energy future, I'll think of other ways to spend my time."

And later, downstairs on his kitchen phone, John assures Nick's mother's scientist boyfriend Ed that we will all share equally. John's cryptic comment after he hangs up—"Ed is a viper"—indicates they did not reach a meeting of minds. "I'm getting tired of everyone's complaints," he says, and not long after, Nick tells me John wants to talk to me about something that makes Nick sick.

"John wants to get rid of me?"

"Buy you out."

At Super-Mex down my street, over tacos, John offers me $20,000 for my share of NGV/USA, plus $100,000 if the program works. "Then you go your way, we'll go ours."

In our kitchen our big dog flops over, his blond feet paw the air. He gives me his saber-toothed grin. I rub his ears, hard. "Super submitting, Charlie," I say. Charlie, a hot rod of dogs—too big, too powerful, part Golden Retriever, part wolf. Warm, brown eyes and a big, wild mouth. A pound puppy. He's put his paw through two windows. Debbie's had him fixed. There are staples where his testicles used to be—"Mommy had your nuggies chopped off," I tell him—but it has not slowed him down. He makes being a moron look so easy. Debbie thinks he's just going through his "love me or I'll bite you" stage. I guess. At dog training school in our veterinarian's parking lot, Charlie leapt up, wrestled the air, lunged and sunk his teeth into Debbie's arm.

A knock on our front door. Nick. With news. "It's like my whole life, everybody's telling me I'm great and I always win and then I threw in with you, and I'm not winning anymore."

Not this week, anyway. His mother and her boyfriend Ed developed a way to heal scar tissue but may lose rights to the vital scar healing technology, and Corina went on a week-long wheat germ and water diet with her parents and it left her "a little difficult." She got more difficult after Nick told her, "When I become rich and famous a lot of young, fresh, pretty girls will want to be involved with me and I don't think I can resist, because as an artist, beautiful women have always been a vital inspiration."

"What happened?" I ask.

"She dumped me. But how could I be honest," he asks, "and not tell her?" Nick says he cried and I feel bad for him. Getting rich and famous by saving the world is about all he has. But when I suggest that he seek advice about our $21 million program from Pierre Ouellette, Nick says, "Have him call me."

"Why not just get on the phone yourself?" I inquire.

"Truthfully? I don't want to spend money for the long distance."

"This car is a widow maker," Bruce Eikelberger says. "Nothing but Nick's sandbox. A car isn't like a sculpture, a car has to be designed around hard, real things."

I'm at Bruce's shop. On his radio, a familiar refrain:

The eastern world, it is explodin',
Violence flarin', bullets loadin' . . .

"Look," he says, "God isn't making very many Nick Pughs anymore. When I was a kid, the world was full of exciting cars. But now I've got a refrigerator at home sexier than the new Fords. Nick's got so much talent he cannot only get through the industry doors, he can blow the doors right off their hinges."

You may leave here for four days in space,
But when you return, it's the same old place . . .

"But once inside," Bruce says, "the engineers'll laugh him out of the room. He's the rarest thing, a genuine artist, and it can destroy him. He has no technical background. Try to explain something to him he gets lost, and when he gets lost he gets scared, and when he gets scared he has to take control, by dictating what the *real* story is. Nobody'll take that forever."

The Corvette rear end is gorgeous, new and expensive. Woody Gilmore uses a torch like a wand. Sparks spill as he tacks in the engine mounts. John Case points to the transmission and asks me, "That isn't the engine, is it?" When at Super-Mex, I asked John, "Who'd pay me the twenty-thousand dollars? You?" he replied, "No. I'll find somebody." And when I said I would not be bought out of my life's dream for $20,000 he suggested, "Get Pierre to loan you the money to build the car."

"Pierre doesn't think the program will work."

John spoke with pained enthusiasm, bonking the Super-Mex restaurant table with his fist. "That's *eg-zactly* why he should loan you the money. If he's really your friend and thinks our project could be derailed if we screw up, he should loan you the money to see that we don't."

Nick has returned from Detroit, where he and Peter Snyder met with General Motors. GM has "fired" us because we are making such slow progress on the car. After Peter and Nick made their request for $20,000, General Motors PR director Bill O'Neill not only said no, but cut us off entirely. No more parts, no nothing.

In my kitchen Nick, making a ham-and-cheese-and-egg-and-another-slab-of-ham-over-that sandwich, tells me, "When I'm with engineers, it's like I'm at a KKK meeting and I'm black. Bruce. Herman. John. No matter how much you don't know about cars you're still a car guy. They see that in a second. But to me, cars are just clay to make art. Engineers hate that. And big surprise, dude: I've learned my art is hard to sell for big money. The gas industry won't pay for T and A. I know you're not spiritual Mark, but I think God is testing me, seeing how much ego crushing I can endure."

"What ego crushing? How is your ego being crushed?"

"When I was a kid going to school, I could do what I wanted, create what I wanted, my rent was paid—"

"Nick, that's called being a kid who is going to school."

"We were going to build the ultimate car, it would be the finest car money could buy."

I say, "I didn't want to get involved in all the hype, I just want to build one little supercar."

Nick shakes his head. "You ran this on hype from the beginning. You never had the money to build a car. If you were a millionaire you'd write a check and it'd all be fine but you aren't, so it won't. But my heart is getting fucked up. Nothing we do works. We are failures. You held this future out like a carrot and the carrot never happened. I bought the hype and that's that."

WE GET A
MILLION DOLLARS

The patent hits. Nick calls: "It went through! The patent attorney in Washington, D.C., called. Unibody, monocoque, everything. As long as it holds up, we've made it!"

Charlie, the world's best bad dog, barks and barks and my wife says to me, "Timmy fell down the well." He keeps barking and after a minute she adds, "Forget about it. Timmy drowned."

That night we drive by bougainvillea-veined Spanish-style homes we may be able now to afford, on our way to watch Katie at a Wilson High School swim meet. Her freshman team is number one in the state, but it's like she's up against the young women of Russia. Girls who have shoulders to build roads with.

Katie, pacing poolside, is getting ready to race. Her sweet and sour little face: she got three first places and a third last week. She's sleek as a sword. Katie wins the two hundred-meter freestyle and her relay team wins two five hundred-meter relays.

My daughter knows how to get things done. For instance, she is, I believe, trying to arrange an abortion for a friend. I heard her say, "I've called twenty clinics" and afterward, by the phone I see that she has written, on my notepad: WHY? WHY? WHY? WHY? WHY? WHY? WHY? WHY? WHY? WHY? WHY? WHY? WHY? WHY? WHY? WHY? WHY? WHY? WHY? WHY?

"It's fantastic," Nick thrills at Bruce Eikelberger's shop. Bruce has cut chunks off the car, lowered the roll bar and slimmed the chassis. Nick walks around it as if he is seeing a mechanical Lazarus risen from the dead. He just got a job designing a cartoon show for $1,000 a week and I haven't seen him so happy in ages.

Bruce says we will put a fiberglass "speed form" on the chassis and speeds of "toward three hundred" are possible. And based on our long-range chassis patents, we may qualify for a $500,000 Advanced Research Projects Center grant. Someone once told me that after forty there are only three careers that tend to really take off: architect, writer and fat cat. So there is hope.

John, Nick and I meet with Mike Gage at Calstart. Calstart's major funder, Lon Bell's technological development corporation Amerigon, has left, moved out of the Lockheed facility into sixty-thousand square feet of brand-new manufacturing space in Monrovia. This leaves a huge vacuum, and kindly, big Mike Gage is courting us. "We'll give your program legs and credibility. Two naturals for you would be Southern California Gas and the Gas Research Institute. Very substantial players."

John asks, "Do you want to go after them?"

Mike says, "Yeah!"

But.

In Washington, D.C. May on a too-warm day in our nation's capitol. Jackie Kennedy has gone to heaven and Dan Rostenkowski is going to jail. Bruce and I find ourselves booked by John into a motel in a concrete and asphalt-skinned neighborhood that called to mind an East Berlin populated by vagrant black people. The phone has been ripped from the wall in my room and when Bruce saw his room, he went across the street to the Comfort Inn.

John has arranged for us to meet with the leaders of the natural gas industry. We present our formula for the long-range natural gas chassis at a conference downtown—a lot of people talking about a lot of ways to make money from natural gas while drinking a lot of coffee from a lot of Styrofoam cups. John introduces our "million-dollar" chassis program based on a little model that sits on a conference room floor like a big cardboard bug. He hasn't briefed Bruce, so Bruce can't provide a technical background.

An executive from the department of energy points to the model as if it did not represent patents but a punch line. "So that's the future?" he chuckles before walking out the door.

"A million dollars," Bruce says when we are done, "there won't be any million dollars." I am surprised his words do not emit steam. He approaches John, who has moved to the back of the room, and says, "This is crazy. There's got to be preparation. You've got to plan your work and work your plan," and John simply turns his back on him so that Bruce is talking to John's cowlick.

"John flies me across the country, for what? Last night, all he wanted to talk about was the pie-in-the-sky promotion. He's got patents to double the range of any car no matter what fuel it uses. Meaning *unbeeeee-leeeeve-able* money if John played his cards right, but he's still obsessed about making Nick more famous than Michael Jordan. It's batty. I told him, *That didn't work, that's not what we're here for,* and he looked right through me." Bruce runs a hand back through his bushy gray hair, stares out at the vast grid of graves. We're at Arlington National Cemetery checking out his soldier relatives. "Talk about pulling defeat from the jaws of victory. I like John. He's made more contacts in the natural gas industry in two years than I have in twenty, but he knows nuuuuu-thing about cars and listens to noooo-one. You only get so many chances. If this fails, John can go back to real estate. Nick, he's young, he can just go onto the next thing. But what are you—forty-four? Forty-five? You're getting old."

In the middle of June, John arrives at my doorstep and says, "Nick said I should level with you. NGV/USA is a failure and it's over. You were right, the twenty-one-million-dollar promotion plan was a bust."

But John has an idea. We go to a satellite campus of Long Beach City College. Low, blockish, smudged buildings, it resembles a minimum-security prison farm. John introduces me to a big-gutted, soft-shouldered guy who looks like Homer Simpson with hair. John's pitch: "A best of the best car" built by the best of the best of Long Beach City College's apprentice shop rats. Leaving, I say, "No way," and John replies, "I'm not responsible for the car."

"The fuck if you're not."

"Georgia," John says behind me, "is very upset about the money we've spent."

"Georgia is upset? Talk to Debbie."

"Mark, you dove in at the deep end. I'm sorry, but I won't do that. I'm spending money on the car I need for the baby. It's as simple as that."

"Nick's right," my wife says. "You told Nick that Gideon would pay for the car without ever getting a contract from Gideon. You tell people John is Matt's godfather. But it's never been official with a church. You tell people Nick is the best car designer in the world as if that were a fact like his height and weight. You've been involved in almost as much hype as anyone."

One last shot. Headed to Newport Beach to meet with members of the Natural Gas Coalition, I am, in Nick's little Honda, almost screaming: "We spent a year chasing promotion, now are we going to spend a year chasing technology?"

Nick says, "The atmosphere between you and John is so bad I don't know if it's worth going on."

We meet at Fashion Island, a lap of local lux. At the tall, posh Four Seasons Hotel, where new Mercedes, BMWs and Jaguars curl the semicircular drive in front, John tells the natural gas executives that Americans are see-it-to-believe-it people and that the natural gas industry needs proof of a natural gas concept vehicle—to counter all the vehicle development by the electric industry. Bill Morse of Columbia Gas, a substantial-looking man of fifty or so, says, "We have a litany of a lack of success as visionary thinkers."

"Like lemmings," Doug Horn, of Atlanta Natural Gas, adds.

Steve Takagishi, principal technology manager for the Gas Research Institute (GRI), says, "ARPA needs a lead lemming on this one." That would be the Advanced Research Project Agency; who developed the Internet as well as a number of visionary new fuel schemes over the last twenty years.

Nick explains that we will use stock suspension, braking system, steering system, et cetera, that the dimensions and drivetrain will remain essentially unaltered, yet we can build a van that will provide a twenty-five-gallon equivalent of gasoline and a range of three hundred and fifty miles.

"I don't see any real new technology here," Doug Horn replies. "Send this to the PR people, send it to the fuzzy thinkers, not GRI. This is a PR project." He puts his arms on the table. "It's not gonna impress the Fords, Chevys and Chryslers, they'll do anything not to build a natural gas vehicle."

Bill Morse says, "If you present this as a million-dollar program, the NGV product advisory group would have a shit fit."

Doug Horn says, "The cylinders can't bear load."

I say, "The cylinders bear no load. This is a whole new series of chassis designs. The chassis bares the load. We have applied for over a dozen different design patent iterations."

Bill Morse says, "You mean this isn't just a box with some cylinders in it?"

"No!" Nick says, "It just looks that way."

John asks Bill Morse if he would support an engineering study. Morse nods. "Yeah. Pending. If you guys want to change the world, fine. But I'm not interested in the happy horseshit aspect. Your patents must address problems of space, weight and safety. I want to see that it's valid, relevant and that it works."

The next day the patents are approved officially and it is not long before we have a deal to do a $140,000 feasibility study.

"I don't want you interrupting," John tells me, dialing the Gas Research Institute office. We are about to have a conference call to Atlanta Gas, Southern California Natural Gas, Bill Morse from Columbia and a bunch of other natural gas executives. I pick up an extension. John says, "I can hear you. Put a towel over the receiver."

I put a towel over the receiver. Steve Takagishi from the Gas Research Institute says, "Chrysler won't participate. It is a waste of money unless you have full backing of an original equipment manufacturer." By that, he means a Ford or GM.

"If we sat down with Chrysler engineers they'd laugh like hell," Bill Morse says. "We've got to take initiative ourselves."

"You are marrying a gorilla," Lon Bell, the trim, professorlike energy mogul who founded Calstart, tells John at a hippie deli near his new facility in Monrovia.

Bell is worth a quarter billion dollars yet drives a years-old Honda. He advises, "Use your patents to show a clear path to production. The car companies want risk reduction. A platform manager is approaching the end of his career, he's not about exploring new ideas. He has to be convinced it's bulletproof. You engage these guys without unduly raising expectations. You must be very careful. They have no intent of stealing your patents, but they'll go to a body maker like A. E. O. Smith and say, 'How do these guys from the land of fruits and nuts beat you with a patent?' Your advantage? If your patents are strong, they'll ask themselves two questions: What's it cost to go with you? And what's it cost to go around you?"

Intellectual property is apparently where the action is. Nick describes his mother's boyfriend, the scientist Ed, this way: "Ed's a razor, he'll fuck you up." Ed advised Nick to "lose" John Case. "My mom and Ed think John will do anything to make the deal, that if we sign what he wants us to sign we'll lose all our rights."

I've elevated our landlord from businessman to patron of the arts: We still have not paid the rent. A lady checker at our grocery says, "Your wife has such a great figure." I do not say that part of the reason for that "great figure" is that Deb is so worried about our finances she doesn't eat.

We've borrowed money from Debbie's stuntwoman sister Sally, who earned it the hard way during the filming of *Drop Zone* by "jumping out of an airplane without a parachute on," and who, for her efforts, ended up breaking her leg.

So what to do? My novel *Aloha* got a great prepublication review in *Publishers Weekly*. My new movie agent names three Pulitzer Prize winners and a Nobel Prize winner among his clients, but my money is already spent and no movie money has arrived.

"Just tell your dad you are in a jam. Not as an investment opportunity, not as a way to change the world, 'Dad, I. Am. In. A. Jam. Please. Help.' Period," Nick suggests.

I am flying back to Portland.

My father is going on "one last" fishing trip in the deep, deep wilds of Canada, it sounds like *Deliverance* for eighty-year-olds and my mother is worried half to death.

I'd like to "reason" with my father about this, tell him I'm afraid he'll die out there, but no. We do not talk much about personal things. After my dad bought me the Porsche when Debbie and I got married, I had a few beers in celebration, called him and said, "I love you," and afterward felt guilty. I figured it probably meant I had a drinking problem, and I do not have the heart to try to talk him out of his last fishing trip or the gall to ask him for the money it would take to finish the car. The car is my problem, not his.

———

Nick is designing new cartoon bad guys and the new Flash Gordon, and is standing over a new drawing of the bad guy headquarters building: a shattered globe at the top where the bad guy plans his worst. I say, "So in the off-hours they could use it for Kiwanis Club meetings and stuff."

"No," Nick says. "The bad guy has to be able to be bad in there all the time."

As for the grant, who knows. At least with the $21 million promotion program I knew we were doomed, but with this?

Nick says, "If it doesn't work, I'm histo." He is a candidate to be designer of the next *Star Wars*. "I'm going to the movies. I'll send you money in five years or something so you can finish the car." He concludes that, in any event, he is "leaving for cyberspace" where "there is no perspective."

Protecting our patents may be hard. Attorney Steve Scherzer, my friend since eighth grade, suggests we request that the Gas Research Institute either: A) Release and waive any rights to the patents; B) Buy us out lock, stock and barrel; or C) Draw up a separate joint venture/ licensing and royalty agreement. But John, at his office, and on the phone to our patent attorney, Mike Stone, says he has already taken action regarding the lead utility contract.

"I signed it," he says.

"You signed it?" Mike Stone asks.

"You signed it?" Nick asks.

"I signed it," John says.

Nick makes a pistol of his fingers and puts it to the back of John's head.

When Nick dies he wants to be placed in an aluminum canister—"After they chop off my head and freeze it"—and be blown up in the desert, "preferably with a nuke." Afterward, he'd like a shrine, linked by a "homite homing device" to a geosynchronous satellite, to "lead pilgrims to the site." I promise to see what I can do.

John Case calls me at home, "Aaaaaahm, good news, we got the grant money."

"How much is it worth?"

"When it's all said and done, when all the utilities and the government pay off, at least a million bucks."

SECOND COMING

"The patents will be worth millions. Four, six, eight, twenty, who knows?" Nick predicts a million dollars to reconstruct one Dodge van, a van to demonstrate how to triple the fuel storage space in almost any vehicle so that your Ford Explorer or Chevy Blazer or even your Honda Civic will drive a month between stops at the gas station. No one has ever devised a way for a natural gas vehicle to get more than about a 120-mile range. Nick's patents provide for a range of up to *one thousand miles*.

This should mean new life for the Xeno, now sitting as still and empty as a new casket in my garage. But as my friend David Noonan says of Los Angeles, "Even in a town renowned for eating its young, there is no free lunch." It is expensive to make a "blueprint in steel." Everything on this Dodge van must be replanned and refabricated to the millimeter. First, the fuel storage chassis has to prove itself in cyberspace. Only then do we get the van and the money to turn it into what Pete Snyder has named "the Long Ranger."

We've had to hire engineers from a private consulting firm to create the van inside the computer and do a simulated crash test, a twelve-day, fifty-thousand-dollar venture on a Cray computer once used to calculate the anticipated path of incoming Soviet missiles during the end of the world. Crash testing is a huge, nonlinear problem—the computer analysts only get within 15 to 20 percent of a "real-life" crash, but it can add credibility to a program. Helpful, because the million dollars will be awarded in increments—each new increment dependent on the successful implementation of the last increment.

NGV/USA has approval for thirteen different versions of a long-range chassis, *every* viable means short of mounting fuel tanks on the roof (someone in Brazil already patented that approach), and the market may be huge. Take airports. They are the biggest single point of pollution in any large city and are being mandated nationwide to run their land transport on nothing but natural gas. The military has already contacted us. FedEx, UPS and every other long-range transport company from here to Kazakhstan is a likely customer.

Wrong, I was wrong. Why? "Because," Nick says, "It was too obvious for you. You can patent almost anything no matter how simple so long as it hasn't been patented before. Like the wheel. Round thing. Rolls down hill. Who owns the rights?" Nick laughs. "We should check it out!"

"Two hundred and fifty thousand people dead isn't enough, nobody cares about two hundred and fifty thousand dead anymore, two hundred and fifty thousand dead is old hat, everybody has to die."

This according to my dark, affable new editor here at the Beverly Hills Hotel. It is white and stately, like a plantation house. Snacks, drinks, on Dominick. A fan. "I stayed up all night rereading *Aloha*. You're funny, you're scary. But blowing up Maui isn't enough." *Aloha*'s original editor quit before the book was published and his replacement, maneuvering a fat comma of shrimp across a plate laked with red hot sauce, concludes, "*Aloha* is finished."

"But," I say, "it hasn't ever been officially published yet."

"It's an orphan," he clarifies. "I haven't got the time. My advice? Write a new book, and take more drastic measures—readers are jaded. Readers want more. Kill everybody."

El Mirage. A prehistoric lakebed. Flat as a mirror, moon dry mud from one side of the desert sky to the other, nothing but nothing all the way to dim mountains. First light provokes a line of wild, ancient cars. Their engines sound like machine gunfire. A Depression Era Ford coupe so dirty it looks unearthed swings onto the endless track, sails down the course, raising a rooster tail of dust that can be seen for a hundred miles. Here is where we can break the land speed record for piston-engined automobiles powered by natural gas. Toward that end, Peter Snyder has found us a sugar daddy: Gerry Clinton, who owns a Budweiser distributorship in St. Louis, races cars on the side and who is building the St. Louis Rams football team a new coliseum.

Bruce Eikelberger has driven out here. This is where hot rodding originated in the 1930s. It is quite a scene. Some of the cars have been running on this dirt for fifty years, a couple with the same drivers. I gaze at the '32 Ford stuffed with a blown Ford flathead engine that is older than I am. Its dirty top has been chopped so low that its windshield reflects only half of my face. Bruce is reengineering our Chevrolet Racing V-8. The engine's cylinder bore will be increased to about 515 cubic inches and will use computer-controlled direct port injection. "We'll run two sets of injectors in each port," Bruce says. "We'll run off one set to a certain RPM point, then a second set will kick in to deliver an incredible amount of fuel to make power you won't believe."

To pay for that power we will have to rebuild a Dodge Ram Van to accommodate our newly patented fuel storage chassis. A cool morning on what will be a hot summer day. Completion of the Xeno II depends now on the success of the million-dollar truck, "the Long Ranger," about to be built here at MetalCrafters, owned by the Argentine émigré Gaffoglio family—dad, and his natty sons. Their facility is long and low. Porsches in the parking lot, but nothing special out here in the flat Southern California heartland, realm of industrial park after industrial park. Inside, however, another world. Big, superclean construction bays, many behind locked doors—birthing chambers for Detroit's secret concept cars.

We are met by dapper Alberto, slender, wearing a three-piece suit. He ushers us into a conference room. "Our portion is to see that the proposal is feasible, containable and doable in the time frame. We need to show strength and efficiency and performance not changed—and, of course, that whatever we present we can do at a certain level of cost."

Nick assures him that we are using available materials. "No pie in sky."

Alberto nods. "What I perceive happening is that this car will have better conditions regarding the torsion, it will be a much more rigid car because we'll be *boxing* it."

Bruce Eikelberger says, "The idea is to create the maximum onboard fuel storage, the largest cavity we can without interfering with suspension pickup points. We don't want to modify anything, but facilitate a path to production that will require the least amount of retooling and reworking. The cylinders must withstand eight-G shock loading—a force eight times their own weight—in eight different directions." He points to a diagram Nick has made. "This shaded area indicates crush structure—honeycomb structure or waffle structure that would increase the crush resistance."

"In case of collision," Alberto says, indicating an oval Nick has drawn to represent a natural gas pressure tank, "if we crush this thing, it will crack, right?"

Bruce shakes his head. "I've worked with these tanks for years, they'll take an enormous amount of impact. A stick of dynamite tied to one just bounces it around. Chrysler would like a chassis still viable for gasoline use so they could use it across the entire line. It can be a CNG chassis or gasoline chassis or in the future, liquid natural gas or hydrogen. There'll be an enormous market. The shuttle van industry. The law now requires any new vehicles that service the L.A. airport to use natural gas. They need at least a three hundred and fifty-mile range, which now requires four thousand dollars in upgrades. This year I've had four hundred thousand dollars' worth of business just in range extenders for Chrysler B vans out of just one shop."

"He's hot for it," Peter Snyder says. "He's a racer and wants that land speed record badly." That would be, Gerry Clinton, our new benefactor. Well, Gerry, you're getting a bargain-basement deal. Bruce needs only $61,000 to cover everything from the cost of two drag parachutes and $35,000 to modify the motor, plus another $25,000 for the body. Tack on the cost of the chassis, and it is only $85,000, all in all.

Nick's rendering of the new car is a sleek ground-hugging wedge bannered with Budweiser, slick and smooth as a bar of soap. This is not the Xeno I, which he originally designed for Mazda, or the Xeno II he designed at the huge studio he shared with Henrietta, or the aluminum-bodied car John Mason was to build, but a new fiberglass-shrouded machine. "It'll be neat, cool," he promises, gazing at his effort.

"Great," I say.

"No!" Nick smacks his drawing. "Neat and cool is stupid. I want people to look at my stuff and say: 'Is he crazy? Is he out of his mind?' That's not neat or cool, that's *radical*."

We mail the proposal to Peter Snyder's public relations office in St. Louis, but before it gets to Dorf and Stanton it is seized by the FBI. Who mistake it for a bomb sent to Peter by the Unibomber, thought by the feds to be targeting the nation's top PR guys.

So we send Peter another one. But no decision yet. "Clinton could hand me a check immediately," he reports, "or the whole project could get lost in the bowels of Budweiser."

"What would be your guess," I ask, "for how long?"

"Off hand? Fifteen minutes to four years."

"This is the last time construction will stop," John Case says. "It is time to build the car. We have the money. Mark, it's time you showed leadership. Tell Bruce: Build the engine, now or never."

In the name of producing record-breaking power, John has just paid for $5,213.36 worth of Dart racing heads. Two intricate aluminum slabs, they introduce fuel into the combustion chambers above the top of the pistons. Developed for drag racing, Dart heads create a very small combustion chamber—simply by providing a very low "ceiling" for each chamber—to get compression up without having to put a dome on the piston. Bruce's pal Yo's shop is using a "flow bench" to push air through the ports of the cylinder head, measure it and determine how much air will pass through the ports under different conditions before modifying the ports and setting up the valves.

"They're enormous," Bruce says. "The intake valve is on the order of two and five-eighths inches in diameter—we'll get great airflow, but the downside is that it's a manhole cover, very heavy. Their inertial mass will create valve float very early—that's the point where the valve overcomes the ability of the spring to close it. It doesn't follow the cam. It stays up in the air, and the cam drops away from under it. You want to keep the lifter in contact with the cam at all times. Otherwise the flow of fuel *into* the combustion chamber and exhaust *out* of the combustion chamber can be completely fouled up."

So we are using titanium valves half the weight of steel. Those valves cost $1,325.

Christopher Robin, QB. My little boy took the hike, scampered across the grass as the fourteen-year-old rusher chanted, "One potato, two potato . . ." and just as the big kid got to the "four potato" and came sprinting after my son, Matt cocked his arm back and whipped the ball spiraling into the end zone defined by the sidewalk and a palm tree. The ball dropped into the receiver's hands, touchdown.

Matt plays touch football at the park down the street after school but today nobody showed up except a half dozen kids from the Wilson

High School freshman football team. Matt threw the ball to me, long; a boy said, "He's got an arm," and what if they play and he quarterbacked for both sides? I thought: He's nine years old and not even five feet tall, what a dangerous way for him to get humiliated, but Matt, worry paling his face, shrugged and said, "Cool with me."

The first play, Matt dropped back and hit the kid running out on his left with a short throw so accurate that he could not have done better if he had just handed the boy the ball. Then three or four passes one way down the field, touchdown, a couple more passes down the field, interception, but then Matt threw one long, the ball hovered in the sky and came whacking down into the receiver's hands, TD.

Now one of the kids says, "Okay, you go out" and at the hike Matt only lopes forward like he's scared, dogging it. The boy covering him drifts in front of Matt and Matt takes off across the field. The kid bolts after him and Matt stops dead, his feet spread, his arm up, a stick boy X, and gets drilled in the end zone. The boys start calling him Jerry Rice, then I amend that to Little White Rice and I get him off the field before his luck runs out, wow.

We walk home, my feet occasionally touching the ground. I am building my 1953 Chevrolet all over again, as well as two 1957 Chevy hot rods and a Corvette, whose body is hanging from a tree in our front yard. I have determined to relive my childhood, except not screw it up this time. But it's hard. First, just looking at the details of my old '53 Chevy brings back memories I don't even want to consider: How could I have been so dumb? Then, as if in answer to the question, I notice that the goddamn glue is blobbing all over the plastic and Matt wants to know, "Dad, don't you think you should read the directions?" and I want to tell my son: *Don't you realize that I've never read the directions to anything in my life?* But all these tiny plastic car parts, a Lilliputian's junkyard.

Matt takes the glue in his slender little surgeon's hand and applies it to the model in straight threads. Later, outside, he takes a can of gray spray paint and finishes priming the model Corvette, the paint misting smoothly over the little body that, hanging by its twine, looks lynched under the tree.

Woodland, Washington, the blown-off top of Mount Saint Helens out there behind the veil of fir trees that stand on the east side of my parents' ranch. Our resident bulls Satan and Sweetheart are grazing beside a bulldozer that stands like a monument when I tell my father Matt's football heroics. He smiles vaguely, and reminds me: "You're lucky you didn't get him hurt."

Right. My dad is being numbed away by Parkinson's disease. When he walks it looks as though he is walking into a head wind. I've been contracted to do another book, *Wild Life*, an anthology, a best of Oregon by the best of Oregon's writers, and have been here working two weeks when Bruce calls to say he's sorry that John is stopping construction of the car.

Come again?

"He's pulled a one-eighty. I guess he waited until you left town."

I call John, who tells me he had stopped construction "because the engine is too expensive. You've got thirty-five thousand dollars budgeted just to build the motor. When Nick saw that, he freaked."

"What do you mean, when he saw it? When was that?"

"Right after you left for Oregon."

"That's impossible," I say. "Both you guys have had copies of that budget for four months. It was part of the presentation for Gerry Clinton."

"I never read it," John says.

"*Never read it*? How could you have never read it?"

"It didn't interest me. It was just a number."

When I ask him why he didn't tell me about stopping the project, he replies, "Because I didn't want to worry you."

So what to do now. My Rx? "John and Nick are chickenshit and I want you here when they come over because I'm pretty sure they don't have the courage to ratfuck me in front of witnesses."

"John is your best friend," my wife replies. "He wouldn't sacrifice the car for no good reason."

"He's got one. He couldn't figure out how to make money out of the car and Nick is so frustrated he's ready to quit."

Outside through the glass-paned kitchen door to our back porch, Charlie, our 112-pound golden wolf, sits poised at attention, mouth open, tongue hanging out, grinning his fanged grin that says: *See what a good boy I am. Let me in.*

I do and Charlie reverts to type, becomes a howling, barking beast. Debbie says, "Now, now," starts to read Charlie the riot act in baby talk. He snaps and lunges at her. I grab his collar and smack him in the face. Eliciting a melodious *"yeeow!"*

"Don't hit him!" Debbie shouts. "Just because you're mad at your partners, you don't have to take it out on the poor dog."

"The poor dog," I say, "has wrecked a thousand dollars' worth of our windows and furniture, the poor dog attacks anybody he thinks he can intimidate, including you, and all the poor dog understands is: 'Do I push you around? Or do you push me around?' Just like everybody else."

Charlie sits down. Wags his bushy tail. A paw goes up. The idiot wants to shake.

When I say there should be no surprise about the engine, that the figures were stated in part-by-part, task-by-task detail four months ago in Bruce's document submitted to Gerry Clinton, John shakes his head. "It's a racing engine. We can't afford it."

I say, "Of course it's a racing engine. It's designed to break a world record. Bruce's formula was the only formula considered in the last year, it passed muster with all of us."

John, in a white shirt and slacks, looks as though he's bitten a lemon. "It's not a car Nick's happy with."

"Every time I make a design," Nick says, fuming, "I expose my creative soul to abuse and compromise. I have no more blind energy for this. I wanted the Xeno II hanging upside down on the ceiling of the New York Museum of Modern Art. Not just a world record car."

I take my head in my hands. "Nick. You have a copy of the budget. You must have looked at it."

"I did, I think, read it. But I forgot."

"Thirty-five thousand dollars," I say, "is a quarter of the cost budgeted for the engine during the late, great twenty-one-million-dollar program."

"Mark," John says, "be realistic. Building a one-of-a-kind car is a rich man's folly."

"And you're not even rich," Nick amends, looking at me.

Murder Without Bloodshed

High noon. "Aaaaaahm, I have an offer," John says, his hands shaking as he unfolds a piece of paper. "So you and Nick can get the car done."

We are seated in a booth at Hamburger Henry's. "NGV/USA will give you eighty thousand dollars, pending all our funding—we'll take the money out of our salaries—plus the ten thousand dollars I gave to Bruce: ninety thousand dollars total for your share of the company, your five hundred shares."

I am shocked, don't know what to say, except that I'm sorry it had to work out this way. *At last, the car will get finished.* We walk back to my house and I have John repeat the offer to Debbie, $90,000. I say that when the car is sold he can recoup his $16,000 put into the suspension and chassis, and I apologize for thinking he was going to cut me off at the knees.

My friend David Noonan says, "It sounds like extortion. He's using your desperation to renege on a deal with you he already made—in order to get your stock. I doubt it's even legal."

I get the car but will lose my rights to the natural gas design patents. It's beginning to sink in: No way do I want to sell my stock in a company to pay for a car that the company had been created to pay for in the first place. Steve Scherzer calls: "I talked to John Case. He told me how real people do business, how he had the vision, you had the problems, the car was a liability, on and on. The ninety thousand dollars he pays you may be nothing when GM or Ford or Nissan buys the rights X amount of time from now. You stand to lose a lot of money. It's a bad deal, but may be the only way right now to continue construction on the car."

Nick says, "No way. You deserve as much blame for our successes as credit for our failures, and here's how much I hate that idea: If John makes you give up your stock I'll give you a ton of mine."

Nick has entered cyberspace, he and his brother are designing Pepsi Cola's website and, this minute, money is no problem.

"But," I say, "that's worse. You came up with both the car and patents."

"We both have done dumb things to achieve our dream—the crown jewel of our fucking up with believing billion-dollar businesses would support my art—but I'll quit before I see you lose your share."

So what to do? Pierre Ouellette votes for the back door. "Forget the car, forget the patents. John Case is not a bad guy—his view is, 'You take your dream, I'll take mine,' but he just makes up the rules as he goes along. And chasing Nick's vision will put you in a nut house. Take the money and run."

Essentially, my choice is: fish or cut bait—actually, fish or get off the dock. If I take the $90,000 and leave the project, no one—including Nick—can say I didn't try. Ninety-thousand dollars can get me out of a financial sink hole that is only going to get deeper if I plunge the money back into the Xeno.

It is spring and I am coaching Little League. Matt cracks a blooper between the first baseman's legs, bolts to second, the ball streaks around the infield, my boy falls onto the bag, gets up, sprints for third, the ball zings by him but ticks off the third baseman's glove and into the fence at the edge of the field. Matt heads, skinny legs churning, for home, the ball whizzes past him toward the catcher and the ump, and as he slides across the plate, I hear, "You're outa there" in a cloud of dust.

Minutes later, he is headed to the mound. He's pitching. His coach got in an argument with the team's manager and gave me a bottle of Coors shaped like a baseball bat and a dozen free movie tickets to take over. I like it. As coach, I advise: "Remember, men, it's not whether you win or lose, but how good you look in your uniform." I pay the kids if they get hits, and leave the thinking to the manager, a psychologist. My boy throws strikes, and is out of the inning in sixteen pitches.

On the other hand, what other hand is there? I don't want to quit. But there is no guarantee that $90,000 will be enough to finish the car, and where would that leave me? Even deeper in debt and by that time with no other avenue than to plough on, no matter what. It has crossed my mind, also, that Debbie has her limits.

Mornings I wake to Katie's stereo down the hall. Usually "Wild Horses," Jimi Hendrix's "Hey Joe" or the Cowboy Junkies' cover of "Sweet Jane." Scary Larry tells me his oldest boy, now six five, sits at their piano playing the "giants." Bach, Beethoven, Led Zeppelin. "He thinks the future stopped happening twenty-five years ago. Jake goes, 'The Beatles, the Who, the Rolling Stones, Dad, why doesn't anybody make hits anymore?' It's bad enough if I'm nostalgic for 1968, but my son?"

My daughter, never lazy, goes dawn to dusk—school, JV tennis, tonight a meeting at a Huntington Beach church with her fellow Christian surfers. Okay by me, as long as she doesn't end up wearing a toga and galoshes and hanging out with God selling chrysanthemums in an airport. I've completed a new novel about the end of the world told from the point of view of movie stars in which Christ comes back to lift us all to rapture. But when I mail it to New York, bad news. The prognosis: It needs a happy ending, plus there are no heroes. Gideon Bosker's advice: "As a novelist you are like the world's best chef at the world's weirdest gourmet dish: blowfish sushi. But too bad for you, unless they're really hip, the eating public doesn't even want to try blowfish sushi. They say 'ick' no matter how good blowfish sushi really is. So what we need to do is transfer your talents to T-bone steak."

Ninety-thousand dollars. Where else am I going to get that kind of money? I spent six months writing a near book-length proposal for a photo history of surfing. The reaction? Publisher No. 1 said they loved it and held the manuscript for four months before revealing they had never done a photo-driven book before and it was too risky. Publisher No. 2 said they loved it and held the manuscript for four months before telling me they wanted something "less serious, more fun pop culture." Publisher No. 3 said they loved it, but wanted to refine it, and we spent another four months dotting *i*s and crossing *t*s before the editorial director announced he was so impressed that he had actually thought of the idea before I did and was going to do the book himself. Publisher No. 4 said they loved it but wanted to know why I had waited a year to send it to them now that, suddenly, there were twenty-eight surfing titles coming out next year—but would $15,000 be okay? That wouldn't even cover the photographer's lab fees.

Gideon suggests that together we write a new novel using the old bromide "an ordinary man in an extraordinary situation." Gideon, who is about as ordinary as plutonium, has, however, come up with a formula to kill us all. I say it is terrifying, and ask: Is it realistic? "Of course," he assures me. "Bad for mankind, but good for our book." So a new novel, *Rx*, about an emergency room doctor, like Gideon, who is an expert on high-tech pharmacueticals, like Gideon, and who is married, unlike Gideon, to a brilliant but unstable scientist who invents a cure for the common cold so fatally flawed that, if mass marketed, will ignite a plague that will return the world to the cockroaches.

Will our protagonist betray his wife and destroy his family to save the world? You tell me.

At a magazine rack, I pick up a *Popular Mechanics*, and see a weirdly familiar shape on the cover, a shape announced as "The Next Ford Taurus." A bulbous junked-up version of Nick's original Xeno.

I call Nick, and he says he's seen it. "Ford stole your design," I say. "They can't do that."

"Sure they can. They're big and I'm small. They can do anything they want."

All right, then. I'm taking the $90,000 to build the car. If Nick's vision is not expressed in a real car, he'll be forgotten. He'll set up housekeeping in cyberspace or fly off to the movies and be gone. The greatest car designer who never was. I can't face that kind of failure. The Xeno has eaten my old Porsche, eaten our new house in Portland, and will doubtless eat everything short of my wife and children if that's what it takes to get the car done. Yet once complete the Xeno will validate Nick as the best designer of his generation and me at least as the coatholder who didn't punk out on the best designer of his generation.

He has already begun a model of a totally redesigned Xeno III—a roadster as linear as a knife. To realize our new design we'll have to lop off the front half of the chassis—a three seater that became a one seater will now be a two seater. Expensive. Good that John has sponsors for the Dodge Van, all six utilities and the Advanced Research Projects Agency have signed up. So I'm surprised at this twist. "I'd never do anything to hurt you or Debbie or Katie and Matt," Nick says, "but we can't start another year without knowing there is money guaranteed to do the car. I just won't do it."

I'm getting the fine print. "Unless?"

"You agree to put the money in a joint bank account."

"You don't trust me?" I ask.

He shakes his head. "It's just that you're so far in debt I know that once we get started Debbie will say, 'Mark, we need money to pay bills,' and the money will have to come from the Xeno stock money John gave you and the Xeno will never get done."

I don't reply. If I say anything, I'll say everything and the five-year project will be over. Besides, he's probably right.

We drive out to MetalCrafters. Nick has to shepherd completion of the "Lone Ranger." He brings his new girlfriend Heidi (Heidi is Nick's *new* new girlfriend, as opposed to his *old* new girlfriend, Corina [actually, there was another girlfriend between these two, a delicately gorgeous Vietnamese woman who spoke several languages and whose dad made gay porno films]. Heidi seems to be sort of a hippie but, like all Nick's girlfriends, is intelligent and very attractive), who has a big smile and short blonde hair. Red-carpeted paths guide us across a big, spare, clean-as-a-hospital-operating-room service bay to our new Chrysler van. A big blue box of a truck, about as generic as a potato, it has been lifted in the air, its bright new metal guts form a ceiling above us. A black-lined grid on the wall called the "problem log" details the process. The van's frame rails have been cut out to be replaced by four steel bows to encase the fuel tanks, each able to store over ten gallons' equivalent of regular pump gas. Major surgery: $400,000 worth.

Say that, to satisfy needs you may never understand, you want to create the most beautiful and powerful street-legal car anywhere. Say you employ a ram induction system suited only for offroad land speed record attempts on a motor, say, already modified to develop near twice its normal horsepower. How will, on the way to the 7-Eleven, this motor survive the firestorm of exploding fuel barely controllable by a conventional throttle?

A change of plan, in the person of Slick, who is as tall as I am, but real big. Slick is married to Mom who is, says engine builder Don Bass, "the sexiest woman I've ever seen," and young Slick is here at the tidy, windowless cave that is Bass's engine shop twenty minutes from my house to negotiate a price for our Dart heads and Tunnel Ram injection. In the door at $6,000, out the door at $3,000. "A fair price," Slick says. He takes my hand. I get a squeeze to compress iron. Slick is a bouncer at a club where his wife, Mom, strips. A nice guy. Gold hair, clear blue eyes, shoulders wide as a gorilla's and a waist as trim as a kid's—like a real-life action figure who should be administering blond justice from the cockpit of a spaceship. He wants our potent but tempermental salt flat parts for his Corvette.

Slick gets those parts at half price. Sadly, top dollar in the current market. But before I can lose my $3,000, Mom has to strip her way through Las Vegas. For Slick is cash poor.

Forget the $35,000 salt flat engine. We can make just as much trouble for ourselves at a quarter of the price. Back to my original plan: The Rat motor ideal, fueled by natural gas. Bruce Eikelberger has subcontracted our motor work to Don Bass, who says the Chevy heads won't give him the compression he was hoping for, but not a big catastrophe. He can go to a belt-driven blower and double the power. "But," he says, "cooling is critical. Double the power you double the heat load. You're putting twice as many BTUs into the system as it was designed to have. And the Chevy stock cylinder head is scary," he warns. "Feel it. There's not much material. It's thin. We don't want to put too much pressure on it or it will break. But the rest should be easy. The crank stays GM, the rods stay GM, but the camshaft will require a different base circle than the stock Five-oh-two. Billet designed from scratch."

Though Bass looks as down to earth as any good dentist, he engineered the first Dodge factory stock car teams in the late 1950s and Bill Strope's Ford racing teams into the 1960s and seventies and his trademark is tough engines that deliver incredible speed.

"We will be making huge power. But we have to be very careful. As the torque curve goes up," he explains, "the valve gears can explode."

48

THE DREAM MUSEUM

The car will be "alive"—self-repairing, able to "reason." The car of 2100 will not look like a car. It will be worn like a jacket. You'll be your own parking space. Your garage may be your closet. The car will envelope its owner like shrink-wrap, penetrate your flesh, bones and nerves, form around your body and through your vital organs to hold them in place, preventing tissues from tearing due to extreme acceleration or deceleration.

Nick is flying. *The New York Times* has hired him to describe the car from 2100 and he just handed me his notes.

I read in the shop. Nick has driven Heidi and me—folded up in the back of his Honda—out here to Pomona. Yes, if not cinder block hot rod heaven, at least a cinder block Palace of Versailles for hot rod royalty. Where So-Cal Speed's belly tank racer white-and-red pod body, once the 315-gallon drop tank from a World War II P-38 fighter, floats between tall, small tires that ring the mirror disks of its racing wheels. It hit a record-breaking 198.34 mph in 1952 at the Bonneville Salt Flats and, restored here to metal virginity, is headed for the Petersen Automobile Museum in Los Angeles.

Why didn't we come here in the first place? I have no idea, it wasn't for lack of pedigree. So-Cal Speed was founded in 1946 by Alex Xydias. Cars fabricated in the original Burbank shop set speed and drag race records all over in the early 1950s. But the backbone of the current operation is Pete Chapouris and "Jake" Jacobs, formerly of "Pete and Jake's"—probably the best known hot rod builders of the last twenty years. In the paint shop, new painted parts are hung up as if in an art gallery. More a museum than a laboratory—most cars here are being created or restored as traditional hot rods—So-Cal Speed restores hot rods that win at the Concours d'Elegance at Pebble Beach. A So-Cal

Speed–built '33 Ford—ZZ Top's Eliminator—was featured at this year's halftime at the Super Bowl.

"This is perfect," Nick says. "The owner Pete Chapouris has got only two requirements if you want a job here. One, be the best. Two, you can't be a dick. So nobody wants to kill me yet." Chapouris is a Marine Corps vet. "The only man ever to be awarded the Congressional Medal of Honor," one of his friends told me, "for extreme cleanliness under fire."

Nick and I stride past a 1933 Chevrolet. No fenders, its knife nose a hair off the cement, the thick roil of exhaust pipes twine from its 500-horsepower, blown Chevy 427 V-8, making it look as if the sleek $300,000 machine has been disemboweled. Nick makes a fist and punches air. "The fabricators are so dedicated some *live* there. I'm learning so much. Like, if you ask a question, they say, 'I don't know.' "

"Awesome," I agree.

"No!" Nick exclaims. "Instead of the usual bullshit, they ask somebody else or call another shop."

On the shop wall, ZZ Top's Billy Gibbons, mad eyes bright above the explosion of beard and his arm around golden-haired, high-heeled pulchritude (his wife? girlfriend? sister?), stares down from a big black-and-white photo on Billy's own supersmoothly redesigned black 1949 Ford, Kopperhed, which sits beside Chapouris's 1932 Ford five-window coupe, the California Kid, painted with flames spilling over its black cowl. This car, so incredibly clean in its execution, defines the meaning of a great hot rod: A machine that is clearly superior in every way to the car from which it was born.

We get the estimate: $111,000 for the whole Xeno. About $30,000 more than I've got to spend, but—"They can't build it for that," Nick says, fuming once more. "Not the way I want it done."

"Nick," Heidi says. "They know what they're doing."

I like Heidi, and Nick's in love. Any worries? "She parties hard," Nick says, after we drop her off at her apartment, blocks from Nick's. "Nothing heavy. Mostly just clubs and vodka." Then looking back at the estimate resting on his lap and propped up by the Honda's steering wheel, he says, "Maybe they will stay on budget. Maybe Heidi's right."

"Yeah," I agree, though I know that as soon as they come to understand Nick's definition of perfection, that estimate doesn't stand a chance.

We bite. We're here. The $111,000? We'll scare it up somewhere. The whole front end of the Xeno has been cut off. This to create a racer capable not only of breaking a land speed record, but of carrying two passengers instead of one, a dream machine able to go 220 miles an hour and be sold for one million dollars. The first great car of the twenty-first century. Nick spent weeks constructing a model of what will now be the Xeno III.

So off with the front end. Six months of work gone in a morning; $10,000 worth of John Mason and Herman Drees's artistry sits in a neat, bent-up pile in the corner of the shop.

"Pete doesn't want it good, he doesn't want it great, he wants it perfect." Nick exclaims, speaking of Pete Chapouris. "Not even Metal-Crafters are as good as these guys. Have you seen Speed's welds?"

Yes. They are perfect. As is the rest of Speed's Mercedes. Sometimes at night I decorate my insomnia trying to figure out how he did it. Our new So-Cal Speed fabricator, Rick "Speed" Lefever, has built one hundred hot rods. His latest is the white Mercedes "funny car" that sits beside the Xeno II, freshly trucked to Pomona from Bruce Eikelberger's shop and even more freshly cut in half.

Though Speed's Mercedes has been stretched one and a half times its original length, he has kept its spatial integrity exquisitely intact, the car's form remains weirdly perfect. Nick says, "But the money. He's spent twenty thousand dollars for his rear end, fifteen thousand dollars on his front end, fifteen thousand dollars for a new Lenco transmission. A hundred-dollar bill is nothing but a little money raindrop on a car like this."

Nick's eyes tick from Speed's Mercedes to the Xeno. We are going to need *a lot* more money raindrops, a monsoon. For example, cooling our supercharged engine requires making a water pump to force water through the engine block at double the normal velocity, as well as building a custom-made aluminum—as opposed to standard copper—radiator. About $3,000. "And it may still run so hot the engine will burn down," Bruce Eikelberger predicts. "Then what?"

Jerry Forster says not to worry.

Our new guru. Young, short, dark, the son of a New York City policeman, he came to California to become a Buddhist monk. And though monkhood didn't pan out, and he went on to become an English teacher and college administrator before his incarnation as general manager of So-Cal Speed, he has a certain Zen certitude I find reassuring. "This will be a groundbreaking car," he says. "If you're committed, we're committed. We'll get it built right no matter what. If you run out of money, we'll get money. All we ask is your commitment."

Nick's crushed. Whomever Nick Pugh may be, boozer isn't it. Two beers is Nick's Saturday night. About the only time I ever saw him tipsy is on the videotape of him destroying the clay model. But his girlfriend Heidi's counselor at AA or wherever she has gone to seek help for what is, I guess, a bad drinking problem, perceives Nick otherwise. "Heidi said she was quitting for good," he says, "but wanted to get loaded one last time. So a night of vodka. I was miserable but she kept drinking and drinking." And the next day Heidi went to her counselor, who told Heidi that Nick was a "facilitator" and that she should never see him again.

"Let him pay his own bills." Debbie is angry at Nick. She is decorating people's homes six days a week while I write my new novel, *Rx*, and, once again, like magic, no rent money. "Same old story. He expects everybody else to pay for his vision except him."

"No," I suggest. "Give the devil his due, Nick was right. Same old story. We are broke and we need money."

"We have money. *Your* money," she says. "I don't get it. You have worked for years, but you can't keep your own money."

"So I have to steal from myself to pay myself."

I say we'll let God decide. I won't forge Nick's signature on our joint account, just apply my own and leave the line for Nick's blank. God, in the person of a fashionably starved teller at our bank, decides in my favor. She cashes the $5,000 check.

But where is the money going to come from? I told John I wanted to keep one hundred shares of stock out of my original five hundred or no deal, and he said fine. So maybe I could sell that too. As one of four partners, I'm left with a one-twentieth share of the company I founded, forced to sell my stock to build the car. Which the company was founded to do. Still, I would not have given two cents to the long-range chassis program. So how angry do I need to be?

Summer's end. It's night and we could be under artillery attack. The Dodge Long Ranger, huge American flags emblazoning both its sides, is going eighty, slamming through the rain past a tractor trailer as big as a house. Lightning cracks down the sky far away, close, everywhere, flashing the black mountains through a downpour that is a million silver slashes in our headlights.

John Case has embarked on the first "unassisted" cross-country trip ever by a natural gas vehicle. He has done a great job. Not to put too fine a point on it, but necessity may be the mother of thinking. Once the patent process kicked in, John suddenly was a details man. No scrap of scructural analysis was too small to escape his eye. The engineers would say things like "The whiizwort is connected to the packaloomer at an eight-point-eight-seven-nine-five-degree angle" and John would say, "Don't forget to figure in the height of the mizmack, that would make the angle closer to eight-point-eight-seven-nine-four degrees," and the engineers would look sheepish, even on occasion Bruce Eikelberger.

It feels nineteen to be out here driving too fast in the revolutionary truck of John and Nick's invention, a truck that will finance my dream if not my rent, and I remember back before all the hassles when Debbie and I first moved to California so I could do my TV book and how John put Debbie, four-year-old Katie and me up in his house rent free for months, and how the only time he ever got pissed at me before this car project was when I informed him I'd run up $2,000 worth of phone bills on his tab and he said, "No, it's only five hundred dollars," and when I replied, "No, it's two thousand dollars, I've got the records," John snapped, *"I said it was five hundred dollars, okay?"*

I'm proud of him. It's a great truck. The van can go 390 miles without refueling. I ask him if he feels like Lindbergh and he laughs and replies: Only a little bit.

PART FOUR

ALL THAT GLITTERS IS GOLD

49

IT'S ALIVE

Funny how the mountain scenery flies by, fir trees nothing but a blur, and how when Katie, who does not have a driver's license but only a learner's permit, passes a Ford Explorer the Explorer truly seems to be standing still. When I look at the speedometer I see that my fifteen-year-old daughter, at the wheel of my wife's newly leased Jetta, is going one hundred miles an hour, on her way to Mammoth Mountain, her dark-haired, high-driver pal Annie curled up in the backseat with *The Great Gatsby*, lost to the Jazz Age, oblivious.

Some very bad news. The publisher who thought creation of the Xeno was such a great idea that they paid me big money to write a book about it is tired of waiting for our ultimate car to be born and is suing me to get their big money back. Steve Scherzer says I have no defense and that the best thing I have going is that I'm broke—no blood from a turnip, et cetera—and that he'll try to reason with the publisher's lawyers but that it doesn't look good.

I tell Katie to slow down but she can't hear over a blaring homemade tape. A girl from a local band, who Katie says will soon be famous, sings, *"I'm just a girl in the world, don't let me out of your sight."* Nick Pugh will be famous too. Before I can suggest to Kate that, for both our sakes, she stay out of the crystal ball business she shouts that I drive like a grandma. The evidence: Last night I stopped at a stop sign at an empty intersection. "That is such! A waste of time." Unlike my father at my age I don't have a Fuzz Buster radar detector mounted beside the rearview mirror of a 300-horsepower road rocket. But frighteningly fearless Katie, already a polished and completely adept reckless driver, has my dad's flair for speed. Snowboarding with her is like free fall with snow in the background.

I look over again and see the needle on the speedometer quivering to 105. "Slow down!" I repeat. On the tape Gwen Stefani of the brand new Orange County ska-pop band No Doubt wails, *"Oooooooooooh, I've had it up to here"* as the Jetta squiggles into a series of turns and I notice, relieved, that the needle has sagged to a far more prudent 75.

"Ford," Nick says, "has been looking for us since before Christmas but lost our phone number, until now." Which is February. "They may incorporate our patents in the whole next generation of Ford trucks, pickups and utility vehicles."

We are driving toward the San Gabriel Mountains to So-Cal Speed along the gray concrete sweep of the Pomona Freeway. A van in front of us has a bumper sticker that reads GOOD GIRLS SWALLOW.

"Does Ford know you know they stole your design?" I ask.

"No!" Nick exclaims. "That's what makes it so weird."

My partners have met with the number three man at Ford. Nick says the patents could now be $20 million, leaving me to wonder—minus 80 percent of my stock—what would be my cut of that?

Speed's pissed, his smooth face burning red. "I can't build a car just from a model made out of paper and Popsicle sticks."

Thirty-seven-year-old Rick "Speed" Lefever is one-stop shopping. He is one of the best fabricators in the country, he also builds engines, designs cars and races them as well. His work is art and the chassis is coming together. "The problem is," he says, "Nick has Corvette suspension—designed *precisely* for a Corvette—and wants me to completely remachine it for the Xeno. That's like asking a plastic surgeon to remake Arnold Schwarzenegger's arm for Oprah Winfrey."

I had no idea that the millisecond it took to light the vision of that front suspension between Nick's ears would cost as much as a year of my daughter's college education: $16,500 in labor alone. All to create "the Falling Water of Cars."

If you have any idea about creating a dream car, here is a tip that will justify the cost of this book: *Never ever create a chassis that requires major alteration of the front suspension.*

What a bucket of snakes. The stock Corvette cross member—the "spine" of the front suspension—left no room for the driver's feet, so Speed had to build fixtures that held all the suspension geometry, and that adapted Corvette geometry to our tubular frame. The Xeno is wider than a Corvette which, of course, demanded an increase in the width of the suspension, which meant a complex and therefore time-consuming and therefore costly reworking. Speed also was able to improve the Corvette suspension by eliminating "bump steer"—the tendency of the front tires to lose their parallel track by as much as a quarter inch, because the suspension warps when it goes over a bump. Which can throw the car out of control at speeds of over one hundred miles an hour. The problem was, in order to reengineer the Corvette suspension, Speed had to call in an Indy 500 racing expert.

The devil is in the details.

Speed's log for the first week in February:

CUT AND WELD BEARING INSERTS. FINISH WELDING BELL CRANKS. SET UP IN BRIDGEPORT FOR BEARING HOLES TO BE MACHINED. BORE OUT FRONT CAMS. GRIND OUT CLEARANCE FOR ROD ENDS AND SHOCK ENDS. FINISH PREP ON BELL CRANKS FOR NICKEL PLATING. CUT OUT AND NOTCH TUBING FOR PIVOT MOUNTS. WELD MOUNTS ON CHASSIS. AFTER MEETING WITH NICK AND MARK, STRAIGHTEN OUT ANGLES OF SHOCKS. CUT OUT GUSSET FOR LEFT-HAND SIDE. WELD IN. CUT REAR SHOCK MOUNTS.

The tab for the week? $1,436.33. Originally, I had $80,000 in my back pocket. Already $36,000 has gone to reinvent the suspension, et cetera three hundred hours in labor. And the hits keep happening. Just the brake and gas pedal cost $1,000. They are Nick's art, truly metal pedals, pedals worthy of Calder or Klee, but pedals that will only be seen by the bottom of the driver's feet. How can we finish the car spending money like that? I try and try to figure that out. Then, eureka, it hits me again. We won't.

Nick's new dream cars are created, observed and destroyed, never to be seen by anyone else, cars gone for good, and when I tell him I find his new vocation strange, even disturbing, he shrugs. "It's the total opposite of how I used to be, dedicated to richness and famousness, which was totally bad."

He just got a job working for DNZ, a design firm in Irvine, where he creates concept cars for auto industry designers to study and be inspired by. "I never know who the designers are or which company they work for. Though before I start a new car I get a 'bible' telling me design cues to include, signature things—like you gotta have an air scoop shaped in a Mustang-y way, you know it's a Mustang, or taillights that look real Honda, you know it's a Honda."

He is not allowed to even sign his drawings and when each car design is finished and everybody has been inspired, all his drawings and models are destroyed. When I ask if that bothers him, he is enthusiastic. "No! I love it. It makes the work king. It's not about me or my ego. It's just about doing my best, which is awesome. Besides," he laughs, "I've got a million cars inside my head. If getting famous or billions and billions of dollars happened, cool, but that means nothing to me now."

If $400 happened to me, that would be, at this moment, pretty cool as well.

But disaster. Time has passed. It is summer.

Little League, the division championship game, I'm coaching. Before the game our opponents, the Pirates in their black-and-gold uniforms, swirl around their kickboxing coach like a black-and-gold tornado. Matt is pitching. I have no idea how he's going to do. He's having growing pains, I think. At night, pain sighs up and down his shins and I massage his legs for half an hour at a time. He still does not weigh eighty pounds—if I pick him up and hold him just right it is as if I am holding nothing. The first batter bats left-handed. On the second pitch he hits a rocket drive that zings past Matt's head, but the second baseman, extending a glove that would look big on Randy Johnson, jumps and snags it out of the sky. Matt strikes out the next two batters, pitches three innings and only allows one run when our manager, Harry Brundle, is thrown out of the game.

In a beach community pervaded by yuppy yacht clubbers, Harry doesn't fit the yuppy mold. In fact, he looks like a walking Wanted poster. A shaved head, no top front teeth, 260 pounds, a tattoo of Elmer Fudd wielding a submachine gun on one forearm and another of matched .38 revolvers on his biceps, and if you hit that muscle, it's like hitting ham.

Back in the days when he was a pigeon rancher Harry drove a hot rod '57 Chevy that ran on straight aviation fuel, but now he's lost his driver's license, "on accounta my ahhhballs." He got out of his car one day and "Ah saw six a my wife."

So I picked him up before the game. Harry manages an apartment complex (!!!UNITS AVAILABLE NOW!!!) in a Long Beach neighborhood where among the only people with steady jobs are the good-looking hookers. When I drove up, he said, "Whaz that, a Beemer?"

No, just my wife's new Jetta. We leased it. Using our real names. Matt was happy to see Harry. Recently my son's pet lizard got its hair-thin fingers stuck on a glue strip that held its cage together. The pet store guy said, "The lizard's had it, he's as good as dead," but when we took the squiggly little reptile to Harry's, he was more optimistic. "Thizza tough one," he allowed. "Thiz happened before. I had a monitor lizard—grew up as big as an alligator, I used to walk it on a leash until it ate a dog, but when it was a baby it got caught in the same crap, lemme see here." Gentle, precise, Harry's stubby fingers tugged the lizard's delicate claws this way and that until the claw was free.

Matt looked happy enough to cry. But at the championship game, trouble. One of our players is called out at home and Harry explodes from the dugout. "Thizzizfukkinridicolous" he tells the Zapata-mustached ump, "The runner slid halfway to the backstop before the catcher even touched him." The brown-skinned umpire makes a jerking motion with his thumb. Lots of yelling, then Harry, "Let's go out behind the snack shack and settle this." Harry is eighty-sixed, and I'm in charge. It's like being in a two-hour-long auto wreck, but, as a leader, I do what I have now learned to do best, what my drag race teacher Frank Hawley first suggested, nothing. I stay calm, my son and the Angels beat the Pirates 8–2—and the following week we go across town to the Tournament of Champions.

Where I plan to sell our old Volvo for $400 to Harry, now that he's getting his license back. He's had to ride tandem with the Angels' assistant coach, Big Steve. A true gentle giant, way over six feet tall and way over 300 pounds, Big Steve has curly hair and a baby face and is great with kids. He drives a yellow Ford pickup powered by a T-bird V-8, and—because he has narcolepsy and can fall asleep any time—he and Harry drive as a team.

But bad news. Harry says instead of my Volvo, he's buying a Cadillac from Pope Ralph.

Pope Ralph?

I am standing outside the dugout, banned from the bench because I didn't get my first aid card completed in time.

Big Steve says, "Most people didn't know it, but the Catholic Church has two popes, the one in the Vatican and the one in Long Beach."

Vinny, our other assistant coach—who, with his trim swoop of hair, looks like a 1950s rock star—is already anticipating our next game. Against the Beverly Hills 90210 team and, planning ahead, is worried. "It's gonna be tough. They'll be the home team and have all their therapists plus all their little pals from rehab rooting in the stands."

John Case says, sitting in the bleachers, "You got it in the bag."

I suppose. It's the fourth inning in a six-inning game and we're up six zip.

A good spring. Katie is the founder and president of her high school's new top sorority—BOTU—Bitches of the Universe—which she assures me is populated with nothing but the smartest girls who have the best bad attitudes. Sorority functions may soon involve surfing and snowboarding trips but seem at this nascent stage to revolve around skipping last period typing class to cruise to drive-in restaurants. The movie *Clueless* has re-enfranchised wealthy, beautiful, daft Beverly Hills girls and, though we live in blue-collar Long Beach and we buy our caviar at Sears, Katie was invited to appear on a Leeza Gibbons–hosted TV show celebrating the best of the best of California's spoiled rich girls. Katie has a smile for the ages and has exercised and not eaten her way to a perfect, delicate, wasp-waisted figure, and looks as if she just stepped out of a Nieman Marcus catalog, so nobody had a clue she is no more spoiled than I am. As for her driving, an amateur race car driver friend of mine says there is a new racing camp in Arizona where talented kids go for six weeks to learn to drive mini-formula cars. It costs a bundle but at least it would keep Katie off the streets.

But anyway, Little League. We are playing an across-town team, the Giants, and have our best first three innings ever. Matt has pitched himself out of the rotation—that is, pitched so much that he cannot pitch in this game—and we have had to resort to a big, sweet Mexican boy, Hugo, who has never pitched a game in his life. Miracle of miracles, the kid throws like he gets paid to do it. He has a shutout going until the top of the fourth inning.

Sitting there in the bleachers, John wants to know how the car is going, and I tell him: great. Except that Nick is insisting that it be fabricated piece by piece, designing almost every bracket and bolt. It's beautiful, but my Xeno money is just about over and, distracted from the game, I am thinking: Shit, maybe I should ask John if he'll buy my last hundred shares—my Lotto ticket to a million dollars for thirty thousand dollars so I can keep the car getting built and not have to realize I'm screwed again until October or so, when John says. "This game is over," gets up and leaves. The minute he goes, the wheels come off. We are ahead six to one, and in go the subs. I plead with Harry not to do it, that it's too early, but Harry says, "Alla kids deserve to play" and puts Lauren—tall and blonde and smart, a future femme fatale and the Angel's only girl—in right field. Lauren is the fastest runner on the team, maybe even the team's best natural athlete, but this is her first year in baseball. She baubles a pop fly. Two runs score. Then our shortstop overthrows to first and allows two runs.

Matt has hit well all year, but last week he went to surf camp, his arms are sore and he strikes out twice. Short story shorter, we lose seven to six.

When Nick vows, "No way I'd ever do anything to risk Katie and Matt's future or education." I say good. Because the only way I can pay for the car is if Katie doesn't get to go to college. Nick continues to design every other part and it will cost double the $90,000 I got for my stock. He is making big money, movie money, and I tell him, "The only way that this car will get finished is if you start paying for it yourself."

Like a nest of metal snakes, the four exhaust pipes erupt from the exhaust ports, then twist and roll over each other and meet in a

O O
O O

pattern at the back of the muffler.

Though the shape is serpentine and complex, it all comes from three- and four-inch radius Us of two-inch pipe. The steel muffler, shaped like the nose cone of a rocket, floats in space beside the trans-

mission, suspended by wires from the shock absorbers, anchored below by a stand. So-Cal engine builder Greg Petersen lengthens and
tightens the wires, to get the right muffler to mirror the left muffler,
already in place.

"I need to know where I'm going and where I've been," Greg says,
holding up his TIG welder, about to begin tack welds. "Watch your
eyes. When this fires, you're looking at a little sun."

The trick is to shoehorn the spaghetti of exhaust pipe into a three-
inch clearance from the exhaust ports to the frame, and to keep all the
exhaust pipe the same length so that four exhaust streams will flow into
the muffler in sync. There are twenty-one segments of pipe per side.
Greg cuts by sight, builds the forward exhaust first, beginning with a
curl of pipe cut about four inches long that will curve from the lead
exhaust port.

He cuts it on a band saw, then dips it in water and grinds it flat on
a wheel—sparks fly—then uses a deburring knife, a handle with an
edged hook at the end. He sets the pieces of pipe together and uses
Magic Marker to indicate the point of his tack weld. There is not a
crack of light, perfectly flush. It's $1,800 worth of work, all in all. Nick
is picking up the tab.

Greg Petersen hits the ignition. The Xeno's engine shudders and
shrugs. "Gaseous fuel likes to walk away." The natural gas executive,
here to supervise the fueling, says, leaning over the motor, "Put the
fuel line to your ear. You'll hear a residual *whoosh*."

Greg does: no *whoosh*. He cracks the fuel line to see if it's clear,
checks the solenoid on the regulator to see that when charged with
electricity it creates a magnetic field to push the rod in its center forward to release the fuel to the line leading to the carburetor, and it
doesn't.

"Bum part," Greg says. He grabs another solenoid, hooks it up and
the motor, fired up for the first time, generates so much heat that the
big, curled snakes of exhaust pipe twisting from the eight exhaust ports
turn a dimly glowing red. The silver tubes of the racing mufflers go
copper and the rear exhaust pipes shade from shining silver to a dusty
black. The engine screams *raaaa-haaaa, raaa-haaa* as Greg tweaks the
throttle lever on top of the blower.

It's alive! The engine snarls. A gray twig of smoke rises off a plastic-
coated spark plug wire, heated by the sudden, near-molten exhaust

headers. Greg gets in, puts the Xeno in gear and the car rolls forward, engine burbling, out into the night, down the alley and to the street. The Xeno is so low it bottoms out. We lift it up by its sides, like guys beaching a dinghy. Then lightless, it screams down the street.

50

AT LAST

My sister Laurie, about to vacation with her husband aboard a Russian icebreaker plying the Arctic, calls to tell me that my father does not have much time left, is very worried about me. "He wants to see you," she says. "He may want to ask some very frank questions. He loves you very much but I'm not sure he knows what has been happening to you."

This: Steve Scherzer calls to say he has talked to my publisher's collection attorney. "You have no defense. We could argue unreasonable enforcement of blah, blah, blah, but talk about an expensive long shot. You're guilty. Your contract gave you three years to finish the book, you didn't, you can't, that's it. On the other hand, the publisher's lawyer knows, even if your publisher doesn't, that you have nothing and that unless you have time to finish the car and with that the book, nobody gets anything, because we have more drastic remedies."

Like bankruptcy?

"Mark, Mark, Mark, let's not go there yet. This lawyer Patrick Barth may be a shark, but he's a good shark. His idea is, let's get the book done, that way his client gets his money and you get your life back. So call him, don't bullshit and let's get the car finished now."

Why not? I can't wait to fly home to tell my dying father the good news.

The problem is, as usual, time and money. If the Xeno will command $1,000,000 it must be worth $1,000,000. This requires execution of spendy detail after spendy detail. As Pete Chapouris says, corners make the car—corners defined by headlights and taillights. Nick is sparing no expense.

Richard Martinez created the main flight assemblies for the Apache

Attack helicopter and the Y-22 fighter plane prototypes and his mill—a superhard electric-powered rotating blade—cuts thin, a swoop that polishes the aluminum bar in his hands as it cuts, gliding a mirror surface across the metal that will be part of the taillight assembly. The mill cuts it one one-hundredth of an inch thinner than it was ten seconds ago and it takes shape as a bladed facet of Nick's new taillight.

We are in his garage. "This blade, there's not a straight angle on it," Richard says, holding the blade in his hand. "Twelve degrees intersecting a thirty intersecting an eight intersecting a thirty-three intersecting a forty-five. Do the math, then figure out how to make it. Eighty-five percent is planning time, the machining time is seconds. It'll take four hours to make one cut of the blade, three hours of tooling."

Nick is spending $16,000 with Martinez, and the plans for each part look like the plan for a house. To make the cones to back our taillights, Richard took a piece of twelve-pound aluminum bar stock, hollowed it out to less than half a pound. Before he began, he studied the drawings for a week. "Nick wanted set screws to bolt the taillight assembly—I talked him into threading it." And thread it he did. So finely that, though the parts unscrew in the middle, it looks like one piece of metal.

Richard puts a brown finger on Nick's plans. "Nick measured by the length of the hypotenuse, he designed all parts with the long diagonal of a triangle. We need to work out north-south, east-west. I had to make four hundred new calculations before I could even begin."

Nick says, "I wanted to do a design that was chaotic and conflicting, but that—using fractal properties—you can give these disparate elements harmony. It is not about form following function, but a collision of form and function. I designed the car so you can look into it from almost every angle—see how the suspension works, see the engineering, see the beauty of function and the function of beauty, see how it works." He explains that the basic sharp-edged language of the design is articulated in simple triangulation, a repeating theme throughout. "It is not conceptual," he says, "but structural. Triangular construction is the most efficient way to create cheap strength. You have three mounting points for the fenders. Three's lots stronger than two, but you don't need four. Triangulation allows you to give, at every level, the car a crystalline form. The resulting aesthetic is geometric, but the reason is organic—from forces that would create a crystal. Grown or evolved rather than something built. The Xeno's design is shot through with self-similarity—something on it that is very tiny resembles the crystalline form you can see at five hundred feet. It is like a first, crude portrait of cars that will be grown, not manufactured."

This has resulted in, perhaps, as much attention to detail as in any other car ever built or grown. Jerry Forster says, "Ask yourself: Is there such a thing as too much perfection? No car I've ever heard of has demanded this kind of attention. Nick wants us to handmake body attachment clamps you could hang in the Getty."

It is the middle of summer. Nick is cutting body parts out in cardboard, taping these pieces in sections to the chassis to make templates for the aluminum body parts that will soon follow. He has got a camera set up on a stand in front of the car, and takes pictures every hour, so that the whole design process will be animated.

The temperature has hit 107 degrees out here, so that Nick can't use his glue gun. The glue melts just sitting there. Nick has skinned the car in paper backward to forward.

"This is a hateful, treacherous angle," he says, making a slashing motion down the flank of the car to indicate where the flat, bare metal body will meet behind the driver. Nick wants the car to look "cut from a chunk of metal crystal." If these So-Cal cars are, as someone suggested, novels written in steel, then Nick may be writing *War and Peace*.

"Dad, guess where I am. Who owns the Lakers basketball team?"

"That would be Dr. Buss."

"I'm at his house! Or his beach house. One of his houses. It's so cool. We're playing pool. We got here by limo. Would it be okay if Dr. Buss bought me a Ford Explorer?"

"Bought you a what?"

"Dad, I know what you're thinking. But it's not like that. The Lakers are soooo cleancut—you would never even say the word 'drugs' in front of them—and soooo nice, they talk to you and you think they're being serious but actually they're just making fun of you, so cool! And to Dr. Buss a Ford Explorer is just like a candy bar would be to you, nothing! Is it okay if I ask him?"

Katie has, without any doubt, left her family to join the world. I can say "No" to a free Ford Explorer, but that's about it. Still, I'm proud of her. I did not want her to become an L.A. hick, and tried to get her to go to school in Oregon or Hawaii or New York, but Southern California is her kingdom—walk down any beach street from Santa Monica to Tijuana and the "Hi Katie's" began to blur—and days later pictures of Katie with Kobe, Shaq and one of Katie with "this all nice, tall red-haired guy about your age named Bill Walton." One of my daughter's bustier friends has just been examined by *Playboy* and this has given Katie, and her more buxomy sidekick, passage to the good doctor's realm.

"You're a sun-fried Southern California lunatic. Lose the goddamned swearing," Gideon instructs over the phone, re: our new novel, *Rx*. He is calling from, I believe, Shangri-la. "Forget the wine. We can't have our hero getting drunk, and take it easy on the moral ambiguity. Readers want good versus evil, black versus white. We need our hero to be a saint. Mark, I'm your biggest fan, but I'm telling you, readers want a linear world."

Because his Doberman and my gold wolf-dog are united by a common bond—the desire to tear each other's throats out—perhaps I shouldn't be surprised that the bald old man with the big nose and big stomach who lives a few houses away wants to sell me his home for half its assessed value. Still, standing in my driveway watering a spindly rose bush, I have to ask, "Why?"

The old man is on the shady sidewalk, his sleek black dog pulling at its leash. "Blacks have moved in around the corner and down the street. You know what that means."

A neighborhood jazz band?

We have moved from near the shore inland to Alamitos Heights—shown on our deed to be twenty-six feet above sea level, a tree-shaded neighborhood by a golf course. We bought the place—for about a dollar down, a big pink old Mediterranean mini-manse fit for a failed Mafia Don—from a local Rolls Royce–driving gun dealer desperate to return to the more right-thinking confines of Orange County.

So how to make the payments? At least Matt will never starve for golf balls. Without a private country club, we live by the least exclusive—that is to say most widely used—public golf course in California, Recreation Park. Foxes slink the bamboo hallows, bunnies hop the fairways at dawn, owls as big as dogs stand sentinel in the palm trees and Matt can play for $3.00 a nine. Games that, like our mortgage, can be financed by credit cards at 19.99 percent.

What makes the guy so scary is that he does not sound like any attorney/doberman eager to tear my throat out, but far more like a very sympathetic and worried physician who is telling his patient that, no, the spot on his lung is not going away, that, no, the chemotherapy didn't work or even cutting the whole lung out either but that, sorry, this is the end. "Unless you can get the car done and resell the book," Patrick Barth, my publisher's attorney, informs long-distance from New York, "they refuse to even read your manuscript in order to reject it. It's 'We want our money back, take Mr. Christensen to court.'"

Not quite the latest triumph in, of course, a lifelong string of triumphs I'm eager to relate back here on this special night in Portland. Dick Donaca's insanely overpowered, sunshiney blue, wonderful chrome-caked flash of a Transylvanian pimp's '54 Ford, Bill Winfree's pure, simple white 1955 Chevy. Art practically before I could spell it. The boys who made those cars float out of the dark, still young, as if from a time machine: Bill Winfree, Dick Donaca. Thanks perhaps to exercise and bad light they look like the guys they were at Beaverton High.

Here at the bar at a suburban Portland country club, my thirtieth high school reunion. I try to explain the Xeno and when I get to the part about Spiro "Ross" Spiros and how he has patented a way for the car to run on water, Bill asks, "How much will you have in it?" When I say $400,000, his reply "Christ, Mark" stings.

What an evening. Dave Mills—the tall, thin boy who saved my 1953 Chevy when it was on fire in my parents' garage by dowsing the flames with flour—is now a tall, big man. He tells me he's building a hot rod 1940 Ford with drag slicks on the back so big that he had to refabricate the whole rear end. Dick Donaca has just built a something, something, something roadster powered by a huge something, something, something motor—the music is so loud I can't hear and it's great. I feel seventeen again, sent back to that time when a perfect world could be a garage.

The next morning I have breakfast with Moon. The same old kid's smiling optimistic face, the same old Nike jock squared-away look, but he keeps saying, "What?" and when I ask what's wrong he asks me to repeat the question and then says last week when he was making Thai food his hearing aid fell out and fried in his wok.

Kit Bowen says, "Fifty'll hit me like a bank safe dropped from a hundred-story building."

"But Moon," I say. "He looks the same as in high school."

"That's because your eyes are shot."

Under the volcano. This morning three dozen elk parked under the trees on my parents' rutted hayfield across the road out front, and I am sitting with binoculars by the dining room table, which has been converted to my father's office. On the table rests my father's empire, all the deeds and stock certificates and pinks slips for whatever it is he owns. No one knows what that is, for my father—who will talk about anything but himself and money—has not revealed even to his wife the extent of his holdings. Not long ago my ophthalmologist sister, Laurie, got a call at her office from a woman demanding that Laurie get her cows off the woman's property. What cows? What property? Evidently my Dad has a cattle ranch in eastern Washington that he forgot to tell anybody else in the family about.

Matt is lying on the floor in my parents' living room here at the ranch, reading a wildbird book, when he looks up to see my father gazing down at him from where my dad is sitting in a chair across the room.

"Is something wrong, grandad?" he asks. On my father's face the closest expression I have ever seen to fear is concern, and I see that now. I have not told him about the pending lawsuit, the probability that the Xeno project will shortly implode, but though he is eighty years old, he still can add two and two.

"No," my father replies, "I was just wondering what will happen to you, that's all."

I take Matt the forty miles south across the Columbia River into Oregon and Portland to see the grease pit at my parents' old house under the fir trees on Woodside Drive. I show him the garage where I committed my first mechanical malpractice—the stripping of the Hudson and the destruction in detail of my 1953 Chevy. I have taken him to the barn down the street where the beautiful sailboat, the *Faux*

Pas, was built and I want to give him my memory of the flaming, falling cars of my grandfather, to give him a memory of the past before he was there to live it. So I take my eleven-year-old to Rocky Butte to see my grandparents' old home. It was a house turned into a nightmare place when my grandparents got divorced, and I haven't been out here in thirty years. My grandmother, whom I loved very much but who was absolutely focused in her hates, made it sound as if my granddad's new wife was a bitch whore. But when I met her, the last time I was out here, she just seemed like a prim little old lady scared I would not like her. After my grandfather died, she sent my mother a note. Barely legible. It read: *He was a wonderful man. I loved him so.*

I don't know where I am. Where is their house? We are driving down a massive new freeway so sweeping that it has completely changed the landscape. As near as I can tell, where my grandparents' house used to be would now be maybe fifty feet straight down—under a vast shoal of earth pushed through here to accommodate this monster road. My grandfather, who spent his life making roads, has had his own home and the site of his construction company completely buried by a vast freeway. A whole world gone. It is like the way things disappear in a bad dream. Only Rocky Butte remains. "Hot rodders pushed flaming cars off that big cliff," I tell Matt, pointing toward the sky. "It was wild."

Stunning too. An entire landscape vanished, buried, gone and taking the past along for the ride. Fifty feet below where our tires whiz over the new pavement, I used to, at Matt's age, crouch by my granddad's coal shed, sighting down the barrel of his sleek .22 carbine at "gray diggers"—squirrel-like creatures that ravaged my grandparents' big cherry tree–shaded garden, aiming down toward the ancient dump trucks I'd first tried to "customize" by ripping apart.

But that world is gone, buried, as impalpable as memory. Now Matt's own grandfather—my father—has been made a living ghost by Parkinson's disease. I want to make sense of this robbery for my son, but for me that would probably be as impossibly reductive as writing CliffsNotes for a stop sign. I was thirty before I realized all the messes I'd made, forty before it occurred to me someone else always had to traipse around behind me to clean them up. As part of a privileged West Coast generation that, as writer Charlie Haas once noted, "grew up under a tremendous lack of oppression." I have been afforded every opportunity. My father, whom a childhood friend once described as "the original angry young man," worked almost full time in a gas station to get through Oregon State. He sent me to five resorts that called themselves colleges—in Hawaii, Colorado, Mexico, a privilege he could not have dreamed for himself—and if I worked a little construction summers to buy racing skis or surfboards or another crazy car, he didn't complain. He had hopes, I could tell—and chances are he loved me not so much for what I was, a hot-tempered, spacy kid who had a sense of humor, but what I could be.

I'm a journalist. But from my first effort, a review of *Deep Throat* (headline: THIS MOVIE SUCKS), my father seemed to have little idea of what I do or why, and now that he is about to die, he is worried and would like an accounting. What have I done with myself? How will I continue to get by, how will his grandchildren get by?

I drive alone to Calvary Cemetery, where my mother is buried. Here, on nearly mile-wide rolling lawns above Portland, I look for her headstone, but where it is supposed to be, it isn't. Rain is flying out of a dark, smoky sky. It is dusk at noon. Who could lose his own mother's grave?

What to tell my dad? I reveal that we will break the speed record for natural-gas vehicles, the Xeno III will become the first great car of the twenty-first century, tour the great auto shows in America and Europe and that the only way I can pay him back for what he has done for me and for being the father he was, is to try to do the same thing for my own son. I want to say, forget me, Dad, your legacy is your grandson—that relevance can skip a generation—but I don't. It could worry him, even frighten him. The Parkinson's has made him dreamy. Last night he hobbled into his little TV room, where I was reading. He was beaming and extended a hand. He seemed thrilled to see me and I was very flattered. But the thing was, I'd been there at the ranch two days.

So before I leave, all I do is hold his hand, tell him that I love him and promise that I will be back soon. He says, "Take care of yourself" and I promise that I will.

Fat chance. I have been sued with complete success. A judgment for well over $50,000 brought against me and a likelihood that my former publisher can take my house. Thank God for my literary agent, who I have known almost half my life and for whom I have provided many profitable clients. He can handle this. It appears, however, that I have gone from fair-haired boy to big fat problem. He says every dog has his day, Nick Pugh has had his, and that the world, the publishing part of it anyway, will no longer wait for the Xeno. He says *Build the Perfect Beast* is about "fair-weather friends who won't stand by you when you get in a jam" and no longer wants to represent my book.

Nick says he wants the car to be dangerous. "Edges sharp as a knife—dude goes to a car show, touches the Xeno and 'Oh no, this is no friendly consumer product, this car cut me. Ouch! Whaaaaa! Mommy, I want to go home.'

"I don't want a bunch of people to like this car, I just want a few people to love it. And maybe even hate it at the same time. It reflects my love and hate for the automobile. I don't want anything PC. The Xeno says: think. Cars should provoke. I want the Xeno to be difficult, maybe even wrong. So maybe another designer comes to look at it and says, 'Nick Pugh is nuts,' and he goes home and—" Nick mimes furious scribbling "—and comes back and shows me and says, 'See, here's how you do it' and I look and see he's right and say, 'Glad to have been of help.'

"I don't think of the Xeno as revolutionary. Not even a car of the future. Huge V-8 engines and tube frames have been around for a million years. So why a humongous supercharged engine? It's rude, crude, incredibly powerful, exciting, fun! Why metal construction? Because it will last forever. Get in the Xeno and you'll never forget the ride, never forget the look. But I think to design a true car of the future will be more like designing a lightning bolt than a BMW. Because the true car of the future will be organic, constantly, instantly changing."

The "Dad!" comes from above. I look back up the white slope to see my son shoot between two fir trees, fly above my head and rip a rooster tail of snow below me as he skids his snowboard to a stop.

We are skiing at Mount Baldy, fifteen minutes away from Pomona, and Matt wants to know if he can go ride in the car. "Not today," I say. "But soon." Imagine, you double the range of almost any car at almost no extra cost. That's twenty million dollars. It may take weeks or years. John says no matter, it will happen.

"Any time you change the configuration of a major automobile system like the brakes," Jerry Forster says, "you take a big risk."

Jerry Forster came to California as a college student majoring in religion. He was studying to become a Buddhist at the Los Angeles Zen Center at Mount Baldy—a twenty-minute drive up the road from where we are now. He began a sesshein, an intense seven-day period of meditation with twenty or thirty others. There was to be no talk, nothing but "living inside your head." After two days something went wrong, he began to hallucinate that he was buried in sand up to his neck on a beach, that the tide was coming in and he was about to drown. "I was terrified. I asked my roshi, my instructor, what I should do, and he said, 'drown.' "

Jerry could not bring himself to do that, so instead, sometime after midnight he slipped out of the Zen Center, trampled through the snow down to the highway and hitchhiked back to his apartment and his girlfriend.

"What happened," Jerry says, "was that you lost the brakes and almost crashed because there was no room in Nick's small footbox to mount the brake power assembly in a stock configuration. When you mess with systems like this—which companies like General Motors have invested millions of dollars designing to work in a very specific way—you can wind up with an abortion."

Or worse. We were in the alley that serves as an occasional drag strip beside the long, low shop at So-Cal Speed. My son was there to take his ride in our $1,000,000 car. No seat belts, or even seats. He sat on plywood. The Xeno was little more than a metal skeleton with racing wheels at the corners and 600-horsepower motor in the middle. But one ride wouldn't hurt. I did not know yet that the brakes lacked their boosters and, thus, had only a third of the power they needed to stop the car.

Matt beside me, I hit the gas. The Xeno, rear tires ripping rubber off their treads, accelerated so fast that the cinder-block wall beside the alley became nothing but the aforementioned blur, and we were going way too fast when the carload of Mexicans popped out from the parking lot. Foot to the floor, I was flying into the horizon, and the big, fat, wide racing tires behind the screaming motor were still spinning so wildly that the asphalt beneath the Xeno might as well have been ice, and suddenly I discovered Nick was right, there were no brakes—or at least no brakes until my leg felt fully extended, then, thank God, the car slowed enough for me to whip it off the road, tires yelling, as we swung into the parking lot, missing the Mexicans and coasting to a stop.

Matt, gripping my arm, beginning to breathe again, laughed. "Nice driving, Dad," he thrilled, a wonderful boy safe and so alive in a world without peril.

EPILOGUE

There is a danger the supercharger that may boost the Xeno to a land speed record may also backfire so powerfully that the supercharger—perched two feet behind my head—will become a one hundred-pound hand grenade that will explode when the Xeno accelerates.

Our steel hallucination sits in a garage at So-Cal Speed like a captured UFO. How fast can we make the Xeno go? 200? 210? Or will the Xeno hit, say, 170, rise, fly, flip and crash? Despite its now super powerful brakes and fighter-plane construction, it is a death trap. I crawl into our $1,000,000 machine through the open, glassless driver's-side window. Perhaps to guarantee that the Xeno is even more art than ultimate car, Nick has declined to spend an extra $10,000—on top of the $400,000 we have spent already—to hinge the roof so driver and passenger can simply step into the vehicle. Inside, my hands on the little Indy 500 MOMO steering wheel, I lay back as if in a glass-topped coffin. Nick has just made a final payment on construction of the headlights and taillights. To build them took three years.

Eight months of work just on the body. Once again Nick has burned the rule book. The Xeno III will look like no other automobile. No compound curves. The body has been made from 3003 H14 aluminum. H14 indicates the alloy's degree of hardness—H14 is midrange, not too hard to bend, but hard enough to withstand collision. The .090 sheets—ninety-thousandths of an inch thick—are thicker than the .060 standard. Normally a thinner metal would have been used and curved slightly, "crowned" to give it more tensile strength, but Nick demanded wide, flat surfaces to give the car a "diamond" shape. Rolling jewelry.

Nick made extremely accurate templates out of paper, cardboard, balsa, plastic tubing and plastic dowls. Then he hot-glued the shape of the body together and fabricator Bryan Fuller set to work building. He began with the rear quarter panels. First he took Nick's cardboard rear quarter and laid it over aluminum sheet. Each sheet was covered with a plastic film to protect it from scratching. Brian used an X-acto knife to cut the shape of the cardboard quarter panel into the plastic, then peeled the excess plastic away.

He then cut the panel using a hand shear or a "stomp" shear—an eight-foot-long cutting tool. Panels were bent when necessary with a sheet metal brake or a huge press brake.

The Xeno has a chromally space chassis, like a race car. And like a race car, the panels were designed to "pop" off, to be removed section by section. Normally this would be done with Dzus fasteners, which resembled little dome-headed rivets—you give them a quarter turn and they pop right off. But Nick insisted that, on the top of the body, there be no exposed fasteners, so Brian used "click-bonds" a stainless steel bolt with a one-inch flat washer on the bottom, which he glued to the back side of each body panel with Lord Fusor, a superhigh-strength glue now used on a lot of factory production cars to replace spot welds. It is so strong, the sheet metal will break before the glue. Brian then filed down all the perfectly straight external bends in the body metal to make each edge perfectly sharp when the body is bolted on.

Things have happened fast. Nick got married last fall. He met a beautiful young woman, a brilliant creator of special effects, a sane young woman who understands, the girl of his dreams. The world just keeps getting richer. The *Los Angeles Times* noted that Microsoft's Steve Ballmer lost $164,000,000 yesterday when Microsoft stock dipped a few points. That's enough money gone to fund a state university. Enough money, Steve, for you to build Xenos IV through CLVI and jump start a fresh future of automobile design.

But is that likely in a world where nobody even builds old-fashioned modern houses any more? Sixty-year-old Frank Lloyd Wright designs look like science fiction compared with the five-bedroom $850,000 mock-1920s-era Gatsby mansions contractors are throwing up in our neighborhood. Forted sameness expressed in a California Cape Cod style last best explored by architects dead since Prohibition.

Nick shrugs that the immediate future of design is nostalgia, that people have become afraid of too much change, that the grass was greener yesterday. After all, though car design is considered a most aggressive expression of tomorrow, even Porsches and Corvettes change silhouettes rarely. People may crave shock, but familiar shock, time-honored shock. Nick says, "By 1960, cars had already began to run out of technological wonders—driving a 1960s car and a year 2001 car isn't much different. A blaster CD, better-handling radial tires, air bags, computer fuel management systems so engines are ten times harder to fix, but what else? By 1970, people began to fall out of love with cars. Smog wasn't fun, fuel shortages weren't fun, endless traffic jams weren't fun, road rage isn't fun—and the marketplace determined cars weren't art, cars were products. You can make a lot more money selling refrigerators than you can Picassos. Exotic and adventurous and creative was not necessary to profit. Still, the future is happening maybe faster than ever before, but it is harder to see. Huge tail fins and huge rocket boosters, that was when progress was manifested outwardly—going to the moon. Now progress has gone inward: Microbiology, nano-technology and, obviously, computers."

But who would have thought, thirty years ago, that the sexiest progress would be the latest digital office equipment? Once futurists like Nick Pugh, Tim Leary and Werner Von Braun were a dime a dozen. Back in the days when I figured I'd be smoking pot on Mars by now.

"You would be," Nick insists, "except nobody ever figured out how to make a buck off Mars."

Meanwhile, Southern California stays Southern California. A perfectly emaciated friend of my wife just spent thousands on a full body liposuction and, black-and-blue from sternum to knees, told her husband she got the bruises falling down a flight of stairs.

John Case has bought a new house and has transformed it, sledge hammered out walls, torn the backyard down to nothing but dirt and one big, gnarly old tree, sanded floors creamy and perfectly flat, laid sod, a silk purse from a sow's ear in six weeks. The other day I came home and found my khaki shorts lying soaking wet on the toilet seat in the bathroom downstairs, and a note.

Mark: Got real dirty working on new house. Let myself in, took a shower. Was going to borrow your shorts, but dropped them in your toilet by mistake. Sorry. John.

I finally borrowed from so many Peters to pay so many Pauls that Debbie felt we had no choice but to sell our house, even at a loss. I'd like to say that I stood firm because I'm tough, but the fact is that I didn't put our house up for sale because giving up would be too much work. I'd have to go buy a FOR SALE sign, then bash its stake into our front yard, and then I'd be hassled by real estate agents and, besides, I figured, if we did nothing, something was bound to save us.

Something did. My father died.

A lovely nightmare vision. White sand, black water, white fog as opaque as a bed sheet. The thickest fog I have ever seen. I stood on the beach at "the cliffs" just north of Huntington Beach last week at first light. My son and two of his friends had paddled out into surf that was who knows how high because the surf was invisible. Matt was out there somewhere.

He does not mind risk. Co-Captain of the Seal Beach 14 and Under Soccer Club, he plays stopper on defense. A reasonably violent world. Last week the referee's back turned, a boy a head taller than Matt cracked him in the face and knocked him down. For some irrational reason I did not run into the field and pound the man-child into the dirt.

No need. Matt got up and followed the big kid everywhere on the field, attacking the boy's position whenever he had the ball, orbiting the lunk like a mad moon, stealing the ball over and over and over. Matt—five three and not yet one hundred pounds—is, by weight, the smallest boy on his team. Bigger boys, often all elbows and trash talk, rarely get past him. A flick of his foot, the ball pops away and, *boom*, a quick kick and bye-bye. His teammates are not boys like my brother and me. These are new boys. They get good grades and don't fight with each other. Never. No cigarettes, drugs or alcohol. Those temptations, in this grassy gladiator pit, only make you dumber, slower, weaker.

The fog does not lift. Someone on the beach says a riptide has surely pulled the boys north.

Scary stood at the head of a table in a dark Italian restaurant a half mile or so from my childhood home on Woodside Drive, a restaurant at the asphalt shore of the Fred Meyers shopping center where, at Matt's age, I skidded my bike to a stop one day and realized that life was one long moment with death at the end of it. "My name is Larry Wobbrock, I am a medical malpractice attorney, the kind of person most of you in this room hate. I knew Leonard Christensen since I was a boy. I never heard one word spoken against him. His record as a researcher, surgeon and physician was immaculate. There was no finer physician anywhere."

A requiem.

My father had saved me in death as he saved me so many times in life. I was given money—no fortune, but enough to pay off most of the Peters and Pauls. I told Matt about his grandfather's passing when I picked him up, in my dad's old Mercedes, from school. I explained that his grandad died peacefully, at home, in bed. Matt was as still as porcelain for blocks, and then his face dissolved.

"I just told him about my dad," I said to Deb when I got out of the car, worried that she would think, for some nut reason, I had hit him.

Debbie, Katie, Matt and I flew to Portland. My father forbade a funeral, forbade a wake, so the best my mother and sister could do was a party at my sister's house months after my father was buried. Laurie and her husband have a beautiful home, down the street from the Donacas' old house, former home to every great hot rod in my childhood world.

"Dad would love this," Laurie laughed. "His favorite kind of party—one he doesn't have to attend."

My brother Scott was at the front door. He's in his late forties but, tall, his face nearly lineless, he appears as exercised as a pro football player and I was glad, at this time of reflection, that he quit drinking. Otherwise, he might remember that I was an enforcer jerk when we were kids, invite me out to my sister's big backyard and deliver nine from the sky.

He told me he was represented by Anybody But a Mime Talent Agency. Scott is a solo act, except when he plays with Phil the Pretty Good, a balloon artist. My brother said that nobody can categorize his guitar playing. Old black men hear him play and say, "You ain't da blues." Young guys with nose rings hear him play and say, "You're no punk, fucker." Hairy-legged girls in Birkenstocks hear him play, and say, 'You are soooo not New Age.'

Scott has done something more significant with a car than I ever will—created a recording system in his 1988 Chevy Caprice that sounds absolutely live.* My brother has many times my natural technological

---

*The way he does it is: Using a $5.00 gooseneck clip, he attaches an Ibanez IM-80 condenser mono microphone—"The mike uses a nine-volt battery that makes the mike so hot it's crazy." He hooks the microphone to a Korg Pandora Box, which is

ability—and if he had been me perhaps the Xeno project would have been wrapped up five years ago. Oh well. There is more news. My father's will is lost. Lost? Who has it, I ask my sister—one of his lawyers, an accountant? "No," Laurie replied, it's bound to be at the ranch somewhere. "Don't worry. As usual, our secrets are safe in chaos."

The wake that was not a wake, I am not ashamed to say, was fun. His doctor friends were owners of Corvettes, Jaguars, Ferraris. One old surgeon, holding up his Merlot, his wineglass sort of floating in the air between us, told me, "No moonshiner could drive like your dad. God never made a cop who could catch him once he put his foot in it."

Yeah, and for some reason I was struck with this memory: On the Lewis River Road below my parents' ranch you can see where my father had, so far as I know, his only car accident, racing home at night at age sixty-five or seventy after another ten-hour day of seeing patients and surgery, when he fell asleep at the wheel of his Mercedes. He recovered quickly. Eight fence posts knocked down, one telephone pole standing up, two fence posts knocked down, and he was back on the road headed for home.

I was listening to a story about how during World War II he served in Australia as a navy doctor in charge of inspecting Sydney hookers and how he resembled the young British Prince Philip—said to be serving incognito with the U.S. Navy—and how my dad had the officers who accompanied him to the cat houses follow a respectful half dozen steps behind, flabbergasting the whores about to have their plumbing inspected by His Majesty, when Kit Bowen, bigger than ever, stepped

---

a mono in-stereo out. "It's got a compressor to tighten the sound." The Pandora's Box has a number of effects. He uses a little compression, a little reverb, a little "chorus." I leave the eq flat—no treble, no bass. The stereo signal is routed into a Sharp md-mt fifteen-mini-disc recorder—"yours for $187.95 at Best Buy." Scott then runs a stereo Y jack into the mini-disc recorder that splits the signal again. He runs one stereo signal from the Y jack into an auxiliary input on his Chevy's CD player. That signal goes into the amp of the car stereo and is broadcast through his Chevy's four speakers. "I control the volume, the other signal on the Y jack goes into my headphones. I do a sound check, I turn a bit of the volume on the car stereo up so the sound of the car is picked up by the mike—which adds presence and depth, widens the sound and gives it the 'live' effect. Most recording studios are known as 'dead' rooms that absorb all sound. What makes the interior of a car great, is that half of it—anything upholstered—is 'dead,' while the other half—the windows and anything metal—is alive, sound ricochets off hard surfaces like bullets shot off inside a big steel box. The microphone picks up the ambient sound of the half dead, half alive 'room' and that is how I get such a cool effect."

through my sister's front door and told Katie, "Get me a Diet Coke or I'm going to hit you right in front of your dad."

I love her laugh. Katie is shaken about her grandfather, but happy otherwise. She is excellent at her many worlds: college, art, writing, computers, misdemeanors, snowboarding, surfing, boys. She was in the new *Skateboarder* magazine four times. "Tacky. Never again," was her reaction to pictures of herself modeling what I guess were skateboard hot pants. She wants to be a newscaster.

Kit's idea: We build a dream house. Does that sound good?

Sure it does. I like dream houses. I like dream houses a lot.

Bowen has gone from Ford sales to housing contractor. He designs the home, builds the home, sells the home, everything and he's enraptured by the work of Oregon architect Pietro Belluschi. "We'll find one of his top apostles," Kit suggested, "and work from one of his old designs."

Who will pay for this, I asked.

"You."

My cousin Jerry was here. Maybe the last time I saw him he was on stage at the San Diego Civic Theater or some other big hall. He played one of the fathers in a *Fantastiks!* revival. The cast had the polished, familiar look of people from TV shows. How did he fit in? "If you live in California," he explained, "you gotta be an actor." How did he get the part? "I went to a casting, the director said, 'Here's a script, read a few lines,' I did and he said, 'You're in.'" Jerry even belted out some tunes. Impressive, like what would happen if gravel could sing.

I tell him that I've a new literary agent and a new publisher. He says he just sold his 700-cubic-centimeter Suzuki racing bike, a motorcycle capable—if tuned right—of hitting one hundred and seventy miles per hour. "I'm getting too old for that crap," he admitted. With my dad gone, Jerry will be the family patriarch. He looked, as did my brother and sister, like he did when I was a kid. Twenty-two then, sixty now, but the same strong arms, same granite-on-granite voice. A testament to the illusion that time does not pass. Wasn't it last night I was home, feet up on a gold, stuffed chair under the oil painting of the naked Polynesian girl in my father's den, Jerry and my dad talking eyeballs, me—Matt's age now—fighting with my homework, picking my way through a ketchup "seafood cocktail" Jerry had prepared and wondering why I was me instead of the shrimp I was swallowing, then pleading "Could somebody please tell me how to spell 'misspell'?" while Jonathan Winters was singing a silly song on the stereo?

Ride my Harley,
Ride my Indian, too.
My face broke out the other night.
But I'm in love.
Gonna ride down that highway all the time.

I remember, too, my dad cancelling our subscription to *The Saturday Evening Post* because he didn't want sanctimonious mother and apple pie magazine writers telling him how to live and subscribing instead to the avantplush magazine *Show* and the muckraking periodical *Fact*. Too bad *Show* soon plushed itself into bankruptcy and *Fact* was sued out of business after publishing an article suggesting Barry Goldwater was too crazy to be president. I remember as well a rare effort to abridge my God-given civil rights, his refusing to let me tape up a red, white and blue FUCK COMMUNISM poster above my bed.

Reading obituaries, I have learned more about my father's career in four minutes than I had in forty years. That he performed the first corneal transplant in Oregon before I was born, developed some of the first ocular instruments used in microsurgery, identified the infection—cytomegalovirus—that is the major cause of severe visual impairment in people with AIDS, founded the eye bank and cofounded the bookstore at the University of Oregon Medical School and the ophthalmic pathology laboratory named in his honor. Nothing he would want me to know.

Jerry wants us to write a book about our bomb-throwing, free-loving ancestors. "My great-great-granddad formed a cult to build a huge circular outhouse so his cult could all poop together in harmony," Jerry told me, "inspiring Jesus Christ to descend to the circle of the ring. When Christ didn't show up, they burned down half of Tacoma. So you probably got this idiocy in your genes."

There was a crowd here now, Laurie had turned her kitchen and dining room into a bar-and-grill and claustrophobia told me red wine was the new air. Someone asked if I could make sense of my father's death, what he meant to me and what I mean to my son. *Huh?* Annoyed, I replied that I am not paid to think, that eighty-six is eighty-six, and that the secret to life is that it ends, but that since you asked, my father was a myth that was true, there but not there—I was probably ten before I realized that not all dads worked seven days a week. But me? I do not live in a medical coal mine—anybody who claims to write more than four hours a day is either a liar, a hack or Stephen King—

I maybe missed two Little League practices in seven years, and what was the question again?

"What do you want?" Jerry asked. To keep doing whatever it is I'm doing until the lights go out, more specifically to mirror Tennessee Williams's goal of enjoying the glories of martyrdom with the comforts of success. Though at this instant I'd settle for a Pulitzer and a face-lift.

Jerry is going to restore the Hudson. We talked about all the chrome I ripped off, curled away from the body with a screwdriver and destroyed. Where will new fifty-year-old chrome come from?

I felt as freshly stupid as I did at fourteen, that screwdriver still in my spidery hand.

Scary, who has had such wonderful cars—a metallic blue '62 Chevy with chrome rims, an Austin-Healey that drove like a rocket-powered stagecoach, a black Porsche 914, the Saleen Mustang and many others—said he'd had it with hot cars. "They take all your money and break your heart."

Gideon arrived, his face pale as candle wax. He was about to publish an anthology, *Beach: Stories By the Sand and Sea*, tales by Albert Camus, Doris Lessing, John Cheever and Vladimir Nabokov, and he said we should forget having our hero a saint, that we must make our novel real. The doctor was sick. Just the flu or something, he said, but whatever it is it appears to have drained him of his blood. He called me last week with news of Tiger Warren. Tiger. Remember Tiger, the luckiest man in the world? No more. Do you remember Kit Bowen talking about Tiger's seaplane, the one he landed with such a dramatic splash in the Willamette River? Tiger had three sons, boys a little younger and older than my own son, Matt, kids who grew up playing in the stable where my sister Laurie kept her horses and who were, by every account, wonderful. "Like young elk," Kit Bowen said. Last month Tiger loaded his sons into the seaplane. The seaplane took off, banked, slid out of the sky and crashed in the Columbia River. Everybody drowned.

The fog began to lift to reveal a big surf tinted with sickly brine. But no Matt. He had to be out there someplace. Surfing. A hot rod would be safer. All that steel. Matt wants a mid-1960s high-performance Mustang fastback like Jimmy Huygens's.

No dual quad carburetors, no supercharger, just a tight-as-a-haiku

289-cubic-inch Ford V-8 balanced and blueprinted with one four-barrel carburetor and a nice little *lubba-lubba-lubba* racing cam and tuned exhaust headers. No trick ignition, no heavy-duty truck clutch to wrench the tendons of a barely teenage left knee already tortured by ten years of soccer. A four-speed tranny, sure, and American mag wheels. A 225-horsepower setup like Scary Larry's Saleen Mustang—gone now to a junkyard or a museum. I remain unhandy. So I won't do the work. So-Cal Speed will. Nick and I have been there so long that we have evolved from clients to part of the woodwork and I know Matt's Mustang will be fast, clean and safe, and I will be charged an arm but not a leg.

I've been walking the cold sand north. A beer can and a several-gallon plastic gas can bobbed in the shore break.

I heard something, a voice? I gazed out to sea again and saw a blond stick figure in a black wet suit paddling at the top of a real roller. Matt's surfboard sliced a spitting white wake across the face of the dark wave, he leapt to his feet and deftly crouched like a superskinny sumo wrestler, took the drop, his board flying across the water, waving one arm high in the air before the white water crashed on top of him and threw him tumbling into the soup.

The engine muttering and screaming behind me as I tap the accelerator, I try to provoke a backfire in the supercharger small enough to spare my skull. It pays to be on the safe side.

I've been asked: What have I learned from all this? My answer: *Absolutely nothing.*

Nick has been solicited to create a new car. He says his client has only $350,000—"So we'd really have to scrimp"—but would I like to be involved? Of course.

Because Nick Pugh is the best automobile designer in the country, and as Willie Loman—or was it Willie Loman's wife—used to say: "Attention must be paid." In a rational world, Ford or General Motors or Mercedes would give Nick a million dollars to pry out a dozen or so of the one hundred new car designs that remain locked in his head. It would be the bargain of the new century.

Nick wonders what my father would think. "Seven years just to build one car!" Tack onto that the time it took to raise the money. I told him I'm not sure it matters. That what matters may not be so much what you do as who you leave behind.

Katie called with the news. "To be a newscaster you have to declare officially as a journalism major. Dad, it'll be hard. To get into the program, first I have to take a test proving I can spell. You know how most people spell ridiculous 'R-E-D'? Actually, it's 'R-I-D.' "

Katie has been chosen by the publishers of a new English-language South American newspaper to be "the symbol of America" at a huge party thrown to celebrate their debut. "They said they wanted a glamorous young woman, me! To give a speech about how America means freedom and opportunity. Me, Dad. The symbol of America. It'll be like the Academy Awards and they're buying me a gown and everything. I have never been so flattered. Me! Can you believe it?"

Not for ten minutes it took me to get to the bank where, standing in line thinking: Katie Christensen, the Symbol of America. My eyes stinging—I wonder what my father would think of that?

So here I am, little Indy 500 steering wheel in hand, our 600-horsepower hand-grenade Rat motor quaking behind my head, in the Xeno III's glass-coffin cockpit. Though, like so many things about Nick Pugh, that image is about to change. Nick has designed a new revolutionary spandex, shag-carpeted, half-womb interior that is infinitely changeable, that will be like riding around in your mother's stomach, except with a big window, so you can see where you're driving at one hundred and thirty miles an hour. Also, though it looks stunning now, everything stark polished metal, Nick is about to plate the whole car gold or platinum. This could evoke the spirit of noble Pharaohs, a renaissance in outlandish cocaine deals or simply Newport Beach bathroom fixtures, but what is life without risk?

I slip the Xeno into gear, let the little car roll forward, hit the throttle gas and the engine ignites, the tires scream and I am slammed back in my seat, the whole world racing toward me, new asphalt gone as soon as I can see it and my foot still nowhere near the floor.

Postmortem: Spring 2001

A woman just called from a funeral home, inviting me to invest in the inevitable. When I said that I wasn't going to die any time soon, she replied, "Are you sure?"

So best now thank Mike Hamilberg for handling this book, and David Kelly, Tom Congdon and the late Tom Bates for their early editorial guidance. I'm likewise very grateful to my original editor at St.

Martin's, Barry Neville—if not for Barry, you'd be reading something else—and to Sean Desmond as well as everyone at St. Martin's for their unfailing help. I'd also like to thank Steve Scherzer. Patrick Barth worked hard to defuse this mess and buy me time so I could get the car done, get the book done and thus get Doubleday their money back. Michael McGuire went so far as to facilitate the refinancing of my home loan.

I have tried to make this story as accurate as possible. But I know enough lawyers, so I have changed a few names and made some prudent excisions. My apologies to those who helped out who got left out, particularly Woody Neeley and his wonderful tale of his battle against dope-dealer astrophysicists.

As for everybody else. Gideon Bosker still lives in the sky, flying the world to remind physicians that many, if not most, antibacterial and antiviral pharmaceuticals are, in fact, microscopic mass murderers who just happen to kill germs faster than they kill you, and to please try and use them with care. Scary Larry Wobbrock continues to practice law in Portland. Kit Bowen is constructing houses and has a new plan. "Let me paint the stage. Art's out. You have bigger mountains to move. Let me build you a mansion in Costa Rica, *dream house in paradise*." John Case has attracted a lot of excited attention for his plan to build a beautiful luxury hotel straddling the Long Beach Grand Prix track. Nick is working for the very influential Rhythm and Hughes film company and doing very well. My son, Matt, has a great grade-point average and has acquired, recently, his granddad's smooth snapping golf swing. The ball, clicked off the tee, becomes a tiny far-away daytime star. His golf instructor shrugs, "If he learns any faster you'll have to pay me to just stand here and keep my mouth shut." He's a miler on his middle school track team and at night strums Weezer anthems on his guitar and chats on his computer with girlfriends from school, Little Hottie and Flirtmagnet69. Deb's fine. Katie's fine.

When asked finally to define his masterpiece, Nick says, "With luck, it'll be the ultimate street-legal concept car." At this second, though, the Xeno III no longer exists. Nick has had our dream machine completely disassembled so that its parts can be repainted, plated, power coated and/or polished. He wants the car to evoke a sort of flash-forward timelessness. He shows me the final gold-and-platinum color schemes, and when I say the "treasure-like" metal surfaces remind me of something archeologists might dig up from an ancient Egyptian tomb, he says, yeah! He wants the Xeno III to be "like an artifact from the future."

As for that Xeno. Unless you're reading this in the year 7000, you can probably see it in any number of auto shows or in a museum or in Nick's garage. Wherever he's displaying it (you can also see photos by going to www.nickpugh.com). The car is viciously quick, and Nick said something about wanting to drive it as fast as it can go as long as it can go. Or maybe he'll rip out the engine and install an electric motor from a Japanese bullet train—or some Japanese guy will buy it for a million and stick it in a safety deposit box for three hundred years. It's hard to tell.

It's summer. Most mornings, I take Matt surfing. Though he drives. He didn't have to sit in my lap or crash into rhododendrons to learn how. He just got behind the wheel and took off. The waves he rides now are often overhead. Scary silver hills of ocean off the beach rise up, up, up to crest and he cuts speeding across them, in water bas relief. He and Nick went for a ride in the Xeno the other night—and the car set off half the alarms in a shopping mall parking lot just roaring by. It may not be groundbreaking eye surgery, but he was impressed.

Nick has, pretty much, got it make. He designed the dog and the monsters for two movies that were hits last month, *Scooby-Doo* and *Men in Black II*, respectively. Now, if you'd like him to design a totally original car for you, he'd be delighted. He has the time, if you have the money.

When the Xeno was finished there was a big party at the Art Center in Pasadena. A mob of people in basic black. Gideon arrived grinning with a vampish ingenue on his arm. Most all the TV networks had camera crews there, it was so crowed a lot of people never even got to see the car—the upstairs balcony at the gallery was so packed people hung off the railing pushed by people behind them. It could have been the stern of the *Titanic* after the iceberg.

The car looked great, and shortly thereafter Nick and I went out and had a million drinks and he said that he didn't know about me, but "I don't care if people say we're crazy flakes who had a crazy time building a crazy car for crazy reasons, *let them go try and build the greatest car ever*—We never gave up and I am just incredibly happy."

So am I. Though when asked about the ultimate point or fate of the Xeno, I have no more idea than I have about my own point or fate. "Art for art's sake" is about the best I can do.